Funk & Wagnalls Guide
to Personal Money Management

By the Author

Dun & Bradstreet's Guide to $Your Investments$

Funk & Wagnalls Guide to Personal Money Management

Funk & Wagnalls Guide to Personal Money Management

by C. Colburn Hardy

Funk & Wagnalls
NEW YORK

Manufactured in the United States of America

Library of Congress Cataloging in Publication Data

Hardy, C   Colburn.
    Funk & Wagnalls guide to personal money management.

    Bibliography: p.
    Includes index.
    1. Finance, Personal. I. Title. II. Title: Guide to personal
money management.
HG179.H28   332′.024   75–17830
ISBN 0–308–10213–4

1 2 3 4 5 6 7 8 9 10

Acknowledgments

With Professional Assistance from:

American Association of Retired
  Persons
American Bankers Association
American Bar Association
American Medical Association
Apartment Life
Associated Credit Bureaus, Inc.
Babson's Reports
Better Homes and Gardens
Business Management
Business Monthly
Business Week
Business Week Letter
Canadian Business Service
Changing Times
Chase Manhattan Bank
Citicorp Leasing, Inc.
College Entrance Examination
  Board
Connecticut Mutual Life
  Insurance Co.
Consumers Insurance Information
  Bureau
Continental Bank

Daley, Coolidge & Company
Dental Economics
Dental Management
Dun's Review
Federal Deposit Insurance
  Corporation
Federal Energy Administration
Federal Trade Commission
Federated Funeral Directors of
  America
First National Bank of Chicago
Fundscope Magazine
John B. Halper
A. S. Hansen, Inc.
Hertz Corporation
Household Finance Corporation
Insurance Information Institute
Institute of Life Insurance
Institutional Investor
Investment Company Institute
Kemper Insurance Companies
Lebenthal & Co.
Media & Consumer
Medical Economics

Merrill Lynch, Pierce, Fenner & Smith
Money Magazine
Moody's Investors Service
Motor Vehicle Manufacturers Association
Moving and Storage Industry of New York
National Association for Hospital Development
National Association of Home Builders
National Association of Insurance Agents
National Association of Life Underwriters
National Association of Real Estate Investment Trusts
National Association of Securities Dealers, Inc.
National Foundation for Consumer Credit
National Underwriter Company
New York Insurance Department
New York Stock Exchange
New York Times

Paine Webber, Jackson & Curtis
Pennsylvania Insurance Department
Physician's Management
T. Rowe Price, Inc.
Reynolds Securities, Inc.
Standard & Poor's
Conrad Teitell, LLB, LLM
The Exchange
Trusts and Estates
U.S. Department of Agriculture
U.S. Department of Health, Education & Welfare
U.S. Department of Housing and Urban Development
U.S. Internal Revenue Service
U.S. Treasury
University of Southern California School of Medicine
Veterans Administration
Virginia Commonwealth University (George Hoffer and A. James Wynne)
Wall Street Journal
Wright Investors' Service

Contents

A Note to the Reader

In writing this book, attempts were made to assure the accuracy and timeliness of all information. Every chapter, chart, table, and statistic was checked with an authority in the field—attorneys, bank trust officers, executives of trade and professional associations, authors, and editors.

If the data vary from what is available elsewhere, it is probably because of differing interpretations or accounting methods. We believe the principles are correct.

If there are errors, we apologize. But remember, this is a *guide,* not a dictionary. *Personal Money Management* is designed to explain concepts and approaches rather than to provide definitive information. Before you take any action based on examples in this book, check with an agent or a firm with whom you do, or plan to do, business. In these days of inflation, consumerism, and changing legislation, specific figures become outdated rapidly.

Preface

This is a personal money management cookbook. It is designed to provide ready reference for information on various phases of financial planning, spending, and investing. In some areas, the chapters reflect personal experience; in others, the advice is based on suggestions made to younger people in our family; throughout, the concepts represent counsel from experts in the fields of interest.

These data are presented as background to help the reader use common sense and his/her experience to make important financial decisions. In real life, of course, most of us live on a less planned, less logical basis than recommended here. We do many things by rote, tradition, convenience, and ignorance. It may be difficult to change ideas and procedures for older people, but this book can be useful to everyone—especially to younger people who have yet to face the many problems of personal money management.

Specifically, this book was written for the fairly affluent, relatively sophisticated individual and family. It attempts to present guidelines and examples that skip over the basics to explain how to approach, analyze, and utilize opportunities whose details may be unfamiliar to most people. *One important point:* You do not have to be rich to benefit from estate planning, trusts, tax shelters, and leveraged investments. Whether you're 19 or 90, have savings of $1,000 or $100,000, this book can help you manage your money better.

There are plenty of excellent books for beginners on taxes, real estate, insurance, the stock market, etc. Generally speaking, *Personal Money Management* starts where they leave off. This book is written for people who are financially and educationally able to use more complex techniques.

Some of the chapters do provide routine checkpoints, partly because such data are not readily available elsewhere but also because such information can be helpful in making decisions in a hurry, under stress, and without adequate preparation. Overall, if you get one useful idea from each chapter, your purchase investment will pay off handsomely.

Making Money Work

Most people work hard to earn money to build an estate for their family and/or retirement for themselves. Too often, they are so involved in making money that they neglect (or postpone until too late) important actions that will make that money work for them. With the knowledge and examples in this book, every reader should be able to use earnings-savings more effectively and with greater rewards.

Money is not something to be hoarded and left idle. It should be put to work—to grow in investments; to reduce costs of living; to expand insurance coverage; to build security; and most important, to enjoy life more fully.

In a broad sense, each family is a little bank. Paychecks, dividends, interest, and inheritances come in; cash, bill payments, and deductions for taxes and benefits go out. Hopefully, in between, there will be a balance that can be used to assure a better life for you and your children now and in the years ahead.

Think of that "balance" as your capital to be invested for the greatest returns, not only in dollars but in protection and pleasure. Smart investors can make money under *all* conditions. This requires flexibility, a realistic approach to money management, and a willingness to use common sense to act on facts, not hopes or outmoded concepts.

When I was growing up, the prevailing advice was:

- Keep six months' pay in a savings account for emergencies.
- Never spend more than 25% of income for housing.
- Save at least 5% (preferably 10%) of your salary in insurance or savings accounts.
- Never borrow more than 1½ times your monthly salary.

Fortunately, circumstances were such that over the years, more by happenstance than by wisdom, I broke every one of these "rules." I concluded that these guidelines must have been set by a committee composed of a Boston banker, a Philadelphia insurance salesman, and a Vermont attorney.

Such aphorisms, especially the caveat against debt, were of little value in the waning years of the Depression, when interest rates were low and almost everything could be acquired for a bargain price. Nor were they viable in the post–World War II period, when the values of real estate and securities moved steadily upward. The people who profited were those who voided these shibboleths and used their common sense.

Don't get the idea that I recommend ignoring these old mottos completely. They will keep reckless spenders out of trouble and prove a leash on your own enthusiasm. But broad guidelines are no substitute for tough-minded, keyed-to-needs/life-style financial planning. Even those who were doubtful before the 1970s should be convinced by the tremendous pressure of inflation. *The old rules are no longer fully valid. There must be flexibility.*

To keep pace these days, people have to think differently about spending and saving. My first insurance policy (purchased in 1932, at age 22) was an annuity that would pay me, beginning at age 65, $150 per month for life. This munificent sum, I was assured by the middle-aged agent, "would provide a strong base for happy retirement for both myself and my as-yet-undiscovered wife." The salesman was an old friend of the family and, I am certain, honestly felt this was a wise choice. In those years, most people had to look up the word *inflation* in the dictionary!

Fortunately, later counsel—and experience—persuaded me to shift those premium payments to a more useful life insurance policy. Its cash value is now invested to bring a return of over $3,000 a year plus prospects of substantial capital appreciation and a welcome inheritance for my daughter. *Moral:* In financial planning, few things are as sure as they seem. You must never get locked in.

In those days, borrowing may not have been a sin, but it was no virtue. I remember my banker's scowl when I decided to renew, rather than pay off, my first loan—for $500. With inflation, it's an entirely different ball game. When the value of a dollar drops at a rate of 8% to 10% a year, borrowing makes a lot more sense than saving for most people. That's why this book has scores of ways to use OPM (Other People's Money).

Equally important has been the shift from individual to government-corporate benefits: Social Security, unemployment compensation, group-life-medical-health insurance, and pension plans. These once-optional buffers of security have become an integral part of most paychecks, so that, in the majority of families, personal protection has become a supplementary rather than a primary responsibility.

On the other hand, many onetime luxuries have become necessities—automobiles, air conditioning, college educations, annual vacations, etc. With few exceptions, Americans are better educated, more prosperous, and more knowledgeable than they, or their counterparts, were half a century ago. They have good reason to ignore old rules of thumb in favor of commonsensical decisions. Nor need anyone ever feel guilty because his spending habits don't fit the "ideal" family budget extolled in some national magazines. Nobody but nobody is average anymore. That's why this book does not show "typical" budgets except as the basis for comparisons with future needs.

Inflation has forced greater financial discipline, but it does not mandate slavish adherence to old formulas. Once the wage earner (or earners) has provided for the basic costs of food, housing, clothing, and protection, other expenditures should be geared to personal and family goals. If you and your wife want to take the children to Europe every summer, plan your finances so you can afford to do it. You will probably have to rent rather than buy, drive your car longer, minimize entertaining, and forgo membership in the country club. But you will have an important-to-you goal.

Use Common Sense

Your brother and his wife may prefer to concentrate their plans-savings on a dream house and spend their vacations at home. That's their privilege. This book shows both families how to achieve these objectives with adequate knowledge, careful planning, and consistent adherence to fundamentals of money management.

The most important single factor in all phases of managing money is common sense. The "experts" are little different from you. They may have more knowledge, greater experience, and special skills, but they all put their pants on one leg at a time. Your task is to use their wisdom without succumbing to their wiles.

Before you make any major decisions—the purchase of a home, automobile, or insurance policy; an investment in real estate, stocks, or shares of an investment company; etc.—*be skeptical*. Take a few minutes to look at the proposition from the other fellow's point of view.

> Why does a corporation have to issue a convertible instead of a straight bond?
> What are the extra benefits to the insurance agent when he sells that particular policy?
> Is this form of legal agreement more rewarding to the attorney than the alternative?
> What would be your stance if you were selling instead of buying?
> Today and 20 years from now?

This does not mean to distrust people whom you have come to respect and like, but it does stress the necessity of making decisions based on facts, not emotions or acquiescence. You worked hard to make that money. Now it's time to make that money work even harder for you!

Finally—and probably most important—do not expect immediate results from any financial planning. Successful investing requires patience. Insurance policies provide protection, but not rewards for many years. And it takes time for property to grow in value. Remember: The tortoise won the race with the hare!

There is always one rule to heed: *Investigate before you invest.* In every phase of financial and personal money management, get the facts, project your hopes, and develop your plans flexibly so they can be canceled, contracted, or expanded as resources permit and common sense concludes. You'll worry less, enjoy more, and hopefully, live a happier, merrier, and more rewarding life if you learn to manage your money.

Funk & Wagnalls Guide
to Personal Money Management

I

Net Worth: Guide to Economic Growth and Future Security

One of the most important annual routines for better money management is calculating your NET WORTH. This shows what you really own in dollars: your assets minus your liabilities—your personal balance sheet. Use your own form, similar to the one on pages 4 and 5. You may be surprised to find how valuable you are!

Your net worth is an important basis for planning your estate, targeting your retirement, and preparing an effective budget each year. Work it out now and update it annually—early in the year.

There are three parts to the table—what you had last year, what you have this year, and what you hope to have next year. Once you have established a pattern, use the results to see how closely you are holding to the net worth growth as shown in the table on page 4. *Your goal should be to increase your net worth each year by a percentage that is great enough to provide the total resources you will need for enjoyable retirement.*

Before you set down any figures, determine your personal financial goal (much as you do with estate planning). The most convenient target is retirement and the assumption that you can get along comfortably with one-half to two-thirds of your last working year's income.

But every family—and every individual in that family—is different, so you will have to set your own scale.

Suppose you decide you will need $20,000 a year from your personal funds at age 65. You are now 35, with a family income of $30,000 before taxes. But your net worth is zero—after paying for heavy medical expenses, private school for the children, a second mortgage, a car loan, etc.

Fortunately, you are just getting out of the woods, and this year, can count on $4,200 net worth. To reach your retirement goal of $230,000 (which will assure you and your wife a lifetime income of at least $20,000 a year), you will have to add 14% to your net worth every year—on a compounding basis.

At 5% a year, these assets will grow to $230,000 in 30 years. To counter inflation, you'll be wiser to shoot for a 9% growth—to $475,000 at retirement.

These may sound like big bundles, especially that original $4,200. But you may already be doing that well through reduction of your mortgage, increase in the value of your home, repayment of installment loans, premiums on life insurance, and savings. Figure it out for yourself!

Getting the Data

In preparing the work sheet, assemble all of your records: checkbooks, list of securities, mortgage receipts, etc. Then estimate the value of your properties: *For the house,* use the latest evaluation from the city assessor's office or what you believe to be the probable price at resale; *for your car,* write down the market (not the trade-in) price, etc.

Then, with your wife, inventory the contents of your home and record their values—of appliances, furniture, fur coats, etc. *Be realistic.* If that washer is 5 years old, it might bring $50. But that Oriental rug which Aunt Lois gave you 10 years ago may be worth double if it's in good shape.

Call your insurance agent to get the approximate cash value of your life policies and contact the industrial relations department of your employer to find your equity in the company pension plan (if you have not already received an annual accounting).

If you have a stamp or coin collection, art, or antiques, make a guess now, but every 5 years, consider a professional appraisal. This information can do double duty—make it possible to update a loss-damage rider on your homeowner's insurance policy.

On your work sheet, leave extra spaces at the end of each grouping—to fill in future acquisitions such as a new painting, your share of the family farm, or borrowings to buy stock in your company.

Be just as realistic on your liabilities—all credit-card charges, your 3-year pledge to the alumni fund, and even that note you cosigned for Brother Fred.

Watching Assets Grow

Once you know what you are really worth, figure out how much these assets will have to grow to reach your age-65 goal. Check the chart to find where the age line crosses the growth line, then look to the left for the assets you'll hope to have.

> *Note:* This chart starts at age 35, as most people are too busy spending money (for mortgages, maternity bills, car loans, etc.) and have little or no net worth in prior years.

The earlier you start boosting your net worth, the better. If you are not pretty well set by age 40, it may be a tough task. If you are worth only $75,000 at age 52, you will either have to boost your savings, lower your retirement sights, or count on a sizable inheritance. On the other hand, if your NW gets over $200,000—at almost any age—you're in great shape!

What Net Worth Means

Age Bracket	Could Be Trouble	All Is Well	On Easy Street
30–39	$ 20,000	$ 50,000	$150,000
40–49	40,000	100,000	225,000
50–59	75,000	150,000	275,000
60–69	100,000	200,000	350,000

Your Net Worth Work Sheet

	Year I	Year II	Projected Year III
Assets			
CASH OR EQUIVALENT			
Checking account (his)	_____	_____	_____
Checking account (hers)	_____	_____	_____
Cash value life insurance	_____	_____	_____
Current value annuities	_____	_____	_____
Equity in pension plan	_____	_____	_____
Funds held in trust for husband or wife	_____	_____	_____
Debts owed to you	_____	_____	_____
Other	_____	_____	_____
INVESTMENTS			
Common stocks	_____	_____	_____
Preferred stocks and bonds	_____	_____	_____
Mutual-fund shares	_____	_____	_____
Sideline business	_____	_____	_____
Participations—oil, cattle, timber	_____	_____	_____
Stock options	_____	_____	_____
Country club certificate	_____	_____	_____
Other	_____	_____	_____
REAL ESTATE			
Home	_____	_____	_____
Vacation cottage	_____	_____	_____
Other land	_____	_____	_____
Other holdings	_____	_____	_____

Your Net Worth Work Sheet (*Continued*)

	Year I	Year II	Projected Year III
Assets			
POSSESSIONS			
Automobile (his)	_____	_____	_____
Automobile (hers)	_____	_____	_____
Appliances	_____	_____	_____
Equipment-furniture	_____	_____	_____
Recreation-hobby items	_____	_____	_____
Collections	_____	_____	_____
Antiques	_____	_____	_____
Furs	_____	_____	_____
Art	_____	_____	_____
Jewelry	_____	_____	_____
Other valuables	_____	_____	_____
TOTAL ASSETS	_____	_____	_____
Liabilities			
Current bills due	_____	_____	_____
Department store accounts	_____	_____	_____
Credit-card charges	_____	_____	_____
Balance on mortgage	_____	_____	_____
Balance on installment loans	_____	_____	_____
Margin account	_____	_____	_____
Insurance loans	_____	_____	_____
Federal-state taxes due	_____	_____	_____
Pledges to charity	_____	_____	_____
Other liabilities	_____	_____	_____
TOTAL LIABILITIES	_____	_____	_____

Net Worth: Assets $_____ — Liabilities $_____ = Net Worth

$_____

Guidelines for an Annual Audit and Review

Managing your personal money is much like running a business. You must know your assets and liabilities, how much you expect to earn and spend in the next year, and have a general idea of major expenditures in the next 5 to 10 years.

The same basic techniques that work in the office can be used at home. The place to start is with a personal audit. This should be fully discussed and prepared at the beginning of each year, reviewed quarterly, and totaled annually.

There are 4 major entries:

Personal Cash-flow Statement

This forecasts income and expenses in the coming year, matches salary and unearned income against fixed expenses, and shows how much is left over for discretionary funds. In this case, the young family has very little discretionary money.

Personal Balance Sheet

This measures personal assets versus personal liabilities and ends with current net worth. Each year, estimate what your net worth will be at year-end. Then you can see if your estate is growing as fast as it should—and could.

Family Budget

Because life-styles differ, this table shows only major fixed expenses and bulks the rest as "living costs." Every family should prepare monthly and annual budgets for each basic category—food, clothing, recreation, medical bills, and so on.

Long-range Plan

This is a separate agenda (not shown here), which lists major spending-needs goals—new car, new furniture, club membership, special vacations, boat, education, etc.

Follow the corporate policy and plan at least 5 years ahead; keep all records up-to-date; set down your projections carefully; revise them as conditions change; review all data annually —year-by-year and against long-range plans.

At best, you will develop good planning habits, not go overboard when you get a raise, and be able to plan a better future for yourself, your family, or your widow and children.

At worst, you will have ample warning that you are not reaching your goals and must take specific steps to bring your expenditures in line with economic-financial realities.

For advice: Consult your banker, insurance agent, corporate planning official, or if you can afford it or are in real trouble, a financial adviser.

This budget is for a young family that has made substantial commitments in expectation of ever-rising income. At the present time, their savings-investments are low. This is an actual situation prepared as a base. With added income, there can be improved living facilities, greater recreation, substantially more savings, and hopefully, a fuller life for everyone.

You can revise this general format to fit your income, lifestyle, and dreams, but DO IT NOW.

Personal Balance Sheet—Budget Projections

Cash-Flow Statement		Projected for Year
Income		
Salary	$20,000	
Bonus	1,000	
Dividends-interest- gifts	2,000	
Cash receipts		$23,000
Disbursements		
Taxes and Social Security		
Federal	3,000	
State	500	
Social Security	825	
Pension plan	475	
Total		4,800
Take-home cash		18,200
Interest expense	300	
Mortgage interest	2,280	
Real-estate taxes	1,750	
Living costs	9,000	
Total		13,330
Net cash before debt		4,870
Amortization and savings		
Mortgage principal	600	
Installment debt	1,000	
Education fund	800	
Savings	600	
Insurance	600	
Total		3,600
Net spendable income		1,270

Personal Balance Sheet

	January 1	December 31
Assets		
Current assets		
Cash and checking accounts	$2,000	$1,000
Savings accounts	800	1,400
Education account	500	1,300
(Mutual-fund shares)		
Investments		
Bonds and stocks	23,800	28,000*
Insurance cash value	5,000	5,500
Vested pension	7,700	8,500
Total	39,800	45,700
Fixed and other		
long-term assets		
Home	45,000	45,000
Personal property	8,500	9,000
Fixed assets	53,500	54,000
Total Assets	93,300	99,700
Liabilities		
Notes payable	2,500	1,500
Mortgage	35,000	34,400
Total Liabilities	37,500	35,900
Net worth	55,800	63,800

* Appreciation in value

Based on data from Aims Group, Inc.

Value of Annual Review

An annual review is valuable not only to see what's been accomplished but also to plan what must be done in the next year. Use the chart to discover how close you meet projections.

If you are falling behind, finecomb every expense to find where you have to tighten up or expand your investment-property returns.

In cutting, consider major items such as trading your car in every 4 instead of every 3 years; taking a 2-week vacation and spending the third week at home, etc.

In stepping up your savings (and that's where most people have the greatest flexibility), make sure that your assets are earning a proper rate of return. You should average at least 9% a year—from quality bonds, more from total returns of good growth stocks, from real estate where there's income plus appreciation.

As with all long-term savings plans, you must allow for inflation. You can do this arbitrarily each year: Add 5% to 8%, or (better for a regular review) try a 5-year average. This will eliminate arbitrary calculations.

At all times, use common sense. Just because the rate of inflation is 10% a year does not mean that you have to use that high figure. Some of your major expenditures—mortgage payments, insurance premiums—are fixed. And to a certain extent, your assets will appreciate with inflation.

Most important, do not skimp so much that you cannot enjoy life. If you are an only son and your widowed mother has assets of $100,000, a good share of that will probably be added to your net worth someday.

Net worth is a tool, not a goal in itself. Use it wisely and review it often.

II

How to Prepare and Plan Your Estate

Estate planning has as much to do with living as with dying. When you accumulate some wealth, it's important to organize your assets so that the taxes on your estate—and that of your widow—will be modest. But right from the start, wise planning can help you reach your goals faster and more easily, and less expensively, than just going along on a week-to-week basis . . . as most people do.

What do you want your money to buy next year? In 10 years? In 20 years? When you retire?

The answers to these questions grow out of your values, your interests, your ambitions, and sometimes the needs over which you have little control (illness, tragedy), or on the pleasant side, unexpected good fortune.

The important thing is to start NOW. People who wait until they have "enough" seldom get down to the hard decisions of financial planning. The first thing they know they are 52 years old, have a helter-skelter of assets and only 13 years to build adequate reserves for retirement. Or worse, they die suddenly and leave their family with little knowledge of the estate and less experience in handling money.

First, decide with your spouse—and as soon as they are old

enough, with your children—what is most important to the family and to each individual member. It's wise to bring the children in early. This will give them insight into money responsibilities, what it costs to live, and why it is so important to make wise financial decisions. (If nothing else, they will learn from your own inevitable mistakes.)

Very few incomes are large enough to cover all wants, so do not be discouraged when you develop a long shopping list. Nor should you be surprised that the list gets longer with affluence. The more we have, the more we want or think we need. *The important thing to remember:* At all times, the power of choice is present with incomes of all sizes.

Once you have a broad plan, you must determine, even if only in a general way, how you are going to get the money to achieve your goals: directly, through earnings or investments, or indirectly, through insurance on your life.

Proper estate planning requires help from professionals: a lawyer, an accountant, an insurance agent, an investment adviser (at the outset, your banker or broker, and later, a professional organization), and in case of death, an executor, trustee, and guardian. Information on how to choose these is provided in other chapters.

Briefly, your immediate financial goals should include:

1. READY CASH RESERVES. These should be equal to 2 months' net-after-taxes income—for a $20,000 annual salary, about $2,500. This should be in liquid or readily convertible form: bank accounts (savings and checking); listed securities; cash value of life insurance, pensions, and profit-sharing plans, etc.

2. ADEQUATE INSURANCE. For home, valuables, health, and life.

3. POSSESSIONS. New home, automobile, appliances, furniture, recreational items (golf clubs, skis, boats), and later, art, stamps, coins, and/or other hobbies.

4. EDUCATION. Private school, college, graduate work.

5. VACATIONS. Summer home, trips abroad, etc.

6. ESTATE NEEDS. Fees, taxes, charitable gifts, etc.

7. RETIREMENT.

8. SPECIAL NEEDS. Care for older relatives, funds for medical costs of handicapped child.

Most young people handle the first two steps—setting aside cash and buying insurance—rather well. The trouble comes when they assume that their incomes will continue to rise and that inflation is here to stay. Unfortunately, the second premise is a lot more valid than the first.

Under the free-enterprise system, even tenured jobs are only relatively secure, as thousands of teachers learned in the early 1970s and automobile workers found out in 1974–75. Fortunately, society has developed some buffers: unemployment insurance, supplementary unemployment benefits, and early retirement. But they are stopgaps, not solutions!

Over a lifetime, almost every wage earner will be without a job for at least one significant period of time. That doesn't mean we advise squirreling away every dollar for that rainy day, but it is a sound reason to think twice before you make an expensive, long-term commitment. *Managing money means just that: recognizing the risks as well as the rewards.*

On the other hand, the old axioms of "Always pay cash" and "Save first, spend later" are no longer fully valid because of the erosion of inflation. In grandfather's time, the dollar saved might buy $1.25 in another 10 years. Today, a saved dollar will buy about 30¢ worth in the same span. That's why so many people are willing to borrow heavily while they are young. They look forward to ever-rising income and the opportunity to repay the loans with depreciated dollars. That higher income may not materialize, but there is almost sure to be inflation!

Not so long ago, it made sense to postpone that new wing to the house because the $5,000 loan would cost 12% or more. Not now. With the cost of materials and wages rising as much as 20% a year, you'll be better off to borrow and build IF you can do so without overstraining your budget. Inflation has changed many a long-standing tenet of financial management!

There's no one answer to inflation for the individual or family. How much you save or borrow depends largely on your personal viewpoint, background, job future, family stability, and increasingly, the overall economic situation.

Personally, we are confident of the future. America has always had the ability to grow and prosper, to provide more and better goods and services to more people, to protect and to improve standards of living, and to offer greater opportunities. We believe this nation and, gradually, the world will continue to do this. But there will be occasional rough times. That's what a free society is all about. If you accept the joys and rewards of prosperity, you must also be willing to endure some of the disappointments and frustrations. Within bounds, there's much to be said for "Nothing ventured, nothing gained."

Calculating the Costs of Inflation

It's not easy to guesstimate the costs of inflation. When the time comes to buy that new car or boat, you can settle for a cheaper model. But when you are making long-term plans, ALWAYS factor in (mentally or actually) the pressures of inflation.

Example: Back in 1965, your father probably thought that a net worth of $200,000 would be an ample estate for his family and assurance of a pleasant retirement for himself and your mother. By 1975, he had found that $300,000 was more realistic. By 1985, he—or you—will need $400,000 to keep pace!

Estate planning consultant Martin Geylin used this table to show what has happened in recent years—between 1965 and

1973. (If 1974 had been available, he would have added another 10%.)

Base Year to Now	To Stay Even % Income Increase
1965–73	28.84
1966–73	26.81
1967–73	24.70
1968–73	21.54
1969–73	17.32
1970–73	12.42
1971–73	8.66
1972–73	5.65

To use this, dig out an old income tax report. If you found one for 1967, you had to boost your net worth, in 6 years, by 24.70%; from 1969: + 17.32%—TO STAY EVEN.

You can devise your own inflation table by taking your income total every 3 months. Subtract expenses and taxes to get your cash flow. Add this to the first-of-the-year net worth. If your assets are growing at a rate of 2.5% per quarter, you are matching the annual inflation rate of 10%.

Things You Want

Budgets vary so widely by areas of the country and by size, type, and personality of each family that there's no good reason to repeat them here. At best, they would be only a starting point.

Estate planning, however, is a long-term program to make your life more enjoyable and to take legitimate advantage of opportunities to save taxes.

It's elementary that you start with your income and adjust your expenses accordingly. Then you know what savings can be used to develop plans: for 1 year, 5 years, 10 years, etc.

Here's how one family set up its 5-year program as of January 1, 1975:

Objective	Amount Needed	Target Date	Months to Save	Amount to Save Monthly	Amount to Save Annually
New car for wife— down payment only, balance financed	$ 900	7/76	18	$50	$600
Washer-dryer	360	1/76	12	30	360
European vacation	2,400	7/78	30	80	960
Investments- education fund	1,500	12/79	60	25	300

Note that we've listed the monthly amounts to be saved. Realistically, you won't be able to put aside that amount every month, so plan on an annual basis. Try to meet the monthly savings schedule, but if you don't make it, add to the set-aside when you get a tax refund, win a lottery, receive a gift, or work overtime. *Be sure to keep close to the schedule and revise plans annually.*

If you have a regular income, planning is easy. If your income is irregular (from commissions, seasonal work, etc.), it's difficult. The best approach is to decide the minimum annual income you can expect: salary, dividends, interest, etc. If you prefer to operate quarterly, divide the total by 4. When you take in more than anticipated, put the extra money in reserve for lean months.

How Large Are Your Expenses?

Expenses can be broken down into two categories: fixed (the *musts*) and flexible (the balance). To some people, some expenses may seem more fixed than flexible, but experience shows that, to varying degrees, flexible expenses can be curtailed or expanded according to family resources—and discipline.

To prepare a monthly plan of savings, take the total amount of large, periodic payments—say taxes—and divide by 12. Then relate the amount to the time available for savings.

Example: You owe $600 in taxes next April. That means you must set aside $150 a month during January, February,

March, and April. But in May you need to put away only $50 per month to be ready for next April.

Here's how to set up your basic program:

Fixed Expenses: must be paid every month or so.

Housing: rent, mortgage payments.

Taxes: federal, state, local.

Utilities: electricity, gas, water, telephone, fuel, garbage, cable TV.

Installment payments: automobile, appliances, furniture, charge accounts, credit cards, personal loans, Christmas Club, investments-savings.

Insurance: life, auto, health, fire and theft, Social Security, other.

Education: tuition, room and board, books, other.

Transportation: auto license and registration, commutation, parking.

Personal allowances: husband, wife, children.

Personal improvement: music lessons, dancing lessons, other.

Membership dues: union, professional association, clubs.

Contributions: religious, charity, college.

Emergency fund: loss of job, illness, accident, major repairs.

Subscriptions: newspapers, magazines.

Flexible Expenses: can be increased or decreased.

Food: at home, meals out.

Clothing: new clothing and accessories, laundry, dry cleaning, alterations.

Household equipment: new appliances, new furniture, repairs.

Home improvements: maintenance, remodeling, expansion.

Household supplies: cleaning, first aid, miscellaneous.

Household help: sitter, yard care, housecleaning.

Gifts: birthdays, weddings, anniversaries, showers, illness, graduation, other.

Transportation: gasoline, repairs, bus-train-taxi.

Health (not covered by insurance): medical, dental, drugs.

Personal care: grooming aids, barber, beauty shop.

Entertainment: extra food, liquor, theater, sporting events, clubs, parties.

Recreation: hobbies, sports equipment and fees, vacation.

Miscellaneous: periodicals, books, postage, stationery, tobacco, other.

To Make Your Spending Plan Balance

Totals	One Planning Period	One Year
Income		

Fixed expenses

Flexible expenses

Total expenses

Savings for goals

> If not enough: Where can you adjust expenses? How can you shift schedule of payments (to bank, insurance company, etc.)? What can be done to build extra income?

Then, says the Household Finance Corporation, keep summaries like this:

	Planning Period	Annual
Fixed expenses: regular		
periodic		
Flexible expenses: regular		
periodic		
Balance (savings)		
Total		
Income		

Things saved for	date started	date wanted	estimated cost	amount saved	total saved

Professional Assistance

If you don't have the time and do have—or hope for—increasing wealth, you may want to retain a full-service financial management organization. These are teams of highly specialized professionals who start with in-depth interviews of your wants, review your assets and needs, and then set up plans to maximize your resources by tax shelters so that only 10 to 15% of your gross income is paid to Uncle Sam.

Most of these firms prefer to start with assets of $1 million, but some will consider clients with incomes of $25,000 and a net worth of $100,000. Fees run from $1,000 to $5,000. These experts are most helpful when sudden wealth is involved.

Example: A middle-aged professional, averaging $35,000 annual net income, inherited land which he sold for almost $1 million. As the result of the $100,000 down payment, his tax seemed sure to zoom. And he still had to decide how to handle an extra $190,000 a year ($100,000 installment and $90,000 in interest).

The experts advised him to:

- Put the down payment into tax-free municipals until the right tax shelter could be found.
- Use income averaging to cut his immediate tax liability.
- Invest in income-producing, commercial real estate. By using the unpaid note as collateral, he was able to borrow to buy prime property. He repaid the loan from the rentals and deducted the interest, depreciation, etc.
- Revise his insurance and other estate plans by creating trusts for his family, making gifts to his favorite charities, etc.

.Long-Term Estate Planning

Other chapters provide information on how to protect your family and reduce your estate taxes. This subject is so important that some of the facts need to be repeated.

Broadly speaking, all estates have 2 major deductions under federal tax laws:

> *Marital Deduction.* The marital deduction is 50% of the value of the estate. When one spouse dies, half of the estate (after legal fees and probate costs) goes to the survivor tax-free. (See Chapter V, "Trusts," to learn how to save taxes on these assets.)
> *Estate Exemption.* The estate exemption is $60,000 off the top. Logically, this should mean a total exemption of $120,000 for a married couple. But the IRS has different ideas. If the wife dies first, the estate will get $60,000 tax-free. But when the husband dies, only the same $60,000 (and no more) will be tax-exempt from his estate.

Proper planning can assure substantial savings in estate taxes —as much as 63% in a $200,000 estate:

Size of Estate	Estimated No Planning	Taxes and Costs Planning	Average Savings Through Planning
$ 200,000	$ 49,000	$ 18,000	63%
300,000	93,000	47,000	49
400,000	139,000	79,000	43
500,000	186,000	100,000	46
1,000,000	432,000	282,000	35

Keep these goals in mind as you plan your estate.
The cost of NOT PLANNING is almost 2 to 3 times that of planning!

These figures show why it is important to get a lawyer with estate-planning experience. Never settle for a standard form. It may cost $200 or more to get a tailored-to-your-needs will, but it can be very important to your heirs. The only thing worse is having no will at all!

To help your executor, your widow, your lawyer, and your own plans, fill out (and keep current) the following data:

Estate-Planning Data

Name_____ Date of Birth_____

Address_____ Place of Birth_____

Name of Spouse_____ Date of Birth_____

Address_____ Place of Birth_____

Names of Children	Date of Birth	Address .

Names of Grandchildren

_____

_____

_____

Other Beneficiaries	Relationship	Address

Assets

	Bank	Account Number	Approximate Amount
Checking Accounts			
Savings Accounts			
Other Savings: Certificates of Deposit			
U.S. Savings Bonds			

Estate-Planning Data (*Continued*)

Investments

	Face Amount	Cost	Approximate Value
Bonds			
Stocks			
Mutual Funds			

Retirement Plan	Trustee	Approximate Value	
		Now	At Age 65

Real Estate

	Location	Title	Cost	Approximate Value
Residence				
Vacation Home				
Other				

Life Insurance

Company	Face Amount	Cash Value	Beneficiary	Loans

Other Assets

	Obligor	Amount Due	Interest	Maturity Date
Loans Due You				
Royalties, Interest in Other Properties				

	Location	Approximate Value
Personal Collections (Stamps, Coins, Etc.)		
Other		

Estate-Planning Data (*Continued*)

Liabilities

	Lender	Amount	Due Date
Loans			
Mortgages			
Installments			
Taxes: Federal			
State			
Local			
Other Debts			

Gifts Made

Recipient	Amount	Years of Gifts

People to Contact

	Name	Address	Phone Number
Lawyer			
Banker			
Broker			
Accountant			
Funeral Director			

Other pertinent information: _____

Set Aside Cash and Liquid Assets

One of the most frequent and disastrous omissions that can be made in estate planning is to leave your family rich in assets and poor in cash. A study of more than 45,000 federal estate tax returns showed that expenses accounted for more than 23% of taxable estate. Yet there was cash and liquid assets sufficient to meet only 13.6% of these costs!

When there are insufficient available funds, your widow and children may be caught in a severe, terrifying squeeze. And because he must pay the federal tax within 9 months, your executor may have to sell assets at forced-sale prices.

> *Note:* The executor can ask for an extension of tax time on grounds of undue hardship—at an interest rate of 9% on the unpaid balance.

As these tables show, the cash requirements can be very substantial.

The Cash Your Widow Will Need

Most estates can be settled within 6 to 12 months, but some can take as long as 5 years. To make sure that your family won't be caught in a cash bind, your estate planning should provide immediate cash and sufficient liquid assets to pay for at least 1 year's expenses and preferably 2. Your widow won't need the full $20,000 as there will be Social Security payments—the amount varying according to your coverage, ages of widow and children, etc. These basic needs should be reviewed periodically and revised according to changing conditions: mortgage repayments, educational costs, etc.

Expenses	Widow's Needs
Home (mortgage-insurance)	$ 4,000
Taxes (property-income)	2,600
Educational costs	4,000
Home maintenance-repair	600
Food, etc.	1,500
Car	1,800
Clothing	1,400
Heat and utilities	700
Telephone	400
Health and personal care	1,000
Recreation	1,500
Miscellaneous	500
Total	$20,000

The Cash Your Executor Should Have

An estate total of $300,000 may seem high, but the figure is used to point up the impact of the costs of settling an estate. Actually, it's not a great amount when you add the value of your home ($75,000), other personal property and investments ($75,000), and life insurance ($150,000).

Wise planning should have placed more assets with your spouse, directly or through a trust. The point is that you cannot keep on building assets without considering the high costs of death as mandated by law.

Here's what will be needed by your executor:

1. Total gross estate $300,000
2. Death expenses (debts, funeral costs, and estate administration) Rule of thumb:
   7.5 % of line 1   22,500
3. Adjusted gross estate (line 1 − line 2)   277,500
4. Estate after marital deduction (up to half of adjusted gross estate goes to wife tax-free)   138,725
5. Specific exemption (from federal taxes)   60,000
6. Taxable estate (line 4 − line 5)   78,725
7. Estate tax*   15,745
   Rough estimate: If your net taxable estate is:
   $50,000–$100,000, multiply line 6 by .20;
   $100,000–$250,000, multiply line 6 by .25;
   over $250,000, multiply line 6 by .30
8. Total cash need by executor:
   Add line 2 to line 7   38,245

   * Before credit for inheritance tax.

Here are steps you take to build cash and liquid assets in your estate:

Real Estate

Sell properties that are far away and not a part of your overall financial program. It's all very well to continue to hold that New England farmland you inherited from Uncle Joe, but if you are not going to use it in the near future, start putting up a for-sale sign. Of course, if it is in the path of development through new highways, etc., or your youngsters want to build a log cabin, hang on, as its value will increase.

If your executor has to sell in a hurry, those shrewd Yankees won't be averse to helping a "neighbor"—if the price is low enough.

Buy "Flower" Bonds

These are one of the most profitable estate-planning investments. They are "die-to-win" obligations of the U.S. government. They carry low coupons, but in times of high interest rates, sell well below par and so provide a modest return of 6.5% to 7.5%. Their big advantage is that, regardless of purchase price, they are worth par ($1,000) when used to pay federal estate taxes.

"Flower" bonds are especially useful to older people who have sufficient assets to have to pay estate taxes. For middle-aged people, they are worthwhile when planning for retirement or when able to afford to take lower returns that are taxable as ordinary income.

For further information and lists of available bonds, see Chapter XXV on How to Make Your Savings Grow.

Use Gifts to Reduce Potential Estate Taxes

Liquid assets can be enhanced and tax levies reduced by the wise use of gifts. You are allowed to give away $3,000 a year to any individual without paying taxes. Above that sum, you are entitled to a lifetime exemption of $30,000. Beyond that, there's a modest gift tax to pay.

As a rule of thumb: The gift exemption applies if the

giver no longer controls the gift, i.e., a man can give the house to his wife and continue to live there. But if he retains any income from the property, he still owns it, according to IRS rules.

Warning: Don't assume that because the husband holds the house jointly with his wife, he has given her a half interest. Such property will be taxed in the estate of the spouse who dies first unless the survivor can prove she (or he) helped to pay for the property.

Taxwise, it's OK to give your wife the house and take the marital deduction, annual exemption, and any unused part of the lifetime gift exemption. But better be sure your marriage is secure!

The same general rule applies to life insurance. Unless the policy is given away, the insurance proceeds will become part of the husband's estate. "Gift" means a complete divestment of all rights to name the beneficiary and to borrow against the cash values. The gift tax, if any, would be based on the cash value of straight policies. Term insurance has no cash value.

Securities, especially listed stocks that have appreciated in value, make excellent gifts. The donor has the tax advantage of deducting the current value even though his purchase price was far less. The recipient gets securities that can be turned into cash promptly.

In such a case, the burden of taxes falls on the recipient if and when the stocks are sold. He/she must calculate the capital gains on the appreciation—the difference between the first cost and the price at the time of the gift. Thus, if Uncle Al buys 100 shares of Eastman Kodak at 40 and gives it to Cousin Judy when it is 140, the tax will be on the 100-point gain if Judy sells. The rate would be one-half that of Judy's regular federal tax up to a maximum of 25% —for most people.

Gifts are an essential part of long-range estate planning. They should be used wisely—always on the basis of desire or need and not solely because of tax benefits.

Older people should establish patterns of giving if they

want to avoid difficulty with the IRS on "contemplation of death," which bans gifts made within three years of demise. People who have been giving regularly for a number of years have a strong case. And recent court rulings have eased strict interpretation.

An 80-year-old lady who had made substantial gifts to relatives and charity died suddenly. The IRS tried to tax the gifts as part of the estate. The court ruled otherwise "because she had shown so much zest for life": celebrating her birthday at the Waldorf-Astoria by dancing until 2:00 A.M., leaving for California soon afterward, and ordering tickets for her next summer vacation!

III

Choosing and Using Your Family Lawyer

A good lawyer can keep you out of trouble, protect your interests, save you time and money, and assure your family's peace of mind. Whether called attorney, counselor, barrister, solicitor, or just plain lawyer, he—or she—is authorized to practice law in your state and, occasionally, elsewhere. In that role he has special rights and responsibilities that are closely related to the protection and distribution of property.

Your family lawyer is the most important selection you will make in effective personal money management. Selection should be done carefully on the basis of *your* present and future needs, *his* experience and ability, *your* feeling of respect and trust, and *his* empathy with you, your wife, and your children.

For most families, legal problems are routine matters that must be handled within prescribed limits and under well-established procedures. It's more important that your attorney be dependable than that he be brilliant.

If you anticipate difficult problems involving taxes, criminal law, damage suits, etc., special expertise should be a key factor in your choice. With few exceptions, the same lawyer can handle, or supervise, the family "nuts and bolts"—preparing wills, closing a real-estate purchase, settling an estate, or setting up trusts. But when you get into special areas of litigation or contracts, he will have to call for help from a partner or a fellow practitioner. The expert's fees will probably be higher than those of a generalist.

It is always wise and often imperative to consult a lawyer on such major life events as:

Building or buying a home or leasing an apartment.
Making or revising wills.
Entering into any contract for employment, partnership, services, or expense sharing.
Setting up a personal pension plan, trust, or similar tax-avoidance, tax-postponement program.
Making an investment in an outside business—real estate, franchise operation, new enterprise, etc.
Defending against legal action.
Seeking payments due you under laws (workmen's compensation), damages (insurance policies), contracts, etc.
Answering questions on interpretation of tax regulations and tax returns.
Contemplating family changes such as separation, divorce, or adoption.
Accepting authority from—or delegating authority to—someone else—as executor, trustee, guardian, power of attorney, etc.

Too many people waste their money and their lawyer's time with minor problems that they can handle themselves—traffic tickets, internal family quarrels, collection of money, and other inevitable irritations. *Before you run to a lawyer, make sure that it is* (1) something that you cannot handle yourself, directly or through some community agency; (2) a real legal problem.

Examples. If you are unable to collect money, go to small-claims court. For about $10, you can start suit for debts up to $500 or $1,000 (depending on the state and municipality). A hearing is usually held within 60 days, and the judge will render a verdict promptly. If necessary, a sheriff or constable will enforce the decision.

If you think you've been cheated by a store or businessman, complain to the local Better Business Bureau or governmental agency such as the Bureau of Consumer Protection (see the phone book or call the local Chamber of Commerce or nearest federal office).

If there are family problems, ask for help from your clergyman or from some United Way agency such as the Bureau of Family Service, Associated Catholic Charities, or Jewish Community Federation. Counseling and remedial services are readily available at a cost far less than that of an attorney, and in most cases, with better solutions to your problems.

If you have to battle the landlord for heat or the neighbors over noise, call City Hall or the Police Community Relations Department. That's one of the reasons why you're paying taxes!

How to Start Your Search

Most people choose lawyers on the basis of tradition (family retainer), propinquity (his office is above the bank), social relations (he belongs to their church or club), or public recognition (he's a member of the City Council or School Board). None of these criteria can be called discriminating standards. Nor do they necessarily relate to the individual's legal knowledge or ability to provide the services you need at the price you can afford to pay.

Then there's the very important question of trust. According to Herbert S. Denenberg, former Pennsylvania Insurance Commissioner, "You probably can't trust twenty percent of the lawyers in this country." This may be a bit of political rhetoric, but it does point up that a law degree is no guarantee of competence or integrity.

Broadly speaking, you have three choices in selecting your attorney—a solo practitioner, a partnership, or a law firm. Remember that, in every case, you are hiring an *individual*. His associates can be helpful and can provide a backup, but one man—or woman—will be primarily responsible for your family's legal needs!

A lot depends on where you live. In a small community, most lawyers work alone. In a medium-size city, partnerships involve 4 to 8 members. In metropolitan areas, a 20-member firm is considered small.

The pros and cons are obvious: greater (and probably slower) personal service in a small office; broader skills with larger firms. As a rule of thumb, look for lawyers who have had at least 7 years of experience as generalists, 10 years when specialists.

If your needs are routine (as most will be), don't skip youngsters. They will be energetic, hardworking, up-to-date, and usually less expensive than their established colleagues. You will, of course, do better if they are associated with at least one veteran barrister.

The first step is to write down just what kinds of legal services you need now and for the next 10 to 15 years. You should assume that the individual you choose will handle everything, even though you know he will need help from his colleagues or outside specialists. You are selecting YOUR lawyer.

If you are new in town, ask friends, neighbors, and business associates for recommendations. Lawyers are not allowed to advertise, but the American Bar Association's comment gives you a good base: "The most . . . effective advertisement possible . . . is the establishment of a well-merited reputation for professional capacity and fidelity."

Ask for recommendations from people in whose judgment you have confidence—your banker, physician, and business friends. Be skeptical of suggestions from those whose self-interest is involved—stockbrokers, realtors, insurance agents, for example. They may get "kickbacks" in dollars or favors.

Names from judges and court clerks also have limited usefulness. These people see the lawyer only in court—the one place you do not want to be.

Also be cautious of individuals named by corporate executives. Their legal contacts are likely to be with large firms whose members have special contacts and skills that are seldom adaptable to family needs.

One corporate source where you can probably get helpful leads is the "house counsel," the lawyer employed by a business organization or governmental agency. He may be most valuable in eliminating "bad" candidates.

Another Convenient Source

A handy source is the local Bar Referral Service. This is available in some 300 communities across the country and in 1974 handled more than 300,000 applications. From personal experience, I know this can be beneficial, but Commissioner Denenberg is not so enthusiastic. He feels that the list is all-inclusive, and because it is compiled by nonlegal personnel, it does not provide enough information to enable you to select the "right" lawyer. All the same, it's a valuable source of names.

An off-beat gambit. Call a friend in a distant city and have him ask his local lawyer whom he would consult if he needed legal aid in your community.

When you have a list of 8 or 9 more-than-once-recommended people, check their qualifications in the *Martindale-Hubbell Law Directory*. This may be available at your local library and will surely be on file at the bar association office. This lists almost every attorney by age, college, law school, specialty, firm affiliation, legal associates, and types of clients. And believe it or not, it shows his financial standing and how his fellow lawyers rate him.

Such information should enable you to cut your roster in half. In your editing, be realistic: Try to select people who are likely to have an understanding of your needs and problems. This means individuals who have similar backgrounds and interests and are about your age—or better, that of your wife. Hopefully, most of the lawyer's time will be spent on planning and settling your estate.

The next step is to arrange for an interview with your No. 1 choice. Over the phone tell him exactly what you have in mind —a meeting to discuss the possibility of a long-term relationship, or if you face a crisis, an outline of your problem. To avoid the possibility of future embarrassment, ask if there will be a fee for this preliminary consultation. If he says yes, you can say thank you and move on to the next name.

When you sit down in his office, use your checklist to review your needs, or if you are facing possible litigation, your problem. *Tell him the whole truth, even if you have been guilty of poor judgment.* Your information will be kept confidential. Knowing the full story is the only way the lawyer can know what he is expected to do and whether he has the experience— and time—to represent you properly.

If he's interested, he'll ask you questions. This will give you a chance to get a feel for his approach, his view of his role, his personality, and whether he will wear well with you and your family.

If he is a member of a firm, he may point out that a partner would be better equipped to handle your needs. Or if you are concerned about suing or being sued, he may refer you to another attorney outside his office.

Before you leave, ask about fees. As explained later, they will probably be quoted in ranges—fairly narrow for standard items such as wills, personal pension plans, settlement of an estate, etc.; very broad for lawsuits, collections, tax counsel, and special problems.

Even if there's rapport and general agreement on fee schedules, delay your decision until you have had a chance to review your needs against his qualifications, and of course, until you have talked to your wife.

Between the information in the *Law Directory,* recommendations, and the answers to your questions, you should know:

the history of his practice or firm; his type of clients (individuals, governments, corporations); experience in special areas; possible conflicts of interest (if you are, or expect to be, involved with an insurance company, for example); legal philosophy (whether he prefers to negotiate settlements or appear in court); and how much personal attention you can expect (will he handle routine matters or turn them over to a younger associate?).

If your first interview does not go well, move on to the No. 2 candidate. You must have confidence in whomever you select. If you feel he is not the man, tell him so at once.

It's a good idea to check at least two candidates, but don't look too far. You won't find a Perry Mason or Owen Marshall. Lawyers are just as human as you are. You are looking for trust and common sense more than brilliance, personality, or an impressive courtroom manner.

Don't Do It Yourself!

There are few areas where doing-it-yourself can be more dangerous and costly than in preparing your own legal documents. The few hundred dollars spent for a lawyer to draw a will, real-estate contract, or incorporation papers is a small investment when measured against the possible losses, penalties, litigation, and subversion of your wishes that can result from improperly prepared legal papers.

Examples: "How-to" books make the preparation of wills seem easy. All you have to do is follow a standard form and get witnesses.

But state laws vary and are changed frequently by legislatures or court decisions. Even if you follow instructions to the letter, your will may not meet the legal requirements in your state. The book, written for a national audience, may say that your signature needs only two witnesses. But the state law demands three!

In such a case, your will could be thrown out, and the court would rule that you died *intestate*—as if you had never drawn a will. The judge would then divide the property according to a formula that might have little relation to what you had in mind!

Or take simple incorporation papers. The book says that all you have to do is write to the state attorney general for the necessary forms. That's true, but each state has different requirements for issuing stock and widely different methods of computing the stock value for estate tax purposes. The $250 saved today could mean $10,000 in extra taxes a decade from now.

Most important: Laws are enacted by legislatures whose members are largely lawyers who, quite understandably, are well aware of the economics of their profession.

Little Uniformity in Legal Fees

Getting quotations on legal fees is always difficult and usually impossible. Some lawyers will give you fixed prices for simple projects that can be handled with standard forms (drawing a simple will, incorporating a small business, or handling an uncontested divorce), but for almost all other legal activities, you'll be lucky to get a range of costs based on estimated hours at specified rates.

This reluctance to be pinned down is understandable. Most veterans know that simple requests can turn into complex, time-consuming problems.

There are few financial standards in the legal field. Most legal fees are a combination of tradition, time (and who is to know the hours really spent?), location of work (office, court, or your home), the amount of money involved, and the results obtained. There's also likely to be an over-the-shoulder glance at the client's financial status.

The ranges of some costs are set by law. The fees for probating a will or buying a house are, generally, percentages of the sums involved. There's no necessary relationship to the complexity of the problem.

And as indicated in the table of fees (see page 44), similar work in different parts of the country (and even of the same state) can be 2 or 3 times as expensive as in your area—or vice versa.

Add personal quirks: Rural lawyers often use "loss leaders." They prepare wills for a small fee because they anticipate handling the estate; wealthy attorneys may charge exorbitant fees in an effort to get rid of undesirable clients; and counselors whose firms have been in the same communities for generations usually provide free or low-cost services to nonprofit agencies or families with limited resources. Such expenses have to be made up elsewhere.

What it all comes down to is that legal fees are not exactly a budgetable item. A lawyer fixes his hourly rates pretty much as does the manager of a business. He considers his overhead, out-of-pocket costs, the salaries and benefits of his staff, how much his own expenses are (insurance, pension, etc.), and how much he hopes to earn for himself.

On the average, the basic costs for a one-person law office run close to $20 an hour. To set a profitable fee, the lawyer must add what he wants to take home for his own efforts.

Even when there are flat fees, these are based largely on assumed hourly costs. These vary according to the type of service and the lawyer's experience, location, and ambition. They range from about $50 an hour for consultation to $150-plus a day for court appearances.

Methods of Charging

Usually, lawyers send their bills on time; occasionally they ask for retainers. They prefer to work on contingencies when the case involves damages, insurance, etc., and once in a while, they look for bonuses or income from referral fees. The last two categories are seldom important to individual clients. A bonus might be charged on important cases where the stakes are high and the services demanding. If a good result is obtained, the lawyer might add 25% to his regular hourly billing rate.

When there's a referral, the originator may get as much as

one-third of the total fee, depending on the case, client, and circumstances. This arrangement increases the costs of the legal services but is used primarily in major litigation, especially when out-of-area attorneys are involved. Most lawyers discuss referrals before commitments are made.

A retainer is a fee paid on a regular, periodic basis. A payment of $100 per month, for example, will entitle you to pick up the phone anytime and to drop in for a brief chat once a month. It may also assure prompt action—no small benefit, as lawyers are not noted for their speed of accomplishment.

In most cases, the retainer is deducted from the total monthly bill if there have been other charges.

Retainers are fine for business firms but seldom make sense for individuals. Once the basics (wills, leases, trusts, etc.) are completed, you will probably be better off if you pay only when you need legal help.

Contingent fees are used primarily in negligence cases where one person claims money damages from another—i.e., personal injuries from a motor vehicle accident. If you win, your lawyer receives 25% to 60% of the amount recovered. If you lose, the lawyer has worked for nothing but costs.

When you make a contingent fee agreement, do a bit of bargaining—on the percentage to be paid and the method of payment.

You should pay expenses, but they should be taken off the top of a successful award *before* the lawyer's fee is deducted.

Example: The award is $10,000, the expenses $1,000, and the contingency fee is one-third of the recovery. If the lawyer takes his share straight off, he will get $3,333 plus the expenses and you will net $5,667. By deducting the $1,000 expenses first, he gets $3,000 and you will have $6,000.

What's a Reasonable Charge?

Unlike charges for medical services, which can be determined, generally, by checking the payments authorized by insurance companies, there are no exact definitions of "reasonable" legal fees.

Note: If you are the digging type who enjoys extrapolating information, take a look at the benefit schedules of prepaid legal insurance plans. The payments cover the cost of each service when the policyholder receives routine legal aid from an average lawyer. There are not many such programs, and as far as can be determined, the charges are not materially different from those indicated in the table on page 44.

Many bar associations do have a recommended *minimum* fee *schedule* but you should be concerned with *maximum* charges.

You can get an idea of how fees are *supposed* to be set by these recommendations from the American Bar Association:

To determine if a fee is reasonable, lawyers should:

1. Consider the time and labor required, the novelty and difficulty of the questions involved, and the skill requisite to perform the legal services properly.

2. Recognize the likelihood that the acceptance of one case will bar or limit other commitments.

3. Keep the fee in line with that customarily charged in the locality.

4. Relate the amount involved to the results obtained.

5. Weigh the time limitations imposed by the client and circumstances.

6. Consider the nature and length of the professional relationship with the client.

7. Take into account the experience, reputation, and ability of the lawyer.

There is some hope of better criteria soon. Consumer groups are stirring public outcry against these haphazard (or, at least, nonscientific) methods of setting fees. The response of the legal profession has been scattered and slow but there has been considerable discussion and hopeful action. The most popular proposal for greater uniformity—if not equity—is the establishment of a unit-value system. This would measure the time needed for

the most frequently used legal services—10 units for an uncontested divorce, 6 for an adoption, 2 for a simple will, etc.
The charges per unit vary according to the area, office overhead,
desired work load, etc. Thus, the final standard might be $30
per unit in a small town, $60 in a major city.

Watch for news that the idea has been adopted in your state.
With support from a past president of the American Bar Association, this relative-value approach may come faster than many
legal eagles anticipate.

What to Do When You Are Unhappy with Your Lawyer

Dilatory seems to be the middle name of most lawyers. They
have an amazing capacity for delay, procrastination, and postponement. In some cases, especially when court appearances
are required, your attorney may not be at fault. But regardless
of who's to blame, you have the right to complain, and if the
inaction continues, to terminate his services and retain someone
else. The same advice goes for other derelictions.

If you do decide to take such a drastic step, protect your
position by consulting another lawyer *first*. Describe your legal
problem before telling him of your complaint. Lawyers stick
together, and of course, don't like overly critical clients.

If you feel strongly about the miserable service, incompetency,
or suspect dishonesty, file a complaint with the local or state
bar association. Or if you live in Pennsylvania, write to the
Disciplinary Board of the Supreme Court of Pennsylvania, 100
Pine Street, Harrisburg, Pennsylvania 17101. This newly established board disciplines lawyers who violate the Code of Professional Responsibility. There may be similar services in other
states soon.

In many areas, bar associations have established funds to pay
clients who lose money or property because of the dishonest
conduct of a lawyer. There's also some chance of reimbursement
if your lawyer carries professional liability insurance. This is a

broad policy for negligence or omission—failing to file an important paper with a court, neglecting to complete legal forms, etc. Such a policy does NOT cover dishonest or criminal acts.

Care and Feeding of Lawyers

Once you have made your choice of a lawyer, get yourself organized. The less time spent with the lawyer, the lower your costs!

Update your original checklist of legal needs; get out all your necessary papers from the safe-deposit box and your home file (and your wife's bottom dresser drawer); correct names and addresses for your will; write down the numbers and values of insurance policies and stock certificates; verify the Social Security numbers of all members of the family—from Grandma to Baby (see Chapter V, on Trusts).

It's a good idea to have your spouse sit in on the first conference. She can add some ideas, learn her responsibilities, and get to know the attorney.

This is the time to discuss *every* item in detail. Then set up a timetable for action. In this way, your expenses will be spread over several months. If an emergency arises, you can make changes or postponements.

Rules for a successful client-lawyer relationship:

Do What the Lawyer Says

This is always important, but it is essential when there's litigation. If you do not trust—or agree with—the proposed legal approach, say so, and if the attorney is adamant, get another counselor.

In most cases, you will be wrong. On a majority of legal issues, the rules are well established and the law clear—*even if you disagree*.

According to legal historian William P. Wilkins, "At least one-third of all court cases are lost AFTER the attorney has been called in. The client, either through ignorance or fear, ruins the case."

Don't Expect Free Advice

A lawyer's time is his stock-in-trade. If you get information or advice over the phone, be prepared to pay for it.

Don't Withhold Information

Remember that courtroom oath: "I swear to tell the truth, the whole truth, and nothing but the truth." The role of the lawyer is to present your case in the best possible light. False or incomplete statements can destroy his arguments, or if it's a document, can nullify your wishes.

Keep Him Advised of New Developments

Don't assume that he knows you have moved to a new address, have a new baby, changed your job, or inherited some property. Lawyers are too busy to keep track of *your* responsibilities. Keep a list of important changes and discuss them at your periodic legal review.

Insist on a Complete, Itemized Bill

If the costs seem high, ask for an explanation, including the list of court filing fees, receipts from agencies, and bills for long-distance calls. There's no need to be chintzy, but you should make it clear that you expect him to watch his expenses as closely as you monitor yours.

When more than one person has worked on your problems, the fees should reflect the office scale—$10 an hour for routine work done by a paralegal assistant; $20 per hour for documents prepared by a law clerk; $50 an hour for your lawyer; and if the help of an experienced partner is needed on a special problem, $100 or more an hour.

If you are referred to another lawyer, get details of the other attorney's fee schedule and ask if a referral fee is involved. This could be important in preliminary discussions when the first lawyer makes no charge. He might get extra income from the second attorney. There's nothing illegal about such a procedure, but bar association ethics require that the client be fully informed.

One ease-your-mind solution: Pay reasonable fees to both counselors.

Some consumer advocates make a great to-do about this practice of splitting fees, but it is customary and only rarely involves family legal services.

When you complain, make sure you are not at fault. Much of the success of a client-lawyer relationship depends on your attitude and preparation. Usually, dissatisfaction is due to a lack of understanding and/or communication. You assumed that the attorney knew, or remembered, more than he really did. He assumed that after his detailed explanation you understood clearly the what and why of his recommendation and plan of action. Before you complain too loudly or decide to make a change, review your own case.

Whenever the problems involve charges (which, of course, you feel are too high), look at the results and ask yourself how much that extra $125 really means when measured against a $100,000 estate!

When you select a lawyer, try to make it a lifetime commitment. A good lawyer is like a good physician. He should be an individual in whom you have confidence. He should be consulted at least once a year. And he should be judged not only by what he does but also by what he stops you from doing!

Use the accompanying table as a reference point only. It was based on information originally compiled for *Money* magazine. These data were revised and supplemented later with the help of friends. Their accuracy (and validity) is open to question, but as the editors of *Money* complained with the original chart: "This is further evidence of lawyers' reluctance to discuss their fees."

Ranges of Fees Charged by Lawyers

| | Northeast | | | |
Service	City Firm	Solo	Suburb	Small Town
Drawing Will	$100	$25	$25 to $50	$25
Probating Will		3% to 5% of gross estate		
Closing on Single-Family House	1% of selling price	$400	$300 to $500	1% to 2% of selling price
Uncontested Divorce	$500	$250	$500	$250
Incorporate Small Business	$300 to $400	$300	$300 to $350	$300
Court Appearances (Per Day)	$200	$50 to $100	$50	$175
Consultation (Per Hour)	$50 to $100	$60	$50	$33

| | South | | | |
Service	City Firm	Solo	Suburb	Small Town
Drawing Will	$75 to $100	$50 to $75	$25 to $50	$50
Probating Will	$100	$100	$50	$150 to $200
Closing on Single-Family House	1½% of mortgage	$100 to $300	1½% of mortgage	
Uncontested Divorce	$350 to $500	$300	$250 to $350	$250
Incorporate Small Business	$350	$300 to $500	$300	$250 to $300
Court Appearances (Per Day)	$150	$150	$100	$300 to $500
Consultation (Per Hour)	$50	$50	$25 to $30	$35 to $50

Ranges of Fees Charged by Lawyers (*Continued*)

Midwest

City		Suburb	Small
Firm	Solo		Town
$50 to $75	$35	$85	$15 to $25
$1,100	$500	3% to 4% of gross estate	6% of 1st $10,000 3% of balance
$250	$150	$175	$100
$275	$400	$350	$250
$250	$350	$350	$250
$300 to $360	$150	$500	$100
$50 to $60	$35	$45	$20

West Coast

City		Suburb	Small
Firm	Solo		Town
$25 to $100	$35	$35 to $50	$15 to $100

Calif.: 7% of 1st $1,000 of estate;
4% next $9,000; 3% of next $40,000, etc.

Closings by escrow and title companies
—generally 4% to 5% of selling
price

$250 to $500	$250	$500	$300
$650	$780	$500	$750
$500	$350	$250	$250
$65	$50	$50	$40

IV

Dos and Don'ts of Wills

There are scores of good reasons for making a will, but as far as I know, there are no valid excuses for *not* making one. Yet, less than half of all adults have a will, and about one-third of these documents will be contested because of poor drafting, errors, or angry survivors—all situations that can be avoided by care and concern.

When there's no will, there are always complications. With a single person or a childless couple, this can be inconvenient. When there are minor children, such a failure can be disastrous. If you die without a will—the legal term is "intestate"—the court will appoint an administrator who must distribute your estate according to state laws. The administrator's action will always be inflexible, usually impersonal, and often contrary to your wishes.

Simple wills that can distribute your worldly goods as you desire require only a few hours and seldom cost more than $50 to $100. This last testament can save taxes, ease strains on your heirs, and reduce legal costs. *Every adult in every family should have a will prepared by a competent lawyer.* It should be reviewed and amended whenever a major change in family life occurs.

Once the will is signed and witnessed, keep it in a safe, accessible place—NOT your safe-deposit box, preferably with your lawyer or the person or institution you have appointed as executor of your estate.

Drawing a will is a task for a lawyer. He'll tell you that it is not necessary to mention all assets nor to give specific items, and will show you how to transfer properties outside your will—by trusts and assignment of contract rights for proceeds of life insurance or pension plans. There are many legal ways to by-pass probate court and permit prompt transfer of assets to your spouse and heirs.

For information about wills in your state (laws vary widely), get a folder from your bank or trust company and consult your attorney—preferably with your wife sitting in. And whatever you do, *heed his counsel.*

As with all phases of personal money management, you should have clear ideas of what you want done with the assets you have accumulated over the years when you die. Discuss them with your spouse and family before you meet with your lawyer. He can be helpful with advice, but his primary role is as a legal technician who will prepare the will to fulfill your wishes and keep taxes to a minimum.

Here are some DOs and DON'Ts on planning your will. There's repetition, but the comments are worth repeating.

DOs for Wills

DO Provide Enough Income for Your Widow

Every wife should have some money in her own name—a savings or checking account and/or securities that can readily be sold. In addition, at least one life insurance policy should name her as direct and immediate beneficiary. All of these will provide funds for taxes and administrative expenses as well as for living, so make sure there will be enough!

The No. 1 need will be enough cash to tide over your widow

and family until the estate can be settled. The lack of ready money can be tragic. Her standard of living will drop drastically. She will be lucky to get credit from the grocer and can count on little help from the telephone, utility, and mortgage companies. She might be able to get a small advance against the estate from the executor bank, but otherwise she will have to depend on parents, friends, and possibly charity. (In many areas, the Red Cross and Salvation Army provide emergency loans.)

> *Note:* Be wary of joint ownership. Treat all property (real estate, bank accounts, securities, etc.) like towels—have HIS and HERS. Jointly owned assets become part of the estate of the deceased. *One easy answer* is to arrange for power of attorney—for your wife on your personal checking account, for you on hers, etc. Furthermore, separate holdings will save taxes and expedite the settlement of the estate by avoiding costly, annoying delays while the tax collector determines how much of the joint property should be excluded from the estate.

DO Plan Ahead for Major Expenses

Provide for your children's education and the devastating costs of a final illness.

If you die in August, it will be almost impossible for your child to start college in the fall unless you have set up a trust or built a separate education fund. Check your insurance agent on a tuition-protecting life policy.

Sickness, as you probably know from family experience, can deplete reserves rapidly. If health insurance is not available and medical costs are mounting, make arrangements for such major expenses before you die as well as in your will.

DO Keep Your Will Up-to-date

Have it revised or rewritten when situations change—when children become adults, when there is divorce, remarriage, death of beneficiaries or witnesses, when you move to another state, sell or acquire real estate, etc.

A will drawn 25 years ago is not likely to be pertinent today. Beneficiaries may be different, especially when there have been divorces, remarriages, and children. Without revisions in your will, your estate could go to your first wife and/or *her* heirs! Your old bequests may negate your present intentions and certainly will confuse distribution of estate assets.

DO Choose a Proper Executor

Choose an alternate as well. This should be a trusted relative or friend who has time to take the responsibility, a lawyer, a bank, or perhaps best of all, your spouse. If you feel that there would be controversy if you appointed a relative who is not popular with other members of the family, name someone else. Your heirs will have trouble enough without this added acrimony.

DO Consider Legacies

Consider legacies on the basis of your wishes, the possibility of the deaths of the beneficiaries, and the tax consequences.

Ask yourself where you'd want the gift to go if the individual named died before you. If you do not state what's to be done, the law takes over, and the result could be quite different from what you intended. In some states, such a legacy would be added to your residuary estate; in others, it would go automatically to the estate of the deceased beneficiary and thus to his/her heirs.

Usually, this carry-through applies only when the beneficiary is a blood relation. *Example:* If you left $5,000 to your widower-brother, who died a few months later, the money would go to his daughter. But if you willed the money to your sister-in-law, and she died, your favorite niece would get nothing!

On each legacy, there's always a question of who will pay federal and state estate taxes. When the gifts are small, the estate can pick up the tab, but if the legacies are large, the taxes can deplete the assets you planned for your wife.

Here, again, there should be definite instructions for your executor. In some states, the entire tax bill comes from your residuary estate; in others, taxes will be apportioned to the beneficiaries according to the value of what they receive.

This last situation can be embarrassing if carried to the letter. If you left a painting to your college roommate, your executor might be bound to send him a tax bill for $14.44!

Be very careful about legacies to office staff or employees. If your will states: "$500 to Susie Cue, my loyal secretary," she'll collect even though she was fired for theft two years ago. *Solution:* Add the words, "providing she is in my employ at the time of my death."

And on the chance that you will outlive all beneficiaries, conclude with the name of your favorite charity. Then, at least, your assets will be distributed as you want, not under the unfeeling law.

DO Protect Your Cash Assets

If they are substantial, the will should provide for prompt professional management. This will lessen the possibility of your heirs' making foolish investments or being talked into lending money to a glib relative.

Make sure that when you make cash bequests, there will be adequate assets to fulfill the commitments. If you name specific sums—$10,000 to St. Mary's Hospital, $15,000 to Yale, etc.— these sums must be paid even if your estate totals only $40,000. *Best bet:* Make the gifts on a percentage basis—10% to St. Mary's, 15% to Yale, etc.

Furthermore, if bequests are not paid within a specified time, the estate may have to pay interest. If cash is short, this could mean that a valuable asset will be liquidated at a poor time. Spell out what you have in mind and give the executor leeway to act as he deems best.

DO Be Specific

This gets into legal interpretations, so make sure that your lawyer understands exactly what you have in mind.

Example: "A home is not just a house." A man bequeathed half the value of his home to his cousin. The building was situated on a 60-acre tract of prime land. The question, which ended in the courts, was: "Is the half value that of the home alone or that of the total house and acreage?"

When you bequeath stocks, write: "All my securities," or if it's real estate, say: "Half of my interest in Roving Acres Estate inherited from my father."

DO Insert a Common Disaster Clause

This covers the rare possibility of the joint death of you and your wife.

DO Use Proper Legal Names

This is not so difficult with relatives, as the courts recognize marriages, divorces, etc., but it can be trouble if you make a gift to the National Association for Chilblains when you really meant the National Chilblain Association—if there are two rival organizations.

What Happens When There Is No Will?

Without a will, an administrator appointed by the court takes over. He must work within the narrow confines of statutes that are designed to provide the greatest good for the greatest number of people. That means, for example, that your estate will be fractionally divided among your legal heirs or next of kin. Your lovely antiques and valuable stamp collection will be sold and the money distributed!

Your widow will get one-third to one-half of the estate, with the rest split among the children, regardless of age. She will have to post bond, make periodic financial reports, and petition the court for some of the children's money to pay for their care.

That's not all. The judge can name a guardian for the children—usually, but not necessarily, the widow. This could be a political hack with little interest in your loved ones. After all, everything is charged to the estate!

Letter of Instruction

This is an informal document that has no legal standing but can be helpful to your heirs and executor. It should be available immediately after your death. In it:

List the names, addresses, and phone numbers of people to be notified—your lawyer, employer, bank, friends, class secretary, etc.

Spell out details of loans, income tax returns, bank accounts, numbers of credit cards, location of safe-deposit box key, and other need-to-know information.

Discuss your financial affairs and the details of your personal bequests, such as the disposition of heirlooms too small to be mentioned in the will—your gold watch to Nephew Tom, your gold cuff links to Cousin Lou, etc.

DON'Ts for Wills

As you will learn from your lawyer, there are many caveats in drawing a will. This is a legal document, so you cannot always do the things you want in the way you want.

DON'T Attach Strings to Gifts

This can cause plenty of legal trouble. United States estate tax laws allow the husband or wife to leave the survivor up to 50% of the estate tax-free—the marital deduction. But if the will says that the widow gets the proceeds only if she does not remarry, and she does marry again, there will be a full tax. She lost the gift, so she loses the deduction, too.

The same goes for other conditional terms, so make sure that your lawyer covers each point clearly.

DON'T List Sentimental Bequests

That gold tie clasp may have fond memories and be just what Cousin Willie wants, but being so specific in a will can cause headaches for your executor. Each beneficiary must be formally notified of his gift and sign a release when he receives it. And for tax purposes, all items must be inventoried and appraised. *Solution:* Put these details in your letter of instruction.

DON'T Clutter Your Will with Details

This can be awkward when there's a lag between the will and your death. When you list 100 shares of General Earache to be given to your nephew, he may not get what you intended if: (1) you sell the stock and make no change in the will; (2) the stock splits—say, 3 for 1; he will get only one-third of what you had in mind.

Solution: Instead of giving shares of stock, bonds, etc., use percentages of the total estate or terms broad enough to allow the executor discretion.

DON'T Give to Charities Aimlessly

Make sure that the cause/institution/agency can use the gift —money for cancer research is no good if the hospital does not have the proper facilities.

Also, check the tax-exempt status of the charity. If it does not qualify under IRS rulings, someone will have to pay taxes. This is especially important with foreign groups where there may also be frustrating-to-your-lawyer delays. *Best bet:* Make the gifts in your lifetime.

DON'T Try to Avoid Probate

It may sound smart and money-saving (after all, one man made a fortune with a book on the subject), but too often, trying to skip probate ends up with trouble and expense for your heirs. Most legal requirements in our society are logical and useful even if the procedures are not always efficient.

Besides, there are laws to prevent many of these shortcuts—i.e., providing that your money goes directly to your children if your wife does not live long after you could avoid probate but it will mean the loss of that all-important marital deduction. Ask your lawyer how to accomplish your purpose properly—perhaps by naming an alternate beneficiary if your spouse "fails to survive you."

DON'T Handwrite or Change Your will

In many states, handwritten wills are invalid. Be equally wary of do-it-yourself documents where you buy forms and fill them out. The odds are high that the will will be upset because of a mistake, technicality, or new legislation.

The same warning goes for handwritten changes in your will. Pencil notations, erasures, etc., can make a will invalid. If you want to revise your mandates, have your lawyer add codicils or draw a new will.

DON'T Make a New Will without Revoking the Old

This sounds elementary but it's surprising how many people write a second or third will without telling the attorney who drew the original one. In case of death, both (or all three) wills could be filed. The latest one will probably be upheld, but there are sure to be unnecessary complications and expenses.

Advice: When you prepare a new will, have your lawyer keep copies of the revoked one. This will help to prove your mental soundness and continuity of purpose.

DON'T Make Acid Comments about Those Left Behind

You may think your son-in-law is "a drunken bum," but don't say so. Such opinions can be grounds for legal action. And under no circumstances assign reasons for your decision, especially one that may not please some heir.

DON'T Leave Anyone $1.00

Don't do this, no matter how tempting or storybookish. You only give your executor trouble, trying to get a receipt for this munificent sum.

Be Careful with Codicils

A codicil is a supplement that modifies or adds to a will. It can be useful for minor changes, but when any such amendment will be to someone's disadvantage, it may be the basis for protest when the will is offered for probate.

With your lawyer's approval, codicils can be used when:

You name a new executor, trustee, or guardian—e.g., when your son is grown up and able to accept the responsibility previously assigned to a bank.

You change a legacy because of death or new circumstances.

There's a new child or grandchild for whom you want to provide the same benefits as other heirs.

There's a change in your assets, such as the sale of your summer cottage that you planned to leave to your daughter. Now the codicil gives her money instead.

To repeat: Whenever there are significant changes in your own or your family circumstances, have the will redrawn, signed, and witnessed. It's insurance against future difficulties for your loved ones.

V

Trusts for Tax Savings, Professional Money Management, Estate Planning, Protecting Your Heirs

Trusts can be valuable tools in money management. They can minimize present and future taxes, assure professional management of your assets, and accomplish your goals while you live and after you die. *Proof of their value:* There are over 800,000 trusts administered by commercial banks alone!

You don't have to be rich to benefit from a trust, but it helps, because to a large extent, a trust agreement disinherits Uncle Sam.

The trust concept dates back to the Middle Ages when Crusaders set down the powers that the stay-at-home manager was to have over property and the guidelines by which the property was to be handled and passed on to others. This fiduciary responsibility still exists.

By creating a trust, you turn assets over to someone else (occasionally an individual but usually a bank or trust company) to hold and manage for the benefit of a third party. Since you no longer control the assets, you and your estate can usually avoid paying taxes. But the most important consideration in setting up a trust should be its PURPOSE, not the tax benefits.

Trusts are legal documents, subject to the laws of the state and federal governments and to interpretations by the courts.

Be sure to retain an experienced lawyer when major assets are involved. With holdings as small as $25,000, however, consider a packaged trust where assets are pooled with those of other people and managed, on a group basis, by a bank or trust company.

The key to a successful trust, in creation and management, is to know exactly what you want to accomplish, to be certain that the trustee understands your wishes, and to be sure that the terms assure tax savings and security for some loved one.

Trusts can be flexible. They can run for a generation or be limited to a specific number of years, be funded or unfunded, provide for immediate distribution of income or accumulate income for later distribution. Within reason, they can anticipate the future and establish the means to enforce your ideas for many years.

Specifically, trusts can:

1. Provide that the income and, possibly, the principal be paid to your spouse while living and that the remainder, on his/her death, be held in trust for your children.

2. Defer payment of income for life or specify that your children be paid income during their early years and receive shares of the principal or predetermined portions when they reach certain ages.

3. Circumvent probate and speed distribution of your estate.

4. Keep your affairs confidential after your death.

5. Bar a child from getting control of an inheritance at what you regard as too early an age.

6. Prevent your widow from turning your hard-earned assets over to her new husband.

7. Preserve an estate for your children or grandchildren.

As a rule of thumb, trusts are worthwhile only if there are net assets of over $150,000. But a trust of $10,000 can make sense if the beneficiary is an elderly person or a minor who is unable to handle money.

Even with $150,000, a trust may not be worthwhile if the estate is to be distributed to several people. *Don't set up a trust just because your neighbor does.* Too many people have too grandiose ideas about how much their money can accomplish and how much taxes can be saved. In every case, the No. 1 consideration in establishing a trust should be the *purpose,* not the size.

Types of Trusts

There are two broad types of trusts: testamentary and living. Both are invaluable tools in estate planning and should be discussed in detail with your attorney.

Testamentary Trusts

Testamentary trusts are created by a will and come into existence only when the grantor dies. They keep holdings together so that they can be disposed of as you want and without losses that might result if a quick settlement had to be made. In the absence of instructions in a trust or in the will, the executor must liquidate the estate. This could be inconvenient, costly, and contrary to your wishes.

Living Trusts

These continue as long as the beneficiary lives or for a set period of time. When the trust ends, the principal goes back to the original owner.

Within those two types, there are these variations:

Revocable Trusts

These can be terminated at any time during the lifetime of the creator. The revocable trust holds property that will revert to the donor if he terminates the trust, and it thus becomes subject to taxes—on any income earned by the trustee, and at death, on the full amount of the assets.

Advantages: The owner shifts responsibility to the trustee. In effect, a revocable trust permits the owner to take a look at how his estate plans will operate. If anything is unsatisfactory, the trust can be amended, altered, or dissolved.

Irrevocable Trust

These trusts cannot be changed or revoked. The irrevocable trust provides tax savings because: (1) the property involved is considered a gift and is not subject to death taxes; (2) the owner will not ordinarily be taxed on the income of the trust; (3) the beneficiary will pay the tax on the distributed income; and (4) the beneficiary is entitled to a credit for any tax paid by the trust on income the trust accumulated before distribution.

The only control that the donor has is in the imposition of conditions on the use of the gift. And those have to be carefully limited to avoid trouble with the IRS. Never set up an irrevocable trust when you are angry. Have your attorney point out all possible contingencies.

Short-Term Trusts

These are irrevocable trusts that run for at least 10 years or the lifetime of the beneficiary. The principal reverts to the grantor at termination. This is useful to reduce taxes when the beneficiary is in a low income bracket.

Trusts for Minors

The trust for minors is a convenient—and tax-saving— method of making gifts to minor children. It provides greater flexibility than the Uniform Gifts to Minors Act and can avoid problems for the parents should the child die before reaching his or her majority.

Note: For further information, write for *More for Your Family,* from the Connecticut Mutual Life Insurance Company, 140 Garden Street, Hartford, Connecticut 06115.

Choosing the Right Trustee

In selecting a trustee, you have the choice of an individual or an institution, primarily a bank or trust company.

Generally speaking, it's not wise to name a friend. Unless the trust can afford to hire professional help, the trustee will have to do a lot of work and accept more responsibility for small remuneration. The trust may be immobilized at his death, and if he becomes careless or senile, he'll be difficult to remove.

The effective management of a trust requires knowledge of law, taxation, and asset management. Almost all banks provide trust services, but before you make your choice, check these points:

Convenience to the Beneficiary

The bank should be within easy driving or commuting distance for your widow or heirs—now and in the future.

It's nice to do business with hometown people, but they may not be able to provide proper service if your widow winters in Florida or the kids work abroad. Look for a larger bank with the facilities and the experience your heirs will need.

Know the Men Who Run the Account

This means not only the VPs but the junior executives who will be doing the work, and hopefully, who will have moved up by the time there are problems that need mature judgment.

Make Sure the Bank's Investment
Philosophy Matches Yours

If the bank is oriented toward large estates of older people, their staff will have difficulty adapting to an aggressive approach you may want for your estate. If you expect your heirs will choose growth over income, stay away from ultraconservative institutions. On the other hand, be cautious about "aggressive" trust departments that were hard hit by the debacle of Famous-Name, Glamour-Growth stocks in 1973 and 1974.

Are Their Financial Reports Easy to Understand?

Remember that your heirs will want complete, clearly spelled out information on dividends, interest, capital appreciation, distribution of income, etc. And they will want it on time!

Check Their Investment Performance

Get the annual reports of their common trust funds for the last 5, and preferably 10, years. These will show results in the value of units that correspond to shares of mutual funds. You will have a tough time comparing results year by year because the banks are shrewd enough to start their records at odd times—February 28 or September 15. This makes it difficult to make direct comparisons with stock market averages, but over a 5-year period, you can get a good idea of how well money was managed.

Two quick checks: (1) Ask your broker to check the bank's record against the Dow Jones Industrial Average. (2) Get the latest edition of *$Your Investments$* from your library and compare the tables of stock market gains and losses with those of the bank.

Look for the bank that does as well as—or better than —the Dow in both up and down markets. In fiduciary investments, consistency is essential.

Talk to People Using the Trust Services

Consult your lawyer, accountant, business friends, etc. Find out their praise and criticism, and especially, their attitude toward the service they have received.

And if you are young and vigorous, test out the bank by giving them a revocable trust to manage for 3 or 4 years.

Arrange for a Change of Trustee

Have your lawyer draw the trust agreement so that the beneficiaries (not you) can remove the trustee if investment performance is poor or the handling is not up to their expectations.

Finally, if you are still not enthused about the bank, appoint a cotrustee—your wife or a qualified investment adviser. This individual can direct the bank's investment policy—even though this won't sit well with the trust officers.

When to Use a Revocable Trust

With a revocable trust, you will lose the tax advantages (because the IRS considers you the owner), but you have greater flexibility. You can amend or terminate the trust at any time— this is valuable when you want to pay out proceeds of life insurance, pension, or profit-sharing plans, etc., in case your wife dies first, or in case there are emergencies or special needs of dependents.

Example: One of Dr. Fuzz's children has a severe physical handicap and often needs supplementary income. The concerned father sets up a revocable living trust with $25,000 life insurance. At the doctor's death, the proceeds go directly to the child.

When such trusts involve income-producing investments, the donor can name himself as trustee. This saves the $500 (or more) bank fee. And because few banks can afford to provide much service for accounts under $100,000, it may save taxes, too. The bank will probably invest the money in a common trust fund. When the trust is terminated, the bank must sell the fund units and distribute the proceeds, which are then taxable as capital gains.

But if the father serves as trustee, the proceeds of the trust will go directly to the beneficiary and there will be no taxes until the investments are sold.

Short-term Trusts

In setting up a short-term trust, remember that, while the tax savings are welcome, the final decision should be made on the basis of what is best for the beneficiary. The advantages are: (1) shifting income and tax liability to someone in a lower tax bracket; (2) providing assured protection during the span of the trust; (3) leaving assets directly to the beneficiary without probate; (4) keeping creditors from getting a crack at the estate; and (5) making possible minimal setup and operational costs.

Examples: A 70-year-old widow, with no taxable income, can receive $3,200 tax-free—$1,500 exemption, deductions and exclusions of $1,700. In the 40% tax bracket, her son would need to earn $5,333 to provide this sum.

But he can set up a 10-year living trust for $40,000. At 8% annual return, his mother will get $3,200 tax-free, and at the end of 10 years, or her death, he will get the $40,000 back.

You inherit property worth $10,000, which provides income of $1,000 a year. If the income is included in your regular tax return, you might have to pay $350 in taxes.

By creating a 10-year living trust with the assets, you can arrange for your 8-year-old daughter to receive all of the income and pay no taxes. Since you still provide more than half her support, you'll be eligible for the $750 dependency exemption. When she reaches 18, you will get the property back and can then make gifts to minimize the tax bite.

Warning: In some states, putting a child through college is part of the parent's legal obligation, so income from such a trust *might* be taxable after the age of 17 or 18.

If you should die before the 10 years are up, your daughter will get the property at once—without taxes or court delays.

Your son is due to start college in 10 years. Your taxable income is $37,500, so you are in the 45% tax bracket. A short-term trust of $10,000 will produce $1,000 a year—tax-free. With compounding, there should be enough money to pay the entire bill!

In setting up any form of short-term trust, consider these points carefully:

1. Whether annual distributions should be left to accumulate or be distributed. Current payouts will be subject to little or no taxes; reinvestment income will be taxable, as capital gains, when withdrawn—at a time when the child, for example, may be in a higher tax bracket.

2. Provision for the trust to pay taxes, if the assets are large enough to generate taxable income.

3. Retain some funds, outside the trust, for emergencies for the beneficiary. And for your own protection, make arrangements so that you can borrow from the trust when you put up proper security.

4. When the money involved is $1,000 or more, make sure that the trustee opens a trust bank account for the cash earned by the trust. Always give a copy of the trust indenture to the bank to avoid future problems with estate valuation and IRS levies.

5. Purchase securities in the trustee's name or have them held in the name of the trustee. This avoids the trans-

fer agent's administrative requirement of obtaining copies of the trust agreement each time a transfer takes place.

6. Obtain a tax identification number for the trust by filing Form SS-4 with the IRS.

Help for Older People

Temporary trusts may be useful for elderly people who are fearful of senility or disability. By putting assets in a revocable trust under bank management, the senior citizen can avoid the indignity of a court-appointed guardian if he or she should become incapacitated. And the trust can be revoked at any time.

Trusts for Minors

If the trust is created in connection with a custodian account for a minor child (see Chapter IX, on Wives and Children), follow these steps:

1. Set up a bank account entitled: [name of custodian] as custodian for [name of child] under [name of state] Uniform Gifts to Minors Act.

This account becomes a reservoir for cash income received from the trust. There will be complete, accurate records for the IRS and for future reference.

Keep in mind that the custodian should *not* be the grantor parent. *But your wife is eligible.*

2. Get a Social Security number for the child at the local Social Security office.

3. Make sure that the income from the trust is distributed annually and deposited in the custodian account. It's easy to forget.

4. If the trust has taxable income or gross income of $750 or more, the trustee must file an annual fiduciary in-

come tax return, Form 1041, for information, and of course, for taxes when the income is over $1,000.

5. Remember that the account terminates automatically when the child comes of legal age (unless there are special needs that justify special permission from the IRS).

But these special trusts for minors do have drawbacks:

1. The grantor cannot receive back any of the assets until the termination of the trust or until the beneficiary dies.

2. The person who establishes the trust cannot derive any direct personal benefits from the trust *in any way*. Otherwise, the IRS will rule that trust proceeds are taxable to the donor.

Note: If you are not ready to shift assets to a trust, you can establish a "dry" trust as a receptacle for assets when available —from the sale of property, proceeds of life insurance, etc. The bank might charge a nonrefundable fee of $100 to keep the trust open.

Advice: There is nothing wrong, illegal, or improper about setting up trusts to avoid taxes. As the courts have stated: "The taxpayer is not required to take the path which involves the highest tax cost."

How to Use Life Insurance Trusts

One type of trust that does not require substantial assets is a life insurance trust. This can protect a beneficiary, enable the trustee to use the principal for support or special needs, and/or allow the establishment of an investment that can grow with the economy. *But unless the policy is paid up, you will have to continue to pay the premiums and report them as gifts each year.*

A life insurance trust is a gift or a series of gifts. During your lifetime, the terms can be revoked or changed without tax penalty. After your death, provisions can permit the trustee to modify payouts, use the policies as collateral for loans, cash them in, and reinvest or distribute the proceeds.

When there are primary and secondary beneficiaries, the trust can name your wife as beneficiary and set up a second trust to receive the proceeds in the event she does not outlive you. This is worthwhile only when substantial sums are involved.

A revocable trust might be wise even when you have exhausted your $30,000 lifetime gift-tax exclusion. Your wife's estate would have to pay on the *face* value of the policy, which probably would be greater than its *cash* value. And furthermore, the federal gift tax is lower than the federal estate tax.

With life insurance trusts, there are also savings in:

Administrative Expenses

Insurance payable to a trust set up by will usually bypasses probate and is not included in the estate, which is the base for the executor's commissions and attorney fees.

Inheritance Taxes

Most states exempt part or all of the proceeds of life insurance from inheritance tax, IF the proceeds are paid to an individual or trust set up before death. But when the insurance is paid to a trust under provisions of the will, the exemption is lost and there'll be a tax of from 2% to 15%.

If you are worried that the gift will strip you of too much life insurance, put one policy in an irrevocable trust and another in a revocable trust. You will lose some tax savings, but you will have the security of the readily available assets in the revocable trust, and if you continue to prosper, you can switch everything into the irrevocable trust later.

Warning: With an irrevocable trust, you can never use the threat of disinheritance with your wife or children!

If you want tax benefits, you must give away control by: (1) naming your wife and children in the trust and giving your wife the right to revoke or change the terms; (2) giving her the policies so that she can set up a contingent trust for the children.

Either way, subject to the 3-year-contemplation-of-death rule, the insurance will be out of your estate.

Important: Insert a clause in the trust to give your spouse and children the right to withdraw any money added to the trust during the year. Thus, the gift of the policy and cash will be *gifts of a present interest*—the only type of gift eligible for the $3,000 annual tax exclusion. Without this protection, the premiums will be considered a *gift of future interest* and not eligible as a gift tax deduction.

Be very careful of tax considerations. If you pay premiums for 7 years and then die, it is possible that the IRS may rule that these were made in contemplation of death. The estate would then be assessed on a percentage basis—three-sevenths of the value of the policy.

Safe solutions: Arrange for the beneficiary to pay the premiums from his/her own funds.

Fund the trust by putting other assets into another trust and using the income to pay the premiums. This agreement should be carefully drawn and managed so that there can be no criticism from the IRS. It must last three years.

The Many Advantages of a Marital Deduction Trust

This is a double trust to avoid double taxation on the same property—in your estate, and after your death, in that of your widow.

To start, divide all family assets in half and set up Trust A to go to the widow and Trust B—"the remainder trust"—to go to your children. Both trusts should be managed by the same bank.

Your widow can invade the principal of Trust A and in an emergency should be able to ask the trustee to tap Trust B for maintenance money.

If she dies after the husband (as is actuarially probable), her

Reducing the Tax Burden Through the Marital Deduction

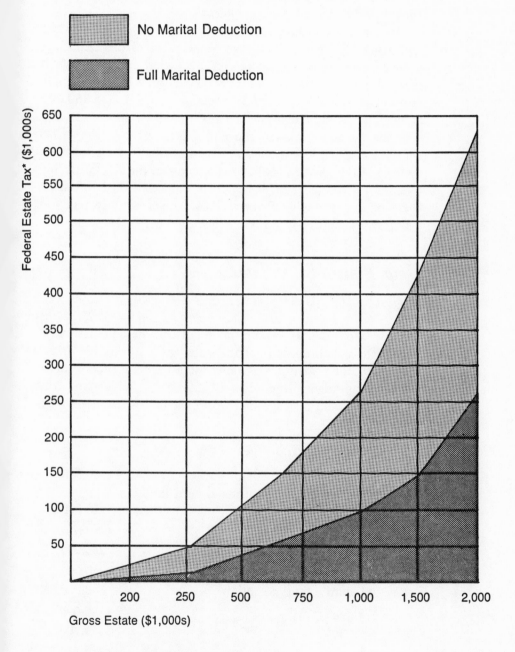

No Marital Deduction

Full Marital Deduction

Federal Estate Tax* ($1,000s)

Gross Estate ($1,000s)

*Includes maximum credit for state death taxes.
Source: Connecticut Mutual
Life Insurance Company.

taxable estate will be only what's left of Trust A, as assets in Trust B will go directly to the children.

The chart shows how these arrangements assure worthwhile tax savings, especially with larger estates. Under this setup, the husband gets the maximum marital deduction and his estate is subject to minimum tax. His estate holds only half the family assets. With the 50% marital deduction and the first $60,000 of insurance exempt, taxes will be modest at best.

If the husband had left the entire property outright to his wife, his estate taxes would amount to one-half of the taxes on the total estate, as before, but she would run the risk of paying a tax on the whole estate at her death unless she died within 10 years of her husband. *Reason:* Estate taxes already paid on property are entitled to a tax credit if paid within 10 years.

How Trusts Save Taxes— with a $500,000 Estate

To spell out the tax-savings value of trusts, here's what would happen to a half-million-dollar estate (as outlined in *Money* magazine). The savings on smaller estates are not proportional, but by using this substantial sum, it's easier to understand why every family with a sizable net worth should discuss trusts with its lawyer.

Everything Willed to Wife:

Gross estate	$500,000
Settlement costs—probate, legal fees, etc.	20,000
	$480,000
50% tax-free marital deduction	240,000
	$240,000
Standard estate exemption	60,000
Taxable estate	$180,000
Federal taxes	$ 44,700

Thus, the widow will inherit a net estate of $435,300. ($500,-000 less $20,000 expenses less $44,700 taxes).

At her death (assuming no changes):

Gross estate	$435,300
Settlement costs	20,000
	$415,300
Standard exemption	60,000
Taxable estate	$355,300
Federal taxes	$144,096

Half Willed to Wife, Rest in Trust:

Taxable estate	$180,000
Estate before standard exemption	$240,000
Federal taxes	$ 44,700
To testamentary trust	$195,300

When she dies, the children inherit $195,300 principal without paying further tax.

Widow's Inheritance via marital deduction:	$240,000
Expenses settling her estate	10,000
	230,000
Standard exemption	60,000
Widow's taxable estate	170,000
Federal taxes	41,700
Net estate	$128,300

Total Federal taxes: $86,400 ($44,700 + $41,700)

Using Two Trusts and Gifts:

Net worth	$500,000	
Puts house in wife's name	50,000	
	450,000	
Gives land and securities to children	120,000	
	330,000	
Trust A established with $100,000 insurance policy	100,000	
Gross estate	230,000	
At death: settlement expenses	10,000	
	220,000	
Marital deduction	110,000	
Net estate	110,000	
Standard exemption	60,000	
Taxable estate	$ 50,000	
Federal taxes		$ 7,000
Trust B gets the net estate	$110,000	
Federal taxes	7,000	
Balance: income to wife for life	$103,000	
principal to children		
Widow inherits: House	$ 50,000	
Marital deduction		
(tax-free)	110,000	
Total	160,000	
She gives securities to children	24,000	
Her estate at death	136,000	
Settlement expenses	10,000	
	126,000	
Standard exemption	60,000	
Widow's taxable estate	$ 66,000	
Federal taxes		$11,180

Total Federal Taxes: $18,180 ($7,000 + $11,180)

Tax Savings Through the "Two-Trust" Pattern of Distribution

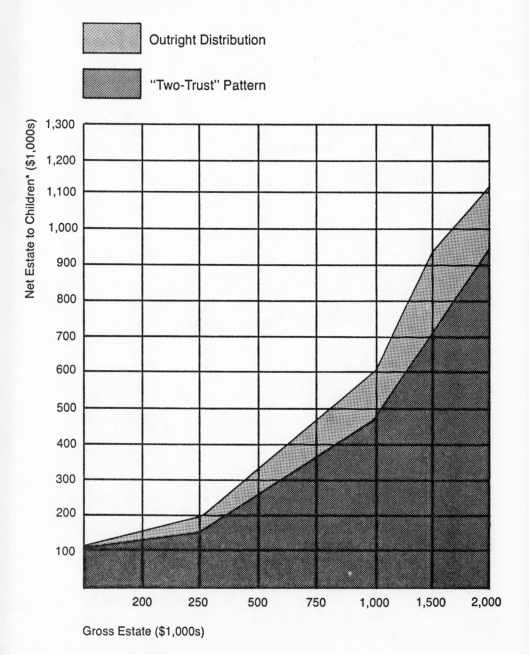

Outright Distribution

"Two-Trust" Pattern

Net Estate to Children* ($1,000s)

Gross Estate ($1,000s)

*Assumes that wife survives husband by 10 years
and does not dissipate any assets.

The Benefits of a Sprinkling Trust

A sprinkling trust is valuable when you anticipate that your children will have different needs at different times. Under this arrangement, the trustee may distribute varying amounts of principal and income as he sees fit. A badly injured child who has to spend months in a hospital might need more income than a successful son. Or the trustee might provide extra money for a daughter who has just had a hard time in the delivery of her baby.

The Value of a Sprinkling Trust—$12,000 annual income

Year	Dorcas, age 18, starts college	Ruth, age 20, married to a student	Larry, age 22, in the Peace Corps	
1	$5,000	$5,000	$2,000	
2	5,000	6,000	1,000	Ruth has baby
3	5,000	3,000	4,000	Larry enters college
4	5,000	2,000	5,000	Ruth's husband gets job
5	3,000	4,000	5,000	Ruth's husband takes graduate work
6	4,000	3,000	5,000	Dorcas marries
7	2,000	7,000	3,000	Ruth ill
8	5,000	4,000	3,000	Dorcas has baby
9	3,000	3,000	6,000	Larry hospitalized
10	$4,000	$4,000	$4,000	

If you so desire, the trust can be written to involve more than one generation. The money that the grandchildren would eventually inherit can go to them directly. A conventional trust could also skip a generation, but it could not provide for the possibility that one of the children might need far more than would any of the grandchildren.

Small Trusts for Modest Holdings

In the last few years, a number of major banks have sought to attract small trust accounts by offering prepackaged plans. New York's Chase Manhattan Bank is typical. Its CompacTrust starts at $50,000 (higher than some) and costs 1% of the first $50,000, then ⅓ of 1% of the portfolio value at the first anniversary date of the agreement.

Trusts can be "living" (during your lifetime), revocable, and according to your instructions, end or continue for someone else after your death. Or "testamentary" (created by will or other arrangement), irrevocable once it goes into effect but subject to revision and updating.

Trusteed accounts are invested in common trust funds with one of the following objectives: long-term capital growth (common stocks); appreciation and income (convertibles and common stocks); taxable income (corporate bonds); tax-exempt income (municipal bonds).

These are discretionary accounts. The bank makes all the investment decisions, acts as custodian, handles all security transactions, and sends you quarterly and annual reports. These show the market value, original cost, income, and at year-end, a tax summary of capital gains and losses.

You start with cash and can add in units of $1,000. Some banks will accept stocks and bonds, especially those listed on the New York Stock Exchange. They reserve the right to sell such securities if they do not fit the bank's investment strategy program.

Income is paid quarterly, directly to the beneficiary, deposited in a savings or checking account, reinvested automatically, or withdrawn up to preset limits.

The trust may be terminated when the principal drops below $25,000, or if proper provision is made, at your request.

Basically, this sort of trust is an investment vehicle and should be so considered. But don't be too impressed. Unlike banks, trust departments are not yet subject to many regulations, and their investment performance, especially since 1971, leaves much to be desired.

Check your local bank, especially one that is a member of a bank holding company, to see if they offer these minitrusts. They are handy, relatively inexpensive, and can be worthwhile if your trust needs are adaptable to a standard plan.

> *Advice:* Trusts can be valuable, but they are not for everyone. First, you should have ample reserves for emergencies. There's no sense in cramping your life-style for tax savings or some possible future benefits.
>
> Unless you have excess assets, through inheritance or wise investing, be cautious about setting up a trust. Project your income and expenses for the next 10 years. If you can reasonably expect to live comfortably without the assets set aside in a trust, go ahead. But wait at least 6 months after you make your first decision before calling your lawyer. Even a revocable trust can be expensive.

VI

How to Choose an Executor for Your Estate

Choosing an executor for your estate is an essential part of every will. No matter what your age or financial status, some individual or institution should be named to handle your affairs after your death. This will save time, prevent legal complications, help to keep settlement costs within reasonable bounds, and provide counsel to your heirs.

The role of the executor is to fulfill your written wishes and to settle your affairs as required by law. He must match your intentions with the needs of your heirs. This means completing all steps mandated for an accounting to your beneficiaries, to tax authorities, and to the court.

The executor serves until the estate is settled and he is discharged by the court. In carrying out his responsibilities, the executor can retain a lawyer and other professionals to carry out your requests. He has considerable power. Heirs and consultants can recommend, but the executor has the final say.

This sounds complicated, but unless you leave a multiasset estate, the executor needs only common sense and the services of a competent attorney and, on occasion, help from an accountant or property manager. *The most important consideration in choosing an executor is not expertise but sound judgment and familiarity with your family.*

More difficulties will come from the heirs than the specialists. When there are minor children, their welfare should be a major consideration. But remember that they grow up fast, so make your selection carefully when you go outside your immediate family. Ideally, the executor should combine the humanity of a clergyman with the business acumen of a successful corporate executive.

Roles of Guardian and Trustee

Guidelines to the selection of trustees and guardians are discussed on pages 60–62 and 107–109, but generally, the role of a guardian is to look after children in the event of the death of both parents.

A trustee takes responsibility for property left in trust. The legal agreement sets limits to his role, but usually the trustee is involved with the investment of funds, payments of expenses, and distributions to heirs. When there are minors, attorneys often advise making the guardian a personal adviser and the trustee responsible for property until—and sometimes after— the children reach maturity. In settling any estate, the executor is the key man and must make the important decisions.

In choosing an executor, there are three general areas of choice—relatives or friends, lawyers, and institutions. The first may save you money, as he—or she—will probably serve with little or no remuneration. Most will need professional assistance.

Do not insist or even suggest that any executor waive his fee. Settling an estate can be a difficult, time-consuming job. If the work becomes too onerous, the lack of remuneration may mean a sloppy or grudging performance. If you select someone outside your family, make sure that your heirs understand this, too.

Checklist for Choice

In choosing an individual as your executor, use these check-points:

The Ability to Get Along with Your Heirs

Especially the ability to get along with your widow (or widower) and children. Death can be a harsh blow to some individuals. They need support and solace from a person who is tactful enough to be able to deal with emotional problems, yet strong enough to get the estate settled quickly and fairly.

Someone Who Can Command Respect

This is essential if you anticipate any controversy—within your family, with business associates, or governments.

Name at Least One Alternate

Do this in case your first choice is unable to serve. Usually, wills are drawn many years before they are used. Your original nominee may die, retire, move away, or shift to a job where he will be unable to act effectively. Look for individuals who are younger than you, in good health, and with time to serve.

Concentrate Your Search

Concentrate on family, neighbors, and business associates in your home area, preferably those who can reach the county courthouse easily. Estate laws date back centuries, so there are many details that require personal signatures or appearances. And legislatures are not quick to make changes.

Furthermore, some states place limitations on executors—blood relatives only, no nonresidents, etc.

Skip Anyone Who Must Travel a Great Deal

There are many legal deadlines that must be met. Postponements can be costly, annoying to your heirs, and inconvenient for your lawyer and the court.

Go Slow on Family Choices

Just because someone is a relative is no assurance of competency. Make the decision on the basis of ability and concern, and recognize that there may be resentment, especially if you are a member of a large family. This is a major consideration with in-laws. And remember that he or she might get divorced!

Take time to review the capabilities of younger members of your family—sons and daughters and their spouses, nieces and nephews, and even cousins. They are not likely to be overly involved in family feuds and should have a good understanding of your wishes.

Don't Overlook Your Wife

The cliché that a woman is too emotional after her husband's death is foolish. If she is smart enough to handle you over the years, she has the ability to retain competent counsel, to make reasonable judgments, and to follow the well-established procedures for settling estates.

If your spouse has had problems, check with your lawyer. A wife may be disqualified because of mental incompetence, conviction for a serious crime, habitual drunkenness, out-of-state residence, overage, etc.

Attorney as Executor

If your estate is modest, you may want to name your regular lawyer as executor. Make sure that he scores well on the checklist used in the selection of individuals, that he has had sufficient experience in handling estates, and that he is willing to accept the responsibility. Just because an attorney is skilled at drawing real estate contracts or conducting labor negotiations is no guarantee that he will be a competent or understanding executor.

If your estate is large, consider naming a lawyer who specializes in estate work or is a member of a firm where he can draw on a variety of skills. This may speed settlement and reduce administration costs.

Before you make any decision, discuss anticipated problems and costs with the lawyer whom you are considering. You may conclude (and he may agree) that he's not the best choice. Be frank and ask his advice. The kind of counsel you want will not accept a job he doesn't feel he can handle properly.

Don't try to bargain on fees. There's no way to know how much work will be involved, and besides, what you want is the best, not the cheapest, service for your heirs. It's OK to ask about hourly charges and double fees—as executor and attorney. Most lawyers will decline to accept both even though some states permit such charges.

Bank or Trust Company

The choice of a fiduciary institution depends on the size and complexity of your estate. Banks and trust companies are experienced, efficient, and skilled in handling taxes, estate planning, real estate, investments, etc. But despite advertising slogans, most bank trust operations are impersonal. To make money, they have to have substantial income—more than is usually available from an estate of less than $100,000. Unless the holdings are likely to be well into 6 figures, no large bank can afford to spend time on giving solace to your widow or on guiding your children.

If your commercial bank considers your estate too small, try a trust company, a savings bank, or a smaller institution in the suburbs or country, perhaps near your summer home.

Do not assume that, just because it's big or a member of a statewide bank holding company, your bank will turn you down. In many cases, acceptance will depend on commercial considerations—the fact that your uncle is a major depositor, that you're an officer of a local corporation, or that the bank president was impressed with the way you handled a committee assignment for the United Way. Most banks have set standards for profitability for all operations, but there's always leeway for exceptions, especially if they create community goodwill or build for the future.

Before you name any institution, take time to visit the trust department, talk with a top officer, and get an idea of the department's capabilities and limitations—i.e., if you have a lot of real estate, be sure there are at least 2 officers who know this field well. Once an executor takes over, there's almost no way he—or it—can be fired!

One final checkpoint—their investment record. These results should be available in the reports of common trust funds. If the performance has been consistently poor, you can revise your will to specify a more aggressive investment policy or name a money-management firm as adviser. *Do not be bashful about criticism.* You worked hard to earn that money!

Responsibilities of an Executor

1. OVERSEE FUNERAL ARRANGEMENTS. The details should be handled by a member of the family, but the executor should have a copy of the burial instructions and be kept informed as to anticipated expenses. If your widow appears to have gone overboard, the executor should comment and possibly act. He has a legal responsibility to see that assets of the estate are spent wisely.

2. HIRE A LAWYER. Generally, this will be the individual who drew your will, but when there are unusual problems, the executor can substitute or add a specialist. To protect himself and the estate, the executor should ask for a written statement of anticipated fees.

And of course, if the lawyer performs poorly or is unduly dilatory, the executor has the power to make a change.

3. COMPILE A ROUGH SUMMARY OF ASSETS. This should be done as soon as possible after death. Such information is valuable in determining future income for the heirs and guesstimating settlement costs.

4. CHECK SAFE-DEPOSIT BOXES. This is usually done, after the will has been probated, in the presence of the attorney, a member of the family, and a tax official.

5. ARRANGE FOR LIVING EXPENSES. If the survivor does not have access to cash, the executor can obtain limited funds by asking for prompt payment of part of an insurance policy, by withdrawing money from a joint bank account, or by selling some assets. In a few states, such action requires a tax waiver.

6. OPEN A BANK ACCOUNT AND RENT A SEPARATE SAFE-DEPOSIT BOX TO RECEIVE ASSETS OF YOUR ESTATE. With legal guidance, the executor should gather assets and arrange for transfer of ownership of securities, real estate, and other property.

7. APPLY FOR DEATH BENEFITS. He should apply to your employer, Social Security, insurance companies, labor union, professional societies, and if applicable, to the Veterans Administration.

8. SAFEGUARD ESTATE ASSETS. This is a broad and often difficult category. It can mean anything and everything—from continuing the operation of a business and collecting rents to paying leases and feeding cats! *Note:* keep these unusual responsibilities in mind when you choose your executor.

9. DECIDE ON THE PRELIMINARY DISTRIBUTION OF ASSETS. He should consider funds for the immediate needs

of heirs and for reserves for future estate expenses. In most states, the executor is personally responsible if he miscalculates the distribution of bequests and then finds there is no money available to complete payment of debts.

10. PAY ALL LEGITIMATE TAXES—FOR THE ESTATE, INHERITANCE, AND FOR INCOME RECEIVED DURING THE YEAR OF DEATH.

Start Planning in Your Will

The time to start helping your executor is when you draw your will. Spell out your ideas on handling major assets so that the executor will be able to make quick decisions and take prompt actions according to your stated wishes.

Example: Include paragraphs that:

- State you are willing to have the executor serve without posting a bond to guarantee his probity. If you do not trust him, why make the appointment?
- Direct him to distribute personal effects within general guidelines.
- Provide wide discretionary powers, especially on handling property. Without an expressly stated right to keep the property in the estate, the executor will be forced to sell off investments that are not in the state's permissible categories—e.g., sell shares of General Skyrocket (which have tripled in value in the last year and, you are convinced, will continue to grow at a rapid, profitable rate) and buy bonds or low-growth utility stocks that are on the legal list of investments suitable for portfolios of pension funds and insurance companies.

- Grant power to borrow and to lend money as well as to mortgage, lease, or sell real estate. Here again, state laws may force prompt—and possibly costly—liquidation.

Check the Fees

Most states set maximums for fees that can be charged by executors. They vary widely—for the first $100,000, from $1,840 in Wisconsin to $10,000 in Delaware and the District of Columbia. Above the $100,000 figure, the fees are more uniform—generally $20 per $1,000, but they may run up to $100 per $1,000. Keep in mind that these are *maximum* fees and not necessarily what the actual costs will be.

If your estate is large enough, you may be able to bargain for a lower fee schedule. Be sure to get such an arrangement in writing. A statement in your will is not enough. In most states, for example, a bank has the legal right to claim a full commission or refuse the executorship!

In some states, the attorney can accept executor's compensation or legal fees but not both. When both fees are permitted, total charges are likely to be below legal limits.

Advice: if you name a lawyer or an institution as your executor, get a written confirmation of the fee schedule—with, of course, some provision for updating or revision.

As noted earlier, fees should *never* be the deciding factor in your choice. But it is part of your responsibility to see that your hard-earned assets are not lessened unnecessarily by high, un-called-for charges.

A wise, conscientious executor can be a tremendous legacy to your family. He can provide sympathy and guidance for your heirs and make certain that your wishes are respected. Choose carefully and give him, her, or it the power to fulfill responsibilities as you would like to do if the situation were reversed.

And if you are asked to be an executor, review both the checkpoints for choice and the list of your ultimate responsibilities!

Charges for Administering Estates

This table is a frame of reference, not a definite guide. It shows the representative or legal maximum fees for administering an estate of $100,000. Exact costs depend on state laws, which may contain special provisions for real estate, life insurance, income earned by the estate, etc. Professional executors, such as banks, may charge less, especially when the estate is sizable. And of course, wise planning can reduce the value of the estate against which the fees apply.

For data in your state, check your attorney or the trust department of your bank. Don't be alarmed; these are maximums, which are seldom charged unless the estate is complex.

State	Maximum Fee for First $100,000	Fee per $1,000 over $100,000
Alabama	$ 5,000	$ 50
Alaska	2,120*	20
Arizona	4,120*	40
Arkansas	3,150	30
California	2,630	20 (1)
Colorado	4,500*	30
Connecticut	2,500 (2)	25 (2)
Delaware	10,000	100
District of Columbia	10,000	100
Florida	2,595	25
Georgia	5,000	50
Hawaii	2,310 (3)	20
Idaho	3,110*	30
Illinois	.... (4)	.... (4)
Indiana	3,700 (2)	20 (2)
Iowa	2,120	20
Kansas	.... (4)	.... (4)
Kentucky	5,000 (5)	50
Louisiana	2,500	25
Maine	5,000	50
Maryland	5,200	40

State	Maximum Fee for First $100,000	Fee per $1,000 over $100,000
Massachusetts	3,000 (2)	30 (1)
Michigan	2,050	20
Minnesota	3,500 (2)	25 (2)
Mississippi	7,000	70
Missouri	3,300	27.50
Montana	2,520	20
Nebraska	2,050	20
Nevada	2,120	20
New Hampshire	.... (4)	.... (4)
New Jersey	5,000	50
New Mexico	5,150	50
New York	2,650	25 (1)
North Carolina	5,000	50
North Dakota	2,080*	20
Ohio	2,120	20
Oklahoma	2,585	25
Oregon	2,630	20
Pennsylvania	5,000 (2)	30 (2)
Rhode Island	.... (4)	.... (4)
South Carolina	5,000	50
South Dakota	2,585	25
Tennessee	.... (4)	.... (4)
Texas	5,000	50
Utah	1,910	10
Vermont	4,000 (2)	20 (2)(6)
Virginia	5,000 (2)	50 (2)
Washington	3,075 (2)	25 (2)
West Virginia	5,000 (2)	50 (2)
Wisconsin	1,840 (7)	20 (7)
Wyoming	2,350	20

* Uniform Probate Code.
(1) Maximum decreases for higher brackets; (2) no legal maximum; (3) plus maximum fee of 7% per year on first $5,000 of income earned by estate, 5% thereafter; (4) executors' fees vary by county; (5) plus maximum fee of 5% on income earned by estate; (6) plus $4 per diem; (7) plus $10 per diem.
Source: Daniel J. Cantor & Co., Philadelphia, Pennsylvania, and Commerce Clearing House.

Lower Costs Coming

As the result of a new Uniform Probate Code, charges for administering estates are coming down. The law, on the books in Alaska, Arizona, Colorado, Idaho, and North Dakota, streamlines procedures, eliminates rigid fee schedules, requires lawyers to charge by service rendered, and makes it possible to bargain with executors for payment of essential requirements. Watch for revisions in your state. It's always a newsworthy subject.

VII

Power of Attorney—What? How? Why?

A power of attorney can be useful, convenient, and an effective safeguard against the unexpected. But it's no cure-all.

Legally, it's a contract granting authority to one or more people to act in your behalf if you are unable or unwilling to do so through absence, illness, or inconvenience. The actions taken by your agent are binding on you, but the power can be revoked at any time and is automatically voided when you die or lose your mental faculties.

Generally speaking, a power of attorney is a wise move when an individual: (1) is away from home or business; (2) is disabled or not physically up to taking part in business, legal, or social procedures; or (3) does not want his identity to be revealed.

Examples:
- A son on military duty grants power of attorney to his father.
- A husband, taking a long trip, arranges for his wife to handle his affairs.
- An aging parent, ill in a nursing home, assigns authority to a relative or lawyer.
- An investor, reluctant to reveal his interest in acquiring property, authorizes a broker to make the necessary purchases.

89

The delegation of power is easy. By signing a simple legal form, you appoint someone to be "true, sufficient, and lawful attorney . . . to borrow in my name . . . to pledge securities or property of mine for the repayment by me of any such loan . . . to sign checks . . . conduct banking affairs . . . to buy and sell securities . . . to adjust, settle, and discharge claims . . . and generally to act as my agent. . . ." This standard form can be amended to meet your specific needs.

Lawyers are often reluctant to exercise such authority, as they prefer to deal in areas where they can use, and be paid for, their special expertise.

Usually, as a matter of convenience, the power of attorney is given to some relative, or in business, to a partner. The choice should be carefully made, and when the immediate need is passed, revoked.

In all cases, the individual should be not only honest and loyal, but preferably, should be familiar with the areas where he has power to act. For personal affairs, this could be wife, father, or son; for securities, consider your lawyer or investment adviser.

Unless there are strong reasons to continue the power of attorney, tear up the agreement when you are willing and able to accept your normal responsibilities. My lawyer tells the sad tale of one of his clients who, when ill for a long period, gave his partner the power of attorney on all business transactions. When the grantee came back to work, he did nothing about canceling the assignment.

Two years later, after a serious disagreement, the partnership was dissolved. But relying on the power of attorney, the former partner sold a building owned by the business—at a sizable profit for himself.

"When my client wanted to sue," my lawyer said, "I had to point out that the sale may have been morally and ethically improper, but there was no legal case. The power of attorney had not been revoked!

"The same caveat goes for relatives," he added. "More than

one trusting husband has found that one of the penalties of separation is the loss of money from a bank account for which the wife had power of attorney. And if there should be a divorce and you have granted any powers to your brother-in-law, review the situation promptly!"

As a rule of thumb, it is not a good idea to give power of attorney to someone who shares in your business interests—at least, not without some protection. One way to avoid trouble is to split the responsibility between two individuals—one with power to handle your investments, the other to hold the actual stock certificates, mortgages, etc. Neither can act without the other's cooperation.

Such an approach can be especially useful with a stockbroker. His income depends on commissions, so there's always a temptation to buy and sell frequently. Investors are protected against "churning" (too-frequent transactions), but in erratic stock markets, this can be hard to prove—and mighty costly.

When you do authorize someone else to manage any type of property, do so only after careful evaluation of the experience, the record, and the investment philosophy of the individual or organization. Then, follow *all* transactions closely for 3 or 4 months, and if you are not satisfied, end the arrangement.

Dealing with Grandma

Another dangerous area is when you are dealing with an old person who is slipping into senility. If there is any proof of incompetency at the time the power of attorney was granted, the agreement becomes worthless and all transactions become void and voidable. Worse, you could be held personally liable for any losses suffered by outsiders!

The only way to handle management of an incompetent's property is to have a guardian or conservator appointed by a court (see Chapter VI, on Guardians and Trustees). If the elderly relative is still competent, however, the best solution may be to put all her assets in a trust. This can continue to operate regardless of her later condition.

Hometown Property

If you move, for business or retirement, and leave property in your old hometown, be sure that you have withdrawn all powers of attorney unless you are convinced that your assignee can be trusted. It's wiser, safer, and more businesslike to have your affairs handled under a contractual agreement—with a real-estate broker for property management, with a bank for investments, etc.

One more important point: The person you authorize to act for you does not have to reveal your identity. This technique is used frequently when developers want to acquire land without spreading information that would boost prices beyond economic feasibility.

It's also useful when a financier or corporation wants to acquire or buy an interest in another business without management's knowledge or, often, approval—i.e., when aggressive young executives of a family-owned corporation team with an outsider to buy control before the old-timers can build legal barriers.

Such secrecy can have harmful results. Many a deal has fallen through because the third party did not trust the power of attorney and was fearful of the unknown. When you plan such an approach, be prepared to reveal yourself if the need arises.

Here are some areas where a power of attorney can be used effectively:

- Buying and selling real estate.
- Investing in land, buildings, or securities.
- Personal banking transactions such as payment of taxes, bills, insurance, contributions, etc.
- Claims and litigations.

- Benefits from military service.
- Personal relationships.
- Records, reports, and statements.

Power of attorney can also be effective in any other dealings that require signed approval.

VIII

DOs and DON'Ts of Contracts

Contracts are meant to be fulfilled by both parties. If they are not, there are probably grounds for legal action, with the possibility of significant damages. Before you or any member of your family signs any contract involving any financial obligation, be sure to read every word carefully, and if possible, check with a lawyer.

A contract is an agreement between two or more parties. One promises to do, or not to do, something. In return, the other party promises to do, or not to do, something. To be legal and sustaining, a contract must have mutual consent, involve consideration, be free of fraud, honest mistakes, and coercion, and be signed by people who are mentally competent and 18 years of age or older.

Typical contracts are insurance policies, mortgages, promissory notes, deeds, and certain receipts for goods and/or services. With some exceptions, oral contracts are just as binding as written ones if there is confirmation. And an oral agreement may invalidate a written contract.

> *Example:* John Andrews signs a contract to have his home renovated. The decorator agrees to complete the work by June 20, the week before the wedding reception for the Andrews' daughter.

94

The work was not finished on time, the reception had to be held elsewhere, so Mr. Andrews refused to pay the full bill.
In court, the judge upheld the refusal because the time promise had been overheard by 2 witnesses.

Contracts are of two types—*implied* and *express*. When you give your wife's dress to the clerk at the cleaners, there's an *implied* contract—the retailer agrees to clean the dress, and by paying for it, you provide the essential third part of any legal agreement—*consideration*.

In such situations, there are few grounds for damages if the store uses standard methods and is unable to remove a spot or fulfill your requirements. You might win in court only if you could prove that improper materials or methods were used.

With an *implied* contract, payment is due after the services have been rendered; with an *express* contract, terms of payment must have been discussed before acceptance, and in most cases, a written agreement is prepared.

A contract is valid even if one party attempts to imply otherwise. *Example:* a parking lot might post signs warning that "Management accepts no responsibility for damage or loss, etc." But if the attendant bangs up your car (and you can prove it), the lot owner is still liable.

And vice versa. If the appliance salesman makes numerous promises about performance and services that are not spelled out in the warranty or installment sale agreement, the store is liable only for what appears in the printed agreement.

Written Contracts

By law, written contracts are required when:

1. Selling real property or leasing it for more than one year.
2. Establishing a trust or other financial settlement.
3. Guaranteeing payment of someone else's debt.

4. Providing for someone in a will.

5. Making an arrangement in consideration of marriage —i.e., a property settlement.

Canceling a Contract

1. There was fraud—usually concealment of material facts.

2. There were honest mistakes—not caused by ignorance, negligence, or failure to read the agreement.

3. The agreement breaks a local, state, or federal law.

4. The contract was signed under duress.

5. One of the signers was insane or drunk.

6. The written agreement has been materially altered.

DOs and DON'Ts

DO Read Every Word Before Signing

If there's fine print, get a magnifying glass.

DO Keep a Copy of the Agreement—As Signed By Both Parties

DO Make Sure That the Contract Covers All the Details You Want

DON'T Leave Anything to Inference or Subsequent Interpretation Unless the Terms of the Possible Revisions Are Spelled Out

DON'T Rely on a Stranger's Explanation

If considerable money or responsibility is involved, have the document reviewed by a lawyer, or when dealing in special areas, by an expert.

DON'T Sign Anything You Do Not Understand—Paragraph, Word, or Condition

IX

Wives and Children

The typical male spends nearly 90,000 hours of his life in moneymaking activities. Yet he sets aside less than 10 hours to discuss how his widow and children can get along if he should die or become disabled.

Worse, 30% of college-educated, presumably smart business and professional men NEVER complete the most basic of all family protections—a will. And 60% of their wives are equally careless.

This lack of constructive action is difficult to understand because, on the average, a wife will be a widow for 10 years. Usually, the male is 4 years older than his wife, and the female has a significantly longer life span.

Death is a traumatic experience, but learning to live independently can be even more devastating if the widow is suddenly confronted with the awesome task of raising children, and later, of living alone for another 10 to 20 years. Only a small number of widows remarry.

Few women can learn to be widows overnight. The time to start such planning and before-the-job training is when the first child is born, and to review the situation when the youngsters are old enough to understand the basic facts of personal money management. For most people, that means NOW.

Teach Your Wife to Be a Widow

The place to start is with estate planning: (1) to determine the family's net worth (the value of the husband's estate after reductions for mortgages, debts, taxes, fees, etc.); (2) to detail all sources of future revenues (insurance, pension, Social Security); (3) to outline the cost of living as a widow; (4) to estimate how many years' income will be required, first until the children are able to support themselves, then for the life of the widow.

In these projections:

DO Make Provisions for Inheritances from Parents or Relatives

A hard-pressed widow is more likely to be remembered fondly than a successful nephew.

DON'T Assume That the Widow Will Remarry

The odds grow greater with age.

DO Remember That, Legally, Morally, and Practically, the Husband Has the Responsibility for Providing for His Wife as Long as She (Not He) Lives

Regardless of how good the husband's health may be, substantial provision must be made for the high cost of dying. In one study of 1,700 men who died before age 65, 50% were hospitalized for one month or more and had an average medical bill of $2,800, only 60% of which was paid by insurance.

Add $1,500 for funeral and miscellaneous expenses, so there's a need for nearly $3,000 in cash or quickly convertible assets—even before the widow has to worry about living costs.

These funds should be available from:

INDIVIDUAL CHECKING AND SAVINGS ACCOUNTS. Funds in joint accounts will be impounded, uncashed checks in the deceased's name must be held, and safe-deposit boxes will be sealed.

As soon as copies of the death certificate are presented, from:

LIFE INSURANCE. Proceeds will be paid promptly, especially if arrangements have been made to attach a sight draft to the policy. This resembles a check and will be treated as such by the insurance agent/company.

Later, payments can be made monthly, or the widow can take out as much as she needs and leave the rest at interest.

EMPLOYER. Checks for vacation and sick pay and any salary or wages earned but not paid.

> *Note:* If the family is really strapped, it may be possible to get temporary funds from some United Way agency such as the Salvation Army or Red Cross. Or if you are well-known in the community, your widow may be able to swing a modest bank loan.

In a month or so, additional funds can be obtained from:

SOCIAL SECURITY. This provides a burial benefit, and depending on the age of the widow and/or children, monthly checks. Red tape will slow payments at the outset.

CIVIL SERVICE. (If the husband has been working for the government.) The payments will be based on the average of the last 3 years' earnings. At $13,000, the widow will receive about $281 per month (more with minor children), unless she remarries before age 60.

VETERANS BENEFITS. These provide up to $250 for burial expenses plus a headstone or marker. If death occurs in a VA hospital, the government will pay to transport the body to a burial place. And if other income is not large, a widow and dependent children may be entitled to a small pension.

Within a few months, there will be estate-settlement costs. Federal taxes begin to be significant when the net adjusted estate is more than $25,000. On the average, the total deductions for taxes, legal fees, etc., will be about 10% on estates up to $100,000; 15% when $100,000 to $150,000; 19% when $150,000 to $200,000, etc.

As emphasized elsewhere, when the prospective estate is more than $150,000, consideration should be given to setting up trusts and to providing insurance, investments, and other liquid assets to meet taxes and costs. A frozen estate (where assets cannot be sold quickly) can frustrate the best plans and even destroy an inheritance if assets have to be offered at bargain-basement prices.

Beware of Joint Ownership

It may sound trusting to have joint bank accounts, ownership of property, etc., but it will probably prove foolish and costly. When one person dies, a joint bank account, for example, will not be available until the survivor has a tax waiver indicating that officials are satisfied there are other estate assets to meet tax levies.

Even if both the husband and wife made deposits in a single account, the IRS will treat the account as property of the deceased—unless the widow can prove how much she contributed. That's not an easy task over a 5- or 10-year period.

Be especially wary of putting assets in joint names and forgetting them for years. Professor Stebbins paid $25,000 for farmland in 1954. A few years later, he gave his wife half ownership on her birthday. By 1974, when the good man died, the land was worth $100,000. He thought only half would be included in his estate.

The IRS ruled otherwise: The entire property should be included in the estate because all jointly held property is taxable in the estate of the first coowner to die, except to the extent that the survivor can prove his or her contribution. And since Mrs. S. had never paid a nickel for the land, the estate had to pay the extra taxes.

There are also lifetime tax problems:

WITH PROPERTY. In 1965, Mr. Loeser bought a ski lodge–
chalet for $60,000, including $20,000 inherited by his
wife. In 1975, in planning his estate, he wanted to transfer
title to his wife. By now, the property was worth $135,000,
so the transaction would require a gift tax on $90,000 (his
two-thirds). Even after using his exemptions, Mr. Loeser
would have to pay a hefty gift tax.

*About the only type of property that presents no tax
problem is that put into joint ownership before 1955—
prior to the present tax laws.*

WITH STOCKS AND BONDS. The act of putting securities,
which the husband paid for, in his wife's account creates a
gift situation. This can be compounded when a joint account is broken up. The securities must be divided equally,
preferably on the basis of "One for you, one for me."

Best solution: Transfer title to both names as "tenants in
common." This makes each the owner of one-half of the
holdings without any right of survivorship.

Or of course, all securities could be sold and the proceeds
divided.

Stock in street-name broker accounts (held in the name
of the broker, not the owner) can be handled differently. If
either joint owner can deal with the account alone or withdraw without the consent of the other, no gift takes place
until the noncontributor withdraws shares.

Another possible problem occurs if the wife dies first.
Then the husband will have to have records to prove that
the securities were acquired entirely with his funds.

> *Warning:* DON'T try to terminate joint ownership with-
> out legal counsel. The IRS does not permit a marital de-
> duction for a gift to a spouse if the property has been held
> as community property under the law of the state.

Working Out the Widow's Income

Just because you set up a trust fund for your wife does not assure her an income when she is a widow. If the assets include properties (real estate or securities) that are producing ample income today, there's no guarantee that the yields will continue or—more likely—that the income will be sufficient to meet the ever-rising cost of living.

To guesstimate how much income your widow and family will need, refer to Chapter V, on Estate Planning, and use this type of table. On the average, figure that she will need at least 60% of your present income. At the beginning, the major savings will be in insurance and taxes. Later, she will have to decide whether or not she can afford to stay in the same house or apartment. *Note:* There's no provision here for educational costs for the children.

Item	Present Average Expenses	Widow's Expenses
Housing and utilities	$ 4,500	$ 3,000
Food and clothing	3,000	2,000
Telephone	200	250
Insurance and Social Security	3,000	200
Car	1,500	1,250
Health care	750	600
Recreation-vacations	2,200	1,750
Income taxes	3,300	750
Charity	750	600
Savings	500	300
Miscellaneous	300	450
	$20,000	$11,150
Inflation		850
		$12,000

To determine how much money will be needed, use the retirement-planning approach. Start with what's left after the estate has been settled. Then the widow should ask the insurance agent how long she can expect to live, according to the actuarial tables.

Next, set aside a portion of the insurance proceeds as a nest egg. This would not be touched until other resources have been exhausted—an annuity, a trust where income is taken from both interest and principal, etc.

If the widow's life expectancy is 18 years, every $1,000 invested today will be worth $3,160 when needed. This projection is based on a 7% after-tax return, compounded annually. With $10,000 from insurance, she would have $31,600, which, with Social Security, should last unless she lives to an unusually ripe old age.

How Fast Will Money Grow?

(At 7%, After Tax, Compounded Annually)

Year	Value of $1,000	Year	Value of $1,000
1	$1,000	11	1,970
2	1,070	12	2,100
3	1,140	13	2,250
4	1,230	14	2,410
5	1,310	15	2,580
6	1,400	16	2,760
7	1,500	17	2,950
8	1,610	18	3,160
9	1,720	19	3,380
10	1,840	20	3,620

Where to Get Help

Most widows need all the help they can get. The best place to find it is within the family, where the advice should be unselfish, relatively unbiased, and sympathetic. Proceed cautiously.

If things don't work out, it will be difficult to make a change.

The best choice is someone who understands how to handle money, is in an income bracket close to that of the late husband, and is respected by the children.

Advice to widows: Don't choose Uncle Bill just because he is an officer of a small-town bank. His experience and views may be too limited if the widow plans to live in a metropolitan area where life-styles are more progressive and children react to different pressures.

On the other hand, don't overlook Cousin Sam, who owns a hardware store. He built that business by his skill and acumen and knows the real value of a dollar.

Under all circumstances: Retain a lawyer who can rule on the legality of what you and your children want to do and also make suggestions that can avoid or postpone taxes. If the estate is large enough, an accountant or tax consultant can be valuable.

Make your own decision. It's your money now, and if you don't really trust your brother-in-law, choose someone else, or better yet, turn to an institution, preferably a bank or trust company.

When the assets, beyond real estate, total over $100,000, an investment advisory firm is justified. A good one should be able to boost total returns more than enough to pay for the annual fee of about $1,000.

But don't buy reputation. Look at their complete investment record for 5—and preferably 10—years. You are paying well for results and should be able to anticipate returns at least as good as those of standard stock market averages. That's a lot better than most banks and trust departments have done lately.

Give Your Wife Some Investment Experience

With more people owning securities for their own accounts or through mutual funds, every wife should be familiar with the stock market. There's no reason to become overly involved or expert. All that's needed is to learn enough to judge the quality of the advice from other people. It's a sad fact that a large portion of so-called professional counsel, especially on the stock market, is of dubious value. A little knowledge and a lot of common sense can separate fact from fiction.

Wife, unmarried woman, or widow should understand the different types of securities and how to use stocks and bonds to build a profitable, rewarding investment program. The details can be left to the broker or investment adviser.

A good way to start is to help your wife open her own account with her savings or a gift from you—$3,000 annual maximum to avoid a gift tax. If she proves successful, keep on adding funds each year. Many a wife has done a better job of managing the household budget than her husband has in handling the family savings.

Unless you are extremely knowledgeable and patient, do not try to be the schoolteacher. She can learn the fundamentals from books, articles, local adult education courses, and seminars sponsored by brokerage firms.

Most important, let her work directly with the broker (probably yours because no registered representatives can make money on a $3,000 account).

It's OK to keep an eye on the monthly statements, but let her make her own mistakes and achieve her own triumphs. Do not belittle her ideas. One of my friends scoffed so long and so loud about his wife's reluctance to sell Cluett Peabody as it dropped from 39 to 14, that his wife sold all her securities and bought land in Florida. Three years later, the husband was still trying to get rid of the swamp acreage!

Guidelines for investing wives:

Invest Regularly in Quality Stocks

It's always better to buy the right stocks, even at the wrong time, than to buy the wrong stocks at the right time. With periodic purchases, the investor is dollar-cost-averaging and thus eliminating the difficult decision of timing.

Pay as You Go

This means no margin borrowing against stocks you own. This can be dangerous for widows with limited resources.

Be Tax-Conscious

Married couples usually file a joint return, so it's important to understand the tax difference between short- and long-term capital gains.

Guardians

FOR THE CHILDREN. The only way to be certain that your minor children will be cared for if both you and your wife die is to arrange for a guardian while you're living. It's good business, not a dolorous portent of disaster.

There are two types of guardianship—custody of the children and management of the property that they own or acquire. In both cases, the general procedures and responsibilities are spelled out by state laws. Terms vary, so consult your lawyer now and when you move to another state.

One thing is constant: The probate or surrogate court must approve the guardian. And if you have no will or make no choice, the court will make the appointment, probably with no knowledge of the real needs of your children or your own wishes.

If you prefer to keep this decision out of your will, write a detailed letter to the county probate judge and attach it to your will. It has no legal force but will probably prove helpful. Besides, it's cheaper to write a new letter than to revise your testament.

Steps to take in the selection of a guardian for children (remember they are legally adults, in most states, at age 18):

Make a Joint Choice

Choose one or preferably two persons who meet with approval from both you and your wife. Only one can serve, but the other can be a successor.

Try to Name a Member of Your Family

Choose a sister, brother-in-law, cousin, etc., who has good rapport with the children. Skip grandparents, as they may be overwhelmed and not able to relate effectively.

Choose a Couple

They should be near your own age, in the same general economic bracket, and with similar interests. Be sure that both are willing and able to handle the responsibility. If you suspect there might be a separation or divorce, name one person with the realization that he or she may remarry.

Consider an Institutional Guardian

This might be a children's home supported by your religious group.

Once you and your wife have made your choices, check out further by taking these steps:

Spend a Weekend with Them

If possible, stay in their home. This will give you a chance to see how they actually live and to determine how your youngsters might react. One wife, a tidy housekeeper, couldn't stand the sloppy kitchen of her cousin. Another husband came home convinced that his sister-in-law was too narrowminded to handle his extrovert son.

Ask Whether They Will Be Willing to Serve

Your request may impose a greater burden than you anticipate. Or they may be planning to move to another state. Keep flexible by naming several successive guardians and telling each of them what you've done.

Draw Your Will to Make Guardianship Easier

If you have a large house and your sister has agreed to be the guardian, leave the house to her. Or if she probably won't want to move, allot enough of your estate to her to pay for an addition to her house.

FOR PROPERTY. In naming a guardian for property, use a person if your estate will be under $50,000, consider an institution if it's larger.

All guardians must be bonded and file accounting reports with the courts. You can cut costs by requesting a waiver of the bond in your will, but there's no way to skip the reports, which, for proper handling, should be filled out by a lawyer.

If you appoint a bank to handle assets until the children are of age, spell out exactly how you want them to manage the money. If left alone, most banks will conserve the funds. That's never as important as education and a life-style that will please and benefit the children. The capacity to learn, to work, and to earn is far more valuable than just money. *You saved the money to use for living, not for preservation.*

Teaching Children How to Manage Money

Children become aware of money at an early age—from family conversation (and arguments), from TV, from school arithmetic, and from shopping with their parents. What they learn will influence their adult attitude—to be cautious or impulsive, to understand that money is never a goal in itself but only one of the resources of living, and to recognize that wise money management will go a long way toward providing personal satisfaction throughout life.

No one is born with a ready-made ability to manage money.

It takes careful training, good examples, and long experience. A child learns basic economic rules when he finds that his wants must be subordinated to his needs, which, in turn, must be assigned priorities in relation to financial resources. *One of the best investments of time that parents can make is to help their children use money wisely—to make choices, to solve problems, to promote resourcefulness and confidence, and eventually, to build independence.*

Give your children reasonable allowances, help them to plan their spending, let them experience disappointment and joy from their own decisions, and keep stressing the wisdom of savings and the lifelong value of personal money management.

Here are general suggestions, based on the long experience of the Household Finance Corporation, for teaching-training your children:

ALLOWANCE. This is a key policy that should be carefully considered and executed according to a long-range plan. The money should be in line with family income and costs of living, NOT what the neighbor's children get.

Allowances should start no earlier than age 5, with payments of a dime 2 or 3 times a week. As the outlay grows to 25¢, 50¢, and dollars, widen the time gap—every week in elementary school, every 2 weeks in junior high, every month in high school. *Always pay regularly, just as if it were a paycheck.*

When the allowance is up to $10 a week, the best approach, says a Harvard professor, is an annual allowance of $520! If you can afford to do it, this should provide some valuable lessons in managing money.

Caveat: At all ages, be cautious about setting an allowance that is considerably higher than that of school friends. The children will feel guilty, will probably waste the money, and may never learn the importance of frugality.

Once the youngster is past the candy-gum stage, help keep a record of necessary expenses—school lunch, bus fare, Scout dues, Sunday school gift, etc. Then add a reasonable sum to buy extras and to start a savings account.

Review this "budget" every 3 months and be ready to grant increases for both *needs* and *wants*. At 13, for example, add a clothing allowance. If Mother does all the shopping, Sister won't make her mistakes until she goes to college, when her clothes will be much more expensive.

The most difficult time will be the early teens, when most children will want more than they (and you) can afford. When their plans include expensive items such as camera, stamps, etc., make them prepare a pay schedule—savings of X dollars, with the balance to be "borrowed" from future allowances.

Don't make the "loan" deductions too large, as the value of the training will be lost. And if there are special emergencies, advance the money with the understanding that it will be repaid from earnings or gifts from relatives (knowing, of course, that if they do manage to repay half, you'll probably forgive the balance).

Teentime is also when children should be brought into discussion of family finances. There's no need to bare all your assets or problems; just discuss rent, insurance, charge accounts, and loans. Answer questions, but don't make a big thing of it. *Never create anxiety by forcing the issue with their—or your—* plans.

At every age:

Provide Help

Young people have difficulty in planning for long-range goals. Help them to work out schedules and stick to them. (Be sure you set a good example!)

Be Consistent, Yet Flexible

After you've agreed to a fixed sum or money policy, hold fast. But not too fast if there are extenuating circumstances.

Be Realistic

Point out the false premises in unrealistic goals or monetary projections. But DO NOT force a change.

Respect Individuality

Each child differs in temperament, rate of development, ability to learn, and approach to money. (As if you didn't know!)

Keep Suggesting New Experiences

This will help tone down the "big spender" and broaden the viewpoint of the "hoarder."

Offer Praise for Success, Mild Criticism for Mistakes

Learning by doing is always a trial-and-error process.

Encourage Savings

As a frame of reference, suggest that 20% of the allowance be in savings—half for future purchases or pleasures, the balance in a savings account, in insurance, securities, or mutual-fund shares. A good way to make savings important (and fun) is to use part of special gifts from grandparents for sale purchases and the rest for investments.

Don't Use Money as a Threat

Discipline problems should be handled apart from an allowance unless the offense is directly related to the use of money.

Do Use Money as a Reward—on a Matching Basis

If Junior wants a new bicycle, make a deal whereby the $10 he gets for an improved report card will be matched by his after-school income.

Encourage Earnings

Money earned by a teenager is always more significant than money given. In your own home, pay for chores only if you would have to hire someone else to do them. *Under no circumstances should there be any payment for routine family responsibilities.*

> *Warning:* Before you permit any child to accept an outside job, make sure there's time for fun, sleep, study, and school and family responsibilities. Children underestimate their family's ability to cope with financial problems and overestimate their own ability to handle varied activities.

Encourage an Understanding of Money

You can do this by urging the children to participate in school fund-raising projects, join Junior Achievement (which operates as a stockholder-owned, moneymaking corporation), buy stock, shop for food (a sure way to learn the ravages of inflation), and take special courses in money management with the Scouts, etc.

Using Credit

Many stores now offer teen charge accounts or permit family credit cards to be used with parental consent. Review the pros and cons in a family session, encourage prompt payments, and if installment sales are used, keep the monthly obligations within bounds.

Handling Problems

When something goes wrong with money, there will be anger and probably tears. Your role is to find out what happened, to suggest solutions, and to develop preventive measures.

If it's a loss or theft, be ready to replace funds for essentials but not for extras. If your daughter went on a spending spree, pay the bills and help her work out a schedule of repayments to you.

If your son has broken a neighbor's window, have him apologize and arrange for repairs. If the cost of damage is substantial, stick with him but make sure he understands how this extra outlay dents the family budget.

If there's stealing, try to understand why. It's usually a passing phase but may reflect an inadequate allowance, lack of peer approval, or insufficient family acceptance.

Always Treat Money with Respect

Teach your children how to manage it for their personal goals and to realize that it can and should be used unselfishly. The money habits and standards you set will affect your children all the days of their lives.

How to Provide Protection for Children's Funds and Save Taxes

If you or your relatives have resources enough to make gifts to children, ask your attorney about the Uniform Gifts to Minors Act. This will help the youngsters in the future and save the donor taxes, too. The income is tax-exempt (in most cases), so the assets will grow rapidly. In 15 years, with all dividends-interest plowed back, every $1,000 can grow to $4,000—a welcome aid to college costs.

These custody accounts must be under the direction of someone other than the donor—wife, friend, or bank (whose fee will reduce the income). Choose someone who is likely to live until the child is 18. There can be only one custodian and one minor in each account—no joint custodians or beneficiaries.

The funds must be invested for the child's benefit. That means no speculations such as options or commodity contracts. But the custodian could authorize a loan to the donor.

In setting up a custody account:

USE THE STANDARD FORM AS PRESCRIBED BY STATE LAW. Improper wording can affect the legal nature of the gift and your—and the child's—ability to transfer the property in the future.

PUT THE CHILD'S OWN SOCIAL SECURITY NUMBER ON THE SAVINGS ACCOUNT OR SECURITIES. If he or she does not have a number, file Form SS-5 at the nearest Social Security office. If you make the mistake of using your own Social Security number, the IRS computer will store up the information and will tax you.

If the donor has already named himself as custodian, check a lawyer to start resignation proceedings. Some states do not provide for a successor, and it may be necessary to apply to the court for permission to make the change.

Gifts and Tax Savings

As gifts, the initial assets are tax-exempt when the annual amount is $3,000 or less ($6,000 if the wife gives, too)—more if the donor uses part of the lifetime maximum exemption of $30,000. When large amounts are involved, a trust should be used. Generally, the best gifts are securities or shares of a mutual fund, but other money-earning properties are legally acceptable.

Older people should be careful when continuing annual gifts. Deposits made in the 3 final years may be considered as "in contemplation of death."

Example: Grandpa Norcross gives $1,000 a year for 8 years, then ups the amount to $3,000. The next year he dies. The first $8,000 is OK, but the IRS might question the $3,000.

The tax savings occur on assets up to about $12,000. All income is credited to the minor, who will have an effective tax exemption of $850—$750 individual exemption and $100 dividend credit (under present laws). When the income is over $750 a year, an income tax report must be filed. There is no standard deduction, and you must use the tax-rate table of the IRS instructions, not the form for one exemption.

Be careful not to use the income from the custody account to satisfy any legal support obligations. If you do, the income will be counted on your tax return.

Example: If the account throws off $300 in dividends, and because of a temporary bind, you use $175 of this to pay the child's dental bill, you're stuck. That is now your income.

You can continue to claim an income tax credit for dependency as long as you provide the majority of support—to age 18 or older if the child is a full-time student.

Bank Trust Account

There are no tax savings with a bank trust account set up in the names of both the donor and the child—"Charles Chipmunk in trust for Charles Chipmunk, III." The income will be credited to the adult. But at death, the money will be transferred directly to the child—without probate proceedings or administrative expenses.

When a Wife Works

The second and third columns below show how much will be left from the additional income of the wife after deducting the additional federal income tax resulting from her part of the income in a joint tax return. With state and local income taxes, the residue will be even smaller.

Wife's Income	Husband's Income	
	$20,000	$30,000
$ 5,000	3,390	3,125
7,500	5,005	4,599
10,000	6,515	6,027
12,500	7,989	7,385
15,000	9,417	8,710

Problems of Divorce

The strong shift to women working is forcing major changes in the payment of alimony. Today, a woman with good potential earning power (whether she is working or not) can expect hard bargaining over alimony.

Generally speaking (and it depends a good deal on the area of the country), a working wife can expect relatively little alimony. Her strongest argument is custody of the children. There are no precise formulas, but she must be able to show exactly how much it will cost to raise the youngsters.

Settlements seldom are more than 50% of net income. Typically, they are 30%–40% when there are children, 20%–25% when there are none. Increasingly, there are escalation clauses to offset the pressures of inflation.

Laws and customs pertaining to divorce are changing rapidly. Nationally, there's a trend toward no-fault divorce (either party can get the divorce without having to show grounds). *The big advantage is speed and lack of emotional strain.*

Today, nearly 95% of cases involve no-contest divorce. In 36 states, there's an equitable division of property acquired during the marriage. In 28 states, alimony is payable. And usually, child support comes from both parents.

Divorce is not cheap. Fees range from $2,500, when there's no contest, to $7,500 or more, when there's a custody battle and long negotiations on settlements. There are clinics in some states, and for $100 you can buy a do-it-yourself kit. But in many cases these "settlements" end up with extra costs and failure to achieve the anticipated goals.

State	Breakdown of Marriage	Standard Faults*	Incompatability	Separation†	Alcoholism, Drug Abuse	Court Cannot Distribute	Court Can Distribute‡	Community Property Joint Ownership	To Either Spouse	To Wife Only	No Alimony
	Grounds for Divorce					**Division of Property**				**Alimony**	
Alabama	●	●		●	●	●				●	
Alaska		●	●		●		○		○		
Arizona	●							●	●		
Arkansas		●		●	●		●			●	
California	●							●	●		
Colorado	●						●		●		
Connecticut	●	●		●	●		●		●		
Delaware	●						●		●		
District of Columbia		●		●			●			●	
Florida	●					●			●		
Georgia	●	●			●	●				●	
Hawaii	●	●				●			●		
Idaho	●	●	●					●		●	
Illinois		●			●		●			●	
Indiana	●	●					●		●		
Iowa	●						●		●		
Kansas		●	●		●		●		●		
Kentucky	●						●		●		
Louisiana		●		●	●			●			● §
Maine	●	●					●		●		
Maryland		●		●		●				●	
Massachusetts		●			●	●			●		
Michigan	●						●		●		
Minnesota	●						●		●		
Mississippi		●			●	●				●	
Missouri	●						●		●		
Montana	●	●					●		●		
Nebraska	●						●		●		
Nevada		●	●		●			●	●		
New Hampshire	●	●		●	●		●		● II		
New Jersey	●			●			●		●		
New Mexico		●	●					●	●		
New York		●		●		●			●		
North Carolina		●		●		●					● #
North Dakota		●	●	●		●			●		
Ohio		●		●	●	●			●		
Oklahoma		●	●		●		●		●		
Oregon	●						●		●		
Pennsylvania		●				●					●
Rhode Island		●		●	●	●				●	
South Carolina		●		●	●	●				●	
South Dakota		●		●			●			●	
Tennessee		●		●	●		●			●	
Texas		●		●				●			●
Utah		●		●	●		●		●		
Vermont		●		●			●		●		
Virginia		●		●		●				●	
Washington	●							●	●		
West Virginia		●		●	●		●		●		
Wisconsin		●		●	●		●			●	
Wyoming		●		●			●			●	

*Include adultery, cruelty, desertion.

†Means living apart with normal financial support provided.

‡When court cannot make distribution, property goes to husband or wife, depending on who has legal title.

§Limits alimony to one-third of husband's income.

II Limits alimony to three years, subject to renewal.

#Only if spouse is unable to work.

SOURCE: *Business Week*, law journals.

The Property Split

When there are children, the wife will almost always get the house. Without children, she *may* keep the family mansion. Much depends on how the property is split. On the most frequently used 50-50 deal, the wife gets the house and furnishings, one of the family's two cars, and the proceeds of all or part of the husband's insurance. The husband settles for the other car, the stock portfolio, a few extras (possibly a boat, skimobile, etc.), and the balance in cash.

Note: Forget about any extra benefits if one party has been guilty of marital misconduct. The courts pay little heed.

Watch the tax angle. The husband must pay a capital gains tax on appreciation of property turned over to his wife. This decision made one husband liable for taxes on $420,000 when he turned over stocks worth $500,000 but costing only $80,000.

Support and Alimony

Child-support payments vary greatly. They depend on living standards, type of schooling, and the wife's ability to work. Unlike alimony, such outlays are never tax deductible by the husband nor taxed as income to the wife. *The only break:* The parent who contributes more than 50% of a child's support may deduct the $750 exemption and medical expenses. The husband can get the exemption only if he pays $1,200 or more a year to support the child.

Advice: For the wife, get some guarantee of payment to safeguard against the husband's skipping alimony and child-support payments—e.g., stocks or real estate held in escrow.

For the husband, settle only for a fixed sum per month, based on present income. DO NOT make it a percentage of earnings, as you might move up to a better-paying job.

Tax Consequences

Since alimony is a tax-deductible expense, a heavy payment can drop the husband into a lower tax bracket. That's why such payments should be specifically termed "for wife and child."

Example: Mr. Whistlestop has a taxable income of $32,000. With a joint return, his federal tax is $8,660, so his after-tax income is $23,340. As the result of a divorce, he pays $10,000 a year in alimony. This cuts his taxable income to $22,000, so his tax drops to $5,990, leaving about $16,000. Thus, the alimony costs $7,340—$23,340 less $16,000. Obviously, the wife should understand this advantage in her payment negotiations.

The ex-Mrs. W. earns $5,000 from part-time work, so her gross income is $15,000, with a tax of $3,520 and an after-tax net of $11,480.

As long as that $10,000 is termed alimony, there's no problem, but if it should be half for alimony and half for child support, Mr. W. can deduct only $5,000 plus a $750 exemption. His taxable income is now $27,000, his tax $8,040—some $2,000 more than when the full payment was for alimony.

The wife benefits, however. Her income is now $10,000, on which the tax is $2,090—a $430 savings.

Far more important than the dollars is the traumatic experience. Divorce is difficult, often searing.

X

Making the Most of
Bank Services

Your grandfather would hardly recognize the modern bank. Today, even the small neighborhood branch (and there's one on almost every corner and in almost every shopping center) provides a score of financial services unheard of a few years ago. As part of a bank holding company, many a small bank has access to departments, or affiliates, to offer everything from *B* (bankers' acceptances and bonds) to *T* (Treasury notes and trusts). Next time you cash a check, stop by the literature rack and find out the wide array of available aids and services. You may find new ways to save time and money and to avoid trouble.

The distinctions are narrowing, but basically, these financial institutions fall into two groups: commercial banks—the largest and most visible; and thrift institutions—savings banks (primarily in the Northeast) and savings and loan associations (stockholder-owned in the Far West and Ohio, and mutual organizations in the rest of the country).

To oversimplify, the following descriptions assume that checking accounts are in commercial banks and that savings accounts are in thrift institutions. Actually, of course, there are many overlaps, and with the development of long-term certificates of deposit at commercial banks and the advent of special checking accounts in thrift institutions, the differences are narrowing.

Most people use commercial banks for checking accounts, personal or installment loans, safe-deposit boxes, and trust departments. Many more services are available, so don't hesitate to ask when you need financial counseling or extra funds.

The majority of the services discussed here are offered by large banks, many by medium-size banks, and some by small banks. But every bank can call on its correspondents—bigger banks with whom it works. The success of every financial institution is directly related to its ability to serve customers.

When you make a deposit in a checking or savings account, the bank acquires legal title to the money—subject to certain commitments to you. Usually, you pay for the convenience of checking and ancillary services, and the bank pays you for savings.

How to Save Money on Your Checking Account

If you want to save money on your checking account, shop around. Banks often make special offers—reduced rates for certain types of accounts, free checkbooks when a new branch is opened, package deals where, for $3 a month, you can get a set number of checks, a safe-deposit box, automatic loans if you overdraw your account, and similar conveniences.

Charges for checking accounts vary widely, but on the average, a commercial bank will fix a price of $1.50 to $3 per month for each 10 items (one for each deposit, one for each withdrawal) *if* you maintain an average $100 balance. You get a few more free services for each additional $100 balance. In many areas, you may also be able to get free checking if competition is keen.

When you open a new account, determine exactly what you want the bank to do for you and find the bank that will do it. If you can save money, too, that's a bonus!

After a couple of months, study the rate structure of your

account to find out how to cut costs. It may pay you to transfer $500 from your savings to your checking account. At 5% interest, compounded quarterly, you will lose about $26 on your savings but you might get 30 free items. At 10¢ each, plus a reduction in the flat monthly charge, you can save $40 to $50 a year for a net gain of $14 to $24!

Other money-saving techniques:

CONSOLIDATE YOUR PAYMENTS. Instead of making out a weekly check for laundry, newspaper delivery, etc., pay the bills monthly. This can mean 40 fewer checks a year.

AVOID OVERDRAFTS. Keep your checkbook up-to-date; subtract each check as it is written; review your balance against the bank's monthly statement; and if you need help, take your problems to your banker. If there are insufficient funds in your account, a returned check can harm your credit, cause cancellation of charge accounts, and even lead to the bank manager's asking you to take your business elsewhere.

SPACE YOUR TRANSACTIONS. Make your deposits in midweek, but don't write checks until Friday of the following week. This will give about 10 days to build a higher average balance.

ASK FOR SPECIAL SERVICE. If you have checks for deposit from a prime business organization or government agency, ask the bank manager to approve the deposit for "immediate credit." This will avoid the usual 5-day clearance and the embarrassment —and extra charge—of having your bill-paying check returned because it was "drawn against uncollected funds."

Mechanics of Check Writing

In writing and endorsing checks, follow the advice of the Continental Illinois National Bank and Trust Company:

DO Use a Typewriter or a Pen

Pencil writing can be smudged, erased, or changed.

DO Sign a Check at the Time of Payment and Only after You Have Filled in All the Other Required Information

DO Sign Your Official Signature

If the check is made out to "Wellington Napoleon Smith," write that name when endorsing, and then, "W. Napoleon Smith," the name in which the account is maintained.

DO Avoid Careless Endorsements

If the check was written by someone else, then endorsed by you, you guarantee its validity. If it bounces, you are liable. *For protection, add, after your signature-endorsement: "without recourse."*

DO Remember That Checks Made Out to "Cash" or "Bearer" Can Be Cashed By Anyone

DO Record Each Check Promptly

It's easy to forget that payment to the dry cleaner when you are rushing to pick up someone at the station.

DO Cash or Deposit Checks from Others within a Month

Most banks will refuse to honor a check after 180 days (but if you mail it in, chances are the computer won't catch the date).

DO Write "For Deposit Only" on Checks Put in Your Account

This eliminates possible misappropriation if the check should be lost or stolen.

DO Destroy a Check When You Make an Error

Erasures, cross-outs, and alterations can void the check or mess up your accounting.

DO Keep Canceled Checks in a Safe Place

This helps to prevent forgery if someone wants to practice duplicating your signature.

DO Destroy Old Blank Checks When You Order New Ones

And these equally important DONT's:

DON'T Sign a Blank Check (without All Required Information)

This can be very tempting, even when you are dealing with local merchants.

DON'T Leave Room for Alterations to Your Check By Someone Else

Fill the space between the printed dollar sign and the figure, and before and after the spelled-out amount. It's easy for a crafty crook to insert a numeral and take you for a substantial sum—$500, not the intended $5.

DON'T Leave Your Checkbook or Supply of Blank Checks in Any Place from Which Others Might Take It

DON'T Cash an Incorrect Check

If it is marked "payment in full" and you feel you are still owed money, don't scratch out this phrase. This will eliminate your case in court. Give the check back and try to get a new, correct one.

How to Handle Stop Payment on Checks

If a check has been stolen, lost, or made out to the wrong person, stop payment.

But be careful how you do it: (1) Telephone the bank with details of the check. (2) Get the name of the teller for future reference. (3) Confirm your request in writing. A verbal stop payment is good only for 2 weeks. A written one (and most banks have special forms) is binding for 6 months and can be renewed.

If the bank slips up and pays the stopped check, you are entitled to damages—usually the sum wrongfully paid out.

If the stopped check is cashed at a store, *you* are responsible.

Note: If your name is forged to a check, you probably will suffer no loss. If you can prove you were not at fault, the bank must make good.

How Much Interest Do You Really Earn?

Thrift institutions are permitted, by federal authorities, to pay higher interest rates on savings accounts than can commercial banks. The actual amount of interest earned varies because of bank policies and the variables used in calculating interest. But the difference is a lot less than you might be led to believe by some advertisements. The maximum legal difference is one-fourth of 1%—on a $100 deposit, the one-year gain from the savings and loan would be only 25¢ more than available from a commercial bank savings account!

The federal government does control the maximum interest rates but has little to say about how interest is computed. According to the American Bankers Association, there are 54 methods of calculating interest. So while the ads may stress the 5% or 6% rate, the actual yield may be less—or more. Use this chart, developed by Jackie Pinson at Kansas State University, to find out the best deal. Once you have made your choice, pay attention to the requirements—minimum balance, grace days, penalties for early or excess withdrawals.

Using your present passbook, fill in the entries for the past 6 to 12 months, then telephone or write other banks and thrift institutions to ask how they would figure the same savings.

How to Find the Best Savings Deal

DEPOSIT TICKET

DATE	WITHDRAWAL	DEPOSIT	INTEREST	BALANCE	

Interest earned_____.
Annual percentage rate_____.
Method of calculation_____.
Frequency of compounding_____.
Frequency of crediting_____.
Number of deposit grace days_____.
Number of withdrawal grace days_____.
Penalty for excess withdrawals_____.
Actual time in interest-paying period_____.
Other variables or comments_____.

$79.13 or $29.25 in Interest?

Here are examples of some of the variables in computation of interest, at 6% a year, on a savings account:

Deposit Ticket

Date	Withdrawal	Deposit	Interest	Balance
1. January 1				$1,000
2. January 10		$2,000		3,000
3. February 6		1,000		4,000
4. March 5	$1,000			3,000
5. March 20	500			2,500
6. March 30	500			2,000

Over a full year an account like the above would work out as follows:

Type of Account, Terms	Annual Interest
Low balance; compounded and credited semiannually; no grace days; penalty for withdrawals when more than 2 per month.	$29.25
Low balance; compounded and credited semiannually; no grace days.	29.75
Low balance; compounded quarterly; credited semiannually; no grace days; 3 withdrawal grace days at end of period.	29.97
Low balance; compounded and credited quarterly; no grace days.	44.93

First in–first out (on beginning balance); compounded
and credited quarterly; no grace days.*   52.44

First in–first out; compounded and credited quarterly;
no grace days.*   53.93

First in–first out; compounded and credited quarterly;
10 deposit grace days (1st–10th).*   56.94

Last in–first out; compounded and credited quarterly;
no grace days.†   58.44

Low balance; compounded quarterly; credited semiannually; 10 deposit grace days (1st–10th); 3 withdrawal days
at end of period.   59.95

Low balance; compounded and credited quarterly; 10
deposit grace days (1st–10th).   59.95

Last in–first out; compounded and credited quarterly;
10 deposit grace days (1st–10th).†   62.28

First in–first out; compounded and credited quarterly;
10 deposit days (1st–10th) and 3 withdrawal grace days at
end of period.*   63.70

Low balance; compounded and credited quarterly; 10
deposit grace days (1st–10th); 3 withdrawal grace days at
end of period.   67.46

Day of deposit to day of withdrawal; compounded and
credited quarterly; no grace days; 3 withdrawal grace days
at end of period.   75.46

Day of deposit to day of withdrawal; compounded and
credited quarterly; 10 deposit grace days (1st–10th of each
month).   79.13

---

* First in–first out: The yield is calculated from the day of deposit to the end of
the interest period, but withdrawals are charged against the first deposits of the interest period.

† Last in–first out: The yield is figured from the day money is deposited to the
end of the interest period (compounding period). Withdrawals are subtracted from
the latest deposit, so earlier deposits accrue more interest, having remained in the
account longer.

With *low balance* accounts, the yield is calculated only on the lowest amount of
money in the account during the interest period.

Deposit grace days (1st–10th) means that money deposited by the 10th of the
month will draw interest from the first day of the month. The more deposit grace
days, the greater the interest.

Withdrawal grace days indicate the number of days at the end of the interest
period when money can be withdrawn without losing interest.

The effect of compounding is very important. This means that the bank is paying interest on interest.

Example:

$1,000 compounded quarterly	= $61.36
compounded monthly	= 61.68
compounded daily	= 61.83
compounded continuously	= 61.84

Source: *Media & Consumer.*

Other Bank Services

Here are some of the most widely used bank services offered by the Chase-Manhattan Bank, North America, one of the nation's largest financial institutions. They will give you an idea of why it may be easier to stop by your neighborhood bank instead of looking for a specialist or waiting until you get to the big city.

Almost every bank will help you invest in such securities as:

CASH EQUIVALENTS. These include Treasury bills and notes, commercial paper, bankers' acceptances, and municipal bonds. Original issues of T-bills have fixed maturities of from 91 days to 1 year, are bought at a discount, and may be sold before maturity. Normally, their interest rates run 1% to 2% above those of savings accounts. The minimum original purchase amount is $10,000, but there's an active secondary market.

TREASURY NOTES. These mature in 1 to 5 years, pay interest semiannually at close to the discount rate, and are readily negotiable. They are available in units of $10,000.

COMMERCIAL PAPER. This is issued by finance companies and major corporations and pays top interest (depending on the credit of the borrower). It may be difficult to sell, since there is no secondary market. The minimum purchase is usually $100,000, but if you are a good customer, your bank can probably arrange for participation with as little as $25,000.

BANKERS' ACCEPTANCES. These are short-term obligations of customers that are guaranteed by the bank. They can be bought in units as low as $1,000 and carry yields above the prime rate. They carry varied face amounts and maturity dates, so you could own a $3,325 obligation of a local merchant due in 100 days.

TAX-EXEMPT BONDS. These "municipals," offered with maturities from less than 1 year to more than 20 years, are exempt from federal income tax and—in some states—from state and local taxes. Banks are large buyers, so you can probably arrange to buy a relatively small amount. (As explained in Chapter XXV, on Investments, these are worthwhile only for people in tax brackets above 40%.)

Help in Estate Planning

When you have accumulated extra funds for investment, talk over your plans with your banker. If you have a sizable sum, he can call on a team of specialists to look at your total financial picture and make recommendations on insurance, investments, tax shelters, etc. Such a study can be expensive—up to $5,000.

Most banks will be glad to refer you to experts if you need the tax benefits of depreciation—to a real-estate firm, a builder, a syndicator for oil drilling, etc. The bank may also provide a loan and/or mortgage and for a fee (usually 5% of the equity investment) will monitor the deal.

Smaller banks provide similar services in relation to their size, location, and expertise. Almost every bank has someone who knows local real estate and is able to anticipate changes in the community. When you plan to buy a house, building, or land in your area, check with your banker first.

Investment Counsel

Larger banks, directly and through trust departments, handle pension and profit-sharing plans and provide professional money management. The fees for investment counsel run from 1% of the total value of the holdings up to $100,000, then decrease to one-half of 1% up to about $1 million.

In recent years, as part of their thrust to become "financial department stores," banks have been moving into smaller markets with broader services. Some major banks will handle portfolios as small as $10,000 for fees of $250—and up. The more money you invest, the broader the service. For holdings under $100,000, you get a list of recommended stock changes several times a year. You do your own buying and selling. Larger portfolios get more personalized service—advice that tailors the securities more closely to the individual's goals and needs.

Generally, the bank will invest your money in common trust funds, which are like mutual funds and provide diversification and professional management. A more recent development is the package plan, such as that offered by Continental Illinois National Bank and Trust Company: a choice of 4 portfolios: for longterm growth, growth and income, income, and tax exemption. The minimum fee is $350 on a $25,000 account. In most cases, you can switch funds as your investment goals change. It's too early to know how well such funds perform, but you can be sure of convenience and frequent reports.

Special Services

Almost all banks can be helpful on trips and business abroad. In addition to the standard traveler's checks, they can provide tourists and people who live or retire abroad with letters of credit, introductions, and routine assistance such as:

CUSTODY SERVICE. This involves safekeeping of securities, record keeping, collecting interest and dividends, and buying and selling securities.

FINANCIAL SECRETARIAL SERVICES. This service handles all financial payments while you are away—bills, monthly remittances to children or dependents, salaries to household employees, etc.

Other tailored services may include:

INDIVIDUAL TAX SERVICE. A year-round operation that prepares and files quarterly estimated tax payments as well as annual income tax returns. Fees range from $150 to $400.

CREDIT CHECKS OF CORPORATIONS AND INDIVIDUALS. The reports, which cost $50 or more, provide only facts, no comments. Such information can be helpful if you are thinking of buying a business in another community or selling your own to a buyer from out of the area.

ESCROW SERVICE. Where the bank acts as stakeholder for cash, works of art, formulas, and other valuables as a guarantee from one party to another that certain specified conditions will be met. This can be useful in business buy-outs and divorce cases.

Less-Expensive Loans

The truth-in-lending law has brought a major change in the way personal loans are handled. In most areas, banks are shifting from discounted loans to simple interest ones. The reason, as one New Jersey banker told me: "If you have to advertise how much you charge on an annual basis, you should be sure to get it. With discounted loans, customers who took advantage of the ten-day grace period before making their payments, got a short, free ride. That's not possible with simple interest loans."

The difference can be important, especially when you repay a substantial portion of the loan early. Here's what happened to a $3,000 loan for three years:

Old method: The 4.96% discounted translates into 10.75% interest a year. Thus, the borrower takes out a loan for $3,522.90, of which $522.90 represents the interest.

New plan: At 10.75% simple interest, the loan would cost $517.43—a savings of $5.47.

But if you paid off $1,000 at the end of 18 months, the interest cost on the discounted loan would be $470.61, compared to $402.25 simple interest—a welcome savings of $68.36!

Insurance on Money in the Bank

Deposits in most (but not all) banks and thrift institutions are insured up to $40,000 for each saver—by the Federal Deposit Insurance Corporation (FDIC) for banks, and by the Federal Savings and Loan Insurance Corporation (FSLIC) for savings and loans.

The maximum coverage for any one individual in any one institution is $40,000. You can be protected on larger sums by setting up accounts in the names of your wife and children or in combination or trusteed accounts.

The insurance covers all your funds. If you have a checking account with $9,000, a savings account of $18,000, and certificates of deposit of $20,000, you are insured for only $40,000—not the total of $47,000.

XI

The Joys—and Tax Benefits—
of Charitable Gifts

One of the privileges of being an American is to be able to help others—directly by volunteer service, indirectly by contributions of money or property. In both cases, the greatest joy will come from giving, but there can also be substantial tax benefits. Governments, at all levels, encourage gifts—to heirs, to friends, and most of all, to nonprofit organizations such as the United Way, educational and religious institutions, special-interest groups, and community agencies.

The percentage of your income you allocate to "charity" depends largely on your family background, your personal interests, and your concern for others. Some religions call for tithing—donating 10% of gross income ($2,000 on a $20,000 salary); others feel that, because of withholding for taxes, Social Security, etc., tithing should be on a net basis (about $1,500 for that $20,000 income). Professional fund-raisers urge that contributions should be not less than 5% of gross income for anyone filing a federal income tax return; and tax consultants advise their clients in the 42%-plus tax brackets to set up a planned, long-term gift program.

Before we go into tax advantages, let's outline your personal and family responsibilities for charitable donations. You will always be under pressure for small contributions—for tickets to

135

the Firemen's Ball, $10 for the Boy Scouts to buy a trailer for weekend camping, or $5 to help a neighbor collect for her favorite charity. *But major gifts should be an essential part of every family budget—planned, argued about, and determined in a businesslike manner.*

1. Make a list of your family's charitable and "cause" interests-responsibilities—United Way (especially if companies in your area have payroll-deduction plans); church or synagogue; prep school, college, graduate school (of both you and your wife); organizations in which you are involved (Girl Scouts, Red Cross, hospitals, etc.—even if they are in the United Way, they need extra funds for capital and equipment expenditures); environmental groups (Sierra Club, Clean Air Association); and any other non-profit agency-foundation that is important to you and/or your community.

2. Classify the charities by groups, then set priorities and degrees of interest. (It's easier to eliminate if you use percentages and concentrate only on those agencies scoring 50% or higher.) Be flexible, as conditions, and needs, can change during the year.

3. Decide what dollar amount or percentage of income is to be budgeted for charitable gifts. Let's say you and your wife agree on 7% of your $20,000 income—$1,400 a year. This may seem like a lot, but you will be surprised at how much those small, unplanned donations add up to in a year! As a rule of thumb, break this down to about 1% for the United Way, 1% for church, 1% for school-college, 1% for fund-raising events such as charity balls or testimonial dinners, 1% for your favorite cause or institution, and the balance ($400) for smaller gifts. Remember, your goal is to zero in on a few worthwhile gifts and minimize the $5 donations.

4. Establish a special checking account by setting aside a set sum each month. This will make it easier to keep accurate records and to make that *big* gift—perhaps even a life membership in some important-to-you organization.

5. Take into account that approved gifts are deductible for income tax purposes—every $1,000 in gifts provides a tax benefit of $250 when you are in the 25% tax bracket, $350 when it's 35%, etc.

If that $1,400 is too big a bite out of your cash budget, keep the total figure but substitute services-goods for some charities. The IRS permits deductions for expenses of volunteer work (mileage, parking fees, etc.) and for the current value of donations—old clothes to a rummage sale, books and furniture to the Salvation Army, etc. *Be sure to get a written acknowledgment stating the approximate value of the gifts* in case your return is flagged.

This schedule, which represents recommended giving for the United Way, will help you project dollars on a percentage-of-income basis:

If You Earn			Your Fair Share Pledge		
Weekly	Monthly	Yearly	Weekly	Monthly	Yearly
$115	$ 500	$ 6,000	$ .60	$ 2.50	
154	667	8,000	.80	3.40	½ of 1%
192	833	10,000	1.00	4.20	
231	1,000	12,000	1.15	5.00	
288	1,250	15,000	2.25	9.50	¾ of 1%
385	1,667	20,000	3.85	16.70	
481	2,133	25,000	4.85	20.85	1%
577	2,500	30,000	5.85	25.00	

Remember, because of the tax deductions, the dollar you give costs less. If you itemize your deductions and are a married man filing a joint return, here's how it works, according to the Research Institute of America:

If your taxable income is:	A $100 contribution costs you:
$12,000	$78
16,000	75
20,000	72
24,000	68
32,000	61
50,000	50

Making Your Gifts Count

Once you have adopted a planned program of giving, try to make your donations count.

LOOK FOR SMALL ORGANIZATIONS. Here your "big" gifts will do wonders, and you will get more recognition (and satisfaction) than when your funds are just part of a big pile.

SEEK OUT AREAS OF GREATEST RETURN FOR EACH CONTRIB-UTED DOLLAR. Many nonprofit agencies need matching funds to obtain larger grants from foundations or enable them to get extra government aid—e.g., every $25 to day care may help to get $75 in federal aid.

DON'T BECOME ROUTINE IN YOUR GIVING. It's OK to support basic groups, but save some of your money, especially when your income is growing, for worthwhile community projects—scholarship aid for an outstanding student, to start a drive to purchase a historic building, or as a commitment for several years so that the community center can replace its furniture.

BE SURE THAT YOUR DONATION IS TAX-DEDUCTIBLE. Not long ago, the Sierra Club, a major national conservation organization, long approved as tax-exempt, ran a full-page ad in *The New York Times* protesting the construction of dams in the Grand Canyon. Next day the IRS withdrew its tax-exempt status. You will have to decide whether it is better to give $100 to a tax-exempt organization to maintain operations or to a taxable group to get things done (and lose your tax deduction).

DON'T BE AFRAID TO MAKE LONG-TERM COMMITMENTS. Such a commitment might be a pledge to a college alumni building fund. If you believe in the organization, you will be providing a strong boost for their campaign and not overextending yourself.

In 5 years, an annual gift of $400 totals $2,000—a significant sum in any fund-raising campaign.

> *Note:* Don't confuse a pledge with a contribution on your tax return. Charitable gifts are deductible only in the year when paid. For tax purposes, it may be wise to speed up your payments. *Example:* Mr. Allen pledged $2,000 to the new "Y" in December, with plans to pay over 4 years. But this year he's in the 40% tax bracket, so he can save $800 in taxes ($2,000 × 40%). Next year, after retirement, he will be in the 25% tax bracket, so the tax benefit will total only $500.

How to Be a Big Giver at Small Cost

You don't have to be a Rockefeller to consider making special gifts, but you do have to understand the tax rules.

The gift tax is unusual in that the *giver,* not the recipient, pays it. This is to prevent people from avoiding estate taxes. But there are enough exemptions so that most people do not have to pay it, and even when they do, they will not find it onerous.

Annual Exemptions

These allow anyone to give away $3,000 to each of an unlimited number of individuals-recipients *every year.* The limit can be $6,000 if both you and your wife sign the gift-tax return jointly—even if the money belongs to you.

Lifetime Exemption of $30,000

This starts after the annual $3,000 exemption is exhausted. Anyone may give up to $30,000 ($60,000 with spouse) during a lifetime. This can be all at once, scattered over the years, to one person or to many. The carryover privilege permits deductions to be taken annually until the full $30,000 is used up.

Example: The IRS rules that charitable gifts or money or appreciated securities or real estate, when held for more than 6 months, is deductible "at full present fair market value" up to 30% of the adjusted gross income, with a 5-year carryover for any "excess." The ceiling may be increased under certain conditions.

Federal Gift Taxes

Taxable Amount (In Excess of Exemptions)	Tax	Rate on Excess
$ 5,000	$112.50	5.25%
10,000	375	8.25
20,000	1,200	10.5
40,000	3,600	16.5
60,000	7,125	21.0
100,000	15,525	22.5

Major Gifts to Charities

If you are responsible for handling the financial affairs of aged parents (or parent), consider having them make a gift while still able to enjoy the recognition and praise. This can be done so that your mother, for example, can count on higher income as long as she lives.

The two most widely used plans are *life-income contracts* and *trusts*.

Life-Income Contract

Under this plan, the donor makes the gift with the assurance of income from the property as long as she lives. There are substantial tax benefits, savings in estate taxes and settlement expenses, and often, higher income.

Example: Your mother, aged 70, plans a $10,000 bequest to a local hospital. She has 400 shares of Becton Dickinson, now selling at about 25 a share and paying a tiny 40¢ per-share dividend. The stock was acquired many years ago, so if she sells, there will be a sizable capital gains tax.

She can have her wish and income, too, by transferring the stock to the Pooled Income Fund (PIF) of the hospital, taking the income tax gift deduction at the current value of the stock and waiting for the monthly checks.

Since the PIF investment policy calls for income rather than capital appreciation, the annual returns have averaged over 8% a year. Your mother will get about $800—a welcome increase over the $160 annual dividends.

The gift is not available to the hospital until after your mother's death.

A PIF is sort of a mutual fund set up for the benefit of a non-profit institution. In return for a donation of securities or money, the charitable institution agrees to pool and invest contributions, and in return, pay the donor a proportionate share of the earned income for the life of the giver or a designee. On the death of the beneficiary, the proportionate shares of the fund, based on units issued when originally donated, is withdrawn from the fund by the institution for its own use.

Note: While designed primarily for older people who want assured, ample income, PIF also provides a tax break for current income of high-tax-bracket philanthropists.

Ted, aged 53, has a net taxable income of $43,000 and has just made a substantial profit on a stock sale. He gives $20,000, in cash, to the hospital with the provision that it be added to the PIF. On the basis of his age and the fund's past rate of earnings, the IRS sets the value of the gift at $16,238 (the $20,000, less a tax benefit of $3,762). With a 7% return on the $20,000, he will get $1,400 a year on an effective investment of $16,238—over 8.6% annual return.

The tax break is even greater with gifts of appreciated securities. When 100 shares of stock have grown from a price of 110 to 200 a share, a sale would mean a capital gains tax of about 22% ($1,980) for Ted. By transferring the stock to PIF, the out-of-pocket costs will be only $14,258—$20,000 value, less $3,762 of realized income tax savings of the gift and $1,980 in avoided capital gains taxes.

Trusts are also useful in making charitable gifts. The two most popular forms are:

Charitable Remainder UniTrust

This is similar to an individual PIF. It is a separate trust agreement that provides a fixed percentage-of-assets income to the donor and the property to the institution. The income is variable and calculated annually because the fair market value of the assets may fluctuate.

This arrangement permits the giver to avoid capital gains taxes, to provide current income tax deductions for gifts, and to make certain that the charitable organization gets the securities or real estate at death. Here again, it is most beneficial when it assures a higher income for the donor.

Charitable Remainder Annuity Trust

This is like the Unitrust, but income is a fixed sum rather than a percentage of assets. Other terms are pretty much the same.

Under both types of trust, the income beneficiary must get at least 5% of the value of the trust.

All of these gift-income arrangements must be carefully checked by a competent tax-estate attorney. Generally, the IRS regulations on deductions and taxes are as described, but there are exceptions, special rulings, and frequently, changes by Congress.

Giving Insurance Policies

A life insurance policy can be used to make a donation in several ways:

As a Straight Beneficiary

There are no advantages for an individual to pay for such a policy, but many college classes use this approach to boost their 25th reunion gift. The class pays the premiums on policies of several classmates and gets a check for the paid-up value or for the death benefit.

Most insurance companies do not feel this is the best way to use life insurance.

As a Co-beneficiary

The institution gets the money if the primary beneficiary is not living at the time of the insured's death. This is useful when there is only one heir.

As Contingent Beneficiary

The institution receives the annuity checks (when payable for a certain period or up to a certain sum) after the annuitant dies.

As a Straight Gift

As a straight gift both *of smaller policies* of $1,000 or $2,000 that are no longer needed for the purposes for which they were originally purchased, and *of larger policies* for a memorial—for your father or mother, for example. If you don't have the cash for such a tribute, you can donate a sizable policy, say $10,000. You will have to continue to pay the premiums, but you can take deductions annually (in the 40% tax bracket, you will save about $100 a year in taxes) and have a gift deduction based on the cash value of the policy at the time of the gift. As with all gifts, the exemptions can be spread over several years.

The recipient also benefits; it can use the insurance policy as collateral for loans at 5% or 6%—less than half the interest rates on commercial loans.

Annuity Plus Gift—Split Life Insurance (SLI)

This is a plan that enables a concerned individual to build an annuity for himself and make a sizable gift to his favorite charity. It is best suited for well-to-do individuals who want to make substantial donations and can benefit from the tax advantages.

With SLI, there are 2 separate but related insurance policies that must be acquired together—an annuity and term life. Each dollar invested in the annuity permits the purchase of up to $100 worth of life insurance, usually, but not necessarily, on the owner of the annuity. The annuity becomes the gift, and the term insurance protects the giver.

Example: Dr. C. is 55, in the 50% tax bracket, and owns $200,000 in life insurance, much of it term. He has to earn $6,000 to pay the annual premiums of $3,000.

Dr. F., same age, same income, wants to aid his hospital but also wants to protect himself and his family. He buys a $2,000-a-year-premium annuity and gives it to St. Barnabas's Hospital. This entitles him to buy $200,000 in renewable, 1-year term at a low rate of about $944 a year. He needs only $3,888 income to pay for both ($2,000 for the annuity, a tax-deductible contribution, and $1,888 for the insurance). That's an annual savings of $2,112 over Dr. C.'s total outlay! And most important, Dr. F. has made a meaningful gift.

There are problems: Dr. F. must pass a physical exam (not always easy at age 55); the term policy can be renewed (to age 95) only as long as the annuity is in force; he must pay premiums on the annuity for 10 years before any income will be paid out; the insurance premiums climb rapidly—to $2,544 at age 60, to $4,342 at 65; and the IRS has not clarified how the deductions are to be handled.

SLI can be practical on a smaller scale if you are determined to provide a substantial gift to your college, church, or community agency. But it should be considered only after you have adequate protection for your family and feel sure you will be able to continue annual premium payments.

Work out the figures with your life insurance agent and then check with your tax adviser. It's a great way to be a BIG giver!

XII

Credit—Where to Get It, How to Use and Keep It

Good credit is the foundation of financial success and personal money management. To get the most for your money, for your business, or your family, you must utilize OPM (Other People's Money)—directly through loans or installment purchases; indirectly through charge accounts, credit cards, and other forms of delayed payment.

Used properly and in moderation, credit can ease your life, enhance your resources, and make immediately available goods and services that otherwise might take years to attain. *To get credit,* you must have assets and/or a good reputation. *To keep credit,* you must pay your bills promptly, hold your borrowings to reasonable limits, and be able to explain delays if you are temporarily unable to meet your obligations.

These days, it's usually easy to get credit. The problem, for too many people, is keeping it. Once you are marked as a poor credit risk, it will take many years of good behavior to regain a good paying record. These are hard facts that should be clearly understood by every member of the family. If anyone has the habit of buying too much and paying too slowly, separate his or her purchases from your own and make it clear that you will not be responsible for these debts.

Most marriages founder on financial shoals, which in many

145

cases is just another way of saying poor management of money and credit.

Credit Limits

As a rule of thumb, never commit more than 20% of your take-home pay to consumer credit—charge accounts, installment loans, etc. The total of such short-term obligations should stay between 1½ and 2 times your monthly income—e.g., if you bring home $1,500 a month, keep the sum of loans-accounts due within one year under $3,000, preferably $2,250.

It's OK to boost this limit if you have no other heavy commitments, but if you are already paying out 25% of your income for a mortgage, another 20% can be tough to handle, especially when costs of food and fuel are rising so sharply.

Borrow for Positive Purposes

It's always better (but seldom easy) to borrow for positive purposes—a mortgage for a home that, hopefully, will increase in value, a car that can help produce income or save expenses, a washer-dryer to reduce laundry bills, etc.

Except in emergencies, do not borrow for negative purposes—to pay old debts or back taxes. Credit should always be used constructively—although, of course, most of us bend that description at Christmastime!

Getting Credit

Short-term credit involves banks, retailers, and finance companies—any business that extends credit for 3 years or less. To get credit, the prerequisite is someone's assessment of your ability (and willingness) to pay for goods and services. In most cases, this is based on information available at the local credit bureau.

When you fill out, or are asked for, credit information, be accurate, complete, and timely. This is a business proposition, so don't try to be cute or evasive. Provide exact data on names, dates, employment, personal history, earnings, etc. Make it easy for the retailer or credit bureau to write your profile. If you have had a charge account with a national organization (rental car agency, department store chain, etc.), note the number on your credit application. If you have been sued for debt, have filed for bankruptcy, or had tax liens recorded, say so and explain the circumstances. *Businesses want you as a customer if they feel there's a good chance you can and will pay.*

The most important criteria are your stability of employment and the size and regularity of your income. If you are young and single, the lender may want your parent to guarantee your account for a while. If you are new in town, you'll need a friendly word from your employer or business friends, and probably, a sizable bank account. *A quick solution:* Use your savings account or securities as collateral for a small, 6-month loan. Meet your payments promptly, and your credit should be OK.

Start opening charge accounts slowly, and preferably with large, reputable firms such as department stores. In a few months, you can charge almost everything IF you want to go that far.

For Women Only

In some communities, working women still have difficulty in establishing their own credit. In addition to heeding the general advice, OKs can usually be speeded by:

KEEPING AMPLE FUNDS IN THE BANK. This will show good money management and look good on your credit report.

MEETING WITH THE STORE CREDIT MANAGER. Meet to get and give answers to questions, and if necessary, to ask for counseling.

STARTING WITH SMALL, SPECIAL-LIMIT BUDGET ACCOUNTS AND GRADUALLY ASKING FOR ADDITIONAL CREDIT AS REQUIRED.

PAYING BILLS BY YOUR OWN CHECK. Do this even if the account is in your husband's name.

If you are a widow or divorcée, you may have to reapply for your own charge account even though the original was in your name (in most communities).

If you feel you have been discriminated against, talk to your banker, call the local chamber of commerce, and write the city or state consumer affairs department.

Getting the Most from Charge Accounts

For promotional purposes, there are a score of different, catchy titles for charge accounts at retail stores. Basically, however, they can be classified in one of the following categories:

REVOLVING CHARGE ACCOUNT. There are usually three types: (1) when paid within 30 days, there's no penalty or charge; (2) if not paid within 30 days, the account is automatically charged 1½% per month on the outstanding balance; (3) by agreement, payments of a set amount are made each month. Purchases above the limit must be paid within 30 days of billing. The store sets the maximum on the basis of income and credit record.

RETAIL INSTALLMENT CREDIT. There is no penalty for monthly payments; 1½%-per-month interest on the unpaid balance with monthly payments of one-sixth of the total, usually with a $10 minimum.

FLEXIBLE CHARGE ACCOUNT. Payment according to a regular schedule—$10 a month when the bill is $50, $40 when it's $200, etc.

OPTIONAL ACCOUNT. When the balance is $50, pay $5 per month; when $200, pay $10, etc. The interest on the unpaid balance is 1¼% per month; 1% when the total is over $500.

EASY PAYMENT PLAN. Payment of a predetermined monthly amount until the specific merchandise is paid for. The 1½% interest usually applies to the original price.

How Add-ons Are Handled

When new purchases are added to the unpaid balance, the new payments are prorated. Thus, if you owe $150 on an air conditioner and agree to pay $25 per month, the balance at the end of 4 months will be $50. You buy a sewing machine for $100 and agree to continue the $25 monthly payment. Your total bill was $250. Since the original agreement ($150) was three-fifths of the new total, future payments will be reallocated on that basis—$15 to the old account, $10 to the new.

Money Savers

To avoid being charged for interest, pay promptly—no later than the 20th of each month. If you did pay within 30 days of the billing date and are charged interest, contact the store credit manager at once. Otherwise, future purchases will extend the service charge to debts you don't owe.

To get free time, make your purchases a few days after the billing date (shown on the statement). Thus, if the billing date is the 24th, buy on the 25th and you will get an extra month's time to pay.

Benefits of Credit Cards

There are two major types—membership cards (American Express, Diner's Club) and bank credit cards (BankAmericard, Master Charge, etc.). The first requires an annual fee, can be used around the world, and permits quick loans almost anywhere.

Usually the bank cards have no membership fee, make cash immediately available at cooperating banks, are widely accepted (primarily in the United States but, increasingly, abroad), and provide the convenience of one monthly statement for numerous expenditures.

If either card is lost or stolen, the owner is not liable for unauthorized charges in excess of $50 if he notifies the issuer promptly with a form and reply envelope provided without charge.

Caveat: With the bank credit card, the issuing bank has the right to take money from your checking account to pay your bill if you are late in payment.

How to Protect Your Credit

When you cannot pay your bills, DO NOT make partial payments to everyone. You will be swamped by a host of creditors. It's better to pay key bills in full, then communicate with the other lenders to work out a planned payment schedule.

You may be surprised to find that some companies will agree to skip a couple of months, while others will prefer small sums regularly. At the first sign of trouble, call or write the credit department of the retailer or finance company and ask for help. They are seldom eager to go to court. If the account is already in the hands of a collection agency, you may have some difficulty, but the forthright approach will usually pay off. By showing that you are not trying to dodge responsibility, you will delay, and probably avoid, a black mark against your credit rating.

If you are in deep trouble, ask your banker for the name of the local credit counseling service or write the National Foundation for Consumer Credit, Inc., 1819 H Street, N.W., Washington, D.C. 20006.

If you are refused credit, the 1971 Federal Fair Credit Reporting Act requires the credit grantor to give you a straight answer and the name and address of the credit bureau. There, you are entitled to learn the "nature and substance" of what is in your file, including the source of damaging information. If you call the credit bureau within 30 days after you are denied credit, there may not be a charge. Agencies are not required to let you see your credit report or give you a copy. Most will cooperate in some way.

If you can prove that the credit report is wrong, the erroneous information must be deleted. If there's a difference of opinion between you and the credit grantor, the bureau must investigate, and if a settlement cannot be reached, it must add your written version to the file. Don't wait. Act promptly. Get confirmation.

The keys to good credit are prompt payment, reasonable debt, a financially conservative way of living, and good bank relations.

Despite the law that requires credit bureaus to delete adverse credit information after 7 years, early failures or carelessness are likely to haunt delinquents the rest of their lives, often at critical times when they want to obtain a large mortgage or borrow to invest in a business.

Busyness is no excuse. Failure to pay after repeated promises, especially from affluent professionals or business executives, is doubly dangerous. Poor credit can harm a career, and few retailers are lenient with anyone who permits his wife to conceal her debts or his secretary to "forget."

Borrowing Money

The cheapest way to borrow money is from your bank on the basis of collateral—securities, life insurance, or savings. The interest rate on a secured loan is less than that on an unsecured one, and generally, the collateral continues to earn money so that the net cost is less. And this is reduced even further when the interest is deducted from your tax return.

Example: On a $10,000 loan, at 12%, the gross cost would be $1,200. If you used your savings account as collateral, the 6% annual earnings from the bank would cut this to $600, minus a tax credit of about $400 if you are in the 30% tax bracket.

Here's how much loans really cost:

Collateral	Maximum Loan	Loan Period	Interest Rate	Earned Return on Collateral	Net Cost
Life insurance	95% of cash value	Unlimited	4.5%–5% After 1970 policies: 6%	3% 3%	1.5%–2% 3%
Bonds	75%–90%	Renewable	10%–12%	7%–9%	3%–5%
Savings passbook	Up to 100%	No limit	10%	6%	4%
Stocks	65%	Renewable	10%–12%	4%–6%	4%–6%
Your signature— education loan	$20,000	To 7 years	11%–12%		11%–12%
Your signature— banks, finance companies	$10,000	Up to 7 years	12%–18%*		12%–18%

* Rates can go as high as 36%.
Note: These terms are in periods of historically high interest.
Source: Institute of Life Insurance.

Types of Interest

On all types of loans, there are different methods of charging interest. The most widely used are:

Simple Interest

This is the amount paid on the total loan. You borrow $1,000 at 10% for one year. At the end of 12 months, you pay back $1,100. (About the only place you'll get such a loan is from a member of your family.)

Interest on Unpaid Balance

This is a declining payment with interest figures only on the unpaid balance owed at any one time. At an interest rate of 1% per month, the cost of a $1,000 loan would be $72.51—a low 7.25%. It works out this way:

1. Divide the $1,000 by the 12 equal amounts you pay on the principal—$83.33.
2. Interest on the $1,000 at 1% would be $10.00, so at the end of the first month you would pay $93.33 ($10.00 interest plus $83.33 amortization).
3. Thereafter, subtract $83.33 each month from the remaining principal—$916.67 at the end of month 1, etc.
4. Pay 1% interest on the new balance of $916.67—$9.17. Adding the $83.33 reduction, the total outlay would be $92.50.
5. In month 3 the principal is down to $833.34—interest of $8.33, for a total monthly payment of $91.66.

Monthly Interest Rate

When quoted as 1½% or 3½% per month, the interest sounds cheap. But only for the first month. To get the true annual interest rate, multiply by 12. If paid at the end of each month, the cost would be 18% a year for the 1½% rate; a whopping 42% at the 3½% rate.

To get the real cost, use this handy table:

Monthly Rate	True Annual Rate
¾ of 1%	9%
⅚ of 1%	10
1	12
1¼	15
1½	18
2	24
3	36

Add-on Interest for Installment Buying

This adds the interest to the loan at the outset. Thus, at 6%, the total loan would be $1,060. With 12 equal payments of $88.33, the last check would include interest on the original $1,000. The true annual rate is 11.08% because you are paying interest on money that you have already paid back.

Interest Discounted

Under this arrangement, the amount of interest is deducted from the total loan. Thus, on that $1,000, you would borrow only $940 if the interest is 6%. When paid in 12 monthly installments, the true annual interest rate is 11.78%; over 18 months, 12.5%; over 24 months, 13.1%.

How to Figure Credit Costs

To find out how much extra you are paying for the privilege of a charge-credit account, follow this example cited by the U.S. Department of Agriculture.

From the total cost, subtract the cash price. The difference is the cost of credit.

Example: A chair costs $310 cash. Under an installment plan, you pay $35 down and $17.50 per month for 18 months.

18 × $17.50	$315
Down payment	35
Total cost	350
Cash price	310
Cost of credit	40

On an annual basis:

1. Multiply 2 × dollar cost ($40 interest) = $80
2. Multiply 80 × number of payments in year: 80 × 12 = $960
3. Multiply amount of credit needed ($310 − $35 = $275) × number of payments plus 1 (18 + 1) 275 × 19 = 5225
4. Divide no. 2 (960) by no. 3 (5225) = 18.37% —true annual credit rate.

Borrowing Now

Time was when paying interest was considered poor personal business. You were supposed to save your money until you could afford to buy the new car, air conditioner, or home improvement. With cash, the adage opined, you would buy cheaper.

But no more. Inflation and tax advantages have wiped out most of the savings that might have been available for cash payments. Cash still has its place, but on major projects, borrowing to buy or build now has advantages.

Example: Back in 1971, Mr. Judge decided he needed to add a wing to his home. He estimated the cost at

$10,000. At 10%, paid over 3 years, his monthly outlay would be $322.

Being a frugal New Englander, Mr. Judge got out his handy calculator and figured that the same $322, in a 5½% savings account, would increase his $10,000 to $12,610 in 36 months. So he delayed the building.

But he reckoned without inflation. Material costs jumped some 30%, and labor even more. By 1974, estimates of the new wing were over $15,000.

In today's climate, anyone who has a reasonably sure income, and is not heavily in debt, will be better off borrowing for a constructive purpose than watching his plans disrupted by inflation.

Loans to Relatives

Credit works both ways. There are times when you will have trouble collecting your debts. The best way to avoid such trouble is not to make the loans in the first place. But if you do get tapped by a less-fortunate relative and cannot refuse:

1. GET COLLATERAL. This may be securities, real estate, jewelry, or something that has resale value. *Even if it's in the family, a loan is still a business proposition.*

2. GET A WRITTEN AGREEMENT THAT GIVES YOU AN INTEREST IN THE COLLATERAL. If there's a default, you will be first in the line of creditors, except for tax and judicial liens.

This document should describe the collateral, state what constitutes default, and be signed by both the borrower and the lender. If the loan is large enough to require an attorney, make the borrower pay the legal fees.

3. BE SURE THERE ARE NO PREVIOUS LIENS ON THE PROPERTY. Also, make sure that it's really owned by the borrower and that it's not leased or stolen.

4. IF IT'S REAL ESTATE, TAKE A MORTGAGE LIEN. Also, if the state law permits, add a "power-of-sale" clause so that, in case of default, you can foreclose and sell without a lawsuit.

5. KEEP COMPLETE RECORDS. Do this so that you can claim an income tax deduction if the loan goes fully or partially sour.

6. CHARGE A RATE OF INTEREST THAT IS BELOW THE LIMIT SET BY THE STATE USURY LAW.

And before you make the final decision, consider cosigning a note at the bank. It will eliminate some future hard feelings if there's already family friction.

How to Use Small-Claims Courts

If you can't collect on a small loan, get satisfaction on merchandise you bought or ordered, or are refused payment for repairs or damages, you can sue in your local small-claims court in many areas. The maximum allowable claims range from $200 to $500, depending on the state and type of debt. Costs are low and action fast and sure.

In New Jersey, for example, the only requirement for suit is that you must be 19 years old, or if under that age, must be accompanied by an adult. The base cost is $2.70 plus $2 each for subpoenas to witnesses and a mileage fee to reimburse the constable when he travels to deliver your complaint. If the judge rules in your favor and you are still unable to collect, the constable will be assigned to help you.

But if you settle for less than your claim, you cannot sue for the balance.

Typical small claims:

• Clothes lost or damaged at the laundry or cleaners.

• Merchandise that is not what you ordered but that the retailer refuses to replace.

• Rental deposit that the landlord refuses to return.

• An appliance that was damaged in delivery or won't work but that the dealer won't repair or replace.

Consumer Protection?

Merchants who have offered free credit cannot suddenly switch to a revolving credit system. Laws in most states require a signed agreement to permit the store to charge interest on an unpaid balance.

But, say lawyers, don't count on such protection. If the retailer gives sufficient notice and you continue to do business with the store, the judge will probably conclude that you have agreed to the new terms.

XIII

Owning a Home—How Much to Pay, Where to Get the Best Mortgage, Rent or Buy? How to Get Top Dollar When You Sell, Condominium Cautions

Buying a house is an important decision. It's as subjective as choosing a spouse. It requires careful planning, defining your life-style and family goals, and a review of your present and anticipated financial resources. The old adage was that no one should spend more than 25% of pretax income. These days it's probably wiser to start the other way around—to find out how large a mortgage you can get and then adjust your budget accordingly.

As a starter, think in terms of a house where the mortgage is double your earned income—a $40,000 loan on a $20,000-a-year salary. Then, relate total outlays for mortgage payments, property taxes, and home insurance. When these are 25% of pretax income, there will be no difficulty; at 30%, there may be some problems; at 35%, you'll be lucky not to be turned down. The longer the term of the loan, the lower the monthly payments. Except in money-tight areas, lending institutions are flexible and place greatest emphasis on character, type of house, stability and prospects of employment, and arrangements made by the builder-developer.

You may have to make changes-sacrifices if you want to qualify for the mortgage, but within reason, do not turn down a chance to buy a home you like solely because of someone's insistence that financial security is paramount. A home should be a joy, not a worry. Nobody's spending fits the norm. If you want to put 35% of your income into your house, do it with the knowledge that other spending-savings must be curtailed. Each family should make its own decision on the best allocation of its resources. Always remember that if your father had listened to Uncle Ebenezer he would never have paid $24,000 for the house that he just sold for $62,000!

Once in a while, a family will find an ideal house, but in most cases, the final choice will be a compromise—between the house you want and the one you can afford. The biggest, and usually most costly, mistake is to let emotion make the decision. It's easy to fall in love with the babbling brook or panoramic view, but you will live in *all* of the house, be part of *all* of the neighborhood, and must meet *all* of the payments.

Before you start house hunting, set down the factors you and the whole family feel are important—convenience, privacy, zoning protection, neighborhood, schools, etc., for the location; space, quality of construction, and adaptability for the house; and carrying costs, assessments, and potential appreciation for the budget. (Write for *Your Housing Dollar* from the Household Finance Corporation, Prudential Plaza, Chicago, Illinois 60601, or check your local library.)

Be careful about buying the most expensive house on the block. Its future value is not likely to be pulled up by prices paid when other homes are sold.

PAY SPECIAL ATTENTION TO TAXES. Note the rate of increase in the past 5 years, the probable future trend, the possibility of substantial new levies for new schools, improved water and/or sewer systems, etc. Remember that if you pay much above the present assessed value, your future taxes are almost sure to rise.

The new assessment will be based on the price at which you purchased the property.

ALWAYS ADD 10% TO YOUR ESTIMATED ANNUAL BASIC COSTS. ONCE YOU HAVE NARROWED YOUR SELECTION, REVIEW YOUR CHECKLIST (PROBABLY EXPANDED FROM EXPERIENCE) AND RERATE THE PROPERTY ON THE BASIS OF WHAT IT WILL BE LIKE 10 TO 20 YEARS FROM NOW WHEN YOU MAY PLAN TO RESELL OR RETIRE. If it's an old house in an old neighborhood, the value will increase slowly. If it's a modern house in a stable, protected area, you should be able to count on your investment increasing at least as fast as inflation.

BUT DON'T SPEND THE GAINS. A lot of things can happen over the years—new highways, apartments, commercial developments, etc. Some changes will be beneficial, others harmful. Be realistic. You may still be paying the mortgage by the year 2000!

Realistically, however, the average mortgage is refinanced, usually as the result of a sale, every twelve years.

Getting a Mortgage

Shopping doesn't end with the house. You have a mortgage to get, and despite the news stories about tight money, you can dig up choices. If you are lucky, you may be able to find an individual who will take back a mortgage—an owner who wants a steady income during retirement; a relative who wants a safe investment; or a professional moneylender. The interest rate may be higher, but you will save on points (the charge, equal to 1% of the loan, that is used as a discount to make the total return attractive to the lender—e.g., 3 points on a $30,000 loan = $900).

FHA Mortgage Payment Schedule
(30 Years)

FHA Estimate of Property Value and Closing Costs	Maximum Mortgage	Minimum Down Payment	Mortgage Insurance Premium	Principal and Interest			
				8%	8½%	9%	9½%
$20,000	$19,400	$ 600	$ 8.06	$142.40	$149.19	$156.17	$163.16
25,000	24,250	750	10.08	178.00	186.48	195.22	203.95
30,000	28,750	1,250	11.95	211.03	221.09	231.44	241.79
35,000	33,250	1,750	13.82	244.06	255.69	267.67	279.64
40,000	37,250	2,750	15.48	273.42	286.45	299.87	313.26
45,000	41,250	3,750	17.14	302.78	317.22	332.07	346.92
50,000	45,000	5,000	18.70	330.30	346.06	362.25	378.45

Source: U.S. Department of Housing and Urban Development.

Paying Back Principal

When you have a long-term mortgage and after a few years find that you have extra money, add to the monthly payment. These extras will reduce the principal immediately and thus lower the monthly interest. You'll be surprised at how rapidly the additional $50 or $100 a month cuts down the indebtedness.

Note: Be sure to check the mortgage company, as you may not be able to start this reduction until after the first 5 years or so.

Saving half or a full point on the interest rate on your home mortgage is worthwhile. On a 30-year, $30,000 loan, the monthly outlay for principal and interest is $263.40 at a 10% rate, $241.50 at 9%, and $221.20 at 8%.

As a rule of thumb, each ½ percent is worth about $3.75 per $1,000 per year—$112.50 on that $30,000 mortgage. For more accurate figures, use the table on monthly payments per $1,000 loan. Select the figure according to the length of the loan and multiply by the thousands of dollars of the mortgage. Thus, for the 30-year commitment, $8.78, $8.05, and $7.34 × 30.

That's not all you have to pay. Most mortgage payments include insurance premiums on the FHA commitment, possibly home insurance, and probably real-estate taxes. As you will also have to budget for maintenance and utilities (which average about 60% of the other payments), multiply the total by 1.6.

For that 30-year, $30,000 mortgage, you will need $421.44 at the high rate, $386.40 at 9%, and $352.92 at 8%—a whopping $67.52 *per month* difference.

If you are handy with your electronic calculator, work these data backward—start with what you can pay each month and calculate the size of the mortgage!

Monthly Payment per $1,000 Loan

Length of Mortgage	Interest Rate 6%	7%	8%	8¼%	8½%	8¾%	9%
20 years	$7.17	$7.76	$8.37	$8.53	$8.68	$8.84	$9.00
25 years	6.45	7.07	7.72	7.89	8.06	8.23	8.40
30 years	6.00	6.66	7.34	7.52	7.69	7.87	8.05

Length of Mortgage	Interest Rate 9¼%	9½%	9¾%	10%	10¼%	10½%	11%
20 years	$9.16	$9.33	$9.49	$9.66	$9.82	$9.99	$10.33
25 years	8.57	8.74	8.92	9.09	9.27	9.45	9.81
30 years	8.23	8.41	8.60	8.78	8.97	9.15	9.53

It's best to go mortgage shopping before you select a house. You will learn how expensive a home you can afford, the size of the down payment, the probable interest and repayment terms, and how hefty your balance sheet should be.

(*Note:* If you want to improve your loan prospects, ask your parents for a temporary $5,000 loan to boost your bank account.)

In tight-money areas, you will have to come up with 20% to 25% as a down payment. With large new developments, you should be able to make arrangements for a 10% down payment. *But don't count on it.* There may be other charges that will boost your required cash outlay.

Where to Find Mortgage Money

The basic mortgage sources are savings banks, savings and loan associations, commercial banks, and in some areas, mortgage bankers who package a number of loans. Your real-estate agent (and many excellent books) can give you detailed information, but follow these guidelines:

Try to get:
1. The biggest, longest mortgage. At a 7% inflation rate, the real cost of monthly payments will be cut in half in 10 years. The monthly payments will be about the same

whether you pay off a big loan at a low rate of interest or a small one at a higher rate.

2. An agreement that will permit prepayment, after a reasonable number of years, without penalty. This right is built into all FHA and VA mortgages.

3. The 10-year warranty of the National Association of Home Builders. This is available on many new homes. For the first 2 years, the builder is responsible for major construction defects, faulty workmanship, pool materials, and the proper function of plumbing, heating, electrical, and cooling systems. There's also insurance to assure proper completion if the builder should go bankrupt or be unable to fulfill the warranty. From the third to the tenth year, the quality of most items is covered by insurance.

Note: In these inflationary times, the benefits of an old, low-interest-rate mortgage are tremendous. In our old neighborhood, the first arrivals, in the late 1950s, paid $20,000, with $5,000 down and a 20-year, 5% mortgage. Taxes doubled, but the monthly payment stayed at $99.

Last year, a new family bought a similar—though improved and expanded—house for $60,000. They paid $15,000 down and were lucky to get a 20-year, 8% mortgage for $45,000. Even after the larger tax deductions for interest, the newcomers are spending $250 a month more than their old neighbors!

Hopefully, the value of your first house will increase so that the profit from its sale—and reduction of the mortgage—will be enough to cover the down payment on a new home, etc.

A House Is a Tax Shelter

A home is the best tax shelter most people can invest in. Tax deductions are permitted for interest, for office-at-home, for property taxes, and when the house is resold, profits can be lessened by adding the costs of additions-improvements and may be tax-free if you buy a new home promptly. Before you invest in an oil well to lessen your taxes, look around at your own property for tax-shelter opportunities.

Comparing Costs of Home Loans

The type and cost of a mortgage depends on the area of the country, the community, and the prevailing cost of money. Generally, there will be little difficulty in obtaining a mortgage in a small town or the suburbs, some problems in medium-size communities, and considerable hassle in older urban centers.

Conventional mortgages are shorter-term (usually 20 years), quicker to obtain (seldom more than 1 week), require a larger down payment (up to 25%), carry slightly lower interest rates, and are more flexible (permitting reborrowing for remodeling and expansion).

Loans insured by the Federal Housing Administration (FHA) are limited to $45,000, require 3% to 10% down payment, bear a higher interest rate (currently 9%, plus ½% fee for insurance, plus 1 point for processing), run for up to 30 years, and usually involve additional points to bring the net yield in line with prevailing money rates and substantial closing costs.

Veterans Administration (VA) loans are available only to veterans who served on active duty for 90 days. There's no limit to the size of the loan, but the guarantee applies only to the first $17,500. The loan cannot be over 97% of the first $25,000, plus 90% of the next $10,000, plus 80% of the balance. Current interest is 8%, and no points permitted!

(*Note:* Veterans who have previously taken out a GI loan can get another IF the earlier loan has been paid off.)

On both FHA and VA loans, the rule of thumb calls for the buyer's monthly payments for mortgage, utilities, taxes, maintenance, and home insurance to be less than 35% of monthly take-home pay, with debts of over 10 months accounting for less than 50% of net income.

Comparison of Mortgage Costs
(1975)

	Conventional Mortgage	FHA Mortgage (Owner-Occupied)	VA Mortgage
Amount you can borrow	Usually 75%, but up to 90% of value under some conditions	Up to 97% of the first $25,000 appraised value; plus 90% of next $10,000; plus 80% of excess to maximum of $45,000	Up to 100% of VA praised value; guaranteed repayment of first $17,500
Size of down payment	20%–25%	From 3% of first $25,000 to 10% of next $10,000, to 20% of balance—depending on FHA appraisal	No down payment
Repayment terms	Usually 20 years, but may go to 30	Up to 30 years	Up to 30 years
Interest rates	Fluctuates with money market; now 8½%–10%	Regulated by FHA; now 9% plus ½% for FHA insurance	Regulated by VA; now 9%
Features	Flexible	Insured to FHA	Only veterans (90 days' active service)
	Quick approval—less than one week	Permits prepayment without penalty	Guaranteed by VA
	May be combined with 2nd mortgage	$40 property appraisal fee	Permits prepayment without penalty
	Prepayment usually permitted	Requires at least 4 weeks for OK	Requires 6 to 8 weeks for OK
	Usually allows re-borrowing up to full amount of paid-up loan balance—for remodeling, improvements		

Source: FHA and VA.

If you feel you may be paying too much, ask about "tandem-plan" loans. These are available under emergency legislation to encourage housing. The mortgages are passed through from the lender to Ginnie Mae (Government National Mortgage Association) and then to Fannie Mae (Federal National Mortgage Association). Houses at any price are eligible, but the maximum loan is $33,000 at 8%, $38,000 at 8¾%. Tandems are made only with mortgages backed by the FHA or VA. The borrower pays 1 point for paperwork plus the ½% for FHA insurance.

New-type Mortgage

Check your savings institution for a new type of short-term home mortgage. It's the same as offered on commercial properties—a low monthly payment figured on a 25-year basis with a large "balloon" at the end of 5 or 10 years. This assures small monthly payments but requires refinancing or repayment in a short time.

Example: Career girl Dorcas Hardy buys a condominium for $40,000, pays $10,000 down, and takes a mortgage at 8½%. For 5 years, her payments will be $241.75, but then she will have to come up with $28,000. She's willing to take the risk that interest rates will be lower by then, so she can get a new, long-term mortgage at a lower rate, or at least at no higher rate.

Variable-rate Mortgages

In some areas, nonfederal lending institutions offer variable-rate mortgages. By advance agreement, the mortgage interest rate—and thus the monthly payment—goes up when interest rates rise and down when money costs decline.

These have been used in Europe and Latin America for many years but have not yet been OKed for loans involving the federal government. Savings and loans favor national legislation to permit these, as the result would be to assure variable rates on savings and thus keep these institutions competitive with commercial banks in periods of high money costs.

Whether variable-rate mortgages will be more expensive than standard, fixed-payment mortgages will depend on when the mortgage is assumed. A buyer who took a 30-year, $20,000 mortgage at 6¼% in 1960 would have started out with a monthly payment of $123. By January, 1974, the interest rate would have been 8¾%, with a $148 monthly payment. But in 1963, when interest rates dropped, the interest charge would have been 5¾%, and the monthly check, $112.

Over the years, interest takes a big chunk out of your income. The interest is tax deductible on Federal tax returns but, even in the 50% bracket, you'll pay half the cost out of your own pocket.

How Interest Costs Mount

Interest Rate	Interest Cost on a $10,000 Mortgage		
	20 years	25 years	30 years
7%	$ 8,607	$11,204	$13,951
8	10,074	13,154	16,417
9	11,593	15,176	18,966
9½	12,370	16,211	20,272

Note: Obtaining the true rate of interest and principal paid off each month is a complex calculation. *Best solution:* Send $2 to The Financial Publishing Company, 82 Brookline Avenue, Boston, Massachusetts 02215, for *Truth in Lending Tables* or *Comprehensive Mortgage Payment Tables.*

Should You Pay Your Mortgage in Advance?

In periods of high interest, lending institutions may urge you to pay off your mortgage at a discount. They want to swap your modest interest for loans with up to double the return.

Example: A homeowner with $16,000 in taxable income has an $8,500, 5¾% mortgage with 6 years to go. The savings and loan offers a 10% discount, so he can settle all of this debt for $7,650.

To see how attractive this "savings" really is, get out your electronic calculator and make projections. Over the next 6 years, his mortgage payments, minus tax deductions, will be about $9,700. If he invests the $7,650 in a 9% bond, he will earn $3,500 in interest after taxes. After 6 years, he will have about $11,000, and so will be $1,400 richer than if he had accepted the "generous" offer.

Always Have a Lawyer and Read the Fine Print

When you get the OK for a mortgage and are ready to sign the purchase papers, retain an attorney. Do not let your enthusiasm for being a homeowner muddle your common sense. Do not sign anything until you have read *every* word of the agreement in concert with your legal counsel.

Here Are Some Protective Measures:

IF YOU ARE BUYING THE HOUSE WITHOUT YOUR WIFE. Add the sentence: "Contract must be approved by purchaser's wife within 10 days."

IF THERE ARE PROBLEMS ABOUT THE CONDITION OF THE HOUSE OR EQUIPMENT. Add: "Seller represents that the roof and basement are free of leaks and have been for the past 2 years," or "Seller guarantees that all appliances, electrical equipment, plumbing, etc., are in good working order and are subject to inspection by a qualified engineer within 10 days."

IF YOU ARE QUEASY ABOUT THE PRICE. Include: "Purchaser reserves the right to obtain a professional appraisal within 10 days of signing, and if the selling price exceeds the property's appraised value, the sale is invalid."

TO PROTECT AGAINST UNFORESEEN DEMISE. Add: "In event of the death of either the buyer or the seller, the agreement is binding on heirs, executor, etc."

IF YOU DO NOT HAVE A FIRM LOAN AGREEMENT. Add: "Contingent on commitment for financing within 15 days."

IF YOU ARE A PROFESSIONAL WHO PLANS TO USE THE HOUSE FOR AN OFFICE. Make sure you add: "Reserve the right to terminate the agreement and get the deposit refunded if the premises cannot be used for the purposes intended."

TO AVOID THE POSSIBILITY OF DAMAGE TO THE HOUSE BE-TWEEN THE TIME OF THE DOWN PAYMENT AND FINAL SETTLE-MENT. Add: "Seller agrees to assume the risk of loss or damage to property . . . until settlement is held and deed recorded."

And always include a clause whereby "Seller guarantees the property is free of encumbrances except as specified in this contract." This will eliminate the possibility of an unexpected assessment for a new sidewalk or sewer system.

With real-estate transactions, always assume the worst!

Rent or Buy?

Economically, it's almost always better to rent than to buy if the time span is less than 3 years. The equity value of property does not mount rapidly until after the fifth year.

If you are smart—or lucky—enough to choose a home whose value rises 5% or more a year, you will make more profitable use of your money by buying rather than by renting. For a fair comparison, it's important to consider how much your money, not used for the purchase, could earn when wisely invested.

Here's an example of the costs of 2 living units over 3 years—a condominium and an apartment. Both have 750 square feet of space, 2 bedrooms, 2 baths, private balconies, carpeting, and appliances. The family is in the 25% tax bracket.

The condominium sells for $30,000 (10% cash; $27,000, 9½% mortgage), plus $500 legal-acquisition fees, and appreciates in value at 5% a year.

The apartment rents for $270 per month. Costs of furnishings, utilities, etc., are the same.

Item	Purchase		Rent	
	Monthly	3 years	Monthly	3 years
Rent			$270	$9,720
Mortgage charges		$ 500		
Mortgage repayment	$235	8,460		
Real-estate taxes	60	2,160		
Maintenance payments	60	2,160		
Total commitment	$355	$13,280	$270	$9,720
Less $2,000 income tax relief		$11,280		
Plus $670 interest lost on $3,500 (after tax)		11,950		
Less $4,729 appreciation of condominium value		7,221		
Less $720 equity (principal repaid at $20 monthly)		6,501		
Plus down payment		9,501		
Total expenditures		$ 9,501		$9,720

Source: *Apartment Life.*

Over 3 years, the owner comes out $219 ahead of the renter. But if the condominium had increased in value only 2½% per year, the owner would have been $2,000 worse off. And if the apartment had been rented for $240, the renter would have been $1,000 better off. *So, realistically, each situation must be judged separately.*

Buy a New House or Expand the Old?

This time, economic considerations should be tempered with personal prospects. If you plan to stay in the new house 10 years or more, it's probably better to buy than to remodel. But if the children will be away in college soon, will you and your wife want the responsibility and expense of a bigger house?

In addition to higher costs (the mortgage at a higher interest rate, heavier taxes, more expensive maintenance, etc.), there will be major outlays for decorating, painting, new furniture and appliances, and so on. Don't ever let your wife persuade you that "the old furniture will do" (unless it is antiques). And there are sure to be extra costs to keep up with the neighbors—not only socially but also with more elaborate landscaping, automobiles, vacations, etc. The ideal situation, of course, is where the value of the new house is likely to increase more rapidly than that of the old one.

But there are economic advantages in expanding-modernizing the old homestead. From a resale viewpoint, the most rewarding expenditures will be for bathrooms, a family room, and a new kitchen. Note that a first-floor family room is OK but not one in the basement. And the $3,000 or more spent for a swimming pool can seldom be retrieved by a higher sales tag.

What You Might Get for Improvements

Here are guesstimates of what portion of your investment in modernization will be returned when you sell your house.

	Southwest	Middle West	West Coast
Added bathroom	70%	55%	62%
New kitchen	50	50	65
Family room	70	50	62
2-car garage	50	50	60
Modernized bathroom	50	45	62
Modernized kitchen	37	45	62
Exterior siding	55	25	22
Insulation	30	50	37
Basement rec room	. . .	15	20

Source: *Changing Times.*

How to Get More Money for Home Improvements

If you do decide to stay where you are and remodel-improve-expand your house, there are 4 ways to get the necessary money:

Bank Loan

The cheapest way is to take out a personal loan with securities, a savings account, or a life insurance policy's cash value as collateral. This will require only payment of the interest (but your banker will be happier if you make regular reductions in the principal).

The cost of the loan will be offset by the dividends-interest from the collateral. *Danger:* That you will keep postponing repayment and acquire a sizable debt to pay together with the mortgage.

An unsecured home-improvement loan will be more expensive, but you will have to make regular repayments that cover both interest and amortization.

Open-End Borrowing on the Basis of Your Original Mortgage

This will boost your monthly payments, but such loans are easy to arrange since the lending institution already knows you and the property.

Not all mortgages provide this privilege, and chances are, the new loan will be at a higher rate than the original mortgage.

Another handicap may be that the original agreement limits the amount of borrowing to the original loan—e.g., you borrowed 70% ($35,000) on a house purchased for $50,000. The home is now worth $70,000, but your maximum debt will not be $49,000 (70% of the new valuation), but $35,000.

Refinance Present Mortgage

This will involve a much higher rate of interest (probably) and may require payment of penalties. If you move to another lender, the costs are almost sure to be more—extra points, higher interest, etc.

Second Mortgage

Don't be embarrassed by this suggestion. A majority of all homes have or have had one.

Your present banker may not want to handle such a transaction but will put you in touch with someone who will be glad to oblige—an individual investor or a professional specialist in this field. And don't forget your own family—a steady income may be welcomed by an elderly relative. Consult a lawyer. Be sure there are no inheritance-tax problems if the lender dies.

The loan will be limited, probably to 75% of your equity (the difference between the value of your property and the balance of the first mortgage); interest charges will be at least 5% more (maximum set by law in most states); repayment will be rapid (5 to 10 years); and there will probably be a balloon at the end—a commitment to pay one large sum.

Here are typical figures on a $5,000 additional loan on property:

Assumption: Your original loan was $20,000, 20 years, 6¾%, and has 12 years to go. Your monthly payments are $152.08, your equity is $5,003.52, and you now owe $21,899.52.

Financing Terms	Open End	Refinancing	Second Mortgage
	6¾% on original mortgage; 9¼% on new loan, both over 12 years	Combines old and new debt at 9¼% for 12 years	6¾%, 12 years, on original mortgage; 18% annual rate, 5 years on 2nd mortgage
Original Mortgage at 6¾%	$20,000.00	$20,000.00	$20,000.00
Equity after 8 years	5,003.52	5,003.52	5,003.52
New amount borrowed	5,000.00	5,000.00	5,000.00
Estimated payments after new loan	None	500	None
New monthly payments 1st mortgage	$152.08 × 12 years = 21,899.52		$152.08 × 12 years, = 21,899.52
New loan	57.61 × 12 years = 8,295.84	230.44 × 12 years = $33,183.66	126.97 × 5 years = 7,618.20
Total monthly payments	$201.69 for 12 years	$230.44 for 12 years	$279.05 for 5 years; $152.80 for next 7 years
Total payments	$30,195.36	$33,683.36	$29,517.72

Note that refinancing costs $4,165.64 more than a second mortgage and $3,488 more than with the open-end arrangement.

Source: *Better Homes and Gardens.*

Checklist for Home Improvements

Remodeling a home is a major financial decision. Be sure to handle this in a businesslike manner, retain a lawyer, and protect yourself by such steps as:

GET COST OF TOTAL PROJECT. Before you ask for bids, set down exactly what is to be done and specify the type of materials, equipment, etc., to be installed. Changes in the middle of a job can be costly, controversial, and time-consuming.

The contractor has the responsibility of giving you a total price. You (and your wife) have the responsibility of obeying the commitment. *One solution:* Have the work done (or at least started) while the family is away on vacation.

In most states, the contractor's demand for additional money is not valid unless he is able to prove that he had to put more work or materials into the project than were originally estimated. Be wary of too-low bids. A good job, by a reputable contractor, is worth a few hundred dollars more.

DESIGNATE STARTING AND COMPLETION DATES. A friend of mine, Don Smith, ordered a new recreation room and signed an agreement with a local contractor. After the walls had been breached for the extension, Don decided to install a new furnace and gave a verbal OK for the work.

The contractor did finish the recreation room on time but was late in completing the installation of the furnace. *Result:* 4 weeks in a cold house and no legal recourse.

SPECIFY QUALITY OF MATERIALS AND EQUIPMENT. It's easy for an unscrupulous contractor to use second-grade piping or install used sinks, stoves, etc. And of course, he charges for new items.

GET A 1-YEAR GUARANTEE OF THE WORK. Even the best of contractors can make mistakes, so be sure that you do not have to pay for redoing the work.

SPECIFY THAT ALL WORK MUST CONFORM WITH APPROPRIATE LAWS. This will eliminate the possibility that the new porch violates zoning laws or that the plumbing does not meet health-building standards.

MAKE SURE THAT THE CONTRACTOR HAS ADEQUATE INSURANCE. If the work involves a bulldozer, for example, there's always the chance of unexpected damage to your own or neighbor's trees, driveway, etc.

REQUIRE THAT ALL DEBRIS BE REMOVED. That includes carting away old timbers, broken branches, pieces of plaster, siding, etc.

Added protection: Under a recent federal law, you have three days to check a contract and to change your mind before any home-improvement agreement is legally binding.

How to Get Top Dollar When You Sell Your House

To get the best price, you must prepare your house properly, arrange for the best presentation, make sure that prospective buyers know it's for sale, and set a realistic sales figure..

As a starting point, take your original cost, add the improvements, consider the present assessment, and then compare your price with those paid for similar houses in your neighborhood. You can get much of this information at city hall, the county clerk's office, or from a local real-estate agent. If you are willing to invest $50 to $150, hire an appraiser. (Contact your local board of realtors or write the National Association of Real Estate Appraisers, 853 Broadway, New York, New York 10003.)

If you sell the house yourself, you will swap a savings of about 6% for a lot of headaches—being ever available to show prospects through, arranging for a mortgage commitment (or assuming it yourself), being ready to abide by fair housing laws, etc.

If you use a broker, the commission will run from 5% to 8%, but he will handle everything—advertising, selling, financing, etc. You will have to decide whether to approve an exclusive listing, open listing, or multiple listing. Each approach has its benefits, so review the choices with the real-estate agent with whom you want to work. Then, take his (or her) advice and be patient. Very few houses are sold within 4 weeks of the initial listing.

Spell out the items to be included in the sales price—chandeliers, fireplace equipment, refrigerator, carpets, drapes, etc. Some state laws specify what items must be included. By eliminating some of these, you'll have a chance to pick up a few extra dollars. But you are taking the chance that they will interest the buyer. Otherwise, they may end up with the Salvation Army!

Present the best appearance by cutting and trimming the lawn; cleaning closets, storerooms, and attic; repairing leaky faucets and cracked windowpanes, etc. Unless the house is shabby, painting is seldom worthwhile. The new owners may have quite different color schemes.

ONE AREA OF PROFITABLE (AND INEXPENSIVE) INVESTMENT. Put new floor coverings in the kitchen.

Be sure to have copies of all bills for taxes, heating, utilities, insurance, etc. (See box.)

You can also help in the financing by:

Having the Old Mortgage Taken Over if the Lender Agrees

Watch out for penalties, as they may wipe out the higher price you can get.

Taking Back a Mortgage

This could be a good idea for a retired couple who want a steady, relatively good income. But it's an illiquid investment, and the house may be difficult to sell if money is needed in an emergency.

Accepting a Second Mortgage

As outlined elsewhere, this can provide a high yield but it's risky. If there's a default and an auction, you could end up with little or nothing. And don't be too trusting with the buyer. He may have more financial problems than you know of or might die before the mortgage is paid off.

Renting with an Option to Buy

This is a last resort, as your money is still tied up and there's no assurance that there ever will be a purchase.

When it's time to approve the sale, let the broker handle the details—generally, a binder of $100 to $500 with the balance to be paid in 10 days. Be sure that there's no commission paid until the title is closed and the deed transferred. Real-estate agents are not noted for their high ethical standards.

Make sure that you get paid for fuel in the oil tank, portions of the taxes and insurance already paid, etc.

Finally—and most important—retain a lawyer. Costs will be far less than possible losses—a fee of from $100 to $500, depending on the time required.

Papers Needed for Closing and Safekeeping

When you finally decide to sell your old house, be prepared with all the essential documents. And after you have moved into the new mansion, keep all of these papers handy, preferably in an office file, or better, in your safe-deposit box.

The original or a Xerox copy of:

1. Certificate of occupancy (required in some areas).

2. Certificates from the health department approving plumbing and sewer installations.

3. Sales contract.

4. Insurance policies—properly endorsed if they are to be picked up by the new owner.

5. Tax payment receipts.

6. Land survey.

7. Warranties and instruction booklets on equipment-appliances.

8. Maintenance and care instructions from the builder.

9. Deed to the property—although this will probably be mailed to you after being recorded in the county office.

Deferred Taxes on House Sales

The biggest one-time tax benefit from home ownership comes after a profitable sale. The tax on capital gains can be deferred if you buy another home, provided that the cost of the new residence is at least as much as the "adjusted" price of the old one —the actual price, less costs of legal fees, commissions, and fix-up expenses.

If you are 65 years of age and have lived in the house 5 of the last 8 years, there are no taxes if the new house costs $20,000 or less. Above that figure, there are lower taxes on a sliding scale based on the ratio of the $20,000 to the adjusted sales price of the old home.

Example: Samuel Groves, age 66, sells his house for $65,000 and buys a Florida condominium for $26,000. His selling and fix-up expenses are $5,000, so the adjusted price is $60,000.

To determine his capital gains tax, Mr. Groves gets the ratio of the maximum base ($20,000) to the adjusted sales price

($60,000) = 1:3. He then deducts the $20,000 from the $60,000 to get $40,000, and divides this by one-third = $13,333. This is subtracted from the $60,000 to get a readjusted sales price of $46,667. Then minus the cost of the condominium ($26,000) to get $20,667—the profit on which capital gains taxes have to be paid.

Condominium Cautions

If you are thinking of buying a condominium, base your decision on the *living*—not the *investment*—value. You gain equity, have a welcome tax shelter, and a chance for future appreciation. But there are costly dangers from fast-buck operators, unrevealed costs, lack of proper management, inadequate financial reserves, and rising costs and taxes.

DOs

DO CHECK OUT THE DEVELOPER. Do this through the local real-estate board, better business bureau, bank, and tenants in other projects he has built. A national contact: Community Associations Institute, 1200 18th Street, N.W., Washington, D.C. 20036.

DO GET FULL DATA ON ALL LEASE SITUATIONS. Some developers maintain fee ownership of the land, thus creating a leasehold. Others retain control of parking lots, recreational facilities, etc. Prices of these services can be jacked up without your OK.

DO SEE IF COMMON-AREA CHARGES ARE REALISTIC AND LIKELY TO STAY SO. Developers often establish low budgets to make units more salable. A monthly fee of $10 for recreational facilities sounds small, but if there are enough families, the developer can recover his costs in a couple of years and be assured of an ample income for as long as 99 years!

DO Make Sure the Building Will Be Managed by an Experienced, Well-regarded Management Firm (Not the Builder's Brother-in-law). And unless it's a small project, never rely on amateur control.

DO Think of Resale Value. The best location is where property values are rising and where there's a mixture of apartments and fairly expensive single-family homes.

DO Look at Your Neighbors. They are coowners, so be sure they are socially compatible and financially dependable. When maintenance costs rise, marginal owners may default and leave you responsible.

DON'Ts

DON'T Expect Lavish Tax Savings as Ballyhooed in the Promotional Brochure. Your tax bracket is based on your *taxable*—not your total—income.

DON'T Allow Your Deposit to Be Commingled with the Developer's Funds. Insist on an escrow account.

DON'T Take the Developer's Word about Real-estate Taxes. Call the local assessor and check the trend of taxes.

DON'T Buy a New Unit If the Builder's Warranty Is to Expire Soon.

DON'T Believe "Guaranteed" Charges. These can be part of the sales pitch, but once you've signed, can be doubled or tripled.

DON'T Buy a Condominium to Make Money. It's a bonus, not a certainty.

How Much Do You Still Owe on Your House?

This table shows the amount of principal to be paid off on your mortgage after different periods. Figures are for each $1,000 of the original loan. To get the full amount, multiply the appropriate sum by the face amount of your mortgage. Thus, on a $40,000 mortgage, multiply by 40. With a 9% interest rate, after 10 years on a 25-year loan, the balance due would be 40 × $825.83 = $33,033.

	6%	7%	8%	8½%	9%
20-year loan					
after 5 years	$848.60	$862.06	$874.87	$881.15	$886.86
after 10 years	644.36	666.49	688.40	699.60	709.69
after 15 years	368.89	389.29	410.63	422.35	432.37
25-year loan					
after 5 years	898.83	911.47	922.59	927.30	932.10
after 10 years	762.29	785.97	807.29	816.29	825.83
after 15 years	578.19	608.09	635.48	646.67	659.43
after 20 years	329.91	355.91	379.53	387.67	398.93
30-year loan					
after 5 years	930.22	940.77	950.55	954.85	958.52
after 10 years	836.11	856.85	876.85	885.85	893.58
after 15 years	709.20	737.93	767.05	780.47	791.89
after 20 years	537.99	569.29	603.47	619.52	632.72
after 25 years	307.08	330.22	359.79	373.72	383.51

Source: *Changing Times.*

XIV

How to Buy Home Insurance

Every insurance policy is a legal agreement, a contract between you and your insurance company. Whether it provides coverage for life, home, disability, health, or special risk, each policy spells out the rights and obligations of both parties.

One of the most important steps in effective money management is to read each policy carefully. Start with your newest policies, as their format is easier to read and the language more understandable (thanks to the pressure of consumer advocates).

In a guide, *Common Sense Introduction to Insurance,* The Kemper Insurance Companies explain the 4 parts of automobile and home insurance policies. The same general format also applies to most other types of insurance except life and health.

Declarations

This section contains the information you, the insured, gave to the company—your name, address, dates—and the data requested from the company—general terms, coverage purchased, premium charged, and maximum payments that may be made by the insurance company under every type of coverage.

Insuring Agreement

This is the company's promise to pay. It lists the boundaries set in the policy. *Read this carefully.* Payments may be made only on losses or accidents listed here.

Exclusions

This outlines the situations that are beyond the scope of the policy. Some areas are not covered because, actuarily, they are uninsurable. Others have limited protection, and still others involve risks that are so big that it would be unfair to charge all policyholders a higher premium to provide the coverage required.

> *Note:* All insurance is based on probabilities—that certain events will or will not occur. The basic premiums are set on experience over a large area and a long time.

Conditions

These are the rules that the company and the insured agree to use to conduct their agreement—specific rights and duties of both parties. *Pay attention to your responsibilities* on claims, payments, termination of contract, etc. If, for example, you do not give prompt notice of loss or damage, your claim may not be honored.

Home Insurance—Protection Against Fire, Theft, Damage, and Disaster

There are 6 types of standard homeowners insurance policies (HOs). The same general descriptive terms are used by most fire and casualty companies and apply throughout the United States. With all HO policies, it is far more important to buy the coverage you need (and no more) than to try to save a few dollars by settling for minimal insurance. When disaster strikes, your losses can run into the thousands. Yet the maximum spread between poor and adequate insurance, on most houses, rarely is more than $100 a year!

A standard HO policy provides for full replacement cost—with no deductible for depreciation—if the dwelling is insured at 80% of its replacement value. Premiums vary according to the type and location of building, scope of coverage, available fire and police services, and financial and marketing approach of the issuing company. Broadly, these are your choices:

HO-1 (Basic Form)

Provides coverage against loss or damage from fire and lightning, extended peril (windstorm, hail, smoke, riots, etc.), vandalism, malicious mischief, theft, personal liability, medical payments, physical damage to the property of others, and the additional costs of living elsewhere while the insured damage to your home is being repaired.

HO-2 (Broad Form)

The same as HO-1, plus protection for a wide range of hazards such as bursting of steam or hot-water systems, water leakage, freezing, building collapse, etc. Costs about 10% more than HO-1 (with variations according to state).

HO-3 (Special Form)

An extension of HO-2, it assures coverage against almost all loss or damage to your building, but—with exceptions—does not cover the contents. Costs about 10% over HO-2 (again, varies by states).

HO-4 (Content—Broad Form)

Designed for renters and apartment dwellers, it is similar to HO-2 except that there's no insurance on the building.

HO-5 (Comprehensive Form)

Deluxe coverage for expensive homes ($15,000 minimum coverage) with high-value contents. It protects against almost all usual risks-losses. Costs 30% more than HO-3 (with variations by states).

HO-6 (Condominium Unit-Owners Form)

Designed for purchasers of condominium apartments. Coverage is similar to HO-4 but expanded to meet the particular needs of a unit-owner. Costs about the same as HO-4.

Keep this table handy when you discuss HOs with your agent.

	HO-1 (Basic Form)	HO-2 (Broad Form)	HO-3 (Special Form)
DWELLING (minimum amounts shown. These should be increased to the replacement value of your home. Your insurance representative can help determine the value of your home.)	$8,000 up	$8,000 up	$8,000 up on "All-Risk" basis
OUTBUILDINGS AND PRIVATE STRUCTURES ON PREMISES	10% of dwelling coverage	10% of dwelling coverage	10% of dwelling coverage
PERSONAL PROPERTY ON PREMISES	50% of dwelling coverage* (may be increased)	50% of dwelling coverage* (may be increased)	50% of dwelling coverage* (may be increased)
AWAY FROM PREMISES	10% of above but at least $1,000	10% of above but at least $1,000	10% of above but at least $1,000
ADDITIONAL LIVING EXPENSE	10% of dwelling coverage	20% of dwelling coverage	20% of dwelling coverage
COMPREHENSIVE PERSONAL LIABILITY	$25,000	$25,000	$25,000
MEDICAL PAYMENTS	$500	$500	$500
PHYSICAL DAMAGE TO PROPERTY TO OTHERS	$250	$250	$250

Note: Because of local conditions and state requirements, Homeowners package programs vary among states both in coverage details and designation of forms. Basically, the principal and savings offered by package policies remain the same. Mississippi does not have the customary Homeowners programs but has a form of package policy which is somewhat similar. Consult your local insurance representative for further information.

    * Under some existing forms the amount is 40% but this may be increased to meet needs.

    Source: Kemper Insurance Companies.

HO-4 (Contents— Broad Form)	HO-5 (Comprehensive Form)	HO-6 (Condominium Unit-Owners Form)	REMARKS
NOT APPLICABLE	$15,000 up on "All-Risk" basis	NOT APPLICABLE	Amounts may be increased to fit the value of the dwelling. Full replacement cost (no deductible for depreciation) is allowed if dwelling is insured to 80% of the replacement cost.
NOT APPLICABLE	10% of dwelling coverage	NOT APPLICABLE	This is granted over and above the amount of insurance on the dwelling. Additional insurance may be purchased if the 10% is inadequate.
$4,000 up	50% of dwelling coverage (may be increased)	$4,000 up	May be increased to meet the individual need.
10% of above but at least $1,000	50% of dwelling coverage	10% of above but at least $1,000	
20% of personal property coverage	20% of dwelling coverage	40% of personal property coverage	Will pay the *extra* cost (up to the percentage shown) of living elsewhere while your property is untenantable after an insured loss.
$25,000	$25,000	$25,000	May be increased for additional premium.
$500	$500	$500	May be increased for additional premium.
$250	$250	$250	Included at no extra cost. May not be increased.

Before you complete your policy selection, study the exclusions and ask your agent to insert riders or add floaters when needed.

A rider is an endorsement to an existing policy to cover—or exclude—areas or needs. A floater, which may be separate from or attached to an existing policy, insures specific items against all hazards, usually almost to their full value and even when they are not in your home.

EXAMPLES OF RIDERS. The overall contents of your home are insured for $20,000. That sounds adequate until you note that the recovery for the theft, loss, or destruction of any one single item is limited to $250! That means that if a thief got away with your wife's $1,500 fur coat, you would be out $1,250! A rider would provide insurance for such valuables.

Or your furnace explodes and starts a fire. Your HO policy would cover the damage from the fire but not the damage to the furnace, so you would have to come up with an extra $1,500. Again, a rider would provide the extra coverage, at a cost small in relation to the possible loss or damage.

EXAMPLES OF FLOATERS. These are useful for possessions that increase, rather than depreciate, in value—antiques, jewelry, stamps, etc. In the past decade, the prices of many collectors' items have doubled and tripled. Floaters provide the special insurance needed—for expensive jewelry, an extra $1.33 per $100; for paintings and antiques, 3.8¢ per $1,000 for the first $10,000; etc.

If these additions to your policy (officially termed endorsements) boost the premiums of the policy too high, ask your agent about raising the deductibles—the amount of loss or damage you have to pay before the insurance claim starts.

Keeping Pace with Inflation

One of the few benefits of inflation is the increase in the value of your home. Your HO policy should keep pace. A good rule: Raise coverage to the replacement cost rather than depreciated value (the custom in pre-inflation times). The following table shows why. The figures might be boosted another 10% a year to offset inflation-rising costs.

Remember that, on the average, across the United States, the cost of the original house (without land) was less than half of the figures shown: $9,000 for a basic 6 room frame home! If such a house were totally destroyed before the insurance was increased, the owner would get only $7,200 (80% of the $9,000) toward the $20,000 replacement cost.

ROOMS	BASIC		STANDARD		SEMICUSTOM	
	Frame	Masonry	Frame	Masonry	Frame	Masonry
6	$20,000	$21,000	$24,000	$26,900	$28,000	$30,200
7	22,000	24,300	27,000	30,000	32,000	34,100
8	24,000	27,600	30,000	32,200	37,900	40,300
9	26,900	30,000	33,100	34,200	42,000	44,600

If you're worried about the cost of the higher limits, here are ways you can save money:

1. Install an approved burglar alarm and fire-detection system—as a self-contained unit or with a direct connection to the local police and fire departments. In some areas, this can reduce premiums as much as 10%. This equipment can be expensive, so you may want to discuss these other money-saving ideas with your agent.

2. Add an "inflation guard" to your policy. This endorsement automatically boosts coverage by 1% each quarter. That 4% a year won't keep pace with the present 8% annual inflation, but insurance companies are seeking approval for more flexible policies.

3. Review your policy carefully to determine if you can add or eliminate riders. Remember: A rider can *exclude* as well as *include*.

4. Increase your deductibles. This can save money on the premium and still not boost your risks out of reason. If there's a claim, you will have to pay several hundred dollars more but will gain several thousands more coverage.

Example: A shift in the deductible from $250 to $500 on an HO policy would make it possible to raise the overall coverage from $30,000 to $40,000 with no additional premium.

Or to put it another way, the premiums drop sharply with the rise in the deductible. For an HO-5 policy—$60,000 coverage:

Deductible	Premium
$ 50	$359
100	279
250	252
500	226

What to Do When You Need Disaster Coverage

In some areas and under some conditions, some forms of basic insurance are not available. Historically, this gap has been for damage from natural forces such as earthquakes, floods, etc. More recently, however, changing social conditions have made it economically impossible for private insurance companies to write essential insurance (fire, theft, burglary, and vandalism) in some urban centers.

To meet these needs, special policies are now available through high-risk insurance pools, usually aided by federal or state government financing or underwriting of the most severe losses.

Examples: Federal Crime Insurance (burglary and theft), up to $10,000 per home or business, is now available in 14 states and the District of Columbia through regular agents. *One essential requirement:* All doors and windows must be properly equipped with locks.

Fair Access in Insurance Requirements (FAIR) plans were formed after the 1967 race riots and since then have extended their coverage to include basic fire coverage for such high risks as buildings in big cities subject to riots and vandalism, homes on the brushfire-threatened hills above Los Angeles, and rural houses isolated from good fire protection. They are now operating in 26 states, the District of Columbia, and Puerto Rico.

As Ralph Tyler points out in *Money* magazine, some of these special policies are expensive, but others, such as fire insurance in Detroit, cost no more than ordinary coverage.

Disaster Coverage

Type of Coverage	Sponsor	Example of Coverage	Deductible	Annual Premium
Fire, extended coverage, vandalism	FAIR plans	$35,000 on frame houses; $10,000 on contents	$50	$138
Flood in eligible area	National Flood Insurers Assn.	$35,000 on houses; $10,000 on contents	Greater of $200 or 2% of coverage	$122.50
Windstorm, Key West, Fla.	Florida Windstorm Assn.	$35,000 on frame house	$200 down	$131.15
Land sinkage in mining areas of Pa.	Coal and Clay Mine Subsidence Insurance Fund	$35,000 on frame house	$250	$35.25 up
Earthquake in San Francisco	Most property insurers	$35,000 on frame house	5%	$52.50 up
Burglary and theft in 26 states, D.C., and Puerto Rico	Federal Crime Insurance	$10,000 on contents of dwelling	Greater of $50 or 5%	average— $80

How to Settle Claims

Getting your insurance is only half the battle. You still have to get paid off for the theft, loss, or damage. Usually, things move smoothly, but there can be times when there will be a dispute with the insurance company. This is where you need to fulfill your responsibilities to ensure your rights. To get the best settlement, start planning before there's a loss.

Make an Inventory of All Your Possessions

Give a description, the original cost or recent evaluation, and when appropriate, the numbers of: appliances, furniture, furnishings, clothing, furs, jewelry, and if they are valuable, books, hobby collections, etc.

Take Snapshots of Every Room

Also, photograph exteriors (from all four sides) to show shrubs, fences, walls, and other ornaments that might be damaged in a storm.

Call the Police; Protect What's Left; Take Pictures

Immediately after the theft or vandalism, call the police so there will be a formal record for future reference. If there's been a fire, take steps to protect what's left by moving valuables to a safe place or arranging for a guard until a moving truck can be hired.

Again, take snapshots, especially when there's been a fire, accident, or natural disaster. The Before and After pictures can be important evidence.

Do Not Sign Anything Immediately

Wait until you are relaxed and have checked every possibility —of loss, coverage, and replacement.

Don't file your claim until you have gathered all necessary information and verification (but don't wait too long, either).

Then:

Get Your Insurance Agent to Help

That's part of his job. He will tell you what areas are covered by your policy, explain procedures and documentation, help you

fill out the forms, expedite payments, and if there's been a catas-
trophe, may be able to get you an advance of funds.

If the loss is small and he advises not to file a claim, *take his
word for it,* especially if you have had several claims in the past
year or so. The insurance company might raise premiums or refuse to renew your policy.

On the other hand, if the agent is not cooperative, his reluctance could mean that he does not want to get into trouble with
the company as the result of too many claims by his clients.

Don't Settle Too Soon

If there's been substantial damage, don't OK the company-
proposed builder-contractor until you have checked the firm
through your local bank or with former customers. Before work
starts, *get everything in writing*—the work to be done, the material to be used, and if possible, an agreement to repair damages
(such as a torn-up lawn) caused by work crews. If there's a firm
completion date, get written assurance that you will be paid for
extra living expenses if the job is delayed.

Don't Be Afraid to Go Back to the Insurance Company
if You Overlooked Something

Often, it's hard to know the full extent of damage until the
builder has cleared away debris or, perhaps, your wife has had
her antiques checked for cracks.

If it's a reputable firm, chances are they will honor any justified oversights even though their legal obligation was completed with a check.

Consider Hiring a Public Adjuster

Do this if your claim is over $5,000 and you are very un-
happy with the proposed settlement. A public adjuster is an
individual or firm licensed by state insurance departments to

work for clients in settlement of claims. Payment is on the basis of 10% to 15% of what is recovered.

A good public adjuster can make a good case better because of his knowledge of policy coverage and limits, his credibility in appraisal of loss or damage, and his ability to come up with a complete inventory of loss even if your record keeping was not so good.

But don't start spending the extra money just because you hired a public adjuster. They are not miracle men, but their expertise can discover and present facts in a manner that may be more persuasive to the insurance company, an arbitrator, or eventually a judge or jury.

For names, check the yellow pages or contact the National Association of Public Insurance Adjusters, 1613 Munsey Building, Baltimore, Maryland 21202.

With or without a public adjuster, if the "final" offer seems very low, take the offensive.

CONTACT YOUR STATE INSURANCE DEPARTMENT. These are busy and harassed people, so be sure to present ALL of the facts—policy number, limits of coverage, deductible, extent and proof of damage, and the settlement you feel is fair.

If your argument is persuasive, the state official will send a letter of complaint to the insurance company. This implied threat of a public hearing with possible adverse publicity may tip the award somewhat more in your favor—but only if you have a solid case.

TAKE ADVANTAGE OF THE ARBITRATION CLAUSE IN ALL HO POLICIES. This can be used only when the dispute centers on the actual cash value of the settlement. The decision is made by a 3-member panel—the company adjuster, your representative, and an impartial arbitrator. Be sure the claim is large enough to warrant this measure, as you are responsible for half the costs.

SUE THE COMPANY FOR BREACH OF CONTRACT OR FAILURE TO COMPLY WITH THE TERMS OF THE CONTRACT AND MAKE "A FAITHFUL SETTLEMENT." This last resort makes sense only when the company has made a total disclaimer (insisting you are not covered at all), the claim is substantial, and you realize that court action may take years and thousands of dollars in legal fees.

Forget your pride and pique. You're suing for MONEY.

XV

How to Invest in Real Estate—
for Long-Term Profits, for
Income, for Tax Shelters

Real estate is an enormous field with something for every purse and almost every purpose. Shares in a real-estate investment trust (REIT) sell for under $10, properties can be bought with a few thousand dollars, partnerships cost up to $50,000, and participations in syndicates can run over $250,000.

Most real-estate investments can provide good to high-yielding (8% to 16%) tax-sheltered alternatives to securities. But they are usually illiquid, may require additional financing, almost always take years to pay off, and require expertise for real success.

Investments in raw land, commercial buildings, and apartments often involve excellent leverage (small cash and large mortgage), but the greatest attraction of almost all types of real estate is *growth*—added value resulting from population gains, inflation, and/or attractiveness of the property. *At all times, it is more important to know how to get OUT of a deal than how to get INTO it.*

There are few areas of investment where there are greater profits and pitfalls than in real estate. It's no field for the lazy or careless. The major reason for failure is the lack of adequate investigation—of the promoter-developer, the location and quality of the property, the trends of population, government plans,

198

transportation and other changing conditions. (By the same token, thorough investigation of the same subjects can go a long way toward assuring profits.) Before you commit funds to any real-estate enterprise, you should have detailed projections for the next 15 years!

Leonard M. Harlan, New York–based investment banker and real-estate consultant, explains why: In 1960, in Newark, New Jersey, there were 3 real-estate opportunities offered by brokers —the most prestigious hotel, the No. 1 medical center, and a major office building. At the time, each was a profitable operation, and apparently, a prime investment.

Not so. Within the next decade, there were radical shifts in population, an exodus of business and professional men, and rapid decay of the central city, climaxed by the 1967 riots. By 1970, all 3 buildings were in bankruptcy! Adequate research would have flashed a yellow, if not a red, light.

Unlike stocks, where all common shares have the same value, all parcels of real estate are not equal. Some properties zoom in price in a few years; the value of others grows slowly; still others, notably raw land, can lie dormant for generations, their investment worth eroded by taxes; and always there will be land and buildings that will decline in value as the result of new highways, community deterioration, neglect, and just old age. Real estate is an ever-changing investment that must be watched, cared for, and usually, utilized or promoted.

The Importance of Leverage

Leverage is the use of borrowed money to magnify gains and, sometimes, losses. The dream of every real-estate investor is to mortgage out—to get your initial money back as the result of a mortgage that is greater than your investment costs—or better yet, to mortgage to infinity—to get a mortgage that will pay off all costs, and because of the increase in income from the property, provide high carrying charges plus an annual return on what has become a zero investment.

Straight leverage is easiest to understand with raw land where there are no costs for maintenance, depreciation, management, etc. You buy a tract of land with a small down payment and a big mortgage. *Your hope:* The value of the land will rise, so that long before the mortgage is payable, you can sell at a price large enough to repay the mortgage and still have a sizable profit.

Leverage on income-producing property depends on the spread between the interest you pay on the money you borrow and the cash flow from the building.

Example: A broker tells you of an office building that earns 10% on its assessed value. You buy it by putting up 20% cash and borrowing the rest at 8%. You will earn 10% on your equity investment and 2% on the rest. For every $1,000 of property value, your income is $20 on a $200 investment, plus $16 on the mortgaged $800, for a total return of $36—an 18% annual rate of return.

Note: Leverage can work both ways. If there are vacancies in the building or unexpected expenses such as replacement of a boiler or roof, you will have less money to meet mortgage payments. If the situation becomes serious and your financial position shaky, you may lose the property by foreclosure.

Says Robert Allen, a prominent New Jersey builder: "Leverage is fine for professionals but can be dangerous for amateurs. When you own a property free and clear, you will be able to weather almost any economic storm. When there's leverage, even the shrewdest owner can be flattened by a strong wind. The inexperienced investor should use leverage only when he has a strong financial base and a property with a sure, steady income."

Where to Invest

In almost every community there are 3 areas of potential profits from real-estate investments—raw land, commercial buildings, and multifamily dwellings.

Raw land is best for long-term capital gains. It is worthwhile only if the acreage is in the path of progress, so that it can be sold, for an average annual gain of 50%, within a relatively few years—hopefully in 3 years, possibly in 5, and probably in 10 years. That sounds like a high return, but it's not so difficult with leverage.

Example: According to John B. Halper, New York City–based institutional mortgage broker: "When you pay $100,000 cash for property sold for $125,000 a year later, you will make 25% profit. But if you put down 10% and borrow the balance at 10% interest, your investment will be $19,000 ($10,000 cash, plus $9,000 interest) for a 132% profit—provided you sell before interest eats you up."

To determine a fair purchase price, check the current value of land now used for purposes similar to what you envision for the property—e.g., if you expect to sell to a developer who will build a combination shopping center and commercial area, find one nearby. If that land goes for $12,000 an acre, that's your target price. To your anticipated costs, add 8% a year for inflation.

Thus, if you can buy a farm for $4,000 an acre, add about $1,800 for inflation over the next 5 years. This should be a good deal IF you feel reasonably sure the population will expand into your area.

As a rule of thumb, your annual carrying charges (property taxes, interest, and amortization) should be no more than 10% of the face purchase price. To a large extent, inflation will help to offset these out-of-pocket expenses.

The real skill comes in the terms you can arrange. The tax laws are favorable: If the seller accepts less than 30% in cash, he establishes an "installment sales basis," thus pays capital gains tax only on the principal received each year. If he takes more than 30% in cash, he is taxed on the gain of the entire sale—immediately.

The leverage is greatest when:

THE MORTGAGE IS LONGEST. Always try to get a mortgage that will not be due until several years after the time when you anticipate you will be able to sell—if you hope to sell the land in 5 years, get a 10-year mortgage, says Halper.

MORE INTEREST IS PAID IN EARLY YEARS. Interest is tax-deductible, so try to substitute prepaid interest for part of the down payment.

Example: On a $100,000 farm, the seller wants 20% down and will take back a mortgage. Instead of coughing up $20,000 cash, offer $12,000 down and one year's prepaid interest on the $88,000 balance. At 10%, the interest will be $8,800, so the total payment will be $20,800. He'll get the cash he wants and you chalk up a welcome tax deduction on the interest.

Check with your tax man on such deals. The IRS approves deductions for prepaid interest only during the remaining months of the tax year of settlement plus 12 months thereafter. That's an effective limit of 24 months, so make your deal early in the year for maximum benefits.

Another money-saver: Get an agreement that allows you to pay interest only, no amortization. This should include a provision that you can pay in full at any time after the third year. Then, if your dream comes true and an agent for Sears Roebuck wants to buy your land in, say, 5 years, you can get your price and pay off the mortgage.

Making Money with Income-Producing Properties

With commercial buildings and apartments, you can invest as an individual, as a limited partner, or as a member of a syndicate. You can operate on your own in a small way, but when you get into bigger money, it's best to join with reliable professionals. They will do the work, assume construction and management responsibilities, and help to raise money. Whether you invest directly or with others, the costs and benefits are similar—relatively little cash, a large mortgage, welcome tax shelter, and adequate-to-good income.

As a starter, look around your community for opportunities—small shopping centers, professional buildings, free-standing stores for franchise operations, recreation areas (marinas, swimming pools, or campgrounds), etc. In each of these you can decide whether you want to be the active leader, the semiactive partner, or the passive investor.

At the outset, you may want to work alone or with a local broker in the renovation or building of property for a franchised operation such as McDonald's, Exxon, 7–11 Food Stores, and the like. Your agent (and possibly, partner) will arrange the lease so that the tenant pays the rent, real-estate taxes, insurance, and maintenance, and you get a monthly income plus tax offsets from depreciation and interest on your loan. With national organizations, your return will be smaller and the loan larger. With local stores, it will probably be the reverse. Overall, you should look for a return of at least 12% a year.

> *Note:* If you are self-employed or own your own business, consider building your own office-retail center. The same general terms apply, and there are opportunities for extra tax benefits. You can, for example, sell the land to your children under an irrevocable trust, then lease it back on a long-term basis. As long as you own the building, you can claim depreciation.

Limited partnerships are more complex. You put up most of the money, but your liability is limited to a preset figure. The general partner is responsible for the operation and the debts, so he gets the lion's share of the profits.

Partnerships pay no taxes and pass through, to investors, the full benefits of all losses. These can be used to offset ordinary income or be carried back or forward on federal income tax returns. You pay taxes on the income at the full rate; on the long-term capital gains, at half that levy.

Syndicates are usually bigger operations. Shares in a building or apartment or project are sold by a promoter who should have some of his own money in the deal. Outsiders supply the cash, look for returns of 12% to 15% plus substantial tax benefits and, when the property is sold, capital gains.

Generally speaking, half of the yields come from depreciation. This is not taxable because it is a return of capital.

Example: Dr. Soreback, in the 50% tax bracket, puts $20,000 into a syndicate that builds Sunshine Apartments. In the first 4 years, largely because of accelerated depreciation (double the straight-line allowance), he takes tax losses of $10,000 a year. As he deducted half of the loss each year, he gets his investment back. Over 15 years, he should get an average annual return of about 16%, IF there are no problems, the property is attractive, and management is able and honest.

If the apartment should be sold in, say, 10 years, he will share in a capital gain, taxable to him at half his regular rate.

But there's no free ride. If Dr. S. needs his money in a hurry, he will probably have to take a substantial loss, and more important, he will have to pay full taxes on his previous income from the syndicated investment.

And if the apartment should not be successful, he and his partners might end up with nothing but empty apartments and, possibly, personal liability for payment of the construction loan!

Valued by Income

One thing to remember about income-producing property: Lenders are not interested in the cost of the property, only what income it throws off and how secure that income is for the foreseeable future. That's why it's sometimes possible to "mortgage out," and once in a great while, to "mortgage to infinity."

Example: Mr. Burns built an apartment building for $370,000 (with the help of a construction loan from the local bank). Because of its design, location, and rental rates, the unit was filled promptly and soon showed an annual income of $90,000. This was enough to get a loan from an insurance company for $386,-

000. Mr. Burns was lucky to "mortgage out" but he still did not recover all of the $47,000 cost of the land.

Two years late, the rents were raised substantially and the mortgage refinanced for $556,000. *Result:* Mr. Burns had $16,000 a year to infinity.

That's great in prosperous times, but remember that when there's a depression and vacancies, the insurance company won't wait long for its money!

As a rule of thumb, property is capitalized, for mortgage purposes, on the basis of assured annual income as a percentage of $1,000. Thus, the lender would be willing to grant a mortgage, for a property yielding 8%, of $12,500; with $100,000 income, $1,250,000.

From the lender's viewpoint, this is a good deal. If he is paying 5½% on savings or even less on reserves against future policy payments, why not?

Select Your Broker-Partners Carefully

With all real estate, it is imperative to deal with reputable, established, experienced firms. This is a business of entrepreneurs. Regulations are few and standards are more quoted than observed. Insist on full, frequent reports and have them checked with your lawyer and/or accountant. Do not be afraid to question when you are disturbed.

Few businesses have more puzzling accounting than real estate. A syndicate can go "broke" while making a profit! Harlan tells of a $1,000,000 building financed with $100,000 cash and a $900,000 mortgage. At the end of the tenth year, the mortgage was down to $800,000, but depreciation had cut the book value of the bulding to $500,000.

There was an offer to buy the deal at $150,000 over the mortgages—at $950,000. This would result in a pretax profit of $450,000. To the amateur, this sounds like a handsome return on a $100,000 investment. But there was a tax bill of $170,000

Where the Profits Are in Real Estate

Note: These figures represent average returns in the early 1970s. Inflation and rising interest rates have boosted income and down payments on new projects.

	Leased Land—for Ranching, Farming, Other Business	Urban Land Undeveloped	Suburban Land—Undeveloped	Farm-Rural Land—Undeveloped
Cash down, balance by mortgage	25%–40%	30%–50%	30%–50%	50%–75%
Risk	Small	High	Medium	Medium to high
Potential problems	Rising costs for taxes, services; tenant business not profitable to carry land to resale	Zoning, politics; high price and carrying costs	Expansion pattern, rezoning; long wait for resale	Hard to monitor; delays and changes in highways, etc., delay in scheduled resale
Personal management?	Yes, if convenient	Yes, in early stages; no, later when need for political pressure	Yes, but may need help in rezoning, etc.	Probably not
Type of tax shelter	Profits of resale taxed as capital gains; when held over 6 months, at lower rate			

Income and Tax Shelters

	Small Apartment	Large Apartment	Office Building	Warehouse, Commercial Property	Shopping Center
Rates of return	8%–15%	8%–14%	8%–14%	8%–14%	15%–20%
Down payment	20%–25%	25%–35%	25%	25%	20%–30%
Problems	Maintenance, changing area	Maintenance, shifts in transportation, area; vacancies, competition	Same plus competition from old and new buildings	Tenant stability, costs of remodeling, competition	Competition, vacancies, community complaints, MANAGEMENT
Personal management	Yes	No	Maybe, but depends on size	No, unless small	No
Tax benefits	In all cases, income can be offset by mortgage interest and deductions of operating costs, investment tax credits; when sold, depreciation maximizes capital gains				
General terms of depreciation	40 years	40 years	45 years	60 years	40-60 years

Taxable Losses on Real-Estate Partnerships

Some real-estate partnerships sell shares in apartment houses with the understanding that if cash flow fails to cover mortgage payments, the loans will be allowed to go into default. This ignores IRS rules: If partnerships get out of a property within 8½ years (20 months on government-subsidized projects), limited partners pay taxes, at ordinary rates, on the difference between straight-line depreciation and the accelerated depreciation that the partners took.

	Cash Distribution	Taxable Income (Loss)	Tax Savings 35% Bracket	Tax Savings 50% Bracket	Accumulated Net Proceeds (After Deducting Original Investment) 35% Bracket	50% Bracket
90% Mortgage						
Construction Period	$ 0	($1,000)	$350	$500	($650)	($500)
Year 1	100	(380)	140	190	(410)	(210)
Year 5	100	(360)	130	180	490	900
Year 10	100	(250)	90	130	1,510	2,140
Year 20	100	0	0	0	2,820	3,610
80% Mortgage						
Construction Period	$ 0	($1,000)	$350	$500	($1,650)	($1,500)
Year 1	180	(320)	110	160	(1,360)	(1,160)
Year 5	180	(300)	110	150	(260)	100
Year 10	180	(180)	60	90	1,020	1,550
Year 20	180	60	(20)	(30)	2,800	3,410

Source: *Your Investments$.

on the gain. Since the cash payment would be only $150,000, the syndicate would have to come up with $20,000 (more than its ready cash) to pay the taxes!

Whether you are dealing with a partnership or a syndicate, be cautious and conservative. Their sales pitch will stress the tax shelter and yield, but there are potential problems, such as:

Loss of Rentals Due to Overbuilding in the Area or Poor Management

How many times have you seen a new apartment building only half rented a year after its opening?

Poor Marketability for Your Investment

If the project runs into trouble, the word will spread fast and you will have a hard time getting out at any time.

Complexity of the Deal

Some promoters know every legal loophole and tax dodge. Have your lawyer check out contract clauses that can cost you more money or tie up your funds—e.g., to the uninitiated, part ownership of a lease and an equivalent ownership of a leased property sound the same. But the leaseholding is worth much more for income and for sale.

Investing in a Business Rather Than in Real Estate

When the promoter suddenly announces that the owner of the bowling alley, motel, franchise store, etc., has quit and he is taking over, watch out. The yields of self-operation may be higher but the risks are greater (especially with inexperienced management).

Fraud

Real estate involving numerous properties provides hundreds of opportunities for finagling—leasing furniture from the promoter's brother-in-law, double charges for services, finders' fees, and you name it. This is a business where most operators have little capital and lots of hope—and nerve.

Questionable Appraisals

Even reputable firms can become overenthusiastic. After all, they are working the same side of the street as the developer!

On the average, a fair purchase price will be about 4 times annual rents for office buildings, 6 times annual rents for apartments, and 9 times rental income for a shopping center.

Optimistic Projections

To be safe, double the number of years for the predicted payoff from a profitable sale.

Promise of Too-High Yields

Real estate is a competitive business. Above-average returns should be checked. Usually, they cannot be maintained without harming upkeep. It could be that to make cash-flow projections attractive, the promoter cuts the reserve for replacing kitchen appliances or reduces maintenance projections. Always ask questions when operating costs get far above or below 30% to 40% of income—depending on location.

To these caveats should be added these personal responsibilities:

• Always Inspect the Property in Which You Invest

When it's out of town, retain local counsel to make sure that the location, price, yields, and depreciation schedule conform to expectations. *In real estate, it pays to take very, very little for granted.*

• Never Judge Any Project Purely on its Tax-shelter Potential

This should be a plus. You are in business to make a profit, not to establish losses. If there are no profits, all you will be doing is paying money out of one pocket into another!

• Favor Deals in Which the Promoter Has a Substantial Participation

He will be more cautious with his own money.

• Worry about What You Will Make, Not How Much the Syndicator Will Take Out

You are buying brains, so you will have to pay well for top results. As a checkpoint, try to make cash flow, tax shelter, and equity buildup add up to at least 2% more than the prime bank loan rate. Preferably, look for 15% yields on residential and office properties, 20% on motels and shopping centers.

• Look for Syndicates Instead of Waiting for Someone to Call

You can get a list of qualified syndicate brokers from the California Real Estate Association, 520 South Grand Avenue, Los Angeles, California 90017.

Swapping Real Estate

Whenever you buy any real estate, consider how, when, and to whom you will sell. If the buyer is as smart as you think you are, he will want you to take back a mortgage, maintain an interest, or perhaps make a swap. Whatever choice you make, be sure that you receive sufficient cash to pay off the mortgage and your own capital gains tax.

You can postpone that tax by exchanging property. If you are dealing with raw land, try to do so when both properties are free and clear. Otherwise, the IRS will want its money immediately. As they see it, if the property you take over has a mortgage, it's not a tax-deferred sale.

Best bet: Arrange the swap after you have a bank loan to pay off the mortgage. As soon as you complete the deal, get a new mortgage. You still will not have to pay taxes on capital gains until the second mortgage, and not even then if you can keep swapping!

Making Money with Mortgages

If you are the kind of person who wants security and better-than-average returns, think about first mortgages. If you are willing to take extra risks for extra rewards, get into second mortgages. The attraction will be the income and only rarely capital gains.

Interest rates on first mortgages are limited by state laws—usually to 8½%, more recently as high as 9½%. That's a pleasant yield for retirement income, but unless you take back a mortgage on your home, don't invest in mortgages haphazardly.

MAKE MORTGAGE LENDING A BUSINESS. Once you have found reliable people who need mortgages (with the help of your lawyer, accountant, and banker), set up a regular program within your financial limits. Try to get a mixture—old houses, new families, different income levels, and different parts of the community. And don't overlook commercial properties.

If the money market is tight, your bank may offer you participations—from 20% to 90%. These can be good deals. The bank provides expertise in the selection of properties, screening of the borrowers, and administration of the loans. If you have sufficient funds, there can be diversification, too.

When you have more experience and more money, contact a local mortgage banker. He deals in larger properties but may be able to set up joint ventures. He will relieve you of the chores of collecting monthly payments, checking insurance coverage, holding tax payments in escrow, keeping an eye on the property, etc.

To save taxes: Arrange for a trust to hold one or more mortgages. With proper planning, the interest income will never be taxed.

Have your personal pension plan make the loan. Over 20 years, that 8½% interest will quadruple and provide extra comfort for retirement.

If your own Keogh Plan does not have sufficient resources to handle a large mortgage or portfolio, team up with your friends and ask the trustee-bank to build a mortgage package.

Disadvantages: Like real estate, mortgages can be hard to sell in a hurry. If interest rates are higher than when you made the loan, you will have to sell at a loss. But if you are lucky (or smart) and interest rates decline, you might be able to sell at a profit.

If liquidity is a problem, stay away from single mortgages and put your money in Ginnie Maes (see Chapter XIX, on Retirement).

Benefits of Discount Mortgages

If you become active in the mortgage market, watch for discount mortgages: those selling below face value because of their initially lower rate of interest—e.g., when the interest rate is 8½%, a 6%, $10,000 mortgage might be selling at $7,000.

When you buy these bargains, you get a competitive return

and the opportunity for capital gains when you hold the mortgage to maturity.

Curiously, this is one situation where the higher the yield, the lower the risk. *Example:* The original mortgage was $10,000 on a $15,000 house—67% of value. When you buy the mortgage at $7,000, the ratio of loan to value is only 47%!

Rewards and Risks of Second Mortgages

Almost half of all real-estate deals involve second mortgages. For the lender they are riskier, but they yield far more—from 15% to 18%, depending on state laws. You are taking a secondary position, so before you advance any money, lessen your exposure by including in the agreement:

1. AN ACCELERATION CLAUSE. This gives you the option, before the property can be resold, of continuing on or demanding full payment.

2. A PRIORITY CLAUSE. This calls for no increase in the first mortgage until the second has been paid. Without such protection, a shrewd borrower could refinance his original commitment, get his down payment back, abandon the property, and lose nothing. Your only recourse would be to take over the big first mortgage.

3. A NOTIFICATION CLAUSE. If there's a default on the first mortgage, you would agree to continue the payments only if you were notified in advance, in writing, of the foreclosure.

Otherwise, it's possible the property could be auctioned off, and after payment of the prime indebtedness, there would be nothing left for you. With this clause, you could submit a claim to the trustee, and if the auction offer seemed too low, you could bid high enough to cover your claim.

Changing to a Condominium?

Switching an apartment building to a condominium can be profitable but it's difficult. In many states the law requires approval by a substantial percentage of the tenants (35% in New York). It's hard enough to get tenants to agree on the color of the new carpet in the lobby, let alone on a requirement that they buy instead of rent!

If you can swing such a deal, do it. You will probably make more money and avoid future maintenance and management problems than if you continue as the landlord. But you'll be lucky to escape severe criticism and, probably, will have to go to court.

What about REITs?

As of this writing, the less said about Real Estate Investment Trust (REITs), the better. In the early 1970s, they were touted as ideal investments for widows and orphans—high dividends, strong appreciation, etc. But as so often happens with Wall Street's darlings, the promise was greater than the performance. By 1973, REITs were hard hit—by high interest rates, slow payments, loan defaults, and bankruptcies.

By mid-1974, most REITs had cut or passed their dividends. Their shares were selling at one-third—or less—of their previous highs, and several major trusts were asking their stockholders to approve incorporation "to make better use of assets and to take advantage of tax-loss credits." What they really meant was that to maintain their tax-free status, they would have to make payments from their surplus and thus drain their financial structure.

Despite their current troubles, REITs fulfill an essential function in financing real estate. They are so-called real-estate mutual funds that provide a means for the small investor to participate in the ownership of real property. The money paid in by investors is used for long-term mortgages, short-term construction loans, equity positions in housing, commercial buildings, shopping centers, land development, etc. Their shares are traded like regular stocks, and many of the larger REITs are listed on the New York Stock Exchange.

Basically, there are three types of REITs:

EQUITY TRUSTS. Generally, these invest in depreciable properties and distribute all or part of the depreciation to shareholders. Revenues come from rents and capital gains when the properties are sold. They buy income-producing properties, commercial and residential.

The equity position may be direct (as a partner with an owner or builder) or indirect (through "kickers," such as warrants to buy stock in the corporation that owns the shopping center, office building, or apartment house). In good times, equity trusts returned about 10% annually—6% in dividends, 4% in increase in shareholders' equity due to the annual reduction of mortgages on the properties.

SHORT-TERM TRUSTS. These make short and intermediate term loans for construction of homes, apartment buildings, commercial buildings, etc. Their income comes from interest (typically 3% to 5% above the prime rate) fees and leveraging their holdings. The loans are repaid by mortgages from long-term lenders such as insurance companies.

LONG-TERM TRUSTS. These provide long-term, permanent mortgage financing, usually with an equity participation. Their returns are modest, but their risks are usually low. Most of these REITs are operated in association with major financial institutions, such as banks and insurance companies, which look for steady income over the years.

To qualify for tax exemption, REITs must: (1) have 75% of their assets in real estate, mortgages, cash, or government securities at the end of each quarter; (2) derive 75% of gross income from real estate; (3) distribute 90% of taxable income to shareholders; (4) have at least 100 shareholders, no 5 of whom can control more than half the shares; (5) not operate properties; (6) have independent management; and (7) remain unincorporated.

Read those requirements over again and see why so many REITs want to become standard corporations. Some of them, I'm sure, are a bit hasty. If you have an eye for bargains and are willing to tie your money up for a couple of years, shares of some REITs could be well worthwhile. With the better ones, you will be buying participation in quality properties, diversification, and financial strength that eventually will bring welcome income and substantial capital gains. Some REITs will come back!

But if you crave more action and want to invest indirectly in real estate, take a look at some of the land-development companies, primarily those whose shares are traded on the New York Stock Exchange—General Development (controlled by City Investing), Deltona Corporation, Horizon Corporation, and ITT. They all own huge tracts of land in resort-vacation areas, are aggressive marketers, and are likely to benefit from the strong push for earlier retirement made possible by the 1974 Pension Reform Act.

But as with all real estate, *investigate before you invest*. Few businesses suffer more severely from high interest rates and tight money!

Always Risks in Real Estate

The strongest appeal of real-estate investments is growth. But there are also unusual tax advantages. What's income in most business can provide tax deductions. You buy a building, collect the rent, pay the taxes, ante up for maintenance and management, and meet mortgage interest and amortization. What's left would be net income in ordinary business, but with real estate, you can still deduct out-of-pocket costs, a percentage of the purchase price, and annual improvements—as depreciation.

By speeding the rate of depreciation, you can arrange it so that there's no taxable income, and you can deduct this "loss" from non–real-estate income. As Halper says, "With real estate, there are plenty of advantages, but not one is without risk."

XVI

Life Insurance—How Much Do You Need? What Should It Cost? Where Can You Get the Best Buy? How to Get Special Coverage; Benefits of Borrowing on Cash Values

Definitions

Ordinary Life

This is the traditional policy that provides a predetermined sum at death. Available on a participating (dividend-paying) and nonparticipating basis.

Also called straight life or whole life, such policies provide low-interest forced savings in the form of cash values that are built up by payment of premiums larger than needed for protection alone.

Term Life

This type provides protection only, builds no cash values. Like automobile or fire insurance, term is bought for a short period of time, usually one year, and is renewable.

Annuity

At a chosen age, normally 65, the owner and/or beneficiary of the policy receives regular payments until he dies, or for a certain period or up to a certain amount.

Within these broad categories are scores of variations—in premiums, in payouts, in combinations of ordinary, term, and annuities, etc.

Life insurance is so competitive that there's a policy for almost every need and every family budget. You can get adequate information about standard policies from advertisements, folders, and agents, so this chapter will concentrate on out-of-the-ordinary policies and combinations that can be more beneficial and less expensive for many people.

Life insurance is the keystone to wise personal money management and estate planning. Its primary purpose is to provide protection against untimely death, but it can be used for savings, to assure retirement income, to provide gifts, to build an estate, and to avoid or minimize taxes.

Basically, what life insurance does is share the risks of early demise with others, so costs of policies are based on averages. When you pay your premium, you are betting that you will outlive the average American of your age and sex. You have a 70% chance of winning.

Meantime, regardless of the type of policy, your heirs will receive the face value (less any loans taken against cash values) at your death. You get the most for your money by starting to buy life insurance early when costs are low and your health is good. A young family should own the maximum amount of life insurance that can be paid for without undue hardship—directly and/or through company or association group plans. Adequate protection is not as expensive as you may think. By using a combination of straight and term insurance, almost everyone can protect his family properly. *The important thing is to buy it, not talk about it.*

Most people are sold straight life because such policies build equity and the salesman earns a higher commission. But there's a lot to be said for term, especially to bridge gaps.

With the same dollars, a 35-year-old man can buy about 4 times as much coverage with a term policy as he can with straight life; at age 50, it's about 2½ as much; at age 64, the gap is narrowed even more. Up to age 65, the cumulative cost of term insurance is less than straight life. Then, overnight, the overall cost of straight life is cut almost in half, while that of the term policy continues to increase (assuming policies were taken out in earlier years).

Straight life builds up cash value, so that the average $1,000 policy can be turned in for $482 at age 64. Term insurance builds no cash value. It's good only for the period paid for by the annual premium.

Most people should consider a combination of straight life and term insurance—more term when they are young and their family needs maximum protection; little or no term when they own their home, have educated their children, and have other assets for retirement.

Insurance should be planned and revised frequently—every 3 or 4 years until you are in your 50s. Then you can switch to options or policies that meet your retirement schedule.

When you buy insurance, ALWAYS stay flexible and think in terms of the next 10 years or more. Today, when families are small, more women are working, divorce is frequent, and incomes are high, young people acquire more assets more rapidly than ever before. To be sure that their families are able to maintain a comfortable style of living after the death of the major money-earner requires substantial insurance. For later years, protection can be decreased with the anticipation of pension plans and Social Security.

How Much Insurance Do You Need?

As a rule of thumb, insurance agents urge that your insurance protections total 4 to 5 times your annual income—at a cost of about 5% of your salary. That is, if you are married and have

2 children, and earn $20,000, your minimum coverage should be $80,000 to $100,000.

Individual needs vary. A bachelor (unless he is responsible for someone else in his family) needs little but will find it worthwhile; a middle-aged widow with no children can get by with enough to cover the costs of death and estate settlement. A family man needs more—to be certain that there is enough money to do the things the husband's income now does for the family—on the average, 50% to 66% of current family income. *WHEN YOU BUY INSURANCE, ALWAYS CONSIDER THAT YOU MAY DIE TOMORROW.*

Here's the recommended coverage for a family of 5—wife and husband about 35 years old, three children, aged 4, 7, and 10, annual income now $18,000.

Insurance Company	Total Insurance Needed
Aetna	$148,000
Allstate	95,000
Bankers Life (Iowa)	139,000
Connecticut Mutual	189,000
Equitable Life (New York)	180,000
Guardian Life	275,000
Northwestern Mutual	120,000
Prudential	149,000

These figures may seem astronomical but they may be easily in reach or achievable with planning and consistent savings. Social Security benefits are increasing faster than inflation, so the margin of security narrows as you grow older.

Unfortunately, few families provide even basic protection. In a study of widows whose husbands died before age 65, the Life Insurance Agency Management Association found that:

50% collected less than $5,000.

25% had to spend all of the insurance proceeds immediately.

Only 8% received more than $25,000!

Can you think of any better argument to buy adequate insurance NOW?

How to Guesstimate Your Insurance Needs

To evaluate your life insurance needs, you must first calculate your net worth (see Chapter I). Then use the following table to determine what's needed to provide the necessary living expenses for your family, educate your children, and how much extra insurance will be needed to bridge the gap.

> *Note:* This example uses a total 4-year college cost of $20,000 per child. It assumes that Social Security will provide $9,000 over the 4 years and that your son or daughter will work and/or get college loans or scholarships.

How to Estimate Current Insurance Needs for Your Family's Future

1. Family's living expenses (50% of current $30,000 a year income)	$ 15,000
2. Social Security—$5,220 for wife and 2 minor children until youngest reaches 18	5,220
3. Net money needed (line 1 − line 2)	9,780
4. At 8% return need (divide line 3 by 8) × 100	122,250

After death calculations:

5. Net worth—value of cash, savings, investments, home, etc.	25,000
6. Life insurance—own and employer's	75,000
7. Available capital resources (line 5 + line 6)	100,000
8. Pending expenses (debts, college, etc.)	40,000
9. Final expenses, estate taxes, etc. (10% of line 7)	10,000
10. Net liabilities (line 8 + line 9)	50,000
11. Capital left after death (line 7 − line 10)	50,000

So extra insurance needed:

12. Capital needed as base for 8% return (line 4)	122,250
13. Funds after death (line 11)	50,000
14. Additional coverage needed (line 12 − line 13)	72,250

Notes:
Line 1. If there are no dependent children, use 33½% for your widow.
Line 2. For widow alone: $2,214.
Line 5. Use the net value of your home—market value − mortgage.

Cost for Guaranteed Renewable Yearly Term Life Insurance
(Representative, Not Standard)

Age at nearest birthday	30	35	40	45	50	55	60	65
Premium per $1,000	$2.41	$2.71	$3.63	$5.50	$8.87	$15.13	$19.75	$30.83

That $72,250 extra insurance sounds like a major investment, but it can be obtained for about $1,900 a year for term insurance. That's another 6.3% of your $30,000 income, but hopefully you'll be getting a raise next year and part of the bill can be squeezed out by economies and careful budgeting.

It may be easier to think in more concrete terms—$158 a month, $33 a week, or just over $4 per day.

Remember, too, that inflation helps as well as hurts. Every time you make a payment on the mortgage, the value of your home is rising. And the same goes for the cash value of your life insurance.

Converting Income Needs to Life Insurance Needs

The following table provides a base for calculating how much insurance is needed to assure a given amount of *monthly* income. It assumes that the insurance proceeds will earn 5% and that both principal and income will be used to pay the survivors.

Example: A 35-year-old man with a 35-year-old wife and 2 children earns $18,000 a year. If the husband dies, the widow will get $435 a month from Social Security until the youngest child reaches 18—in 14 years. Thus, she needs $380 from insurance to reach the planned $815 per month.

Take the multiplier for 14 years in Column II (122) and multiply by $380 to get $46,360. This will produce $380 per month for the 14 years. For the next 11 years thereafter (until age 60) when the widow will draw Social Security, the total income will be $50,160. But since this amount will not be needed until 15 years hence, multiply it by the discount factor for 15 years (Column II) of .48 = $24,076.

I	II	III
Years	Multiplier	Discount Factor
1	12	.95
2	23	.91
3	34	.86
4	44	.82
5	53	.78
6	63	.75
7	71	.71
8	80	.68
9	88	.64
10	95	.61
11	102	.58
12	109	.56
13	116	.53
14	122	.51
15	128	.48
20	154	.38
25	174	.30
30	189	.23

Source: *Money* magazine.

For the widow's retirement, a lifetime annuity will cost 150 times the extra monthly income of $380 she needs. This amount, $57,000, must be discounted by the factor of .27 for the 27 years between now and Social Security. Thus, the extra insurance needed is $15,390—at a cost of $417 a year for term.

Note: In case you're confused about the various tables, different rates are used to show the different possibilities. That 5% a year return may seem low these days, but it's more than the average long-term interest rate on savings. The 8% is a fair yield on investments in securities and real estate.

Beating Inflation

There's no sure way to beat inflation, but you can get some idea of how much extra insurance you will need just to stay even by using the following table.

Pick the time frame when your needs will be most critical—probably when the children are in college. Then guess the rate of inflation and check the table to see how much each present $1 will be worth in the years ahead. If you have a $20,000 policy to be paid when Junior enters college 10 years from now, the real purchasing power will be between $10,800 and $5,600! That means that, realistically, you will need 2 to 4 times the insurance calculated!

How Inflation Is Eroding Your Life Insurance

Projection —Years	Rate of Inflation		
	6%	8%	12%
5	.73	.66	.53
10	.54	.44	.28
15	.39	.29	.15
20	.29	.19	.08

How to Make Up the Difference

If your budget is already tight, consider these steps to obtain extra coverage:

Use Annual Dividends to Buy More Insurance

With a straight life policy, the dividends will buy from 2½ % to 3% more coverage each year. When used to buy one-year term life, they can add 5% to 10%, depending on your age and the amount of dividends. Be sure that you get a policy that is convertible to whole life.

Join a Group Plan or Increase Coverage Under a Group Plan

You can join a group plan at your company or through your union, trade association, or professional society. This will be term insurance. You may have to pay more than you would for an individual policy because the premiums are based on the average age of all enrollees.

With one large professional group, a member between the ages of 41 and 50 can buy $50,000 coverage, without a physical exam, for $300 a year.

Consider Level-premium Decreasing Term Life

The premium stays constant, but the face value drops. This may be suitable when you are in your mid-40s and can look forward to a paid-up mortgage and no more college expenses. They are expensive when you start young. At age 30, $400 buys a $100,000 policy; at 40, the same $400 buys only $69,200 coverage; at 50, it's down to $8,400.

Buy Variable Life

Do this where part of the insurance company investments are in common stocks, which, hopefully, will grow in value and in dividends to outpace inflation. But those common stock values can also go down! It's too risky for a widow and fatherless children.

Check Cost-of-Living Policies

These automatically increase coverage every year. By using the annual dividends from a straight life policy to buy one-year term, Canada Life Assurance Company boosts coverage by about 8% a year. If the dividends exceed the cost of the extra premium, they are stockpiled for the future. If they are insufficient, you can make up the small difference.

Philadelphia Life Insurance Co. raises the face value of its straight life by 5% annually. This may not keep pace with the rising cost of living, but since the premium is based on your original age, you benefit over the long run.

Warning: Avoid increasing term. At the outset you pay a disproportionately high premium for very little extra coverage. You will do much better with level term.

Example: At age 45, it costs $725 to get $3,310 term. At the end of 10 years you will have $31,300 insurance but will have paid out $7,259. For an outlay of about two-thirds as much, you could have bought $50,000 of level-premium term.

How to Get the Most for Your Insurance Dollar

There are three things to consider in buying life insurance: service, policy terms, and cost—*in that order.*

Service is hard to measure in dollars. A good insurance agent can help you plan your estate, show you how to get the most protection for your money, provide counsel, help arrange loans, hasten payments at your death, and guide your widow and children with their financial problems.

You may pay a little more when you deal with an agent of an established insurer, but it can be well worthwhile. You are buying extra security.

Policy terms may seem to vary, but basically, all life insurance starts with the same fundamentals—actuarial tables that predict length of life. The differences in policies, in large measure, are sales tools—combinations to attract new clients and to serve specific markets. The consumer has a wide, wide choice.

Costs are difficult to compare. The initial low price of term may be offset by the future benefits of straight life. Attempts are being made to provide yardsticks, but by and large, these are not yet widely available nor truly accurate. At this time, the best advice is to determine your insurance needs and shop several companies, directly or through their agents, for policies that will provide the family protection you want now and with the retirement benefits you look for in the future. *And at the best price.*

What $1,000 Insurance Costs

Type of Policy	Age Purchased		
	25	35	45
5 year renewable-convertible term (premium for first 5 years)	$ 3.49	$ 4.45	$ 9.10
10 year renewable-convertible term (premium for first 10 years)	3.65	5.05	10.20
Level-premium term to age 65	7.30	10.60	15.99
Ordinary life	12.64	18.09	27.58
20-payment life	21.48	27.83	36.59
20-year endowment	41.27	42.14	45.54

What $100 in Annual Premiums Buys

	25	35	45
5 year renewable-convertible term (premium for first 5 years)	$30,000	$22,000	$11,000
10 year renewable-convertible term (premium for first 10 years)	30,000	20,000	10,000
Level-premium term to age 65	13,000	10,000	6,000
Ordinary life	8,000	5,500	4,000
20-payment life	5,000	4,000	3,000
20-year endowment	2,500	2,500	2,000

Source: *The Unique Manual.*

It won't be long before you will be able to shop for the best buy in life insurance. Wisconsin and Arkansas already have adopted regulations to require cost disclosure by a standard comparison. Several other states are readying similar rules.

The new rules:

1. Outlaw the calculation of cost based on total premiums that are paid for a policy and that are offset by dividends and cash value accumulated over the life of the policy (a favorite sales pitch to "prove" that your insurance costs you nothing over a period of time).

2. Provide an "interest-adjusted" method of comparing costs of similar policies. This takes into consideration things such as the theoretical cash value at any given time (not just ultimate cash value), anticipated dividends, the alternative investments a policyholder might make with the money involved in the policy, the premiums, and the value of death benefits. Under such a calculation, a policy with a higher premium might prove to be less expensive than a lower-premium one.

3. Establish a formula index that uses a 4% interest rate to calculate the values and costs of each policy at the tenth and twentieth anniversaries. This would eliminate the variations caused when insurers pay dividends at different rates.

Some insurance executives are not happy about this yardstick. They feel that the index is an inadequate measure because it does not take into account such important-to-many-companies factors as conversion benefits, cost when held to maturity, etc. They also argue that the real differences between policies are not as great as would appear by applying the set formula. At any rate, the day is coming when you will have a consistent basis for comparison of costs.

Maybe the best way to consider the cost of life insurance is in terms of buying an automobile. The cheapest model is stripped, but most people are willing to pay extra to get power steering, power brakes, air conditioning, and other add-ons that make driving more comfortable.

To give you an idea of what's ahead, here are the interest-adjusted costs, per $1,000 of face amount of insurance, of some major companies. The base policy is $10,000 whole life issued at ages 25, 35, and 45. *The table should be used ONLY as a frame of reference.*

Interest-Adjusted Costs

Bought by a Man at Age 25

Company	Interest-Adjusted Cost per $1,000 Participating Policy Surrendered at End of	
	10 Years	20 Years
Connecticut Mutual	$ 3.15	$ 2.50
Bankers Life (Iowa)	3.22	2.60
Northwestern Mutual	3.63	2.74
Provident Mutual	3.77	3.21
Massachusetts Mutual	4.25	3.19
Mutual Benefit	4.30	3.39
New York Life	4.84	3.59
Prudential	5.53	4.51
Equitable Life	5.66	4.04
Metropolitan Life	6.34	4.49
John Hancock	6.63	4.94

Company	Nonparticipating Policy Surrendered at End of	
	10 Years	20 Years
Allstate	$3.98	$4.16
Life & Casualty (Tennessee)	4.89	4.13
IDS Life (Minnesota)	4.90	5.22
Travelers	4.91	4.37
National Life & Accident	5.22	4.67
Lincoln National	6.01	5.55
Jefferson Standard	6.24	5.52
Republic National	6.31	4.76
Aetna Life & Casualty	6.32	5.58
Connecticut General	6.46	5.00

Interest Adjusted Costs (*continued*)

Bought by a Man at Age 35

Company	Participating Policy Surrendered at End of 10 Years	20 Years
Bankers Life (Iowa)	$4.35	$4.18
Northwestern Mutual	4.65	4.13
Connecticut Mutual	4.74	4.45
Massachusetts Mutual	5.16	4.72
Provident Mutual	5.30	5.15
Nationwide Life	6.31	5.61
Home Life	6.57	4.54
Occidental Life	6.94	6.58
Franklin Life	7.41	5.80
State Farm	7.45	5.85

Company	Nonparticipating Policy Surrendered at End of 10 Years	20 Years
Allstate	$ 5.76	$ 6.63
IDS Life	6.36	7.48
Life & Casualty (Tennessee)	6.57	6.51
Travelers	6.84	7.05
Occidental Life	6.91	7.34
Southwestern Life	7.28	7.20
Continental Assurance	7.41	7.34
Life of Virginia	7.88	8.17
Business Men's Assurance	8.04	8.36
Liberty National	8.15	8.44

Interest Adjusted Costs (*continued*)

Bought by a Man at Age 45

Company	Participating Policy Surrendered at End of	
	10 Years	20 Years
Bankers Life (Iowa)	$ 8.12	$ 8.53
Northwestern Mutual	8.28	8.49
Connecticut Mutual	8.75	9.03
Provident Mutual	8.98	9.65
National Life	9.06	8.75
Sun Life (Canada)	10.01	9.53
State Mutual of America	10.26	9.92
Penn Mutual	10.45	10.07
Home Life	10.72	8.97
Prudential	12.26	11.70

Company	Nonparticipating Policy Surrendered at End of	
	10 Years	20 Years
Allstate	$ 9.90	$11.85
Life & Casualty	11.07	12.02
IDS Life	11.10	13.32
Republic National	11.39	11.70
Occidental Life	11.71	13.54
Jefferson Standard	11.86	13.11
Franklin Life	12.12	13.06
American National	12.63	13.99
United Benefit	12.77	14.04
Aetna Life & Casualty	13.10	14.03

If you want comparisons on the companies whose policies you are investigating, read *Cost Facts on Life Insurance,* by Price Gaines, Jr., published by The National Underwriters Company, 420 East 4th Street, Cincinnati, Ohio 45202.

Ordinary Life versus Term Life

When you buy ordinary life, you are buying protection *plus* savings. Every premium payment builds greater equity in the form of cash value. This becomes a special reserve fund that can be used as collateral for loans, for emergencies, to pay premiums, or to use in investments. If it's an old policy, that loan may be at a low rate of interest—5% to 8%, depending on your state.

With term insurance, you buy temporary protection. That's why it costs less.

Ordinary policies pay dividends that can be used to buy additional coverage, reduce premiums, or be taken in cash. Over the years, these dividends can reduce the cost so that by retirement time, the cost may be much less than that of comparable term. As the cash value builds up, the net protection decreases.

Here's how two policies of the Philadelphia Life Insurance Company compare:

Age	Face Amount	Cash Value	Ordinary Life Interest on Cash Value— 6%	Pre- mium	Cost Net Protec- tion	Cost per $1,000	Term Cost per $1,000
35	$1,000	$ 0	$ 0 +	$15.71	$15.71	$15.71	$ 4.11
45	1,000	120	7.20 +	15.71	22.91	26.03	7.65
55	1,000	296	17.76 +	15.71	33.47	47.54	16.77
64	1,000	482	28.92 +	15.71	44.63	86.16	25.46

When Buying Insurance

Read the Contract Carefully

Make sure that it's suited to your needs. Will you be able to convert, renew, increase, or decrease coverage? Are you paying for anything you don't need?

Have Your Insurance Agent Explain Any Sections or Phrases You Do Not Understand

Buy Only from Companies Licensed to Sell in Your State

Otherwise, the state insurance department will have no power to act if there are problems. Each state has its own regulations. New York and New Jersey are the toughest.

If You Feel You Have Been Misled Regarding Any Kind of Life Insurance, Write to Your State Insurance Commissioner and the Federal Trade Commission

If You Feel That You Have Been Cheated of What You Were Led to Believe Were Benefits, Consult a Lawyer

You may be able to sue the company under the doctrine of reasonable expectations. That means that if the big print appears to give you a benefit that the fine print takes away, the courts may side with you and help you get all or part of your money back.

Many Types of Term Insurance

Shop just as hard for term life as you do for a regular policy. One of the best ways to get extra coverage, especially for emergencies, is to buy 5-year renewable term. You pay the same premium for 5 years, then pay a higher premium for the next 5 years, etc., up to age 70. You can arrange to have the option to convert to straight life, and the cost is slightly less than that of yearly renewable term:

Age	Premium $100,000 Yearly Renewable	Premium $100,000 5-Year Renewable
30–34	$207–$229	$219
35–39	239–311	270
40–44	338–489	400

Example: Frank Farrell, age 38, has a wife and 2 boys, 20 and 12, and an unexpected new daughter. He realizes the need for extra protection, so he takes out $100,000 in 5-year renewable term. Three years later he finds he has high blood pressure, so he cannot get a straight life policy at a reasonable rate. But all is well—he can continue the term policy until the children are through college, or if he has extra income, he can convert to $100,000 (or a portion thereof) straight life *without a physical exam.*

Note: Some authorities argue that you will make out better by buying all term rather than straight life. According to Professor Joseph Belth of the University of Indiana, if you take the difference between the premiums on the 2 types of policies and invest it at 5%, after taxes, you will have twice as much as the increase in the cash value of your ordinary policy. Maybe so, but much depends on age, income, date of death, etc., and you may not get around to investing that money!

Comparison of Whole Life and Term Insurance

Insurance $25,000, Age 35, Male

With whole life, you have forced savings and increasing cash values that can be used as collateral for loans as needed. The real protection diminishes as the cash value rises—after 20 years, the actual insurance protection is only $15,700 because the balance represents cash value and accumulated dividends.

With term, after 20 years, you have the full $25,000 coverage, but you have to build your own savings by investing the $13,100 representing the difference in premium payments between term and whole life. And you will have to pay taxes on the income and reported gains.

| | Whole Life Participating Policy; Dividends Left to Accumulate at 5% Interest | | | Term Life 5-year Renewable; Premium Difference Invested at 5% Return | | |
| | While You Live, You Have | | Survivors Receive | While You Live, You Have | | Survivors Receive |
Policy Year	Cash Value and Dividends	Insurance Protection*	Death Benefits†	Invested Difference	Insurance Protection	Death Benefits
1	$ 75	$24,975	$25,050	$ 475	$25,000	$25,475
5	2,150	23,300	24,450	2,600	25,000	27,600
10	5,800	20,700	26,500	5,700	25,000	30,700
15	10,100	18,300	28,400	9,200	25,000	34,200
20	15,500	15,700	31,200	13,100	25,000	38,100

Source: *Forbes* magazine.
* Policy amount less cash value.
† includes return of cash value.

Should You Insure Your Wife?

Yes. Every wife, especially when she's a mother, should be covered with a reasonable amount of insurance. The proceeds will help to pay for nonreimbursable costs of her illness, such as wages for a housemaid/cook, baby-sitters, and funeral and estate settlement.

If the children are small when she dies, you'll need to consider some provision for a housekeeper. At $75 a week plus board and room, you will pay out $37,500 plus Social Security and workmen's compensation in 10 years!

To protect your wife, you can buy individual policies, or for less money, get a rider on your own. Under a "family plan" the insurance covers your wife and children for one-fifth of the basic protection on your life and provides the right of conversion for the youngsters when they reach 21.

As a rule of thumb for wife insurance, a $2,500 policy to cover estate expenses, $5,000 for a short illness, $10,000 or more if there are young children.

And of course, if the wife is a career woman and has the right to convert her group coverage, this might be a good idea if the husband is in poor health and near retirement.

Which Policy Should You Drop?

This is a difficult decision, which you must reach on your own. As there are no commissions to be earned, your agent may be helpful but he is not likely to be impartial.

The time to consider dropping insurance is when the need for protection is less—when your house is clear, your children are on their own, and you are looking forward to a smaller income after retirement.

In your working years, hold on to as much insurance as you can, as long as you can. Your premiums on new coverage will be higher and the terms less beneficial. Use dividends and the automatic loan privilege to keep policies in force even if it means depleting the cash values. *You owe it to your family!*

If things get really rough and you cannot continue to pay premiums, review every policy to determine which has the greatest coverage for the least outlay and then consider your needs for protection:

Risk Exposure

(1) How much insurance must you have to protect your wife and raise your children? (2) What will happen if you live beyond your actuarial age and outlast your retirement savings?

In both cases, there are very few situations where you can settle for less than $100,000 if you are married, $50,000 if you are single.

Investment Portfolio

Do you have enough assets that can be readily liquidated to pay your debts and provide a minimum income? If you decide that $100,000 will be enough to get by on and have your net worth of $150,000 now, you can afford to drop $50,000 in insurance.

Consult your insurance agent before you order any cancellations. *Turning a policy in for its cash value is seldom the best answer*. In most cases, your need for life insurance changes slowly. Your agent may be able to suggest shifts that will reduce your costs but not seriously erode your protection. *BUT BE CAREFUL HE DOES NOT WANT YOU TO DROP AN OLD POLICY AND BUY A NEW ONE*. There are many ways to meet your goals, such as:

Extended Term Insurance

This permits you to stop paying premiums and use the cash value in the policy to buy term insurance as long as the money holds out. At age 65, a $10,000 straight life policy, bought at age 40, has a cash value of about $5,000. This is enough to buy $10,000 term for 12 years—almost as long as you can expect to live.

This might be a good idea if you still have children in school. *The risk:* You will live beyond age 77, so be careful if you come from a long-lived family.

Paid-up Insurance

Use the cash value to buy a smaller amount of paid-up insurance. There will be no more premiums. With that $10,000 policy, the cash values should be enough to buy $6,800 paid-up insurance. You will be protected for life and in an emergency can always borrow several thousand dollars.

Minimum-Deposit Insurance

This also stops the cash outlay for premiums. You use the dividends, plus a loan from the cash value, to pay annual premiums on the old policy.

Thus, if the annual premium on that $10,000 protection was $270 and the dividends averaged $150, you would borrow $120 from the accumulated cash value. The interest would be tax-deductible. If you died at the end of 10 years, your heirs would still get $8,800.

Minimum-deposit insurance can also be used in an overall insurance program, but it takes a long time—10 to 15 years—for the difference between term and minimum-deposit insurance to benefit the policyholder. And to qualify for tax deductions on interest costs, a new policyholder must put up 4 of the first 7 years' premiums in cash. Thus, for a 25-year-old the entry fee would be as much as $8,000 on a $100,000 policy—just at an age when he probably needs every dollar he can put his hands on. Minimum-deposit makes more sense when you are in your mid-40s and can put in money borrowed from the cash values. But in both cases the savings of MDI can be welcome and possibly substantial.

When you use MDI, you are, in effect, borrowing from yourself and freeing the premium payments for other, more profitable investments. The decision requires projections of the costs of both MDI and term insurance, the anticipated yield on alternative investments, and the tax bracket of the policy owner. If you are in a low tax bracket (25%) and get 12% on your money, it's much more profitable to buy term than MDI at age 25; it's a stand-off when you are 35 and in a 45% tax bracket, and it's a losing proposition at age 45 in the 35% tax bracket. If you are willing to use the leverage of borrowing, MDI can be a tool for providing family protection and funds for business investments.

In most cases, however, MDI becomes important at age 50. This is the time when people want to cut down on premium payments and still provide family protection. As a rough rule, the higher your tax bracket, the greater the advantage of MDI over ordinary life and—to a large extent—over term.

To Determine if Minimum-Deposit Insurance Is Worthwhile
Age 50, $100,000 Straight Life (New England Mutual), 42% Tax Bracket

1. Present cash value of policy	$26,474
2. Annual premium	2,280
3. Premiums to pay by age 65—15 years × $2,280	34,200
4. Total interest to retirement—$2,280 × factor of 9.7 (Guide to Interest Costs and Investment Growth)	22,116
5. Tax savings on interest—$22,116 × 42%	9,289
6. After-tax interest cost to retirement—$22,116 − $9,289	12,827
7. Cash value at retirement*	54,738
8. Net cash position at retirement—$54,738 − total of lines 3 and 6	7,711
9. Value of invested premiums—$2,280 × growth factor of 26.9 (Guide to Interest Costs and Investment Growth)	61,332
10. Total return—$7,711 + $61,332	69,043
11. Cash advantage of MDI—$69,043 − $54,738	14,305

* Plus any dividends not used for the purchase of one-year term and terminal dividends. Based on after-tax rate of 7% for 15 years.

Guide to Interest Costs and Investment Growth

This table provides a shortcut to find out how much you will pay for money borrowed to pay premiums on your policy. Once you know the interest cost, find the number of years to retirement and multiply the annual premium by the factor in the table.

Annual Interest	Number of Years to Retirement			
	10	15	20	25
5%	3.2	7.7	14.7	25.1
6%	4.0	9.7	19.0	33.2

Annual Growth Rate				
6%	14.0	24.7	39.0	58.2
7%	14.8	26.9	43.9	67.7
8%	15.6	29.3	49.4	79.0

Drop Cash Value or Term?

If you own both a cash value and a term policy, drop the term and consider converting the cash value of the straight life to MDI.

If you own 2 equal-face-value policies taken out at different ages, drop or cash in the newer one.

If you own 2 policies taken out at the same age, one with a mutual and one with a stock company, cash in the stock policy if it is over 10 years old, the mutual one if it's under 10 years old.

Be Wary of "Trade-ins"

Life insurance policies grow better with age. The policy you own will almost always be the best buy. Just because the new policy is described so enthusiastically by the agent does not mean that it is necessarily better.

Once in a while it may be wise to trade in, but in most cases such a switch is likely to be offered by "twisters," sharp salesmen who are not above misrepresentation or misleading policy comparisons. They want to sell a new policy because they can make a sizable commission.

A trade-in can be expensive: (1) You will pay for two acquisition costs and end up with one policy. (2) It will be several years before the dividends on the new policy equal those of the old. (3) The cash value of the new one is less. (4) You may not pass the new physical exam. (5) You will have to wait 2 years before the policy passes the contestable period (the time insurance companies generally give themselves to void a policy because of a policyholder's misstatements in the application).

Advice: Submit the proposal for the trade-in to your present insurance company for comments.

What to Do if You Can't Get Regular Life Insurance

If you are told you are uninsurable, don't despair. There are many ways you can provide the protection your family needs. According to the Institute of Life Insurance, only 3% of the population is uninsurable.

You may have to search for an agent who has special knowledge and contacts, and you may have to bother the home office of some insurance companies, but insurance is available for almost anyone who can still walk around—at a price: +10% for mild defects, up to +100% for more serious impairments.

For a 35-year-old man, an ulcer could boost the premium per $1,000 coverage about $17; for hypertension, +$100; for overweight, +$170.

Before you panic, check your present policies to see if:

1. There are guaranteed insurability clauses permitting you to take out additional insurance at standard rates.

2. Your long-term policy has a conversion privilege that permits you to switch to straight life without a medical exam. You may not get more coverage, but you will extend the time.

3. Your participating policy includes an option to buy additional coverage regardless of health. Usually, dividends can be used to buy (1) small, paid-up, cash-value policies without a physical exam or (2) one-year nonmedical term insurance up to the amount of the cash value of your ordinary policy. By using both of these benefits, you may be able to boost coverage by as much as 50%.

If if appears that you cannot get the extras you need from your present policies, ask your agent to query the home office for an opinion. The company is likely to be more scientific than the agent. It may offer a policy at a higher-rating classification. This can be expensive, as the premiums will probably keep going up with the increase in cash value or dividends. *But your family will be protected.*

Example: A 45-year-old man with high blood pressure obtained $10,000 ordinary life for a $320 premium, $120 above the regular cost. The company also offered a chance to recover all extra charges by means of a rider in the form of an endowment to start at age 65 with a level, standard premium.

Caution: If you are worried about impairment, consider having your application accepted on a nonmedical basis. Withholding information or knowingly making false answers on a medical questionnaire constitutes civil fraud. This can be grounds for terminating the policy in the first 2 or 3 years, or sometimes even a civil suit.

Here's how your chances rate:

Heart Disease

Delay your application until 6 months after the attack (longer if you were hit with a coronary thrombosis or coronary occlusion). There's a good chance if your weight, blood pressure, etc., are OK.

Cancer

Each case is treated individually. Usually, there must be 3 to 5 years with no further symptoms. Skin cancer is no problem, but lung cancer, breast cancer, in women, etc., may require a 5-year clean record.

Diabetes

If the diabetes is controlled by diet or insulin, coverage is readily available at extra rates. Only 1 in 100 diabetics fails to live the normal life span.

Psychiatric Conditions

With mild cases, standard rates; with severe conditions, higher rates are frequently reduced if improvement continues.

No Questions Asked

When you have exhausted other channels, ask your agent about "guaranteed-insurability" insurance. This is regular whole life that is available regardless of your job, health, or hobby (but sometimes only when you have reached a certain age, 45 to 55). There are no physicals and no questions asked. You just put up the money—usually about twice as much as you'd pay for comparable conventional policies.

Example: Kemper Life Insurance Company will insure almost anyone, anytime, up to $10,000, without a medical exam. For a 45-year-old man, the cost is $38.50 per $1,000 (versus the usual $26 to $28), up to $100,000 if you have been employed at least 30 hours a week for the past 6 months. This policy doesn't pay off for 6 years, but there are partial proceeds if you die from sickness or disease—in the first year 5%, fourth year 50%, etc.

Other companies offer special policies with constant premiums, no cancellation, and a maturation period of 2 to 3 years. Or you have the option to buy additional insurance, up to a maximum amount, for an extra premium, at intervals of 3 years.

Rates vary widely, so shop around. Get a complete physical, an "attending physician's statement" on your health, and have your agent check several firms that concentrate on unusual risks.

What to Do if You Are Already Paying Extra Rates

When the conditions that caused the higher premiums have eased or disappeared, you may be able to get a better deal by:

Asking for Reclassification

Ratings cannot be raised once a policy is written, but they can be lowered if the current medical situation warrants—e.g., cured cancer victims can qualify for normal premiums.

Checking Standard Policies of Other Companies

See if their criteria are less restrictive.

Consulting Your Physician

Learn if his treatment has improved your health sufficiently to meet insurance standards.

Discussing with Your Employer the Possibility of Switching from Your Present High-Risk Job to a Safer One with Minimal Hazards and Exposure

Don't Neglect Indirect Insurance Coverage

If you can't get insurance directly, try one of these indirect routes. The policies may be smaller and the costs higher, but you may be able to get all the coverage you really need. And in some cases you can get extra benefits from the services that are covered by the insurance.

Group Insurance

If this is offered by your employer, fraternal organization, trade union, professional association, etc., you may be able to buy extra coverage with the provision of conversion to an individual policy when you retire or leave, while qualifying for new coverage with a new employer.

Savings Accounts

Savings accounts often provide insurance up to $2,500 to depositors under 60 years of age. You pay for it by accepting a lower rate of interest.

Credit Unions

These usually cover loans with insurance (maximum $10,000). By investing the borrowed money, you can minimize the cost of the coverage.

Installment Loans

Such loans often carry decreasing credit life insurance. There's no requirement for insurability. Buy all you can on time if you need that extra protection.

Mortgage Insurance

This can be purchased through group mortgage-redemption plans that pay off the balance at your death.

Mutual-Fund Shares

When purchased on the installment plan, mutual-fund shares can be covered by term insurance. Most funds provide this without a physical exam to investors under age 55 and with a total investment of less than $18,000.

Increase Insurance on Your Wife

In case of death in a common disaster, your children will be protected.

Special Policies for Special Purposes

One of the most intriguing special insurance policies is split life insurance (SLI). It permits you to buy, at the same time, retirement benefits for yourself and insurance protection for your family.

SLI is a combination of an annuity and term insurance put together so loosely that neither need protect the same person nor even be owned by the same person. Your purchase of ordinary life includes a potential annuity in its cash values and what is, in effect, a decreasing term policy. *This is a package deal and cannot be separated.* It's especially valuable with small personal pension funds set up under the Keogh Plan.

For every $1 you put up for an annuity, you can buy $100 of renewable term insurance. Thus, $1,000 used to buy an annuity permits you to buy $100,000 term at a very low rate—in early years.

Example: You are 40 years old, in the 42% tax bracket, and a partner in a small business. You have a Keogh Plan for retirement. This year, instead of investing all of your $7,500 contribution, you use $2,500 to buy an SLI annuity that pays $550 a month at age 65. Then you pay an extra $245 to acquire a $100,000 5-year renewable term policy payable to your wife.

The premium for the annuity will remain the same; that of the term policy will increase with age. If it gets too high, you can drop part of the coverage, as probably your family needs will grow less.

You retire at 65 after selling your share of the business to your younger partner for $50,000—$5,000 down and $5,000 annually for 9 years. You use the cash to buy an extended SLI annuity and a decreasing term policy on your partner's life. This protects your investment, and should the partner die, it relieves the business of possibly harmful pressure.

There are drawbacks: (1) In relation to conventional annuities, SLI has a relatively small cash value. (2) At death, the taxes will be high because of the excess of the death benefits (the cash value) of the retirement annuity over the net premiums paid as ordinary income.

That is, suppose that at the end of 10 years premium payments (even when made through a personal pension plan) totaled $2,500 to provide a death benefit of $36,790. The difference, $11,790, would be taxable as regular income at the rate prevailing at time of death.

On the other hand, this is offset by the fact that the proceeds of the term insurance would be tax-free. Thus, the total death benefit of $125,000 ($136,790 − $11,790) would be greater than the proceeds of an ordinary $100,000 straight life policy, which would have cost more money.

These SLI policies are subject to close scrutiny by the IRS, so be careful to ask your agent to have the proposal checked by the home office of the insurance company. If you own the annuity and your wife owns the term, your estate will have no tax liability. But unless the terms of the purchase and the beneficiary are carefully spelled out, the IRS might argue that since both parts of SLI are interdependent, you have an interest in both policies, and thus your estate might be liable for more taxes—on the difference between the premiums paid and the cash value of the policy.

SLI has a definite cost edge over ordinary life in many situations. If you like the SLI idea, keep your present policies and buy SLI as added protection.

Ask Your Employer about Split-Dollar Insurance

If you work for a corporation that provides extra benefits to its executives, ask the boss about split-dollar insurance (SDI). This provides a way for corporations to assist their key personnel by splitting the cost of the premiums. Unlike pension and profit-sharing plans, which must be inclusive, SDI can be handled on a selective basis.

Split-Dollar Plan

Year	$100,000 Ordinary Life Policy		Split-Dollar Plan	Annual Premium $2,350		Employee's Death Benefit
	Dividend	Net Premium (Annual Premium Less Dividend)	Cash Value	Increase in Cash Value (Employer Pays)	Net Premium Less Employer's Contribution (Employee Pays)	
1	$ 185	$ 2,165	$ 225	$ 225	$1,940	$99,775
2	250	2,100	2,050	1,825	275	97,950
3	315	2,035	3,900	1,850	185	96,100
4	385	1,965	5,775	1,875	90	94,225
5	445	1,905	7,680	1,905	0	92,320
11–20*	12,600	36,200	37,000	33,300	2,490	63,000

* The sum of the 20-year dividends minus the net premiums for the first 20 years.
Source: *Business Monthly*.

Every permanent life insurance policy has two aspects—cash value and death benefit. With SDI, the corporation pays that portion of each annual premium which represents the increase in cash value, while you pay the rest.

There are two beneficiaries—the corporation for an amount equal to the cash value of the policy at the time of your death, and your widow (or children) for the remainder.

Example: A $100,000 SDI for a 36-year-old executive. In year 1 the employer pays $225, the cash value; the executive pays $1,940 (you might be able to borrow this from the company). In year 2 the company pays $1,825; you pay $275; etc. From year 5 on, the companys pays the entire premium of $1,905.

At your death, the company receives an amount equal to the cash value—$225 in the first year to $37,000 by the twentieth year. Your widow or heirs get the balance of the $100,000. *Result:* You get far more insurance than you could afford; the employer is sure of getting back whatever was spent on the policy whether the executive lives, dies, quits, or retires.

This arrangement qualifies under Section 101 of the IRS Code; the company's financial position is unchanged because all contributions remain as assets, and the cash value may be used as collateral for a loan or used to fund a retirement plan.

There are some tax responsibilities: During the executive's life he must pay regular income taxes on an amount equal to the cost of one year's term insurance, at his current age, for the net amount of insurance coverage he has. This amount is reduced, under IRS Ruling 64–328, by whatever premium the executive pays. Thus, the cost comes to no more than a few hundred dollars a year of taxable income—all for $100,000 extra insurance that decreases to $63,000 in 20 years.

Beware of Mail-Order Insurance

There have been so many misleading (if not fraudulent) offers by mail-order insurance companies that the Federal Trade Commission has issued a warning booklet. If you receive what appears to be an actual insurance policy with your name on it, remember that this is a form of advertising. *It is not a valid policy.*

With mail-order insurance, never sign anything until you have checked with the state insurance commissioner to see if the insurance company is licensed to do business in your state. The low rates and touted benefits may be worthless unless you can get help from a governmental agency.

Be equally cautious if the policy comes in an envelope similar to the brown one used by the U.S. government to mail out VA checks and the letter starts out with "Dear Veteran." The same warning goes for "Special Armed Forces Policy" if your son or daughter is in service, and for many accident, health, and Medicare policies.

It sounds great to read: "For hospital care, $5,000; for death natural causes, $10,000," until you read the fine print to find that the payment for hospital care does not exceed $500 for one person and that each death benefit is limited to $2,000!

Never buy mail-order insurance unless it comes from a reliable, well-known insurance company that is licensed to do business in your state.

Found Money in Insurance

When you have to borrow money, take a good look at your insurance policies (including National Service Life). Many older ordinary life policies permit loans against the built-up cash values at low interest rates, usually 5%, occasionally up to 8%. That's a lot less than you have to pay a bank, finance company, or broker.

The disadvantage, of course, is that there's no required repayment schedule, so it's easy to let the loan run and just pay the annual interest.

The money can be used to pay for a new car, appliance, tuition, down payment on a house, etc., but it's better to use it for investments:

To Pay Up a Policy

Do this so that there will be no more premiums—only the small interest charges.

Example: At age 50, Professor Grey notices that the $100,000 straight life policy for which he has been shelling out $2,000 a year has a cash value of $26,000. He borrows the money and pays the policy in full. *He will never have another premium to pay.* At 5%, his annual cost is $1,300—a net savings of $700 a year. And the interest is tax-deductible.

This does reduce the face value of the policy to $74,000, but if he feels he should plug the gap for a few years, he can buy one-year term insurance for about $9 per $1,000. With most companies, there's no need for a physical exam. All he has to do is sign a statement that his health has not deteriorated in any signficant respect since he took out the original policy.

To Set Up Small Trusts for Children

The cost of the loan is small, and as outlined in another chapter, the income will be tax-exempt until the children start paying their own income taxes.

To Invest in Securities

Invest in bonds or quality common stocks that yield 9% to 10%. Since the interest on the loan is only 5%, there's a free ride of 4% to 5%. If the value of the securities increases, there will be the additional benefit of capital gains.

In setting up your financial program, there is no better base than life insurance. When you are newly married or have small children, it's essential for family protection; as you grow older, it can be used to help start a business, buy a house, or educate your children; at retirement, it can provide the extra income needed to supplement Social Security. BUY AND KEEP LIFE INSURANCE, but do it wisely, carefully, and selectively. Straight life policies are basic, but term life and combination-variations can be useful in many situations. Find an alert agent, deal with reputable insurance companies, and always try to get the most for your money—protection first, then cost.

XVII

What to Look for in Health Insurance

These days, the way medical costs are rising, most people get a relapse when they receive a bill from their physician or hospital. Even the best health insurance policy won't pay all of your costs, but some coverage is essential if you want to protect your family against the heavy toll of ordinary illness and the horrendous expenses of major sickness. The passage of some form of national health insurance will be helpful, but for most people such mandated protection will be a base, not a total answer.

Use the information in this chapter to plan your health insurance as one of the most essential of all family protections.

The problem with health insurance is that it provides good coverage against the large expenses that may not happen, but it is least effective against the smaller costs that are almost sure to be incurred. Perhaps this is as it should be in a free-enterprise society. With 9 months to save, most people can pay for the expense of childbirth. What they need is insurance against the very high bills of after-birth complications.

As this is written, health insurance is available through 2 major channels—health maintenance organizations (HMOs) and group and individual health insurance policies.

HMOs require advance payments of fees: quarterly, from

about $60 for a single person to $175 for a family of 3—about the same cost as a broad health insurance policy.

HMOs are prepaid group-practice plans that try to catch health problems before they can develop into major illnesses requiring hospitalization. There are 2 types: (1) Where physicians work at a single center that either owns or works with a hospital. This type is usually less expensive than (2) individual-practice foundations where doctors work in their own offices and are paid on a fee-for-service basis. In both cases, the premium payments cover normal medical, surgical, and hospital charges, some of the expenses of prescription drugs, and—often—up to 50% of certain types of other health care such as dental treatment.

These prepaid medical plans have had varied success. The oldest and most widely used plans are on the West Coast—through Kaiser Hospitals, Ross-Luce, and Puget Sound Health Cooperative. In recent years, with financial encouragement from the U.S. Department of Health, Education and Welfare, HMOs have been started across the country. As most of these new organizations are in urban areas, only about 20% of the population has ready access to them. But this may change under new federal health-care legislation.

If you have the opportunity to join an HMO (through your union, company, or neighborhood center), check these points:

Coverage

How much of your expenses will be paid for in dollars, in number of days, after deductibles?

Will the same benefits hold if you are taken ill outside your HMO area?

Number of Physicians

If there are more than 1,000 patients per MD, you may face a long wait for service.

Certified Physicians

The doctor must be on the staff of or have staff privileges at a hospital to get you institutional care.

Copayment Schedule

Is there provision for extra service for an added fee? Will $2 or $3 more provide house calls or permit clinic visits? (This surcharge is necessary to discourage hypochondriacs.)

Well-Defined Grievance Procedures

Can you appeal to higher authorities if foulups occur?

Participation in Management

Will you have the right to elect one or more members of the governing body and also have something to say about the operations of the program?

Maternity Care

Is this available? Does it require an extra fee?

Special-Needs Coverage

Is it possible to look for financial help (usually 50%) for the costs of more-than-routine dental care? Or mental health? (Perhaps 100 days with a 20% deductible?)

Types of Health Insurance Policies

Most health insurance is bought through group plans, but you can buy individual policies as substitutes or supplements.

As a starter, consider that medical expenses can be classified in 4 groups: minor expenses, hospital charges, major medical insurance, and catastrophic insurance.

Minor Expenses

These include the $10 per visit to your physician, the cost of prescription drugs, etc. These are partially covered by some health insurance policies, but generally, they should be considered normal living expenses.

Hospital Charges

These include surgeon's bills, room and board, consultants, etc. These costs are usually covered by package plans such as Blue Cross for hospital expenses, Blue Shield for surgical and medical bills.

Typically you pay, each year, the costs of the first $60 to $100, then 20% of the balance. The insurer picks up the balance according to predetermined fee schedules. If charges are above these limits, you're responsible.

Advice: Try to get this protection through group plans. Individual policies provide lower coverage, have longer waiting periods, and cost at least 15% more.

If you are young and healthy, a commercial insurance company may be cheaper. As you grow older, the Blue Cross and Blue Shield coverage may become increasingly attractive because of the high 93% average loss ratio (the percentage of premiums paid out in benefits).

For people over 65 years of age, the basic policy is Medicare, which has become an integral part of Social Security. The monthly cost of $6.70 is deducted from your Social Security check if you receive one regularly. If you continue to work intermittently and draw Social Security only occasionally, you are billed quarterly.

PART A. For hospital costs. This picks up most of the tab for the first 60 days in a hospital *after* you pay the first $92. For the sixty-first through ninetieth days, you pay $23 per day; for the next 60 days, $46 a day.

For bills in a skilled nursing facility, you pay $11.50 a day for the twenty-first through one-hundredth days.

Part A coverage does not include such costs as doctors' bills, private-duty nurse, custodial care, etc.

PART B. For medical expenses. This pays 80% of "reasonable charges" after you pay the first $60. There are exceptions—drugs, medicine outside the hospital, routine physical exams, glasses, false teeth, and similar peripheral costs.

EVERYONE NEEDS HEALTH INSURANCE TO SUPPLEMENT MEDICARE!

Just because you are 65 and can count on Medicare does not mean that you can skip health insurance. There are many expenses—the deductibles, over-the-limit costs of hospital care, physicians' fees, and long-term nursing-home care—that are not fully paid by Medicare.

Most insurers permit you to continue their regular group policy protection (at higher premiums) after you retire at age 65, but if this is not available or adequate, you can buy special policies from the Colonial Penn Group through the American Association of Retired People, 215 Long Beach Boulevard, Long Beach, California 90801. Cost: about $115 per year.

Major Medical Insurance (MMI)

This helps to cover the high costs of major surgery and recuperation. Premiums depend on age, health, and deductibles. Your best buy is through group coverage from your employer, union, or trade or professional association. Individual policies may seem expensive, but they can be very valuable, especially when you consider that the odds are high that you, or your wife, will suffer some sort of prolonged illness.

Most MMIs have a $500 or $1,000 deductible, then pick up 80% of the balance. Costs range from about $50 to $250 a year—more if you select first-dollar coverage or a low deductible.

If your employer does not provide or make available a group health insurance plan, get an MMI policy where the deductible starts just above the coverage you get from your basic hospitalization.

Medicare Benefit Summary

	Hospital Care (Part A)			Surgical and Medical Care (Part B)	
	In-Patient Hospital Services	Extended-Care Facility Services	Home Health Care	Physician's Care	Other Medical Expenses
Covered Expenses Include	Semi-private room and board, routine nursing care, operating and recovery rooms, anesthesia, diagnostic x-rays, laboratory tests, oxygen, drugs, dressings, physical therapy, x-ray and radioactive treatments, blood transfusions.* Physician's charges for radiology and pathology.	Room and board, routine nursing care, drugs, physical, occupational and speech therapy. Confinement must follow 3 days of in-hospital care, start within 2 weeks of discharge from hospital.	Home visits by nurses or therapists for physical, occupational and speech therapy, medical supplies (not drugs) and appliances. Must be ordered by physician within 2 weeks of discharge from hospital or 3 days from extended-care facility.	Services of surgeons, anesthetists, pathologists, radiologists, podiatrists, physiotherapists. Psychiatric care. Charges in home, hospital or office. Costs of radiology and pathology (x-ray and lab) during hospital confinement.	X-rays and lab exams, x-ray and radioactive treatment, surgical dressings, rental of iron lung, ambulance service, prosthetic devices, blood transfusions.* Up to 100 home-care visits in addition to those allowed under Part A without requirement of prior hospital confinement. Hospital out-patient emergency treatment, surgical treatment and diagnostic services.
The Out-of-Pocket Deductible	$92 per benefit period.	None	None	$60 combined per calendar year for all eligible expenses.	
Then Medicare Provides	Reasonable costs during first 60 days per benefit period. Then, all but $23 daily for next 30 days, then $46 daily —with lifetime reserve of 60 days.	Full coverage of all reasonable costs during first 20 days of confinement per benefit period. Then coverage of all but $11.50 per day for the next 30 days per benefit period.	Full coverage up to 100 visits per benefit period.	80% of reasonable charges. Full coverage for home-care visits.	

The Individual Co-insures	$23 per day for sixty-first through nine-tieth day of hospital confinement; $46 per day during 60-day lifetime reserve.	$11.50 per day for twenty-first thru one hundredth day of confinement in extended-care facility.	No co-insurance.	20% No co-insurance for home visits.
Limitations	In-patient care in mental hospitals: lifetime maximum of 190 days. With a private room, individual pays the difference from semi-private room rate, except when private room medically necessary.	None, if care is in an approved extended-care facility, *but no custodial care.*		Out-patient psychiatric care limited to 50% of the cost and maximum of $250 per calendar year.
Expenses Not Covered	Private-duty nursing care. Hospital charges for confinement beyond 90 days per benefit period after exhaustion of 60-day lifetime reserve.	Private-duty nursing care. Care in a TB or mental sanatorium or rest home. Extended-care facility charges for confinement beyond 100 days per benefit period.	Private-duty nursing care. Cost of home visits above 100 per benefit period.	Physical checkups, immunizations, cosmetic surgery, dental care, examinations for eyeglasses and hearing aids, routine foot care. Drugs. Private-duty nursing care. Eyeglasses, hearing aids.

* Except the first three pints of blood per benefit period.
Source: The Prudential Insurance Company.

Even if it costs a bit more, try to get a policy that will continue after age 65—for both you and your spouse. This will probably be limited to treatment in the United States, Canada, Guam, and Puerto Rico. So if you plan to retire to sunny Spain, better make other arrangements.

If it is not possible to convert from a group to an individual policy at retirement, consider buying a $100,000 policy at age 64. This will cost only $52 a year IF you agree to assume the first $10,000 in expenses yourself. This sounds like a lot of money, but long illnesses can be financially debilitating—as you probably know from your own family experience.

Whatever plan you buy, be sure that there's a cutoff point— $1,000 or $5,000 while you are working, or as mentioned, $10,000 after retirement. Up to that point you pay all or, with coinsurance, part. From then on, the company pays everything.

Checkpoints for Major Medical Insurance

Provision	Desirable Coverage
Renewability	Guaranteed renewable to age 65, then convertible to the Medicare supplement
Preferred benefits	$100,000 for each member of the family
Deductibles	Family expenses for unrelated illnesses or accidents combined to meet $750 deductible
Coinsurance	20% to 25% for your share with cutoff of $5,000; thereafter, insurer pays 100%
Changes in coverage	No reductions in benefits
Hospital expense limit	If there is a limit, keep it as high as daily semiprivate room charges in your area
Intensive and cardiac care	Fully covered
Private nursing care	Limited, but for both in and out of hospital where physician specifies
Psychiatric care	50% of total bills with $10,000 limit
Convalescent-home care	60 to 120 days—preferably to half of the daily hospital limit
Blood and plasma; prosthetics	Fully covered

Catastrophic Insurance

This starts where MMI leaves off. It is designed to pay for MAJOR bills for heart surgery, prolonged mental illness, cancer treatments, etc. Policies with maximums of $50,000 to $60,000 cost from $70 to $175 a year, depending on deductibles and payments made for hospital rooms, etc.

Such policies can be important if there's a better-than-average chance that someone in your family may be a victim. Unfortunately, such tragedies usually strike before the insurance is purchased.

How to Find a Sound Company

With more than 2,000 health insurance companies to choose from (and many of them unfamiliar), it's important to have some standards by which to judge insurers who offer adequate coverage, assurance of payment, and reasonable rates.

One important key is the *loss ratio*—the percentage of premiums that a company pays back to its policyholders in benefits. A high loss ratio means that you have a better chance to get more money for illness. A company with a loss ratio of 65, for example, will give your family almost double the protection of one with a 30% return.

Annual Premium	X Loss Ratio	= Average Benefits to Policyholders
$500	95%	$475
500	65	325
500	50	250
500	30	150

But do not choose a company only because it reports a favorable loss ratio. A new insurance firm will have a low loss ratio because the policyholders have had little time to get sick and file claims. An overly high payout, on the other hand, may mean that the company is flirting with bankruptcy—as befalls nearly 1 of every 10 health insurance companies each year!

Here's how *Best's Insurance Reports* rated some health insurance companies in 1972:

Company	Earned Premiums in $ Millions	Loss Ratio	Financial Stability
American National	14	76.3	4
Equitable Life	17	68.5	4
Physicians Mutual	60	65.6	2
Metropolitan Life	84	62.1	4
American Republic	37	60.1	3
National Liberty Life	16	60.0	0
New York Life	34	59.2	4
Beneficial Standard Life	20	58.9	1
Mutual of Omaha	127	56.9	4
Union Bankers	17	55.6	1

0 = No Recommendation, 1 = Fair, 2 = Good, 3 = Very Good, 4 = Excellent.
Source: Pennsylvania Insurance Commission.
For detailed information on loss ratios, send $1.50 to the Research Institute for Quality Health Plans, 1611 Foster Street, Lake Charles, Louisiana 70601.

The most important considerations are knowledge of what benefits you are paying for and the limits of coverage. Most policies work on a dollar basis ($40 a day for hospital care, $150 for an appendectomy, etc.), but some use percentages of the total bill or—with MMI—limit payments to 4% or 10% of family income.

Checkpoints in Buying Health Insurance

Never Buy Dread-Disease Policies

Do not buy such policies for cancer, spinal meningitis, leukemia, polio, etc. *This is gambling, not insurance.* The odds against your collecting are enormous.

Never Buy from a Company with a Loss Ratio That Is Consistently Below 50%

Look for Comprehensive Coverage

Look for coverage that will provide benefits for the illnesses that are most common and likely to strike your family.

Buy Noncancellable and/or Renewable Insurance

Otherwise, one major claim could mean cancellation.

Be Wary of Policies That Pay Cash When Someone Is Hospitalized

At best, they are marginally worthwhile. At worst, the costs are high, and if you pay over many years, you will have to be sick a long, long while to come out even. That's not the purpose of insurance!

If You Plan to Shift to Another Company, Don't Drop Your Old Policy until after the Waiting Period of the New One

Deal Only with Companies Licensed to Do Business in Your State

And if you want to be doubly sure, deal only with companies authorized to operate in New York and New Jersey.

Read the Policy Carefully and Review the Definitions of Benefits and Exclusions

In *A Shopper's Guide to Health Insurance,* Pennsylvania Insurance Commissioner Herbert S. Denenberg cited these examples of comparative definitions:

Sickness

More liberal: "Sickness, whenever used in this policy, means a sickness or disease first *manifested* after the effective date of this policy."

That's a lot safer than this *less liberal* definition: "sickness . . . contracted and commencing after policy has been in force not less than 30 days."

Under the first policy, you would be denied benefits only if you knew you had symptoms when you signed up. Under the second, you would get no benefits whether or not you knew you had symptoms.

Injury

More liberal: "Injury means accidental bodily injury sustained while this policy is in force."

Less liberal: "Injury . . . means bodily injury sustained directly and independently of all other causes."

The reluctant-to-pay company would use the second phrase to prove that the accident resulted from other causes, such as your poor medical condition.

Renewable

More liberal: "This policy may be renewed (by the policyholder) for any specified term by the payment . . . of the renewal premium for such term."

Less liberal: "Policy renewable [only] at the option of the company."

When You Leave a Group Plan

If you retire, quit, or are fired, see if it is possible to convert to an individual policy without penalty for preexisting illness. You will have to pay a substantial premium but not as much as if you had started anew.

Always Tell the Truth on the Application

If you neglect to mention a serious illness and get another attack, there may be no benefits. Chances are that if the illness has not recurred for several years, you can get an OK—at a higher premium.

Don't Be Surprised at Differences in Premiums When You Move

Where you live is important. With Prudential, for example, health insurance for a 35-year-old man with a 35-year-old wife and 2 young children is $602.60 a year in St. Louis. In Los Angeles, it costs 35% more; in Peoria, 15% less.

How to Analyze Your Health Insurance Policy

In choosing a specific policy, follow the same general guidelines suggested for other types of insurance—broad benefits, reasonable costs, renewability, financial stability of the issuing company, and prompt service from the agent. Specifically, examine:

Coverage

The higher, the better. It costs only about $5 a year to boost a $50,000 lifetime limit to $250,000.

A lifetime maximum may be OK for the whole family, but there should be at least a $10,000 (and preferably a $20,000) maximum for each separate illness of each member of the family.

Check the exceptions to see if they appear reasonable and not likely to apply to your family—e.g., limitations due to mental illness or to behavioral changes from side effects of drugs.

Exclusions

The fewer, the better. There should be no objection to eliminating coverage for injuries sustained at work, as these should be handled by workmen's compensation. Or for a 6-month waiting period for special conditions that people may neglect until they get insurance—hernia, enlarged tonsils, etc.

But if there are no payments for hospital treatment of mental illnesses or drug addiction or for convalescent care when prescribed by a physician, keep shopping.

Deductibles

The higher the deductible, the lower the premium. But with health insurance, these can be tricky because, unlike deductibles for home insurance which disappear after you fulfill them, they can return. The deductible can start to apply again if the illness persists.

Choose policies that provide a long accumulation period against which deductibles can be taken. A $100 deductible over 3 months is not good. If you had $90 worth of bills in the first quarter, then $105 in the next 3 months, you would collect only $5 overall!

With a $500 deductible, look for at least 6 months for accumulation; with a $1,000 exclusion, don't settle for less than 1 year!

Make sure that the policy covers ALL family bills. The more people and the more illnesses that qualify, the easier it is to move above the deductible minimum. Some companies, such as Prudential, have a per-person deductible, but when 2 members of the family reach their deductibles, no one else has to do so.

Limits

Most policies set a ceiling on individual items the company will pay—$50 for a semiprivate hospital room, $1,500 per operation, etc.

Or when the total runs high, they may pay on a coinsured basis—you pick up 20%, the company pays the balance. Or up to a certain figure, say $1,000, costs may be split, but thereafter the insurer pays everything. You will have a tough time trying to compare different policies when you get into these mathematical probabilities, so it's best to continue to look at policies that seem to give the purchaser a fair deal.

Beware of fixed limits. The insurer prefers these, as his payments won't keep pace with inflation, plus the fact that what's fair in Oshkosh may be far too little in Boston.

New York State, which has strict standards for health insurance, requires minimum payments—$100 of surgeon's fees for an appendectomy, $150 for a hysterectomy, etc. But these are minimal sums, so try to find a policy with higher-than-mandated limits.

Premiums

This is the final, usually decisive, factor. It will pay you to shop for health insurance and to take the cost into consideration, but it's like choosing a physician. You can probably save money by going to the clinic or the VA hospital, but you will feel a lot safer and surer when you find a doctor with skill, experience, and the ability to help all of your family. As with all insurance, buy from a good agent or the representative of a good company.

XVIII

How to Protect Your Income with Disability Insurance

One of the most important and most neglected economic protections is disability insurance. When illness or injury takes a breadwinner off the job for several months, it can be damaging; when the disability lasts for a year or more, it will be devastating.

The inability to work happens more often than you may think. According to insurance industry experience, 45% of all American men now age 35 will be laid up for a period of 3 months or more before they retire. And only 1 of 3 wage-earners has any insurance against loss of income. A large number of these are under mandatory temporary disability insurance in California, Hawaii, New Jersey, New York, Rhode Island, and Puerto Rico.

Disability insurance is most important to the self-employed, but it's worth considering for almost everyone.

In most cases, you will get more and better coverage from companies that specialize in the field. The basic principles are the same as for all insurance—premiums are based on actuarial probabilities of age, health, occupation, etc. For $1,000 per month disability benefits, costs range from about $25 to $50 per month.

Statistically, younger people need greater protection because of their responsibilities to their children, but these are the ones who are likely to be laid up for a short time. High earners get the

270

best deal because of tax savings—in the 50% tax bracket, they receive the equivalent of $50,000 when they get $25,000 in annual benefits because all disability payments are tax-free when premiums are paid with after-tax dollars.

In buying disability insurance, you have three choices—noncancellable, guaranteed renewable, and optionally renewable.

NONCANCELLABLE. As long as you keep up the premium payments, the policy will protect your income—usually until you are 65 years of age—and also permit you to add coverage in the future.

At the outset, the premiums will be relatively high, but over the years they will level out. The major advantage is that the benefits are assured as long as you maintain payments.

GUARANTEED RENEWABLE. This is less expensive than noncancellable, as insurers have the right to boost premiums. Again, the benefits are fixed. By law, companies must make only across-the-board increases, so you will not be singled out for raises because of severe illness, etc. It's best to buy such policies early in your working career as the premiums tend to level out proportionately.

OPTIONALLY RENEWABLE. This is the cheapest because each year the insurance company can decide whether or not to renew and at what rates—also on an across-the-board basis.

Note in the following table that premiums vary widely according to the age and sex of the insured—from $228 to $330 annually for a 27-year-old man; from $515 to $790 for a 37-year-old woman; and from $493 to $688 for a 47-year-old man. *But check the terms and exceptions, as price alone is not the most important consideration.* When dividends are paid, some of those apparently high premiums will prove to be quite competitive. Benefits and limitations can be changed with renewals, so read the wording of each policy and the company's (not the agent's) statements. Use these tables as references, not as final determinants.

Why It Pays to Shop for Disability Insurance

Company	Payment for How Long?	Terms of Payment	Reduce Benefits	Special Benefits	Exclusions	Age Limits	Premium Per $1,000 monthly*		
							Age	Men	Women
Aetna Life & Casualty	10 years	If earn money outside regular job, insurance income cut by 50% of earnings	After 2 years if insurance benefits exceed previous income	If disabled before 45, lifetime income paid	War, pregnancy, attempted suicide, piloting plane, etc.	To age 72 but 1 year income after 65	27 37 47	$330 457 603	$ 473 669 907
Guardian Life of New York	5 years or to 55, whichever longer	As long as can't work at own occupation	Income maximum of $400 a month if woman disabled while not employed away from home†	Lifetime payment if permanent disability from illness before 50, accident before 65; if one disability for 6 months, no waiting, on second, for 5 years	War, pregnancy, intentionally self-inflicted injuries, etc.	To age 72; limit 2 years if result of injury	27 37 47	321 479 688	632 790 999‡
Mutual of New York	2 years	As long as can't work at own occupation; after 1 year can earn up to 75% previous income with reduced payments	None	None	War, pregnancy, disabilities during military service	To age 75, limited to 2 years at age 70; can refuse to renew	27 37 47	270 372 605	461 640 1,048

Company	Benefit period	Definition of disability	Partial disability	Other benefits	Exclusions	Income limits	Age		
Occidental Life—California	10 years	As long as can't work at own occupation; if earn at other job, insurance income cut by 50% of earnings	Income cut 50% if woman disabled when not employed away from home†	Half benefits for partial disabilities	War, pregnancy, attempted suicide, etc.; no more than 12 monthly payments if living outside U.S. or Canada	To age 70 for men; income limited to 2 years	27	294	423
							37	404	545
							47	581	717
Paul Revere Life	5 years or to age 55, whichever longer	As long as can't work at own occupation	Income cut 50% if woman disabled when not employed away from home†	Between 65 and 72, can convert to lifetime hospital insurance	War, pregnancy	To age 72; income limited to 2 years	27	246	390
							37	349	523
							47	494	697
Union Mutual Life—Portland, Maine	To age 65	As long as can't work at own occupation	None	None	War, pregnancy	To age 72; income limited to 2 years	27	228	387
							37	326	515
							47	493	694

* Based on 90-day waiting period; available to executives making over $20,000 a year and some lower-paid professionals.
† New York State prohibits such discrimination.
‡ Dividends will reduce premiums—in 1974, by 16%.
All policies are noncancellable until at least age 65. All pay monthly income until at least age 65.
Many policies provide discounts or extra benefits for annual payments; others stress monthly payments on the basis that premium payments stop with disability.

Extra Benefits from Social Security

If you are overwhelmed by the possible cost of disability insurance, remember that Social Security provides special help if you can show that you are unable to do "any substantial gainful" work for a year. The benefits start after 5 months of disability.

The government terms are stricter than those of most insurance policies, but the payments are significant—a man with a wife and child can get up to $786 per month at age 25, $684 per month at age 35, $580 per month when 45 or older.

Year of Death or Disability
Based on Earnings Base of $12,000 in 1974

Age in 1974	1976	1978	1980	1985	1990
35	$360.50	$368.50	$373.50	$381.50	$386.50
36	356.50	364.50	369.50	378.50	383.50
37	349.70	358.50	364.50	373.50	379.50
38	336.50	347.30	354.50	366.50	373.50
39	320.40	336.50	344.90	359.50	367.50
40	302.20	323.40	336.50	352.10	361.50
41	286.80	308.30	325.00	344.90	356.50
42	274.60	294.60	312.80	338.90	350.90
43	264.50	283.20	300.60	332.90	344.90
44	255.80	274.60	290.10	323.40	340.10
45*	247.40	266.10	281.70	314.40	335.30

* Remains almost the same to age 65.

Benefits are based on the primary insurance amount (PIA), about the same amount a widow is entitled to at age 65. There are numerous special provisions, so see your nearest Social Security office as soon as it becomes probable that you will be unable to work. Apply promptly because you will not be eligible for back benefits if you wait more than 14 months after you recover.

Example: This example assumes that the father, the primary wage-earner, is 45 years old in 1975 and becomes disabled in 1980. He has earned at least $12,000 annually since 1974 and has a wife and two teenage children. The children's benefits are payable until they become 18, or if full-time students, to age 22.

1. Your benefit: PIA (from table above)—age 45, year 1980 $281.70

2. Your wife's benefit: $\frac{\$281.70}{(\text{line 1})} \times 0.5$ $140.85

3. Your children's benefit: $\frac{\$281.70}{(\text{line 1})} \times \frac{2}{(\text{no. of children})} \times 0.5$ $281.70

4. Total benefits: $\frac{\$281.70}{(\text{line 1})} + \frac{\$140.85}{(\text{line 2})} + \frac{\$281.70}{(\text{line 3})}$ $704.25

5. Family's maximum benefit: $\frac{\$281.70}{(\text{line 1})} \times 1.75$ $492.97

6. What you get—lesser of line 4 or line 5 $492.97

What Your Family Will Get if You Die

Social Security provides income to your family if you die before you start taking Social Security benefits. There are benefits for your widow and for children under 18, or children under 22 when they are full-time students. These benefits, like disability payments, are based on what is known as the primary insurance amount (PIA) as shown in the table above.

The family benefits are paid to your widow only while she is caring for the children. She does not become eligible for full widow's benefits until age 65, or for reduced benefits until age 60. But if you had started to receive your benefits at age 62, your widow would receive that amount unless her own earned benefits were greater.

Example: In this example, the father is 47 years old at his death in 1976. He has a wife and 2 small children and a dependent mother.

---

1. Your widow's benefits: $247.40 × .75
   (see table above: last line, 1976 column) $185.55
2. Your children's benefits:

   $$\frac{\$185.55}{(\text{line 1})} \times \frac{2}{(\text{no. children})} \times .75$$ $278.32

3. Your dependent parent's benefit: $\dfrac{\$185.55}{(\text{line 1})} \times .825*$ $153.08

4. Total benefits: $\dfrac{\$185.55}{(\text{line 1})} + \dfrac{\$278.32}{(\text{line 2})} + \dfrac{\$153.08}{(\text{line 3})}$ $616.95

5. Maximum family benefit: $\dfrac{\$185.55}{(\text{line 1})} \times 1.75$ $324.71

6. Total family benefit—lesser of line 4 or 5: $324.71

* If 2 dependent parents, use 1.5.
Note: Use this table to check your own family income, but contact the local Social Security office, as there are some exceptions and some further benefits.

Calculating Need for Disability Insurance

In determining how much income will be needed if you should become ill or injured, add up your "must" expenses of rent, food, clothing, education, etc. You can forget the costs of straight life insurance by paying a small additional premium to guarantee maintenance of the policy as long as you are disabled.

Generally, the total will be between 50% and 60% of your regular pretax income. *Remember: Disability benefits are tax-free.* Thus, if you are earning $20,000, you should consider buying disability coverage to provide $10,000 a year, less if you have reserves enough to handle the first 5 months before Social Security payments start and are pessimistic enough to think you will be laid up for a full year.

Most insurance companies are reluctant to write policies that pay more than $3,000 per month. They are fearful of malingerers who would welcome the opportunity to live in reasonable comfort without working!

If your wife insists on full coverage, see if you can buy through a group plan of your professional association, fraternal organization, or union. It will be inexpensive though limited.

Selecting Policies

Once you have determined how much income you will need to protect your family, it's a question of what you can afford. Your best long-term choice is a noncancellable, guaranteed renewable policy. This protects you against both cancellation and extraordinary rate hikes.

Rates vary according to occupation—lower premiums for individuals who are likely to be able to keep working, even part-time, such as physicians, dentists, lawyers, architects, and accountants; higher costs for factory workers and women.

If you are turned down because of health or occupation, keep looking. There are more than 2,000 companies writing disability insurance.

The easiest way to tailor a policy to fit your pocketbook is through the timing of benefits. The longer the elimination period (the time before the payments start), the lower the premiums. At age 35, lengthening the waiting period from 30 to 90 days will cut the premium about $86 a year. Conversely, the more extended the time of benefits, the higher the premiums.

Best bet: Try to set the elimination period to match the sick leave available from your job, or if you are self-employed, to the time it takes to collect for work already completed.

DON'T GO OVERBOARD. By buying a policy that starts payments after 180 days, you will save about $250 a year over one with a 30-day elimination. But with a $1,000-per-month benefit, you could count on income of some $5,000 in those 5 months! That's as much as your premium savings over 20 years—at the same rates.

If there's a choice between adequate coverage and a longer elimination period, take the coverage—even if you have to settle for less income than you would prefer.

Note: If you are a member of a professional corporation, the corporation can buy a policy with tax-deductible dollars, but only the first $100-per-week income will be tax-free. If you pay the premiums yourself, you can deduct them from your federal income tax return and all of the benefits will be tax-free.

Costs of disability policies for women average about one-third more than those of men. This is because rates are based on past experience when women took more sick leave. With more females in professions and moving up to responsible positions, this discrimination is easing, partly through the insurance companies but primarily because of governmental pressure—e.g., New York State prohibits different payments when based on sex!

Extra Protection

To cover the costs of inflation, ask your agent about riders:

- A cost-of-living adjustment (up to 5% a year) costs $90 per $1,000 monthly benefits:
- A guaranteed-insurability provision lets you increase the benefits every few years to keep pace with your income—regardless of health.

Avoid riders that promise to return a good chunk of the premiums if there are no claims for a certain number of years. Obviously, this will discourage you from making claims. You'll do better to spend the money for added coverage or investments.

DON'T PAY EXTRA FOR SPECIAL ACCIDENT BENEFITS. This is a ripoff—illness, not accidents, is responsible for the majority of all losses of income. If your mother-in-law keeps "suggesting" accident coverage, watch for special offers through your association, union, or local newspaper. Costs are small.

Never buy any policy with delayed benefits for such special illnesses as heart disease, tuberculosis, diseases of the female reproductive system, etc., or those which require you to be confined at home to collect. As with all insurance, read the policy and look for the spirit as well as the letter of the agreement.

New Benefits

In recent years disability policies were improved by: (1) expanding the definition of total disability to insure *job status,* not just to protect income; (2) providing residual disability benefits. *Both of these provisions are very significant.*

1. Under some old policies, *total disability* was defined as the inability to perform any work for compensation or profit. Now it means the inability to engage in your own occupation or profession.

If a surgeon is injured so that he can no longer operate, he will be paid the full benefits for which he bought disability insurance even though he is able to conduct a general practice. If Dr. Taylor had a disability policy providing $2,000 monthly, he'd get $24,000 a year PLUS whatever he earns as a GP. Dollarwise, he might be better off because when properly programmed, that $24,000 would be tax-free!

2. Residual disability benefits are paid on a proportional basis according to ability to continue occupation. Architect Bowser has a heart attack and is able to work only half-time. Under a disability policy, he would receive 50% of his benefits as long as that shorter work schedule continued. If he became worse, he would be paid on a proportional basis up to 75% of his previous income. At that time he would be considered totally disabled and would receive full disability benefits.

The Importance of Definitions

Definitions are even more important when you are dealing with small companies that are better at promotion than payment.
Example: "Total disability during the first 24 months means

that the covered person, by reason of injury or sickness, is under the regular care and attendance of a physician and is *completely* [italics are mine] unable to perform the duties of the full-time occupation in which he was regularly and actively engaged."

The key word is "completely." Some insurers use this to modify, if not cancel, the other important phrase, "unable to perform." If the agent is not able to provide you with a written explanation of the company's interpretation of any statement, move on to another company. You may not be able to collect until there is a formal adjudication, probably by the state insurance commissioner.

Best bet: Look for a policy that provides "residual benefits." You'll get some income as long as you are not able to work full-time.

Quick Check

Ask your state insurance department for a list of the disability insurance companies with the highest number of complaints in relation to their volume. In 1972 this was the scorecard for New York State:

	Complaints per $1 Million Premiums
International Life of Buffalo	192.0
American Progressive Health	40.3
Federal Life & Casualty	22.0
Empire State Mutual Life	19.1
Commercial Travelers Mutual	14.6
Columbian Mutual Life	11.4
Mutual of Omaha (New York)	10.2
Bankers Multiple Line	10.1
CNA (American Casualty, Continental Casualty, Continental Assurance)	9.7
Nationwide Mutual	8.8

On the brighter side, Paul Revere Life Insurance Company reports that "Of 103,000 claims, only $7/10$ths of 1% involved inquiries or complaints to Insurance Departments."

In insurance, almost more than any other purchase-investment, it pays to shop for integrity, service, and a record of proved performance.

XIX

Start Planning Your Retirement
Early

Retirement plans are changing. A 1968 survey showed that 1 of every 3 heads-of-households expected to continue to work after retirement. In 1974, a follow-up survey found that 7 out of 8 want to retire completely.

Whether this shift is due to changing life-styles or to the added security of present and anticipated pension plans, the results make it clear that people are thinking about their retirement, the location of their home, and the funds needed to enjoy it.

General planning for retirement should start at age 45; specific planning should start 3 to 4 years before you quit your job; the final judgments should be made at least 6 months before your retirement deadline.

Three areas that require personal research and long discussions with your wife, lawyer, and investment adviser are: (1) where to retire; (2) how much income you will need; and (3) how to achieve that income with greatest safety. *Taxes and benefits to your loved ones should be secondary.* You worked hard to accumulate some wealth, so enjoy it!

The *where* assumes you will move to some sort of retirement area. (If you stay in your hometown, your costs may be somewhat lower but you will probably want to spend more for vacations and travel. And you have to keep in mind that it will be difficult for you to adjust to a lesser scale of living. The hospital, the church, and the United Way will pressure you to maintain your gifts, and it will be difficult to break lifelong habits of parties at the club, guests for golf tournaments, etc.)

A check with older friends in my area (northern New Jersey) shows that almost half of them plan to go elsewhere, and the majority of these will choose one of these future homes:

Retirement Community

Whether large centers of small houses or small clusters of modest homes, these are neat, ready-made societies that offer homogeneous companionship and instant activity. You will be isolated from youth, dirt, noise, and crime and have a variety of recreational-cultural services. At the outset, you may just want to relax, but as you grow older you will need more stimuli to offset boredom. Checkpoints of the retirement community include:

1. AGE RESTRICTIONS. Usually one person must be over age 50 and there must be no children under age 15.

2. CLUB OR COMMUNITY CENTER. Be sure this is in operation or under construction. With bankruptcies and tight money, many developers are already 2 or 3 years behind promises. Find a community where these facilities are already operating. Costs for membership will run from $300 to $1,000 a year, depending on the type and extent of privileges—swimming pool, shuffleboard courts, tennis courts, golf course, etc.

As most of these projects regard the recreational areas as keys to long-term success, you can anticipate that costs of membership and use will continue to rise.

3. TYPE OF HOUSING. If your wife wants special features in the home, allow 1 year for building and up to 6

months to obtain the furniture and furnishings she wants. Costs will be from $25,000 to $40,000.

4. SECURITY AND MAINTENANCE. You can look forward to protection such as guards, gates, and patrols, and helpful services such as snow removal, lawn mowing, and community gardens.

If you get tired of the same climate, you may want to have 2 homes—an apartment near your old community and a small house in a retirement area.

5. AVAILABILITY OF A NURSING HOME OR FULL-SERVICE RESIDENCE. Until you're 75, you may be independent, but thereafter, you or your wife may need some sort of custodial care. Plan *now*.

For most people, this is a *final* move, so do not be in a hurry. Consider carefully whether you want the responsibility of a house or the convenience of an apartment or condominium. Even in a structured community, a home provides greater individual freedom.

The original investment may be higher than that of an apartment or a condominium, but the monthly carrying-maintenance costs may be lower because most states now provide tax benefits for property-owning retirees.

With multifamily units, you must be a conformist and be ready to accept the social and recreational activities.

Condominiums

With these group units, *always* double the monthly maintenance fees quoted by the developer. In 10 years, inflation will boost operating costs by at least 75%, and unless there are special provisions for major repairs and replacements (central air conditioner, heating plant, roof, etc.), you will be hit with a sizable bill in not too many years.

The cost per unit is $20,000 to $35,000—unless you want to consider one of those very swank deals overlooking the beach!

Mobile Homes

These are smaller and cheaper to buy and maintain. They cost from $15,000 to $20,000, but your mortgage will be less favorable, as depreciation is figured on a 10-year basis—one-half to one-third that of a regular house. Also, the resale value will be small.

One major advantage: A mobile unit can be moved around the country if you and your wife like the thrill of adventure and enjoy hard driving.

Cash Savings

If you pay cash for your new home, your total costs (taxes, maintenance, and modest reserves) should be between $100 and $150 per month. With a mortgage, your monthly payments will be what you make them.

Income Needed

To retire comfortably and maintain a life-style similar to your current standard of living, you will need 50% of your present income; 40% if you plan a sheltered life; 60% if you want to travel. These figures will vary according to location of retirement, health factors, personal preferences, and of course, available resources.

Inflation will boost costs by at least 5% a year, so in 10 years you will need two-thirds more money to maintain the same pace and style. But most people will be able to get along on less—partly because mortgage payments will be lower or completed, partly because of physical limitations, and partly because of a desire to just take it easy.

In retirement, living is easier and cheaper. But you have to modify your life-style considerably. You probably will not have enough money to do everything you want, so you will have to plan your major expenditures—new appliances, trips abroad, anniversary parties, etc.—with great care.

The following figures are based on sample budgets developed by the U.S. Department of Labor with modifications from personal research with people who have already retired. These guesstimates reflect life-styles of 2 income groups: (1) the business-professional man who has been earning $25,000 or so a year; (2) the teacher-civil servant who has had a gross salary income of $15,000 to $18,000 a year.

The Social Security payments are adjusted for an annual increase of 5% a year. (There is no sure way to predict these checks because Congress must review the situation annually.)

By age 75, most retirees will either have reduced expenses or started to invade capital. As explained in this chapter, that's really not so drastic as it may seem—unless you come from a long-lived family or are determined to leave a substantial estate. (In such a case, some of your funds should have been given away or placed in trust.)

In both cases, the tough problem is the erosion of inflation. The estimates are projected on a rule-of-thumb basis—an annual inflation rate of 5%, or for easy figuring, 60% at the end of the next 10 years. This is on the low side in view of the 10%+ rate of 1974–75 but is close to the average rate in the United States over the 20-year 1953–72 period.

To make ends meet, a retired couple will have to cut some corners and do without. We believe these are, basically, realistic projections. Your own budget may vary because of personal tastes or—more likely—your method of allocation. The following are broad categories—food includes liquor; housing covers utilities, telephone, mortgage payments, and taxes; recreation-travel means costs of recreation, clubs, dining out, and vacation trips. Use these as guidelines, not set formulas.

Balancing the Retirement Budget

Item	Budget A 1975	Budget A 1985	Budget B 1975	Budget B 1985
Food	$ 1,800	$ 2,500	$ 1,600	$ 2,200
Housing	3,200	4,000	2,400	3,000
Transportation	1,000	1,600	900	1,400
Clothing	1,000	1,600	700	1,100
Personal care	500	800	300	400
Medical care	500	800	400	500
Recreation-travel	3,300	3,600	2,200	2,650
Family	600	1,000	300	400
Taxes	2,400	2,500	700	800
Charities	400	600	200	200
Miscellaneous	300	1,000	300	350
Total	$15,000	$20,000	$10,000	$13,000
Income				
Social Security	$ 3,659	$ 5,800	$ 3,659	$ 5,800
Wife (age 62)	1,372	2,175	1,372	2,175
Social Security total	$ 5,031	$ 7,975	$ 5,031	$ 7,975
Pension-Dividends	10,000	10,000	5,000	3,175
Total Income	$15,031	$17,975	$10,031	$11,150
Invasion of Capital		$ 2,025		$ 1,850

Here are some general guidelines. Details come later.

As shown by the budget, you will need $15,000 *minimum*. Social Security for both you and your wife (age 62 at the time of your retirement) is about $5,000. You can count on a pension of $4,000. (That's about average. Don't let those 50%-of-last-salary figures of civil servants fool you. Most people who retire in 1975 had little or no pension benefits for many years.) So you need an additional $6,000 annual income now, more later

You own a mortgage-free home worth $50,000, have $2,000 in savings, personal investments of $40,000, and life insurance of $100,000. At first glance, it looks as if you will need a whopping 15% return on that $40,000! Fortunately, you have more assets than you think and several ways to achieve your goal.

Steps to take:

Reduce Your Life Insurance

Since $50,000 is term, drop this, then review your other policies. Be sure to check the riders. Many older policies provide for insurance to be kept in force if you should become temporarily disabled or unable to pay premiums. *Hold these policies as long as possible.*

Then look for other policies that are paid up or where interest has been used to buy additional coverage. These can provide extra income—say, $500 a year in this case.

Now you need only $5,500 annual income.

Start Selling Your House

It will take several months to get the right price and terms. There'll be no immediate capital gains tax if you buy a new home within one year (before or after).

After paying for moving, buying new furniture, and making a down payment against a modest mortgage, you should have some $15,000 free per year. Your total investment assets are now $55,000, on which you need only a 10% return.

Note: These figures provide considerable leeway for emergencies and/or extra costs. If you can swing it, pay cash for the home; if you can't, arrange for a small mortgage or get a bank loan against your securities.

Keep That Cash Working

If there's a delay between the sale and purchase of the houses (while you and your wife take a long-planned trip), put the free cash into short-term, liquid obligations. Your returns will be around 9%, so in 6 months on $20,000, for example, you will earn an extra $900 to add to your nest egg.

Do Not Buy Certificates of Deposit

These pay high interest but in most cases require either large sums ($100,000) or long-term commitments with severe penalties for early withdrawal. You want to be able to get your full investment back—with maximum interest—FAST.

With Your Stocks

Sell those with small profits or losses and hold those with substantial profits until the year you retire when your tax rate will be lower.

Make No Major Moves

Until you are settled, have a clear idea of your cash position, your immediate needs, and your long-term schedule, make no major moves. You will have $55,000 in investments, about $3,000 in savings to handle emergencies and tide you over until dividends-interest arrive. This sounds ample but will dwindle rapidly with payments for club dues, registration fees, entertaining old friends, etc.

And always remember that in 10 years you will have to have about $2,000 more annual income even after sizable boosts in Social Security payments.

How Best to Invest Your Money

Answers to this important question should have been discussed, dissected, reviewed, and tested long before retirement. They depend more on your background and experience than on your wealth.

Whatever you do, *keep flexible.* Unless you are quite well-to-do, do not put all your assets into any one investment. There is no one sure answer. As you know from the fate of members of your family and of friends, conditions can change rapidly under the pressure of illness, death, economic stress, and longevity.

DON'T Look Solely for Security

You need income, too. There is no such thing as absolute security in any type of investment. With annuities and fixed-income holdings, you will get a check regularly but each deposit will buy less.

DO Use Your Assets for Personal and Family Enjoyment

Never sacrifice your last years in an effort to leave a large inheritance. Who wants to be a dead millionaire?

DON'T Be Afraid to Move into New Areas of Investment

You will have more spare time to study operations and supervise the use of your money. Use your skills and experience at a leisurely pace. It's best to start such ventures while you still have a steady income and can deal with people whom you know and trust. But don't be afraid to tackle something new if you move to a retirement area. It can be fun, exciting, and rewarding IF done cautiously within your financial and personal resources.

This advice applies especially to income-producing investments such as real estate—a building with a long-term lease from a prime tenant, mortgages, secured loans, etc. When properly selected, they can provide good income and a not-too-taxing challenge.

Disadvantage: These are nonliquid holdings, hard to sell in a hurry, and difficult to manage by remote control.

Who and What?

The two key decisions—Who? What?—are intertwined. When you buy an annuity or shares in a mutual fund, you automatically turn over the management of your money to someone else. That's fine for *part* of your assets, but don't be in a hurry to walk away from responsibilities. Most people who have spent a lifetime making decisions find it boring when there's no such opportunity.

You can sell the fund shares and invest the proceeds yourself, but once you have bought an annuity, that's it—for life.

Best advice: STAY LOOSE. Keep part of your savings under your own control.

One possible compromise: Transfer a portion of your port-folio-savings to your son and/or daughter in return for an un-secured promise that there will be periodic payments for the rest of your life. This will enable you to make suggestions (if you're tactful) and save taxes. Such a course is best for holdings of $100,000 or more and of course assumes that you have con-fidence in the integrity and money-managing ability of your kin.

In broad terms, the investment-income choices for retirees are savings accounts, annuities, securities, options, and shares of in-vestment companies. Real estate depends so much on available assets, personal experience, and tax advantages that it is usually not a major field for retirees.

The following information refers to the hypothetical budget and $55,000 savings but is designed to be used by everyone and anyone to make retirement years more enjoyable and less wor-risome. Again, let me repeat: Be flexible. Don't get locked into any one plan.

But don't jitterbug! If a change seems wise, try to make it partial and gradual. You are not likely to have a chance to go back to the original program.

Annuities—Guarantee or Gamble?

Retirement annuities take the worry out of living too long. They are the only investments able to guarantee a fixed rate of return for 40 years or more. But they can be expensive, and if you opt for variable annuities, they may not always provide the income anticipated.

The annuity is a form of life insurance that relieves an in-dividual, usually a retiree, of money-management responsibilities and assures a steady income for himself, and if he so desires, for his widow. Such a guarantee makes possible greater freedom—and risk—with other assets.

When you buy an annuity at age 65, you pay about $12,000 for each $1,200 a year ($100 per month) for life—which can be expected to be a little over 15 years. Costs are higher for women—$13,400 because women can be expected to live to 84! With that $55,000, you could buy only some $5,500 a year income—$4,500 less than you need!

Straight annuities pay the highest income of all fixed-pay agreements. They are based on the simple risk-sharing concept that losers pay for winners—i.e., those who die early will provide the money for those who live longer than their actuarially computed life expectancy. With a straight annuity, there will be nothing left for your heirs if you should die one day after the payout begins!

That's why many people choose: (1) a *refund annuity*, where the remaining principal goes to a named beneficiary; or (2) a *period-certain annuity*, where payments continue to a beneficiary for 5 or 10 years.

There are also *deferred annuities*, where you can designate a future date at which the payout will begin. In the meantime, your payment will earn interest either at a guaranteed rate, or if you are optimistic about a rise in the stock market, at a variable rate reflecting the higher returns from the underlying investments. If you die before the payout starts, your beneficiary receives the accumulated funds.

When you buy an annuity, you trade uncertainty for security. You will receive a lifetime income whether you live a few years, your allotted span, or to age 100 or longer. That may not be as munificent as it sounds. If you put the same $12,000 in a savings account at only 6½% interest and draw out $100 per month (from both interest and principal), your savings would last about one year longer than your actuarial lifetime. And there would be a slight tax advantage, as less of your income would be a nontaxable return of capital. But if you beat the odds and live beyond 82, there will be no more money from that source! The annuity will pay slightly less but will continue as long as you live.

In all cases, arrangements can be made to continue payments to your widow or beneficiary or to return the unspent principal to your estate.

Check the guaranteed rate of growth through interest. This is a strong competitive point, so have your insurance agent furnish you with a printout of what portion of your annuity income is taxable. Even a few dollars in savings can be helpful.

Take a hard look at a deferred annuity IF you can afford to wait a few years for your money, because: (1) the later you start the payout, the greater the monthly income; (2) the interest will be building under a tax shelter, and presumably the ultimate taxes will be at a lower rate; (3) you can borrow, at low interest rates, up to the cash value of the policy; (4) you can hedge on your anticipated life expectancy. If your health deteriorates before the annuity starts, you can put your money into something else. People in poor health should not buy annuities for themselves.

Note: Many insurance companies refuse to sell an annuity to anyone in substandard health. The company would probably make money but would open itself to legal challenge on the grounds that such coverage would be against the buyer's interest.

Flexible Annuities

In an effort to provide benefits that can partially offset the inflation-caused erosion of fixed-income payments, insurance companies now offer 2 new types of flexible annuities: participating (PA) and variable (VA). Neither has been in force long enough to determine whether they really will keep pace with rising costs over a period of time. But the principles are logical, and perhaps a rising stock market will enable them to fulfill their promises.

PAs cost more than straight annuities—$13,000 to $13,500 versus $12,000 for that $100 monthly income. They provide guaranteed minimum payments plus hopes of higher income when investment results are favorable. Two insurance companies specializing in PAs are State Farm Life Insurance of Bloomington, Illinois, and Confederation Life of Toronto, Canada.

A variation of PAs is the cost-of-living annuity, where, for an extra fee, you can get a built-in annual 3% raise in your monthly checks. This policy is sold by Colonial Penn Life in Philadelphia and Crown Life in Toronto.

Varying Variables

After long and arduous negotiations with federal and state agencies (and a couple of court cases), insurance companies appear likely to have approval to sell VAs to individuals.

These flexible policies are based on the premise that, over the long haul, investments in quality common stocks will keep pace with (or close to) inflation. In theory, 50% of the funds back of each VA policy are to be invested in fixed-income securities (compared to a mandatory 90% for fixed-income annuities) and the balance used to buy equities where the combination of dividends and capital appreciation will provide continually growing returns.

Depending on how well the stock market is doing, the monthly payments could be lower, about the same, or higher than those of a regular annuity. The income varies, up and down. The hope is that, over the years, the ups will more than cancel out the downs, and the income, by fits and starts, will gradually inch its way up to a more rewarding level.

During the 1973–74 market decline, many VAs (sold on a group basis) paid less than fixed annuities. But better days may be ahead. If the stock market continues its historical rise, VAs will be worthwhile. As Chapter XXV, on Investments, points out, the long-term trend of stock values has *always* been up.

One ray of sunshine: The Prudential Insurance Company says that the returns on its VA investments have been right behind those of savings accounts—not bad when considered against the stock market averages but rather puny in relation to the available returns on fixed-income holdings in the early 1970s.

And even more encouraging were the results of Aetna Life & Casualty, which started selling VAs to employee groups in 1954. Until 1973 the average annual return was 10%!

What You Really Get with Annuities

Guaranteed income for life is not as rewarding as it would seem unless you come from a long-lived family. When started at age 65, the annuity will exceed the original investment in about 12 years—some 3 years less than your actuarial life! You'll do better with a simple savings account, at 5½% interest!

Deferred annuities provide a guaranteed rate of accumulation of as little as 3%, after sales charges. For the individual in a 35% tax bracket, the after-tax return on a 6% savings account will be 4%, and investments in tax-exempt bonds will accumulate even faster. Furthermore, if you need cash in a hurry, you may sustain a loss—because of the front-end sales load, cash values usually do not equal paid-in premiums until the sixth year.

But there are some tax breaks—interest accumulates tax-free, and payouts are partially tax-exempt because some of the money represents a return of capital.

Disadvantages of Annuities

With annuities:

YOU CANNOT LIQUIDATE YOUR HOLDINGS OR ALTER THE RATE OF WITHDRAWAL OF CAPITAL. They are a one-time deal; no changes.

SALES CHARGES ARE HIGH. They are 5% to 8% on the average. That comes off the top, so less of your money is earning interest and/or dividends.

ACQUISITION COSTS VARY, THOUGH SPECIFIC BENEFITS REMAIN PRETTY MUCH THE SAME. As with all types of insurance, price/cost may be secondary to the service and counsel of your insurance agent.

THERE'S NO OPPORTUNITY FOR EXTRA INCOME (EXCEPT WITH VAs).

YOU CANNOT LEAVE MONEY TO YOUR HEIRS. An annuity is just what the name states—income for life.

When You Shop for Annuities:

GET A CAREFUL DETERMINATION OF YOUR HEALTH. Learn if the odds are favorable that you will live as long as anticipated actuarily.

CHECK YOUR FAMILY HISTORY. If there's a record of long life, you are probably OK.

DECIDE THE PAYMENT OPTION. With no dependents and a hard-eyed judgment on your life expectancy, straight life annuities are the highest yielding.

Period-certain annuities are hedges if you distrust your ability to outlive the averages or if you have a dependent child or parent.

For those who have little or no life insurance, the best choice is joint and survivor options to assure payments as long as you both live.

Check Your Present Policies

See if it is worthwhile to convert the cash values into an annuity. Be careful: Older policies, based on shorter life expectancies, may provide higher income than current annuities.

Added advantage: under IRS rules, there's no tax due on cash values used to buy annuities, provided you make a direct conversion from a life to an annuity policy.

Ask about Mortality-risk Fees in VAs

These can vary from 1% to 2% of assets. Over the life of the contract, this small spread makes a big difference in your income, and if you should die early, in the value of the remaining principal.

Ask about Loan Privileges

Some companies offer this with a deferred annuity. But once the payout period begins, not all policies permit borrowing. Check with your agent.

Consider Mixing Your Retirement Assets

Mix in an annuity to supplement Social Security, minimal life insurance, shares of mutual funds, or a portfolio of quality stocks, bonds, and convertibles. And if you have the knowledge and experience, real estate.

Review Your Needs and Assets

Review them with several agents, as there are significant differences in costs, and it may also be possible to find benefits more attuned to your life-style. For a broad frame of reference, the following are recent single-premium prices for some $100-a-month-at-age-65-for-life annuities.

Cost of $100-a-Month Annuities

Men		Women	
Equitable Life	$11,655	Equitable Life	$13,195
New York Life	11,776	Occidental Life	13,222
Occidental Life	11,781	New York Life	13,324
Dominion Life	11,850	Prudential	13,328
Penn Mutual	11,868	Penn Mutual	13,411
Acacia Mutual	12,030	Connecticut Mutual	13,449
Connecticut Mutual	12,073	Dominion Life	13,497
Great-West Life	12,110	Confederation Life	13,498
Confederation Life	12,133	Paul Revere Life	13,555
Pacific Mutual	12,151	Republic National Life	13,555

Typical Annuity Payments—$100 a Month

Option	When Income Stops	One-Time Premium Male	One-Time Premium Female	Residue of Capital for Heirs
No years certain	At owner's death	$12,600	$14,200	None
10 years certain	At owner's death or after the number of years designated as certain, whichever comes *last*	13,600	14,800	None
15 years certain		14,600	15,400	None
20 years certain		16,100	16,600	None
Joint and survivor (male 65, female 62)	At death of second recipient	15,400	15,400	None
Installment refund	At owner's death or when principal is used up, whichever comes *last*	14,000	15,200	Unused principal for monthly income
Lump-sum refund		14,100	15,300	Unused principal immediately
Fixed period (4½% interest)	20 years	15,200	15,200	Unused principal plus interest

Savings Accounts Safe, but . . .

The best thing that can be said about using savings accounts for retirement funds is that they are convenient and safe. The returns, under present banking regulations, are not competitive with those available from other types of investments—bonds, high-yielding common stocks, convertibles, real estate, etc. But in most cases they are more rewarding than the income from straight annuities.

The difficulty is the low interest—at 5.25%, your $55,000 will return only $2,887.50 a year. That's about $241 per month. With special types of accounts, it is possible to boost this a smidgen, but historically that 5.25% rate is well above the average paid in the last 10 years.

The convenience is that you personally can make deposits

and withdrawals and in most cases deal with people who become friends of a sort. But even the safety, in the form of Federal Deposit Insurance, is limited to the first $40,000 in your account. You can get around this by setting up separate accounts in your wife's name, in joint names, as trustee, etc. Of course, you can

How Much You Will Have at Age 65

Present Age	Total Includ- ing Dividends	Amount Deposited	Dividends Alone Will Give You This Amount Monthly
Savings—$100 per month			
25	$164,226	$48,000	$ 719
30	121,049	42,000	530
35	87,839	36,000	385
40	62,296	30,000	273
45	42,650	24,000	186
50	27,538	18,000	120
55	15,915	12,000	69
Savings—$200 per month			
25	$328,452	$96,000	$1,439
30	242,099	84,000	1,061
35	175,679	72,000	770
40	124,593	60,000	564
45	85,300	48,000	373
50	55,077	36,000	241
55	31,831	24,000	139

If you use part of your principal in your monthly withdrawals, these are typical, approximate amounts you could withdraw monthly:

Principal at Age 65	Monthly— 10 Years	Monthly— 15 Years
$124,593	$1,337	$1,002
82,113	881	660
42,650	457	343
27,538	295	221

Source: Dime Savings Bank, New York. Based on 5.25% dividend rate compounded daily from day of deposit when deposits in account for one year. No allowance for income taxes on dividends.

use more than one savings bank. But those tactics may not be convenient.

The only way you can get that $5,500 annual income on a $55,000 savings account is to invade principal. On that basis, your money would last about 15 years!

Types of Securities

In positioning your retirement portfolio, keep in mind that you are looking for total returns—dividends-interest plus capital appreciation. It is also important to make selections on the basis of your investment experience, emotional stability, and time available for research. If you are the least bit worried about your ability to handle your investments yourself, turn them over to someone else—an investment company, a professional money manager, or under rare circumstances, your broker.

The following sample selections of securities assume that you (1) are planning to handle your own investments with as much advice as you can glean from the financial press, investment advisory services, and brokers; (2) understand the basic forces that influence the securities market—economic conditions, interest rates, investor psychology, etc.; (3) realize that these are *examples* of the kinds of stocks and bonds you should consider just before and after retirement; (4) will sell any security when it becomes fully valued and reinvest the proceeds in a more rewarding manner; (5) will not hesitate to make changes if there are unfavorable developments, or more important, when you become concerned about the future of any corporation. *The last thing you want to do in retirement is to lie awake worrying about your investments.*

That goes double for your wife. If she doesn't like GM because it reduced its dividend to yield only 6%, sell the stock and buy a 9%-yielding bond. *Peace, it's wonderful.*

Total returns (income from dividends-interest plus capital appreciation) *must* average 10% to provide the $5,500 you need. That means you have to achieve an even higher yield, as your income will be reduced by the costs of commissions when you switch to meet changing economic and monetary conditions. This does not mean you'll be trading, but few portfolios should remain untouched for more than 3 to 5 years.

All stocks suggested here are top-quality blue chips. The corporations have long records of profitable growth and ever-increasing dividends. These stocks, when selected, were selling at price-earnings ratios well below the averages of the past decade. By fundamental investment standards, they were *bargains* and could be expected to double in value in the next few years.

With their small-to-modest dividends, that growth is essential to reach the 10% total annual return. That goal requires only an annual rise of 1⅛ points in the price of AT&T (plus the 7.7% dividends) or a 4-point rise, in the next year, for Coca-Cola. Even at 75, that quality stock would be selling at half its 1973 high!

But as the debacle of 1973–74 indicated, prices of all common stocks will decline in a bear market. That's why only a portion of your retirement funds should be invested in equities.

(For more information, see Chapter XXV, on Investments.)

The basic portfolio is balanced to provide income plus hope for appreciation. You will get greater returns, immediately, by putting all your funds in high-yielding bonds, but these cannot provide the growth needed to offset the erosion of present and future inflation. In 10 years, you have to come up with an extra $2,000 a year!

Be Cautious with Bonds

If you prefer fixed-income securities, you will do better to buy low-coupon bonds selling at discounts. With these, there are two chances for capital gains: (1) when the interest rate drops (the price of all bonds is related directly to the cost of money, so the discounts will narrow when interest rates decline); (2) when the prices of the bonds rise as the day of redemption nears. All bonds are redeemed at par, usually $1,000.

Convertibles provide a middle ground between bonds and common stocks. They have the yield stability of a bond and the growth potential of a stock. Generally, their yields are lower than those of straight bonds, but here, too, there are 2 chances for gains: (1) when the interest rate drops; (2) when the price of the related stock rises and thus enhances the value of the convertible.

This growth potential is attractive if you plan to make gifts or an inheritance to your children or grandchildren. CVs provide income for you and growth for your heirs.

Concentrate on Quality Stocks

Invest in common stocks according to your financial experience and personal comfort: (1) modest-dividend-paying growth stocks (3% to 4%); (2) good-paying blue chips (5% to 6%); (3) high-yielding utilities or cyclicals (7% to 9%).

All of these securities are *investments,* not speculations. These are long-term portfolios. In some cases, it will take months, even years, for the value of all of these stocks to be recognized by investors. Emphasis is placed on the safety of the bonds and the probability of strong advances in earnings and continuing high returns on stockholders' equity, which in turn will boost the prices of the stocks and CVs.

> *Note:* The explanations are based on research from 4 major brokerage firms and investment advisory services—Reynolds Securities, Inc., an international brokerage firm; Babson's Reports, an investment advisory organization; Wright Investors' Service, professional money managers; and Delafield Childs, a New York broker whose chief clients are banks and investment companies.

Diversified Portfolio for Retirement

Company	Shares	Recent Price	Cost	Dividends	Yield
Amer. Natural Gas	100	31	$ 3,100	$ 254	8.2%
A T & T	100	44	4,400	340	7.7
Beatrice Foods	100	14	1,400	72	5.1
Coca-Cola	100	58	5,800	213	3.7
General Motors	100	37	3,700	340	9.2
Gulf St. Utilities	100	12	1,200	112	9.3
Travelers CV pf.	100	31	3,100	200	6.5
Ford Credit CV					
$4\frac{1}{2}$, '96	10	61	6,100	425	7.0
Tenneco CV					
$6\frac{1}{4}$, '92	20	88	17,600	1,250	7.1
Pacific G&E					
$3\frac{7}{8}$, '84	10	63	6,300	312.50	5.0
			$52,700	$3,518.50	6.7
Alternates					
Diamond Inter.	100	26	$ 2,600	$ 200	7.7%
DuPont	50	91	4,550	275	6.8
Kroger Co.	100	19	1,900	136	7.2
Norfolk & Western	100	69	6,900	500	7.2
Alcoa CV $5\frac{1}{4}$, '91	5	75	3,750	262.50	7.0
Reading & Bates					
CV $5\frac{1}{2}$, '88	5	78	3,900	275	5.7
C & O $4\frac{1}{2}$, '92	10	54	5,400	450	8.3
Liggett & Myers					
6, '92	10	76	7,600	600	7.9
Pacific T&T $2\frac{3}{4}$, '85	10	60	6,000	275	4.6
Union Carbide					
5.3, '97	10	71	7,100	530	7.5
U.S. Steel 4s, '83	10	70	7,000	400	5.7

Within their categories, all of these securities are interchangeable—depending on your own requirements. If you are conservative, select more bonds and AT&T stock; if you are more aggressive and feel optimistic, buy fewer fixed-income securities and additional shares of Gulf States, Beatrice Foods, or Kroger, etc. And of course it is not necessary to have as many different holdings as indicated. As a rule of thumb, investments should total about $5,000 per corporation—e.g., for $55,000, a maximum of 11 different investments.

How the Experts Rate These Securities

American Natural Gas

Extensive underground storage facilities, adequate reserves, contract to buy 5 trillion cubic feet of Canadian gas, and owner of 2.7 billion tons of lignate for possible production of synthetic gas. In the past 10 years, ANG has boosted its dividend from $1.60 to $2.54 per share.

AT&T

Lucrative return on well-protected dividend. Little downside risk. Significant earnings growth despite problems with governmental agencies. Return on common equity back over 10%.

(For **Beatrice Foods** and **Coca-Cola,** see Chapter XXV, on Investments.)

General Motors

GM will be back. Over the long term, this powerful corporation has the capability of producing a high rate of return on investment. Total growth, from capital gains and dividends, should average 20% compound annual rate.

Gulf States Utilities

Pays ample dividends, is in a strong growth area with realistic governmental commissions, and should continue its steady growth.

Travelers Corporation

A major, full-line insurance company that is benefiting from high interest rates, fewer highway accidents, and reduction of industrial hazards under federal safety programs. The preferred, convertible to 1.1 shares of common, is at a small premium.

Ford Credit's Bond

Convertible into 12.8 shares of Ford Motor stock. The income is safe, the growth potential good.

Tenneco

The largest gas pipeline operator, active in petroleum exploration in "safe" areas, prominent in booming shipbuilding, has interests in the manufacturing of automotive, construction, and agricultural equipment. The debenture is convertible at 69⅜ (price of common stock).

Pacific G&E

A major utility in a strong growth area. These bonds are rated Aa, and in 10 years, their value will increase by 66%.

Note: To be sure of attaining that 10% return each year, watch your holdings carefully and review the portfolio every 3 to 6 months. If your projections indicate you will not reach your goal, sell some stocks and buy securities with higher yields. *But do not trade.* Successful investing takes time and patience. There's little fear of lower dividends with stocks like these, but capital gains can be slow in coming if Wall Street sours on an industry group.

Selecting Investment Companies

If you are unwilling or reluctant to invest your own retirement funds, investment companies can provide professional management, immediate liquidity, and many convenient services. But you may not always get the best, or unless you choose wisely, even average returns. Most mutual funds are managed for growth rather than income, but it's up to you to find one—or more— that will fit your specific objectives.

Investment companies are discussed in detail in another chapter, but broadly speaking, the criteria in selection of a depositary-money management fund for retirement income should be: (1) objectives, (2) performance, (3) services, and (4) size of fund.

Objectives

These should be conservative. In retirement, assured income is more important than growth. Capital gains are welcome but *always* secondary (unless you are wealthy).

Your choices are:

STRAIGHT INCOME FUNDS. These invest all or most of their money in fixed-income securities—bonds, convertibles, preferred stocks, government bills and notes, and occasionally, high-dividend-paying common stocks.

Be wary of any fund that reports consistently rising payouts. In an effort to beat competition, some fund managers may take extra risks in short-term paper or low-rated bonds. Concentrate on funds whose returns are closely related to the interest rate. This is always the key factor in income securities-investments.

BALANCED FUNDS. Their primary goal is preservation of capital —good income and moderate growth. Typically, their portfolios will contain a high percentage of bonds and preferred stocks and a small-to-modest holding of high-quality common stocks. Their income may not be as high as that of income funds, but over the years the capital appreciation should be greater.

AGGRESSIVE BALANCED FUNDS. The managers of these funds shift their portfolios with the trend of the stock market—more fixed-income securities when values are declining; more common stocks when they are rising. Income will not be as high nor as steady as that of the first 2 funds, but their capital appreciation, especially in good times, will be substantial—with wise selections.

Performance

This is always important. The only way you can judge the future of any fund is by its past record. Look for funds that have long-term records of annual gains of over 6% (not including dividends) in rising markets and of declines less than those of stock market averages in down periods (hopefully offset by ample dividends).

Check the record of total returns for at least 5, and preferably 10, years. *Do not be impressed by 1 or 2 years of superior performance. You are planning to live at least 15 more years.*

Pay special attention to performance in the bull market of 1962–70 and the bear market of 1973–74. Some funds that scored high in good times bombed when glamour-growth stocks faded. Others, which stressed quality and income, held up fairly well in erratic markets. For retirement, look only at conservatively managed funds.

Remember: You are looking for average annual returns of 10%, so the fund will have to beat that mark in some years to offset less rewarding results in others. One way you could hedge is to shift from one fund to another—in a strong bull market, from an income to an aggressive balanced fund; in a bear market, vice versa. BUT BE CAREFUL TO SWITCH ONLY A PORTION OF YOUR NEST EGG. *And never, never consider a straight growth fund if you must depend on the income from the investment company.*

Fortunately, such a change need not be expensive. Most investment companies manage several different types of funds and permit shareholders to swap for a small handling fee.

Before you make such a decision, check the portfolio of the fund whose shares you own. If the securities are those of quality corporations that are currently undervalued, chances are good that the dividends are ample and that in a rising market their values will bounce back.

But if you spot poor quality, risky stocks or bonds, get out fast. You should not have bought such shares anyway.

Services

Look for extras that can benefit your life-style and make your living easier and more convenient, with such services as:

REGULAR INCOME CHECKS. This is the No. 1 consideration for most people. They have been used to a regular paycheck and need income every month.

This can be achieved in several ways: (1) by buying shares in several funds, each with different dividend months; (2) by arranging for regular quarterly dividends to be paid in monthly installments; and (3) by permitting the sale of some shares if needed to supplement the dividends.

Example: That $5,500 annual income you need comes out to almost $460 a month. If the fund is able to earn 10% a year, your principal will remain intact. But if the fund reports dividends of only 4% and capital gains of 3%, you will have to invade capital—sell some shares to get that extra $140 each month.

Hopefully, of course, the returns will improve to well over 10% annually, so your savings will start to grow again. Still, as the table on page 317 shows, if the fund can average only 5% a year, your principal is almost sure to outlast your life span!

ASK ABOUT BENEFICIARY DESIGNATION. This provision is not legal in some states and not available through some funds. It permits you to name your beneficiary by means of a trust agreement. This will assure that the investment will go directly to your designated heir when you die. There will be none of the delays or expense of probate.

Size

Stay away from the extremes—funds with multibillions move too slowly and are not able to take advantage of fast-growing medium-size companies; funds with less than $100 million in assets are suspect. If they have been operating for some years, their performance must have been poor. If they are new, there's no track record.

Possible Tax Savings

Recently, the Supreme Court ruled that for purposes of estate and gift taxes, mutual-fund shares must be valued at the asking price on the day of valuation. This price is *higher* than the price at which the shares could be redeemed because it involves the loading charge—about 8.5%.

With that $55,000 in a load fund, the difference would be a small $467, but with a large estate, or gift, the gap would be substantial.

If you have received a sizable gift or inheritance of mutual-fund shares since May, 1973, ask your lawyer how the shares were valued. An amended estate tax return might mean a welcome tax refund!

Options to Boost Retirement Income

Writing calls is a technique that offers unusual opportunities to boost income on a conservative basis. For those who want maximum income (about 12% annual rate plus dividends), options can be written to obtain the highest premiums. *The risk:* some depletion of capital if the price of the basic stocks declines.

For those who can afford to take less income (6% to 8%, plus dividends) and still want long-term appreciation, options can be written on an "out-of-the-money" basis.

The best stocks for all types of options are those whose calls are traded on the Chicago Board of Options Exchange (CBOE) and the American Stock Exchange (AMEX). There's also a sure, active, liquid market.

Options can be speculative, but it takes 2 to make a transaction. The opposite side of the deal can be conservative. That's why retirees, with limited funds, should stick to *writing* calls.

The primary types of options are calls and puts. A call is the right to buy a specified number of shares (usually 100) of a specified stock at a specified price (striking price) before a specified date. A put is the opposite—the right to sell. In the future there may be listed markets for puts, but at this writing, calls provide the best, most liquid, and most active opportunities.

Options are written for varying periods of time, but for retirement portfolios, they should be concentrated on those for 190 days (6 months and 10 days) to take advantage of the lower capital gains tax rate.

The cost of an option is called a premium. It varies with the duration of the contract, the type of stock, and the general activity of the market. According to Leroy Gross, director of options, Reynolds Securities, Inc., a national brokerage firm, the percentage ranges for premiums are:

Time of Option	Volatility of Stock	Premium as Percentage of Underlying Stock Value	
		Call	Put
6 months, 10 days	High	15%–20%	12%–18%
	Medium	10%–12%	8%–10%
	Low	7%–8%	6%–7%

Note: Calls for shorter periods are lower, but turnover is faster. Profits are taxed at regular income rates.

Calls on both CBOE and AMEX are traded with exercise dates every three months. With additional listings, you can pick an expiration date almost every month. Usually, there are two striking prices but, in volatile markets, there can be more. With Xerox at 54½, there were calls available at 6 prices: 110, 100, 90, 80, 70, and 60. The premiums ranged from a tiny 5/16ths for the 110 option to 6⅜ths for the 60s.

This means that if you bought 100 shares of XRX at 54½ in

December, you could sell an April call for a premium of from $3.12 to $637.50. For the low price you agree to sell 100 shares at 110 ($11,000); for the high premium, at 60 ($6,000).

The odds are always with the seller, because according to a survey by the SEC, most options are never exercised. *The basic concept of writing options is to accept a limited, assured profit instead of an uncertain but potentially greater gain.*

Investors who write options on a programmed basis hope to average 15% a year (after commissions on the option and occasionally on the stock), plus 3% to 6% in dividends! Most settle for somewhat less.

The 2 ways that retirees can use calls to boost income and/or capital with CBOE stocks are for high yields and for long-term holdings.

FOR HIGH YIELDS. Sell a 190-day call for the premium—no less than 12% and hopefully as much as 20%. With an almost twice-a-year turnover, shoot for total returns of 25%—and settle for a little less. You also get the dividends as long as you own the stock.

Note: All examples are without commissions and fees.

Example: When Kresge (KG) was quoted at 19¾ in December, a July call was 4 ($400 on a $1,975 investment). That's a 20.2% return in just over 6 months.

With such a relatively volatile stock, the chances are good that its price will move above 24, and thus the stock will have to be sold (with the commission reducing your profit). But you would have $400 at the outset, plus $11 in dividends if you held the stock through 2 declaration dates.

When a call is not exercised, the same stock can be used again and again. *The big danger:* The price of the stock will go down. Thus, the next call might have to be written at 15, so even at 20%, the premium would be much lower—$300. Et cetera.

The best way to use this income-first approach is to set aside $4,000 to $5,000 every month and buy stocks whose options are traded on the CBOE, with emphasis on those commanding the highest premiums. Thus, a hypothetical program might be as follows:

January

Buy 200 shares KG for $4,000.
Sell July call at 20 for 4 to get $800.

February

Buy 100 shares of Upjohn at 45.
Sell July call at 45 for 6 to gain $600.

March

Buy 300 shares of Northwest Airlines at 16.
Sell October calls as 15 for 3 to get $600.

Note: From the premium deduct the commission—$25 for one call, proportionately less thereafter.

FOR LONG-TERM HOLDINGS. The "out-of-the-money" approach is best for people who own or prefer to hold high-quality stocks over the years. The premiums will be small—seldom more than 8%—but the chances of the stock's being called are small and the opportunities for capital gains large. The key is to sell calls at striking prices "out of the money"—well above the current quotations of the stock. You want the extra, assured income but also want to hold the stocks on which the calls are written.

Example: (cited by Alph C. Beane, Sr., Reynolds Securities, Inc., a specialist in option writing for older investors):

Mr. May, who has just reached his sixty-fifth birthday, has a portfolio worth about $45,300:

		Price	Value
100 shares	Eastman Kodak	60	$ 6,000
100 "	IBM	165	16,500
100 "	Exxon	60	6,000
200 "	Monsanto	40	8,000
200 "	Sears Roebuck	44	8,800

Mr. May wants more income than the annual $1,856 dividends but does not need regular monthly payments. He asks broker Beane to set up a call-writing program by using computer-based data to select the most rewarding calls "out of the money."

Example: With EK at 60, sell a call, due in 3 months, at 70 for 6⅞—$687.50, a 7.7% premium. The stock would have to go up about 10 points, to 70, to be picked up. That's possible but not probable in such a short period—except in a very strong market.

With IBM, sell a 190-day call at 200 for 18½—an 11.2% premium.

In each case, the call is written to make a modest profit and retain the stock. If EK should move more rapidly than anticipated and hit the low 70s in 60 days, cover the call by buying an option at a price of 5 or less (hopefully for under 1). This would wipe out much of the premium, but the underlying stock would be worth more.

With such a program, it is possible to secure an average annual income of $6,000 to $7,000, *plus* dividends, *plus* opportunities for long-term capital gains with stocks that every intelligent investor would like to own—most of the time.

Special Investments—Ginnie Maes

These are mortgage-based securities that provide high but varying returns representing interest, amortization, and return of principal. They have a limited life but long enough to fit the needs of most retirees. Ginnie Maes are "pass-through" securities backed by both the Government National Mortgage Association and the Federal Housing Administration (or Veterans Administration). They represent pools of single-family mortgages that have been packaged by mortgage brokers. The monthly payments—and prepayments—of homeowners are "passed through" to investors.

Here's How Ginnie Maes Work

A large brokerage firm buys a million-dollar certificate, then sells portions at retail—with a $25,000 minimum investment. The buyer receives a certificate showing the pool number (important for identification), original principal amount, interest rate, and maturity—typically 30 years from date.

The total of the interest and amortization (just like your own mortgage payment) remains steady; the "extras" vary according to the number of prepayments or refinancings. As the average mortgage is paid off or refinanced in 12 years, total income starts to rise after the third year and declines after the twelfth year. There is usually some income for the full 30 years.

Example: You invest $25,000. That's 2½% of a $1-million, 8%-interest pool. You get 2½% of all proceeds. In year 1, a monthly check of $303.45—$162.13 interest and $21.32 amortization. In year 2, one $20,000 mortgage is paid off so you get an extra early payment of $500; in year 3, 3 mortgages, totaling $70,000, are refinanced or prepaid so you get a lump sum of $1,750 during the year. That would boost your average monthly income to almost $450.

Paine Webber, Jackson & Curtis, a national brokerage firm, points out that the taxes on the income are heavier in the early years because this is the period when the homeowner is paying more interest than amortization. This is taxable as ordinary income. Later, when a majority of each monthly homeowner's check is reducing the mortgage, this is a return of capital and so is tax-free.

For wealthy retirees, there are participation certificates, issued now and then by the Federal Home Loan Mortgage Corporation. These are available in units of $100,000, and while similar to Ginnie Maes, have no active secondary market. Usually, however, they can be sold back to FHLMC.

Ginnie Maes are an excellent vehicle for retirees who want security and a regular monthly income. The returns start fairly low, rise steadily after about the third year, reach a peak in the eighth to fourteenth years, and at the end of 30 years are com-

Don't Be Afraid to Invade Capital

When you retire, live it up a little even if you have to invade capital! Unless, of course, there are strong reasons why you feel it necessary to leave a large sum to your heirs.

If you're worried about ending up a pauper, double the number of years of life expectancy and then set up a plan to invade your capital accordingly. If you are a 70-year-old widow, you have, actuarially, about 15 years to live. So arrange your investments (better with a mutual fund) to withdraw one-thirtieth of your capital each year. You won't go broke until you reach 100!

Meantime, that extra money makes it possible to have the extra pleasure of eating out, entertaining friends, taking trips, visiting grandchildren, etc.

And if you reach 75, you may want to review your plan and speed up the withdrawals. By doubling the figure this time, you can withdraw one-twentieth of the remaining principal each year.

Life Expectancy

Age	Male	Female
65	15.92	19.11
66	15.24	18.30
67	14.58	17.50
68	13.93	16.71
69	13.29	15.94
70	12.67	15.18
71	12.07	14.44
72	11.47	13.72
73	10.90	13.01
74	10.34	12.33
75	9.80	11.66
76	9.27	11.02
77	8.76	10.39
78	8.27	9.78
79	7.80	9.19
80	7.35	8.64

Source: Equitable Life Assurance Society.

pletely paid up. *Best bet:* Buy Ginnie Maes as supplementary investments.

How Long Will Your Nest Egg Last?

Another way to find out how much you can afford to invade your capital is to use the following table. It shows how long your investments will last when they provide a fixed rate of return and the same percentage of the original investment is withdrawn annually.

Unless you have all your holdings in fixed-income securities where the rate of return is pretty much predetermined (and even that will change as bonds mature, etc.), use this table as a frame of reference. No stock-based portfolio, whether managed by a mutual-fund or investment adviser, will show the same rate of return each year. The best you can count on is an average based on past performance.

Even that may be deceiving. If you start your retirement when there's a bear market, there'll be no capital appreciation, so withdrawals from capital will be relatively high. Later, when the bull market boosts total returns, there will be fewer assets.

And as many a mutual fund discovered in 1973 and early 1974, there are some years when returns can be small or nonexistent. It is mighty difficult to make sufficient gains to replace such losses in a few years! *Temper all projections presented by your mutual-fund salesman or enthusiastic broker or investment adviser.*

To find out how much of your capital you can withdraw each year, start with the left-hand column and decide how much, percentagewise, you will need each year. Then move to the column under the anticipated rate of return. Thus, you can withdraw 10% of your original holdings each year for 20 years if the average return is 8%.

If it's easier to understand, take the actual dollar figures— 10% of a $100,000 portfolio is $10,000; 10% of that

$55,000 retirement fund is $5,500 a year from 1975 through 1995.

Growth and Withdrawals

Annual Withdrawal	Number of Years Fund Will Last at Annual Growth Rate of							
	5%	6%	7%	8%	9%	10%	11%	12%
5%								
6	36							
7	25	33						
8	20	23	30					
9	16	18	22	28				
10	14	15	17	20	26			
11	12	13	14	16	19	25		
12	11	11	12	14	15	18	23	
13	9	10	11	12	13	15	17	21
14	9	9	10	11	11	13	14	17
15	8	8	9	9	10	11	12	14

Checklist of Itemized Deductions on Income Tax of Retirees

Medical and Dental Expenses

DEDUCTIBLE WHEN IN EXCESS OF 3% OF TAXPAYER'S ADJUSTED GROSS INCOME:

> Medical, hospital, and health insurance premiums when in excess of $150
> Costs of drugs and medicines exceeding 1% of adjusted gross income
> Abdominal supports
> Ambulance hire
> Anesthetist
> Arch supports
> Artificial limbs and teeth
> Back supports

Braces
Cardiograph
Chiropodist
Chiropractor
Christian Science practitioner
Convalescent home (medical treatment only)
Crutches
Dental services (cleaning, filling, etc., of teeth)
Dentures
Dermatologist
Eyeglasses
Gynecologist
Hearing aid and batteries
Hospital expenses
Insulin treatment
Invalid chair
Lab tests
Lip-reading lessons (to overcome handicap)
Neurologist
Nursing services (for medical care)
Ophthalmologist
Optician
Optometrist
Osteopath (licensed)
Physical examinations
Physician
Physiotherapist
Podiatrist
Psychiatrist
Psychoanalyst
Psychologist
Psychotherapy
Radium therapy
Sacroiliac belt
Seeing-eye dog
Splints
Surgeon

Transportation expenses for medical purposes
Vaccines
Vitamins (prescribed by MD)
Wheelchairs
Whirlpool baths (medical purposes)
X rays

Insurance Premiums

One-half of medical, hospital, or health insurance premiums
up to $150

Taxes

Real estate
State and local gasoline
General sales
State and local income
Personal property

Contributions

Up to 50% of adjusted gross income, but only 20% for
certain private nonprofit foundations, veterans organizations, and fraternal societies
Cash
Goods—to fair market value
Purchase of goods or tickets (excess of amount paid over
fair market value of goods or services—e.g., if ticket to
charity ball costs $100, can deduct only portion not repre-
senting cost of meal, etc.)
Out-of-pocket expenses (travel, postage, etc.) while serving
charity

Interest

Home mortgage
Auto loan

Installment purchases
Bank credit card finance charges
Points—required to obtain mortgage loan
Penalty for prepayment of mortgage
Revolving charge accounts (finance charge only)

Casualty or Theft Losses

Losses from tornado, flood, storm, fire, or auto accident, provided not caused by a willful act or willful negligence; theft losses to nonbusiness property

Generally, the amount of the casualty loss deduction is the lesser of (1) the decrease in fair market value of the property as a result of the casualty or (2) your adjusted basis in the property.

This amount can be further reduced by insurance or other recovery, and if property is held for personal use, by the $100 limitation. Use Form 4684 for personal casualty loss.

Child and Disabled Dependent Care Expenses

Employment-related expenses incurred in obtaining care for:
1. dependent under 15
2. physically or mentally disabled dependent
3. disabled spouse

Maximum deduction—$400 per month

When adjusted gross income exceeds $18,000, deduction reduced by $1 for each $2 of income above this amount. For full information, see Publication 503, *Child Care and Disabled Dependent Care,* at an IRS office.

Miscellaneous

Alimony and separate maintenance
Appraisal fees for casualty loss or to determine fair market value of charitable contributions

Business entertainment expenses
Business gift expenses (not over $25 per recipient)
Campaign contributions—up to $100 for joint returns, $50 for singles
Cost of preparation of income tax return
Cost of tools for employee
Dues for chamber of commerce
Educational expenses to maintain position or sharpen skills
Employment agency fees for securing employment
Fees paid to investment counselors
Payments made by a teacher to substitute
Rental cost of safe-deposit box for income-producing property
Special safety equipment
Subscriptions to business publications
Telephone and postage in connection with investments
Uniforms required for employment (and maintenance)
Union dues

Watch the Headlines to Discover Changes in Tax Legislation
If You Have Any Questions, Call the Nearest IRS Office

Tax Returns for Retirees

Filing Status	Required to File Tax Return if Gross Income at Least
Single (under age 65)	$2,350
Single (65 or older)	3,100
Married (both under 65), joint return	3,400
Married (1 spouse 65 or older), joint return	4,150
Married (both 65 or older), joint return	4,900
Married, filing separately	750

EXEMPTIONS. If you are 65 or older on the last day of the taxable year, there is an additional exemption of $750. You are considered 65 on the day before your sixty-fifth birthday. If 65 on January 1, 1975, you are entitled to an extra exemption on your 1974 federal tax return.

DEPENDENTS. Dependents may be claimed if they meet these 5 tests: (1) support, (2) gross income, (3) member of household or relationship, (4) citizenship, (5) separate return. Generally, the taxpayer must contribute more than half the support.

Even if you are single and live alone but support a parent, you can claim a dependent if he or she is a U.S. resident, citizen or national of Canada, Mexico, the Canal Zone, or Panama.

RETIREMENT INCOME CREDIT. To qualify, income must be from pensions, annuities, interest, dividends, or gross rents, and you must be a U.S. citizen or resident and have received earned income in excess of $600 in each of any 10 calendar years before 1973. The credit is 15% of the lesser of: (1) taxpayer's qualifying retirement income or (2) $1,524 ($2,286 for joint return when both are over 65), minus the total of nontaxable pensions (Social Security, Railroad Retirement annuities) and earned income (depending on taxpayer's age and amount of earnings).

If under 62, reduce the $1,524 figure by the amount of earned income in excess of $900.

For those between 62 and 72: Reduce by one-half of the earned income in excess of $1,200 up to $1,700, plus the total amount over $1,700.

Over 72: not subject to earned-income limitations.

Note: The IRS will compute the retirement-income credit on request.

Beware of Deferred Income

If you are, or become, an upper-echelon executive and are eligible for a deferred-income plan, be cautious. Originally, such postponed income was subject to lower, after-retirement taxes. No more, if you are in a high income bracket. There's a 50% limit on earned income, but no ceiling on retirement income or deferred income.

Example: prior to 1969, a corporation executive arranged to have his company set aside $30,000 annually to be paid after retirement. In 1974, he paid $42,000 on a net taxable income of $100,000.

With higher pensions, he can look forward to $82,000 —$52,000 pension, plus $30,000 deferred income. This is taxable at 55%, so he will have to shell out $2,200 more in taxes on that deferred $30,000 than he would if he took the money now.

Another negative: Should he die before collecting all the deferred income (and 70% of husbands die before their wives), his beneficiary might have to pay taxes on the full amount unpaid in the year of death if she has the right to take a lump-sum payment even if the actual payment is spread over many years.

Advice: Eliminate the lump-sum provision or set up a trust that will minimize the tax bite and see your tax adviser at once.

XX

How to Check Your Corporate Pension Plan

Pension plans are undergoing major changes as the result of the passage of the 1974 Employee Retirement Income Security Act. It is too early to judge the full impact of this milestone legislation, but basically it mandates federal regulation of private pension plans and ensures pensions for eligible employees regardless of dismissal, resignation, layoff, sickness, bankruptcy, shutdown, or merger. Starting January 1, 1976, almost all plans must conform to certain vesting, participation, and funding requirements.

Unless you are a corporate executive, in industrial relations, or an official of a labor union, you will probably have little to say in how your pension plan is shaped or managed. But you can judge the merits or failings of the pension plan of your present company or prospective employer by checking these points. Most of the answers can be found in the explanatory booklet available from the company's industrial relations department.

Method of Computing Pension Income

This can be based on your salary or years of employment, officially designated as Credited Service (CS), or both. The booklet will probably contain a sample work sheet so you can guesstimate what you will receive.

A typical plan might provide 1.25% of salary-wages of the last year of employment for each year of CS, *less* 1⅔% of the Social Security benefit for each year of service. Usually, the deduction is limited to 50% of the Social Security payment.

Example: You have worked for the company for 30 years and are earning $25,000. Your Social Security will be $3,648 annually.

$$30 \times 1.25\% = 37.50\% \times \$25,000 = \$9,375$$
$$1.67 \times 30 = 5.01 \times \$3,648 = \$1,828.$$

Since $1,828 is just above 50% of the Social Security, deduct only 50% ($1,824) to get an annual pension of $7,551.

Rules for Credited Service

Find the answers to these questions:

How long do you have to work each year to get CS?
If you leave and return, how much do you lose?
Are these special provisions for leaves of absence, military or government service, illness, etc.?

In many cases, the new law sets standards well above those of old pension plans. If you feel you have been, or are, the victim of discrimination or misinterpretation, consult your lawyer or contact the new federal agency.

Rules for Joining Pension Plan

Under the new legislation, eligibility must be extended to:

- Persons 25 years of age with at least 1 year's employment (exceptions for companies with high turnover).
- Newly hired workers, unless they are within 5 years of company's normal retirement age.
- Part-time workers (1,000 work hours a year).

Leaving before Retirement Age

Broadly speaking, the new law sets the following pattern for vesting (guaranteeing the right to pension benefits): after 5 years, 25% of accumulated benefits; after 10 years, 50%; after 15 years, 100%.

There's also the rule of 45: When age and years of service add up to 45 (after 5 years' service), the worker must be 50% vested, with 10% increase for each additional year to a maximum of 100%.

Some companies permit early retirement with options: (1) full pension if employee waits until age 65, (2) immediate income which, as a rule of thumb, will be reduced 6% for each year before normal retirement date. Thus, the employee who would get $8,000 a year at 65 would get about $6,500 if he retired at 60.

Pension Benefits to Beneficiaries

Under the new law, an employee's spouse may be eligible to receive at least 50% of accrued pension benefits if the employee dies *after* retirement.

Under most corporate plans, the employee agrees to accept a smaller pension if payments will be made to his widow.

It is also important to find out how long before retirement you must decide which plan to choose and if you are permitted to change your mind before you start drawing pension checks.

And be sure to ask if your beneficiary benefits from your pension plan if you die *before* retirement. Such information will be in the company's printed, explanatory booklet.

Financing of Pension Plan

Do so to the maximum. You will receive substantial extra benefits: (1) Your money, deducted from your paycheck, will not be counted as taxable income up to $1,500 per year. (2) You will be dollar-cost-averaging your investment so that, over a period of time, you will be maximizing your funds. (3) Your money will grow rapidly as the result of the magic of compounding the dividends and interest. *BUT you can receive less if the investment performance creates a loss instead of a gain.*

> *Note:* Under the new law, employees in a pension plan are guaranteed protection if the company moves, goes broke, or is merged. Qualified employees can collect up to $750 per month from the Pension Benefit Guaranty Corporation, financed by a head tax on each employee with a company that has a pension plan. This is full assurance that you can count on some retirement benefits even if they are delayed by government red tape.

Provisions for Disability before Retirement

Find out exactly how disability is defined and who makes the decision—the corporation, the insurance company, the physician, or a combination of these.

Are there different benefits if you are not fully vested at time of disability? Under Social Security, for example, the period of disability counts as Credited Service.

Profit-Sharing and Thrift Plans

If your company has a profit-sharing or thrift plan, add these checkpoints:

INVESTMENT OPTIONS. Do you have a choice in the types of investments for all or part of your own or corporate contributions —U.S. Savings Bonds, company stock, growth portfolio, bond portfolio, balanced holdings?

These options make it easier to integrate the profit-sharing or thrift plan into your own estate program.

AMOUNT OF EMPLOYEE CONTRIBUTIONS. Typically, a corporate thrift plan will match employee contributions on an advancing scale (2%, 4%, 6%, etc.) of income up to a maximum, usually 6% to 10%. Thus, an individual earning $20,000 can have $4,000 in a profit-sharing plan—$2,000 of his own funds and $2,000 matched by the company. Often, the company contribution may be made only when the employee participates, and sometimes the total may be limited to 6% of annual profits.

ALWAYS MAKE THE MAXIMUM CONTRIBUTION POSSIBLE. YOU WILL HAVE TWICE AS MUCH MONEY WORKING FOR YOU, AND THERE ARE ALSO TAX ADVANTAGES, AS EARNINGS ARE NOT TAXABLE UNTIL WITHDRAWN.

RULES FOR WITHDRAWAL. Can you withdraw your savings and leave the accumulated income and corporate contributions? It's also well to find out how long you must wait before you can make any withdrawals, whether there are penalties, and whether there are provisions for using the funds as collateral for a loan—from the company credit union, a corporate bank, or your own local institution.

XXI

How to Set Up Your Personal
Pension Plan

Every wage earner can have a retirement-pension plan as the result of the Employee Benefit Security Act of 1974. If you are self-employed or work with a small group, you can choose a Keogh Plan (HR-10) or a professional corporation. Both require that all full-time employees be included.

If you are not covered under a corporate plan, Keogh Plan, or some public retirement fund, you can set up your own Individual Retirement Account (IRA).

Broadly speaking, the decision should be made on the basis of your tax bracket—IRA for those who pay federal income taxes at a rate of 25% or less, Keogh for those in the 25%-to-40% bracket, and professional corporations for those who earn $50,000 or more. *But there are advantages in each.*

All of these personal pension plans provide present and future tax savings:

Annual contributions are tax-free and so reduce your income tax base.

All fund earnings, from interest–dividends–capital gains, accumulate tax-free until they are withdrawn, when, presumably, the beneficiary will be in a lower tax bracket.

Even a modest pension plan will grow to BIG money in a short time. An annual contribution of $5,000, with an average annual return of 8%, will rise to over $70,000 in 10 years and to almost $225,000 in 20 years. It's the magic of compound interest—earning interest on interest. Growth will be even greater when contributions are made quarterly and invested promptly.

Every individual who has reasonable anticipation of annual earned income of over $1,000 not subject to a pension plan should consider his or her personal retirement plan. You can set up your own program if you are already covered on your regular job (or do not want to participate) IF there is earned income from another source—moonlighting, free-lancing, etc.

(Earned income is money paid for work or services. Unearned income comes from interest, dividends, capital gains, royalties, etc.)

Under the Keogh Plan, a self-employed person (a physician, dentist, free-lance writer, accountant, owner of a small business, etc.) is permitted to deduct the smaller of $7,500 or 15% of earned income, from pretax profits and set it aside in a qualified pension or profit-sharing plan.

There must be proportionate contributions for all full-time, nonseasonal employees who have been with you for 3 years or longer. A full-time employee is one who works more than 20 hours per week. A nonseasonal employee is one who works more than 5 months in any calendar year. With a new business, you must include employees who have been with you since the beginning.

Thus, a physician who earns $40,000 can set aside $6,000 a year, plus $1,800 for his long-time office manager (salary, $12,000) and $1,500 for his nurse (salary, $10,000).

In addition, he can make voluntary contributions of 10% of earned income (his own and that of employees) up to $2,500 each. This extra money is not tax-deductible, but its investment income is tax-free until withdrawn.

If you start early—and there's no age restriction—and make regular contributions to the 15% maximum, you will be assured of retirement income as much as you regularly earned! If your savings are invested profitably, your *monthly* income will be as much as one-half of your *annual* contribution.

Example: Over 25 years, $4,000 annual savings will provide $24,000 a year income—at 8% total returns. If that return can be boosted to 10%, the goal can be achieved in 20 years.

As Steven R. Anreder explains in his excellent book, *Retirement Dollars for the Self-Employed,* even a person over 60 can put away funds, save on taxes, and shelter dividends and appreciation of principal until age 70½, when he must take the benefits.

All Keogh Plans must be qualified by the IRS. From then on, all income and realized capital gains can be reinvested without payment of income taxes. Benefits cannot be taken, except in case of death or disability, before age 59½, or with employees, at termination of employment. Withdrawals prior to that time are subject to tax penalties.

Management of the Funds

Most people prefer to work with a standardized plan offered by a bank, savings institution, or mutual fund. This is convenient in that all details are handled for you—paperwork, reports, tax data, supervision of distribution of benefits, etc. But such a course is not always the most rewarding. If you feel competent to handle your own investments, you can be your own trustee under a qualified-by-the-IRS plan.

It's easiest to personalize a standard plan with the help of your attorney and tax adviser. Future changes can be costly and difficult if you try to do it yourself.

The management of private pension plans can be handled by:

The Trust

Legal title of invested funds is transferred to a bank or trust company. The trustee is free to make almost any type of investment—stocks, bonds, savings accounts, real estate, etc., under your direction.

Under some circumstances, an individual, including the self-employed person or a member of his family, can be designated as trustee. Check with your lawyer on this—there are restrictions on coverage, and investments are limited to endowments or life insurance contracts. A firm where no one individual holds more than a 10% interest can serve as its own trustee.

Direct Purchase

This permits you to make direct purchases of certain investments such as: (1) fixed annuities where guaranteed retirement payments are made, (2) variable annuities where the payout depends on the insurance company's success in stock investments, (3) "face-amount certificates" issued by mutual funds. At maturity, the participant receives the face amount in a lump sum, or by prior arrangement, in periodic installments which are nontransferable.

Custodial Account

A bank is designated custodian to take full charge of the contributions and with authority to make all investments, reinvest dividends, interest, and capital gains. The funds must be invested *exclusively* in the shares of a regulated mutual fund (not closed-end funds) or *exclusively* in an annuity, endowment insurance contract, or in fixed-income securities such as certificates of deposit, savings instruments, and bonds.

Group Plan

This is similar to a trust account and is available through professional groups. Commissions and fees are lower than those charged to individuals, but their investments tend to be conservative and inflexible, so, generally, returns have been mediocre to poor.

Professional Corporations for Larger Groups

The professional corporation is ideal for larger groups and for high-income individuals. It enables sole proprietors and partners to operate as a corporation and take advantage of tax deductions, payment of insurance policies and retirement benefits, and make broader investments than are permitted under most Keogh plans. You can contribute more, deduct more, and draw out more at retirement than you can as an individual partner or participant in an HR-10 or IRA.

Example: When a corporate profit-sharing plan is combined with a pension plan, the contribution (tax-free) can be up to 25%. With a Keogh plan an individual earning $50,000 would be limited to $7,500 annual contribution; with a professional corporation, this can be $12,500. Retirement payments are taxable as capital gains.

Other advantages, according to Anreder, are: The corporation can borrow money, retirement benefits start at 50, penalties for excess contributions are less, and corporate funds can be used to buy medical, disability, and insurance benefits. With proper legal advice, it is also possible for the corporation to pay for college costs of children of principals.

There are disadvantages: You must hold regular directors' meetings, record minutes, vote on all proposals, and distribute cash annually. There are also extra taxes: Social Security (paid by both the corporation and individuals), state and local levies, and often, extra insurance fees. Vesting provisions on pension plans must be applied equally, and immediately, to all employees, and must total 100% after 10 years.

How to Use the IRA

The IRA is limited to an annual tax-free contribution of $1,500. If you work for a corporation and do not like their pension plan (nowadays the chances of any employer not having a plan are slight), you are allowed to set up your own IRA. Or if an individual, such as a part-time worker, does not make enough to justify a Keogh Plan, the IRA is worthwhile.

Generally, the procedures are similar to those of the Keogh Plan—a trust fund, custodial account, or self-trusteeship. You cannot buy life insurance, but an endowment contract is OK. In that case, only that part of the premium earmarked for the savings portion of the contract is deductible.

A flexible premium annuity is being offered by several insurance companies, such as Bankers National Life. Premium payments can be reduced, then increased. The policy cannot lapse. Thus, a smaller contribution will keep the policy in force, and you can move up to $1,500 again when you can afford to do so. This is a great advantage if your earnings should fall for a year or two.

This plan locks in your tax benefits without forcing a fixed contribution. Furthermore, there's 100% first-year cash value— the surrender value is always the greater of total premium payments or accumulated cash value.

One of the major uses for the IRA is expected to be as a temporary parking place for pension funds when switching from one job to another or when transferring from a qualified plan. The transfer must be made within 60 days of the original change and can be effected only once every 3 years.

Drawbacks: Contributions above $1,500 a year are subject to a 6% penalty, and if withdrawals are made before retirement, they are taxed at regular income tax rates plus a 10% penalty.

At this writing, the IRS has not issued detailed rules on the IRA, so check with your local IRS office before you start any IRA plan.

Investments for Personal Pension Plans

The types of investments vary somewhat according to the plan, the trustee, and the wishes of the sponsor. Almost all plans can buy: life insurance, to age 60, convertible into retirement-annuity contracts; endowments; annuities; shares of open-end mutual funds; bonds rated BBB or higher; common stocks rated B+ or higher by Standard & Poor's; U.S. government securities; certificates of deposit; and insured/guaranteed mortgages.

Specifically, here are choices and probable returns:

Savings Accounts, Certificates of Deposit

In periods of high interest, the yields will be from about 6¾% to 7¾%, depending on method of compounding. Over the long term, the more realistic range would be 6% to 6½%. There will never be appreciation, nor will there be any loss on amounts up to $40,000, because of government insurance.

Bonds

Currently, long-term bonds (20 years or more) can provide returns of 9% to 11%, depending on the quality of the issuer. Be sure to check call provisions. It's nice to get your money back, but you will have to worry about new purchases.

Capital gains can be achieved by buying bonds selling at a discount. These carry low coupons, so they will rise in price as interest rates drop. Current yields are comparable to those of new issues, but the gains will come when the bond rises to par at maturity.

Preferred Stocks

These are similar to bonds with a little less security but the advantage that there's little danger of a call. Look for preferreds with sinking funds for extra protection.

Convertibles

The yields will be lower than those of bonds—6% to 8½% —but there's always the possibility of capital gains if the common stock appreciates.

Common Stocks

These provide the greatest potential for the highest total returns over the years. Choose quality stocks which pay adequate dividends and have good prospects of strong, continuing growth. With companies that provide automatic reinvestment of dividends, brokerage costs are reduced and funds kept working. *Hazard:* The stock market may be at a low ebb when you retire.

(For further information, see Chapters XVI and XXV, on Life Insurance and Investments.)

Mortgages

These provide good, steady returns over the years. They are best for plans with substantial capital, as few mortgages are available for less than $20,000. Check with your bank on the possibility of participation with banks and/or other pension plans.

Government Retirement Bonds

Government Retirement Bonds, sold in denominations of $50, $100, and $500, are available at the U.S. Treasury, Federal Reserve Banks, and many savings and commercial institutions. They are designed especially for personal pension plans. Interest, currently at 6%, keeps on accumulating, compounding every 6 months. *But they cannot be redeemed until retirement.*

Both savings certificates and retirement bonds are safe but little more. They are illiquid, nonappreciating investments. With the certificates, interest may be compounded daily, but the rate of return is guaranteed only for a relatively short time (now, typically, 4 years). The current total yield of 8.2% is likely to decline.

About the best thing that can be said for the retirement bonds is that they provide a steady return and benefit Uncle Sam.

Note: With all types of private pension plans, be careful about any transactions which could be interpreted as a conflict of interest—e.g., selling mutual-fund shares (on which you will be allowed a large tax loss) to the retirement plan, which, hopefully, will benefit from price rises. Always check with your tax adviser.

Extra Pension Benefits

Participants in a Keogh Plan are allowed an extra benefit if they choose a Defined Benefit Plan (DBP)—an exact number of dollars per year for life. This provision permits tax-free deductions above the $7,500 maximum on a formula based on age. The extra contributions continue at the same rate during a working lifetime, but if there's a lapse, the higher renewal age figure must be used.

Age When Participation Begins	Applicable Percentage
30 or less	6.5%
35	5.4
40	4.4
45	3.6
50	3.0
55	2.5
60	2.0

Thus, under the DBP formula, a 45-year-old physician, earning $50,000 annually, would multiply 3.6 by $50,000 to get $1,800. This is his annual annuity. Since he anticipates working another 20 years, to age 65, he multiplies $1,800 by 20 to get a whopping yearly $36,000 pension. That much income would require a regular contribution of $9,800—tax-free.

DBP must include all employees on the same basis, and the total pension cannot exceed $75,000 a year or the average earned income for the 3 highest years. If you can afford such annual savings, ask your insurance agent to get details from his home office. This program must be carefully tailored to meet IRS guidelines.

Keogh Plan Checklist

Provision	Explanation
Maximum Deductions	
Standard plans	15% of earned income to maximum of $7,500
Defined Benefit Plan	According to formula
Voluntary Contributions	10% of self-employment income not to exceed $2,500; contributions not deductible, but earnings accumulate free
Distribution of Benefits	
When permitted	Not permitted without penalty before death, disability, or age $59\frac{1}{2}$; must commence at $70\frac{1}{2}$; to employees on termination of employment
Tax Treatment	
Monthly payments	At ordinary income tax rates on dollar$_s$ distributed; undistributed balance remains tax-sheltered
Lump sum	If plan opened after 1973, entire distribution is taxed under divide-by-10, multiply-by-10 income-averaging formula
Service Requirements	
for Participation	3 years maximum, but can provide coverage for any full-time employee
Vesting	Full and immediate
Minimum Contributions of	
Owner/Employer	Lesser of 100% of self-employment income or $750
Contribution Deadline	Due date of income tax return including extensions
Excess Contributions	Subject to 6% nondeductible excise tax
Estate Tax	Value of owner/employer's account in estate; beneficiary may take income tax credit for estate tax paid

Source: Vance, Sanders & Company, Inc.

Tax-Sheltered Retirement Plan for Employees of Nonprofit Institutions

If you work for a nonprofit institution such as a social service agency, hospital, or educational system, you are allowed to invest up to 20% of your salary in a tax-sheltered annuity. For tax-free purposes, the money is deducted from your gross income.

Requirements: (1) You must work on a regular-salary basis—not for fee-for-services. (2) The annuity program cannot be part of some general retirement program covering other employees. (3) The plan is nonforfeitable—i.e., you can keep and continue the plan after you leave this job. (4) The plan applies only to income earned after you've signed up—no backdating. (5) The plan must last 1 year. (6) The 20% contribution applies to your gross income *before* the deduction (on $15,000 income, the maximum contribution is $3,000). (7) You can make additional contributions to the plan, but they are not tax-deductible.

Such plans, available from many insurance companies, can be set up by direct contributions or by an agreement with the employer whereby you take less money and the difference is invested directly into the retirement plan.

Example: You earn $15,000 a year at a hospital. You arrange for $57.69 to be deducted from your weekly paycheck, so your actual base pay is $12,000.

You can start taking your benefits at age 59½ and must do so at age 70. Payments can be in a lump sum but usually are on a monthly basis.

XXII

The Family Car—How to Buy for Less, Compare Costs, and Save on Insurance

Driving a car is a necessity for some people, a convenience for others, and a pleasure for many. Until recently, more people bought an automobile for pleasure than for economy. But with higher costs for purchase and operation, there's a strong shift to utility first—but not without some now-accepted "necessities" such as power steering, power brakes, air conditioning, etc.

Usually, the purchase of an automobile is the third-largest family expenditure (next to a home and college). That is why money management must consider ways to make owning, maintaining, and protecting a car less expensive. Obviously, the greatest savings can be achieved by driving the car less and keeping it longer. These are personal decisions dictated by life-style and financial resources.

Car dealers are franchised by the car manufacturers. Under the terms of his agreement with the manufacturer, the dealer is expected to maintain a number and variety of models, strive to meet yearly sales quotas, stock replacement parts, do warranty repairs, and conduct his business honestly and fairly. If you feel you have been misled or mistreated by any dealer and cannot get satisfaction locally, call or write the manufacturer's district or zone office, and if you are still not satisfied, contact its Detroit headquarters. You will get a prompt answer and, usually, the service you anticipated or a logical explanation of why it's not available. The automobile industry is aware of the need for public confidence.

To get the best buy in a new car, ask for the list price without options (not including shipping, advertising, undercoating, etc.). Formulas vary according to dealer and region, but here's a base which, according to Consumers Union, can help you determine the dealer's cost:

> Multiply this base price by 0.77 for a standard car, by 0.81 for an intermediate car, or by 0.85 for a compact or subcompact. Subtract the nonoptional equipment charges as listed on the sticker to get the approximate amount the dealer paid.
>
> Add back the freight and profit (about 10% of cost), and the final figure should be close to the quoted-to-you price. If it's much higher, go elsewhere; if it's somewhat higher, start bargaining; if it's lower, watch out—unless you are convinced that there's a genuine sale in progress.

In most situations, the dealer will settle for about $300 above his cost if he feels you will rely on his service department. Under normal selling conditions, he will be able to get an extra 2% of the suggested retail price ($65 to $125 per car) from the manufacturer, can count on more cars more quickly, and will qualify for sales prizes such as a vacation holiday.

It is usually best to buy from a local dealer, but if you are leery of his reputation or taken aback by his hyperbolic sales pitch, check these points (suggested by an established franchised firm which has to compete in a major metropolitan market):

DOUBLE-TICKETING. After the car purchase, the dealer delays delivery for 60 to 90 days. During that period, there's a price increase which is added to your cost—without explanation or notification.

EXTRA CHARGES. These might include $25 to $50 administrative or clerical fees for processing sales papers. These should be part of general overhead.

DEALER-PREPARATION CHARGES. These average $60 to $100 and should be listed on the sticker price, not charged separately.

FINANCE CHARGES. Some dealers add 2 to 3 percent to the basic loan. Cash is cheapest, but if you must finance, shop around. Compare rates from your bank with those offered, through the dealer, by Ford Motor Credit, General Motors Acceptance Corporation, etc.

Always consider borrowing the money with presently available collateral—your account at the credit union (at about 12% interest), on your passbook at the thrift institution (the cost of the loan will be reduced by the interest earned on your savings), or by a loan against the cash value of your life insurance (usually no more than 6%). In these days of high money costs, it pays to shop for the best deal in credit as well as in the car.

Use This Table to Figure Interest-loan Costs

Facts You Need		Example	Dealer	Other Sources
1. Cash price, including extras and taxes		$3,600		
2. Subtract down payment				
Cash	$100			
Trade-in allowance	880			
		980		
3. Balance due		$2,620		
4. Insurance		208		
5. Principal to be financed		2,828		
6. Am't monthly payments	$ 90.31			
7. Number monthly payments	36			
8. Total monthly payments		3,251.16		
9. Dollar Cost of Credit (subtract principal from total amount monthly payments)		$ 423.16		

Source: Household Finance Corporation

For Extra Savings

Check your union, professional association, or employer to see if there's an auto-buying discount service. Or contact an organization such as Car/Puter International (CPI), 1603 Bushwick Avenue, Brooklyn, New York 11207.

Once you have decided on the make and model, send CPI a check for $7.50. In return you'll receive a listing form where you put down details of color, equipment, and options. This will be answered with a computer printout similar to the sticker on the new car, with retail price, dealer costs for the base car, each option, freight and dealer expenses, etc. You can use this as a bargaining tool when you shop local dealers, or order through CPI by sending in a down payment of $300 or so.

CPI will place the order through one of 400 participating dealers. You'll have to wait a month or two and pay the balance (plus $50 to $75 in delivery charges) in cash to the dealer nearest you. Your total outlay will be $150 to $200 above dealer cost, less the $7.50 originally paid.

You will have to decide whether the savings (small when the car is priced under $3,000) outweigh the delay, the possibility of traveling 50 miles to pick up the car, the worry about getting service under the warranty, and the inconvenience of having to sell your car on your own.

Buying a Used Car

The No. 1 rule in buying a used car is to deal only with a reputable dealer—an established company which has had few run-ins with consumer groups or the local arbitration board (if there is one).

Next, get the name and phone number of the previous owner and ask if there were any particular mechanical difficulties. Then,

344 / The Family Car—How to Buy for Less

spend a few dollars to have the car checked by a friendly repair shop, or if you're not bashful, by a competitive dealer.

Finally, do your own testing by:

LOOKING FOR SIGNS OF ACCIDENTS OR CARELESS HANDLING. Stand back about 40 feet to see if the car sits level. If not, it may mean a bent frame or bad suspension. Examine the sides for ripples, the doors for poor fits.

If the paint under rubber gaskets around the windows or doors is a different color, the car's been repainted. And watch for rusted areas.

CHECKING THE STARTER SEVERAL TIMES. There should be no whine or flooded carburetor.

GUNNING THE MOTOR WHILE YOUR WIFE CHECKS THE EXHAUST. White smoke is OK; black discharges indicate a worn engine.

TESTING BRAKES. Drive on an uncrowded road and make several abrupt stops at increasing speeds of 15, 20, and 25 miles per hour. If the car pulls, the brakes grind, squeal, or chatter, or the pedal goes to the floor on the first push, repairs or adjustments are needed.

RUNNING IN ALL GEARS. If it's automatic transmission, the shift should be smooth. If it's a manual shift, watch out for jerks or stickiness.

Make These Specific Checks

STEERING WHEEL. If there's excessive play, make sure there's an adjustment or replacement.

CLUTCH. Look for about an inch of free play in the pedal before there's resistance.

SHOCK ABSORBERS. Jump on the bumper one corner at a time. If the car moves up and down more than once after you stop, get new shocks.

REAR AXLE AND DRIVE SHAFT. Have your wife sit in the back seat while you accelerate and slow down. If she complains of noise, clicks, or chatter, there may be trouble.

ACCESSORIES. Turn on and off: wipers, defrosters, heater, radio, lights, horn, turn indicator, etc. Even the best dealers get careless sometimes.

TIRES. In addition to examining the tread for uneven wear, wet the tires with a hose and stop fast. If there are 4 tread marks instead of 2, the car has probably been bent in an accident.

OIL. After the car has been warmed up, check the oil gauge. If the oil is unusually heavy, the dealer may be trying to deaden motor noises. If there's a smell of gasoline, the engine may be worn. If there's any sign of water in the oil, the engine block may be cracked.

Then park the car on smooth, clean concrete and let it idle while you talk to the salesman. In 5 minutes, move the car and check for oil leaks—*red* means a loose transmission; *black,* oil; *brown,* gasoline.

As a final check, drive the car about 20 miles an hour and slowly push the foot brake with your left foot while accelerating with the right foot. This will load the engine, transmission, and differential, and will signal mechanical deficiencies immediately. But don't keep this up. Your brakes will overheat.

If Your Car Is Repossessed

If unexpected expenses force you to miss payments so that your car is repossessed, so be it. But if you will owe money, stick up for your rights. The law says that the finance company must resell the car in a "commercially reasonable" manner. That is, since you bought the car at retail, the lender cannot wholesale it to a friendly dealer for $500 when the used-car *Blue Book* lists the retail value at $1,150!

Which Cars Are in Most Accidents?

With growing children, most families are more concerned with safety than economy. They should be. According to a survey of 162,000 cars made by the Highway Loss Data Institute, subcompact cars are involved in more collisions than larger cars, and the average repair bill for small autos is higher! That means that those insurance premium discounts now available for subcompacts are not likely to be around in the future.

Crash Claims and Costs
(1974 Model Cars)

Make and Model	Claim Frequency per 100 Insured Vehicle Years	Average Loss Payment per Claim	Average Loss Payment per Insured Vehicle Year
All Cars	9.6	$495	$48
Subcompacts			
Ford Pinto wagon	8.6	468	40
Volkswagen Beetle	10.2	431	44
Chevrolet Vega	9.9	489	48
Compacts			
Plymouth Duster	9.8	386	38
Ford Maverick 4-door	7.5	568	43
Chevrolet Nova	8.8	526	46
Intermediates			
Chevrolet Monte Carlo	9.4	368	35
Buick Century 2-door	9.4	389	37
Olds Cutlass 2-door	9.2	452	42
Ford Torino 2-door	9.5	468	44
Full-size			
Olds Delta 88	7.1	384	27
Chevrolet Caprice	6.9	540	37
Ford LTD	9.2	439	40

Source: *Money* magazine (digested).

How Much Does a Car Cost over the Years?

A study by the U.S. Department of Transportation calculated that, over 10 years, with total mileage of 100,000 miles, the total cost per mile would be:

Standard Car

Four-door Ford Galaxie or Buick Century with V-8 engine, automatic transmission, power steering, power brakes, and air conditioning: 15.9¢ per mile.

Compact

Two-door Chevrolet Nova, Plymouth Valiant, or AMC Hornet with 6-cylinder engine, automatic transmission, and power steering: 12.9¢ per mile.

Subcompact

Chevrolet Vega or Ford Pinto with 4-cylinder engine, standard transmission: 11.2¢ per mile.

These figures are based on: (1) declining mileage—14,500 the first year, to 10,000 the fourth year, to 5,700 the tenth year; (2) rising repair costs as cars grow older; (3) lowering insurance, including dropping collision coverage after the fifth year.

These data should be used only as a frame of reference. Driving conditions vary, costs are in 1974 dollars, and gasoline was set at a standard price of 52¢ per gallon. The key factors: for big cars, depreciation; for compacts, gasoline; for subcompacts, repairs and maintenance.

Should You Buy a Standard or Compact Car?

With higher prices for gasoline, less driving, and the urge to effect savings wherever possible, many families are considering buying compacts to replace their standard cars. There are savings, but:

1. The chances of serious damage are greater.
2. The depreciation may be more.
3. The savings may not be as great as anticipated.

Trading a big car for a new small car is seldom profitable unless you have rolled up a lot of miles.

Here's a summary of how 2 experts at Virginia Commonwealth University, George Hoffer, economics professor, and A. James Wynne, instructor in information systems, suggest you make your analysis. Their original explanation appeared in *Money* magazine.

The key criteria are: (1) gasoline costs, (2) depreciation, (3) mileage adjustment, (4) maintenance-insurance savings.

Small cars do cost less to operate, but new ones depreciate more rapidly than the older, large car you now own (where the depreciation is already evident). Other things being equal, the smaller the car, the less the *percentage* of depreciation—when both cars are the same age.

Note: The validity of all figures will change now that new cars are priced higher, provide better mileage, and of course, reflect the rising price of gasoline.

On the basis of 1975 data, you can do your own estimates from these comparisons:

Standard Car

Two years old; bought for $4,000; normally to be kept for 4 years; gasoline at 60¢ per gallon; annual mileage, 12,000; average miles per gallon (mpg), 14.

Compact

New, $3,000; mpg, 24; 12,000 miles a year; gas, 60¢.

Example: To determine gasoline costs, multiply the number of years you would keep the big car (2) by the annual mileage

(12,000), to get 24,000. Divide by mpg (14) to get the gallons of gas used (1,700). Multiply by the price per gallon (60¢) = $1,020.

$$\frac{Y \times M}{MPG} = GG \times PG = GC$$

Y = years plan to keep car GG = gallons of gasoline
M = annual mileage PG = price per gallon
MPG = miles per gallon GC = gasoline costs

Standard

$$\frac{2 \times 12,000}{14} = 1,700 \times 60 = 1,028$$

Compact

$$\frac{2 \times 12,000}{24} = 1,000 \times 60 = 600$$

Therefore, you can hope to save $428 in fuel costs in the next 2 years. BUT THAT'S ONLY PART OF THE STORY.

Estimating Depreciation

The decrease in value of every car varies with the model, manufacturer, age, and usage. These tables show how to estimate depreciation. The prices are for basic cars, popularly equipped but without unusual options. For more specific data, consult the *Blue Book* at your auto dealer's or bank.

Note: Finance terms—one-third down, 36 months to pay, at 11% annual rate with all finance costs charged against first year.

To get the depreciation, find the price in the "new" column that's closest to the price you paid ($4,000). Do not include unusual options such as stereo, back-window wipers, etc.

Then move to the column for the present age of your car (2) to get the present worth ($2,131). Since you plan to keep the car 2 more years, move to the 4-year column to get the depreciated value ($1,352). The difference ($779) will be the depreciation to be used in the calculations.

Depreciated Values

	New	1 Year Old	2 Years Old	3 Years Old	4 Years Old	5 Years Old
Big Car						
Cash price	$3,000	$2,096	$1,598	$1,271	$1,014	$ 722
financed	3,360					
Cash price	4,000	2,795	2,131	1,695	1,352	962
financed	4,480					
Cash price	5,000	3,494	2,663	2,110	1,690	1,203
financed	5,600					
Compact						
Cash price	$2,500	$1,809	$1,507	$1,225	$ 980	$ 791
financed	2,800					
Cash price	3,000	2,171	1,809	1,470	1,176	950
financed	3,360					
Cash price	3,500	2,532	2,110	1,715	1,372	1,108
financed	3,920					
Cash price	4,000	2,894	2,412	1,960	1,568	1,266
financed	4,480					

Adjustments for Mileage

To make proper allowance for mileage, find the row in the following table that corresponds to the age of the present car (2), then move to the column showing total mileage (24,000) to get −175. Then repeat this at the anticipated trade-in age (4) and future mileage (48,000) = −100. The difference is −75.

With the compact, start with the number of years you would keep your present car if you did not trade it in now (2). Move over to the mileage column (24,000) to get the figure of −125.

> *Note:* Professor Hoffer suggests that if you drive between 10,000 and 14,000 miles per year, you skip this table. The mileage is average, so the adjustment is minimal.

Adjustment for Mileage

Mileage		15,000–19,999	20,000–24,999	25,000–29,999	30,000–34,999	35,000–39,999	40,000–44,999	45,000–49,999	50,000–54,999
Standard									
	1	− 75	+ 25	+100	+175	+250	+325	+400	+475
	2	−250	−175	−100	+ 25	+100	+175	+250	+325
	3	−375	−300	−225	−150	−100	+ 25	+100	+175
Years	4	−525	−450	−375	−300	−225	−150	−100	+ 50
Old	5	−625	−550	−475	−400	−325	−250	−175	−125
	6	−700	−625	−550	−475	−400	−325	−250	−175
	7	−625	−550	−475	−400	−325	−250	−175	−125
	8	−525	−450	−375	−300	−225	−150	−100	− 50
Compact									
	1	− 50	+ 25	+ 75	+125	+175	+225	+275	+325
	2	−175	−125	− 75	+ 25	+ 75	+125	+175	+225
	3	−275	−225	−175	−125	− 75	+ 25	+ 75	+125
Years	4	−375	−325	−275	−225	−175	−125	− 75	+ 50
Old	5	−450	−400	−350	−300	−250	−200	−150	−100
	6	−475	−425	−375	−325	−275	−225	−175	−125
	7	−450	−400	−350	−300	−250	−200	−150	−100
	8	−375	−325	−275	−225	−175	−125	− 75	− 25

Different Running Costs

The following table, based on a 1974 study by the Federal Highway Administration, shows the savings on annual maintenance and insurance for a compact.

Compact-Car Savings on Maintenance and Insurance

Mileage	15,000–19,999	20,000–24,999	25,000–29,999	30,000–34,999	35,000–39,999	40,000–44,999	45,000–49,999
Savings	$129	$166	$203	$240	$277	$314	$351

To determine the possible savings on the small car, start with the number of miles you expect to drive with your old car (24,000) and drop down to the savings ($166).

For the final comparison, use this table:

	Big Car ($4,000)	Compact ($3,000)
Gasoline costs	$1,028	$600
Depreciation	779	1,470
Mileage adjustment	−175	−125
Savings on maintenance & insurance		−166
Total costs	$1,632	$1,779

Note: Because the savings are subtracted from the costs, they should be entered as minus numbers.

Try it yourself. These 2 examples come out with little difference, but as a rule, the older your present car and the less you drive, the more worthwhile it is to keep the gas guzzler.

Prepaid Repair Plans

One way to counter the soaring costs of car repairs is to buy a prepaid maintenance plan. It's like Blue Cross. For $50 to $75 a year, you get a policy to cover the charges for many automobile mechanical ailments—*generally,* engine breakdowns, troubles involving transmission parts, differential gears, rear axle, intake manifold, torque converter, and drive shaft; *usually not* carburetors, fuel pumps, batteries, distributors, and other "add-on" engine parts.

A typical plan provides a 12-month, 12,000-mile warranty on used cars up to 5 years old with less than 62,000 miles. In case of a breakdown, the motorist calls a central number and is directed either to an affiliated repairman or to one with whom the insurer can work out a price.

Currently, plans are available through Vehicle Protection Corporation, Mineola, New York 11501, and Fleet Aid Corporation, Ridgefield, New Jersey 07657.

How to Get the Most from Your Auto Insurance

There are 3 types of automobile insurance which provides protection against the expenses which may result from an accident:

Liability

This type protects you (the car owner) or others who drive your car with your consent against bodily injury or property-damage claims of another person resulting from an accident caused by your car. Some states have minimum requirements of 10/20/5—the insurance company will pay up to $10,000 to 1 person for bodily injury, $20,000 for all injuries for 1 accident, $5,000 for property damage from 1 accident.

Most authorities feel this is too low and recommend 100/300/50, plus $5,000 per person medical damage, plus an *umbrella* policy. The real test is how much you drive, where you live, the reasonable possibility of a serious accident, and how much you can afford. Unlike life insurance, there are no standard tables to refer to.

With no-fault insurance (mandatory in Connecticut, Delaware, Florida, Maryland, Massachusetts, Michigan, New Jersey, New York, Oregon, Texas, and Washington), accident victims get funds for payment of damages and injuries from their own insurance company. This eliminates costly lawsuits but still permits legal action, on grounds of negligence, for costs above the state-set maximum payments. While generally considered an important advance, this new type of coverage appears to have encouraged some lawyers to seek higher damages through jury trials.

Comprehensive

This type pays for loss or damage resulting from fire, theft, vandalism, windstorm, hail, flood, smoke, falling objects, and other causes listed in the policy. There's always a deductible (the amount you have to pay first), from $50 to $250.

Collision

This type pays you if your car strikes or is struck by another car or object or if your car turns over. You are reimbursed for damage to your car regardless of who caused the accident—including an uninsured driver. The higher the deductible, the lower the premium.

There's considerable room for judgment here—on a new car, you may want to pay a little more for a $50 deductible, then raise this to $100 in 3 years and even cancel when the value of the car drops below $500.

The basic costs of automobile insurance depend on the type of car, the area in which you live, the amount of driving you do, and the coverage you select. From then on, the premiums are more individual, based on the insurer's experience and your conduct-character-record.

There are also variations in costs of competing insurance companies. In Pennsylvania, for example, the premiums on a similar policy for a Chevrolet, driven by a mature, "good-driver" male, ranged from $218 to $544 in Philadelphia, from $267 to $418 in the suburbs, from $153 to $201 in Harrisburg, and from $142 to $212 in a rural county.

For the same policy for a 19-year-old, not-too-good driver, owning a Mustang, the premiums were much higher—in Philadelphia, from $1,083 to $1,716; in the suburbs, from $827 to $1,125; in Harrisburg, from $435 to $652; and in the country, from $414 to $691. These figures were quotations of 5 major, nationally known insurers. No one company was always low or high.

Cost should never be the sole reason for choosing any policy or any company. There should always be other factors—coverage, service, etc. And look for a local agent who is a member of the National Association of Insurance Agents, a nationwide trade association with high standards and strict regulations.

Choosing a Company

There's no sure way to know how you'll be treated until after an accident, but one guideline might be the number of complaints reported by your state insurance department. You can get the information annually.

Here's how New York State listed some of the companies selling auto insurance in 1973. The rank is based on the number of complaints adjusted for the value of company premiums. *Note:* The term *fleet* means that the company sells insurance under more than one name but is most recognizable by the name given.

Company	Number of Complaints	Average of 1972–73 auto premiums (thousands)	Number o complaints per $1 million of premiums f
Great Eastern	111	$ 3,369	33.0
Country-Wide	110	5,993	18.4
Government Employees Fleet	1,370	122,260	11.2
Crum and Forster Fleet	143	16,063	8.9
Home Insurance & Indemnity	205	23,345	8.8
Royal-Globe Fleet	271	46,508	5.8
Aetna Insurance	85	15,161	5.6
Allstate Fleet	1,262	231,822	5.4
Chubb Fleet	169	33,993	5.0
Liberty Mutual Fleet	306	69,565	4.4
Hartford Fleet	447	104,513	4.3
Travelers Fleet	334	77,761	4.3
State Farm Fleet	265	74,196	3.6
Kemper Group	181	50,112	3.6
INA Fleet	101	38,765	2.6
Factory Mutual Fleet	20	15,932	1.3

Shopping for Insurance

Decide on the policy you need. You can always choose alternative coverage if it seems more advantageous. From the yellow pages or newspaper ads, select the local office of half a dozen insurance companies and ask for quotations over the phone. How your inquiry is handled may be a clue of what you can expect in the future. *Note:* Find out if any company is represented by a local politician. If he is conscientious, he'll have more clout in getting a settlement. And you will have a friend in government!

When you have narrowed your choice to 2 or 3 candidates, meet with the salesmen and ask questions. In many cases, you will find that the rate structure reflects different extras or that you may be able to qualify for a discount.

Other ways to save money:

Increase the Deductible

By agreeing to pay the first $250 instead of $100, you can save 50% or more. This may make sense if you are in a high tax bracket. The uninsured part of a loss is fully tax-deductible if the car is used for business, and all but the first $100 is tax deductible if it's a family car.

Consider a Combination Policy

This means coverage of more than one car or together with your homeowner's policy. This can be tricky, so deal with an experienced agent and well-know company and plan well in advance to be sure that both policies will start at the same time.

Ask about Single-Limit Policies

These are not available in every state. The coverage is less because it eliminates duplicate medical benefits (already covered by other insurance). The savings can be welcome, but the surcharges can be substantial if you have a few accidents.

Try to Find a Group Policy

You can do this through a club, society, union, or association. Only 15 states allow such coverage, but there can be savings up to 15%.

Consider Mail-Order Policies

These will be cheaper, but you won't get advice from someone who knows you and your community and you won't be in a position to press claims or become very involved in legal actions.

Added advice: Unless you have strong reasons to do so (or the company makes the decision for you), be slow about switching carriers. The new underwriter will investigate your record and may cancel within the first 60 to 90 days for any number of reasons.

Finally, don't pester a company with small claims. The real reason for automobile insurance is protection against major accidents.

How Insurance Companies Rate You

It's a bit Orwellian, but auto insurance companies pay attention to the occupations, habits, and records of the people whose cars they insure. Being on this Hit Parade can be expensive. If you accumulate 10 demerits, most companies will require their agent/underwriter to justify, in writing, why your policy should be accepted or continued. Rejection will mean that you will have to persuade another company, probably at a higher premium, that you deserve coverage. As a last resort, your application will become an assigned risk—where the state requires some company to accept your insurance. Fortunately, most of the black marks can be erased over a few years—if you and your family make the effort.

10-Demerit Factors

Conviction for: drunkenness or drug use
failure to stop and report an accident
driving while license suspended or revoked
a felony or misdemeanor
75 years old or over
Unemployed
Gambler, entertainer, or professional athlete
Poor reputation or habits
Physical disability or illness affecting driving ability
Souped-up or altered car (5 demerits if coverage limited to liability)
Over 25,000 miles per year business driving
Over 20,000 miles per year personal driving
3 nonchargeable accidents in past 3 years
Held restricted policy

8-Demerit Factor

Age 70 to 74

6-Demerit Factor

One chargeable accident in current year with double demerits for each additional one in same year

5-Demerit Factors

Each speeding or careless driving offense
Married male under 21
Unmarried owner or operator under 21
Resident of blighted, deteriorating area
Union official
Unskilled or menial occupation

Student
Impaired health or physical ability
Sports car
20,000 to 25,000 miles per year business driving
15,000 to 20,000 miles per year personal use
Policy canceled or refused renewal
Policy limits reduced or refused increase

4-Demerit Factors

1 chargeable accident in previous year (double demerits for
  each additional one) in same year
Age 65 to 69
Member of armed forces (not officer or noncom)
More than 1 moving violation in same year

3-Demerit Factors

Driving less than 1 year
3 or more operators in a 1-car family
4 or more operators in a 2-car family
Own current-model-year car
Male under 21, car over 10 years old

2-Demerit Factors

Moving violation, first offense
Chargeable accident 2 years ago (double demerits for each
  additional accident)
Car more than 3 years old
Career officer or noncom with armed services
10,000 to 14,999 miles per year personal driving

1-Demerit Factor

Held driver's license from 1 to 3 years

What it all adds up to is that: You should notify the insurance
company when a young driver goes away to college or is married,

keep track of your annual mileage, double-think before buying a sports car, and most important, drive carefully.

Consider an Umbrella Policy

An *umbrella* policy provides protection against personal-catastrophe liability and almost all perils not covered by other insurance—a neighbor's child hurt by your electric lawnmower, for example.

Initially, this type of policy was designed for affluent professional people who were prime targets for lawsuits. But today, broader policies are being bought by individuals with modest incomes.

Under an umbrella policy, the insurance company provides protection up to $10 million when there's basic coverage—bodily injury $100,000/$300,000 ($100,000 each person; $300,000 each accident); property damage of $10,000; comprehensive of $50,000, and medical coverage of $10,000.

Premiums for this extra coverage with a $1-million limit start at $60. This pays all costs between the standard limits and the $1 million. If you feel you might be the target of a damage suit or are worried about unusual accidents, ask your agent for information. A $500,000 award would wipe out all but the wealthiest families.

Legal Responsibilities

Laws and court decisions show that when it comes to the family car, you and/or your wife can be held liable in most cases regardless of who was driving when the accident occurred.

Illinois Automobile Insurance Quotation Work Sheet

COVERAGE	LIMITS OR DEDUCTIBLE	ANNUAL PREMIUMS				
		COMPANY A	COMPANY B	COMPANY C	COMPANY D	COMPANY E
1 Liability Bodily Injury Property Damage	$100,000 Per Person 300,000 Per Accident 5,000 Per Accident	$ 71 *	$51 45	$73 *	$84 *	$36 30
2 Physical Damage to Insured Vehicle Comprehensive Collision	$ 150 Ded. Per Accident 100 Ded. Per Accident	$18 41	$15 53	$12 40	$18 45	$14 48
3 Medical Payments	$2000 Per Person	8	8	**	6	6
4 Uninsured Motorists	$10,000 Per Person 20,000 Per Accident	4	4	**	4	4
5 Other Optional Coverages						
Total Premium		$142	$176	$125	$157	$138
6 Membership Fees (If Applicable)		0	0	0	9	0
Total Cost of Automobile Insurance		$142	$176	$125	$166	$138

Minimum Rating Information Required:

7

	Age	Sex	Marital Status
Principal Owner or Operator	35	M	M
Youngest Occasional Driver	NONE		

8

Number of Miles if Driven to and from Work ___2___

9

Type of Auto to Be Insured	Make	Model & Year
Auto 1	CHEVY-IMP	1971
Auto 2		

10

Estimate Number of Annual Mileage ___8,000___

11

Number of Accidents or Moving Violations in the Last 3 Years ___NONE___

12

Name _DEPARTMENT OF INSURANCE_

Address _ROOM 512 ~ JEFFERSON WEST #1_

Street _525 WEST JEFFERSON STREET_

City _SPRINGFIELD, ILLINOIS 62706_

*Bodily injury and property damage liability premiums are combined.
**BI/PD includes uninsured motorists and medical payments.

If your wife and child are involved, you are responsible. If you sign Junior's license application, you are automatically responsible for his negligence. Some states do have a "consent statute" that limits your responsibility if you can prove that, at the time of the accident, the family member was operating the car without your permission. *If you don't want Junior to drive, make sure that he doesn't.*

If a friend is driving, you're responsible if he is doing a chore for you. But if the crash occurs as the result of high speed which violates your instructions, you may be free. It's your negligence if you lend the car to an unsafe driver—one with a poor record, history of drinking, etc.

Members of the family cannot sue for damages in most states—unless they can prove sufficient negligence.

If a "guest" is injured, most states protect the driver unless there's reckless behavior which, in legal terms, is more than ordinary negligence.

The key word is *negligence*—falling asleep at the wheel, drunken driving, failure to react when trouble is seen ahead, etc. The worst offense is failure to stop after a hit-and-run accident. The driver must stop, identify himself, investigate, render aid, and call the police.

XXIII

Leasing—Convenient but Costly for Most People

Leasing of a car, typewriter, air conditioner, furniture, etc., has advantages but they are not the ones most people believe. Leasing won't save you money or create tax benefits, but it can pay off in convenience and cash flow.

A true lease 's an agreement whereby the lessee (you) pays for the use of a relatively expensive item over an extended period of time. Most leases cover new products, but when the equipment involved is expensive (such as an X-ray machine used by a physician), it is possible to sell the old model for cash, lease it back, and when the contract is ended, re-acquire it at a fraction of the resale price.

Leasing is not inexpensive. It is almost always cheaper to pay cash and, usually, to borrow from a bank or to buy on the installment plan. This is because leasing is a form of long-term financing whereby the lessor makes part of his profit on the difference between the cost of the money he borrows and the amount you pay him over the length of the lease.

Your monthly lease payments may be less than those under an installment loan, but at the end of the lease, you will not own the equipment. All you will have are options—to return, to buy at a pre-agreed-upon price or at fair market value, or to sign a new lease for a later, and presumably improved, model.

The real dollar plus of leasing is conserving capital, improving cash flow, and eliminating costs of trade-ins. You pay for the equipment as it is used and, hopefully, as it helps you to generate income.

The tax benefits of leasing are not all they are cracked up to be. If you use your car for business-profession, money you pay under leasing contracts is tax-deductible as a business expense. But because you are not the owner, you will not be able to claim depreciation and investment tax credit.

And forget about the idea that leasing makes it easier to justify tax deductions. The IRS uses the same test for both owned and leased equipment-vehicles: How much of the use is related to your business or profession? If it's 50%, that figure applies to *all* expenses.

There are, of course, definite advantages to leasing:

No Cash Outlay

With leasing you do not have to come up with a 25% down payment required with many installment purchases. All you have to do is to have good credit—and the ability to meet the monthly charges.

No Other Investments Affected

If you are planning to ask for a loan from the bank or a mortgage for a new home, you can keep a better-looking balance sheet by leasing rather than by buying on the installment plan. By the same reasoning, leasing may be wise if you have to sell securities or real estate at a loss to come up with cash for a down payment.

Ready Money

When cash can be used more advantageously elsewhere, a leaseback is a quick way to get funds. This makes sense only if the equipment is expensive—an X-ray or copying machine, furniture, and occasionally, an automobile.

The lessor will generally pay above book value because he knows he will get his money back with ample interest. You get the cash and can still use the equipment.

This sounds great, but such a sale and leaseback can mean substantial tax penalties. The IRS will want to get any and all tax benefits taken during the years the equipment was used.

Example: Dr. Zug bought an X-ray machine in 1971 for $18,000. He established a useful life of 8 years and claimed the 7% investment tax credit for a total deduction of $3,780. When he sells the machine and leases it back, he will have to reimburse Uncle Sam for that $3,780 credit!

To point up the economics of leasing, here are examples of car leasing. The same general principles and dollar comparisons hold for leases of other items used in the business, profession, or home. In almost every case, leasing is the most expensive way to acquire products, even when there's a business or profession involved.

Automobile Leasing

With automobiles, there are dozens of different leases. At one extreme, a car lease can be little more than a buy-and-sell contract under which the lessor agrees to purchase a car for a specified price and dispose of it after a certain period, for a fixed fee.

At the other end of the scale, a lease can include a "full-maintenance" agreement which calls for the leasing company to license and insure the car, pay for tires, parts, batteries, servicing, inspections, and cost reporting.

In between, there can be a wide variety of lease terms: One contract may include insurance and licensing but no operating or maintenance work; another may specify a maximum number of miles that can be driven per year or over the duration of the lease; a third may permit limitless mileage, etc. As competition intensifies, more car leases are tailored to the specific needs of customers, primarily corporations but, increasingly, individuals.

As a result of the great variety of terms, lease payments for 2 identical automobiles can differ by as much as one-third for leases of the same duration. "That's why it is almost impossible to quote typical or average costs for any given car in any given locale," says Dennis Israel, vice-president of the Hertz Car Leasing Division of the Hertz Corporation.

(Ads in *The New York Times* confirmed this statement— monthly leases for a Cadillac Coupe de Ville were quoted from $209 to $294; for Chevrolets from $112 to $148.)

"Open" and "Closed" Leases

Perhaps the most common consumer misunderstanding of car leases, says Israel, is the difference between "closed-end" and "open-end" lease contracts. With the former, the leasing company assumes full responsibility for any losses incurred in disposing of the car when the lease expires. At the end of say, 2 years, you turn the leased car in for a new model. Whether the market value of the car has declined (as it did during the oil crisis) or has increased (as has happened with higher new car prices), you will be credited with a fixed value set forth in the original lease. Obviously, the lease payments will be set at a rate high enough to protect the lessor.

The "open-end" lease is the simplest and cheapest. You are responsible for the difference between the actual market price and that in the contract. If the value of the car falls below book value at the end of the lease, you win. If the resale price is higher, the company wins.

"Open-end" contracts can "save" you $10 or more per month during the lease, but you could lose this, and more, at the trade-in.

Added danger: Under such contracts, you are responsible for returning the car in good condition, or as it says in the contract, "ordinary wear and tear excepted." The key, of course, is what constitutes "ordinary wear and tear."

Extra bonus: In some states, car-leasing companies are exempt from sales taxes on automobiles. This can mean a savings of $300 to $500, which will be reflected in your lower monthly payments and comparatively higher trade-in value.

Costs of Car Leasing

Car costs fall into 2 broad categories—variable and fixed. *Variable* charges include gas, oil, service, tires, batteries, etc.—all dependent on the number of miles the car travels and the care given by the driver.

Fixed costs are those that remain substantially the same regardless of the mileage—licensing, insurance, and depreciation of the car, and interest rates on the financing loan or cash used.

Most people forget that last item, says Israel. "If you pay cash, you must figure what the money would have earned if it had stayed in the bank while you leased a car. Even at 5%, the cash buyer would lose nearly $100 a year in compound interest over 3 years. The interest loss adds about ½ cent per mile to ownership costs.

"And if you finance two-thirds of the purchase price, your interest will cost about $165 a year plus another $65 in first interest on the one-third down payment."

Maybe so. But to a family that just saved 10% on a new vacuum cleaner by paying cash, this "logic" is questionable.

"Average" Car Costs

Consumer authorities, in government and public-interest groups, believe that automobile leasing is expensive for low-mileage drivers, may be useful for those who drive close to 25,000 miles a year, and probably can be economically justified for those who pile up 36,000 miles annually.

The statistics, even from the leasing companies, tend to bear out these conclusions. According to Hertz, the average car is driven 10,323 miles a year—13,400 miles is the average for men, half that for women. And men in the 25 to 50 age group roll up an average of 15,950 miles annually.

Estimated per-mile costs range from 24¢ for a standard-size car driven 10,000 miles annually to 11¢ for a subcompact at 25,000 miles per year (MPY). The data in the table below use a 3-year period, assume there was a one-third down payment, finance charges of $230 a year, gasoline at 55¢ per gallon, and depreciation at the rate of 2¼ % per month.

Type of Car	10,000 MPY	15,000 MPY	25,000 MPY
Standard Size			
10 miles per gal.	29¢	21¢	17¢
Intermediate Size			
14 miles per gal.	24	18.3	14
Subcompact			
18 miles per gal.	19	14	11

Source: The Hertz Corporation.

When you use these figures to compare your own car costs, make allowances for the type of driving, weather, conditions of roads, etc. An "average" is a mean between high and low costs.

Checkpoints for All Types of Leasing

Deal Only with Reputable Companies

Leasing is a business that attracts "smart" operators who may be more interested in a quick buck than in building a business. Leasing relies on borrowed money and estimates of resale prices. An established company has the reputation to get money on better terms and the expertise to arrange the best resale terms.

With small firms, there can be savings in overhead and operations, but when these are spread over 24 months or more, the cost difference is seldom enough to justify a rate $20 to $30 per month below competition. *When you make a deal on price alone, watch for the sheriff with a repossession order. Read and understand the contract.* The obligations of both parties are spelled out. Make sure that you are protected against a "lemon" and have the right to turn in the car or equipment without penalty if you receive it in poor or damaged condition.

Check with Your Accountant before Signing Any Lease

He can spell out the alternatives and the costs both before and after taxes. Review the leasing-cost examples below with a realistic rather than an optimistic eye.

Weigh the Convenience in Terms of Your Own Life-style

You can get a more expensive, later-model car quickly and without shopping.

The lessor is responsible for insurance, and if you so request, for maintenance and replacements. And in most cases he will supply a car while yours is being checked or repaired.

> *Special benefit:* Leasing is a lifesaver for those unable to qualify for regular car insurance because of physical or financial difficulties. As car owners, their policies would be assigned by a state agency to a car-risk pool. This provides coverage only for public liability, NOT for damages to your vehicle. With leasing, there's full coverage at modest rates.

Here's how Hertz pinpoints the breakpoint between owning and leasing:

Individual Ownership and Leasing Costs

Auto Expense	Ownership	Open-End Lease	Closed-End Lease	Maintenance Lease
Sale Price	$3,747			
Trade-in	712			
Net Cost	3,035			
Depreciation	1,012*			
Lease Costs†		$1,560‡	$1,680‡	$2,082‡

Individual Ownership and Leasing Cost (continued)

Auto Expense	Ownership	Open-End Lease	Closed-End Lease	Maintenance Lease
Costs per Mile @ 16,666 Miles per Year				
Fixed Charges				
License and Insurance	.0222			
Depreciation (1)	.0607			
Subtotal	.0829			
Time Purchase (2) (3) Interest Charges	.0138			
Total Costs (Lease)	.0967	.0936	.1008	
Variable Charges				
Maintenance Repairs Tires, etc. (4)	.0182	.0182	.0182	
Subtotal fixed and	(.1149)			.1249
Maint. Charges ($1,915)				($2,082)
Gas and Oil	.0520	.0520	.0520	.0520
Total Variable Costs	.0702	.0702	.0702	.0520
Grand Total—per Mile	.1669	.1638	.1710	.1769
Fixed and Variable Costs per Year	$2,781	$2,730	$2,850	$2,949
Cost Differences—Mile		−.0031	+.0041	+.0100
Ownership versus Lease-Year		$ 51	$ 69	$ 168
3-Year Total		$ 153	$ 207	$ 504

* Based on 1974 Ford Torino. With options and delivery costs, retail price of $4,257 less $510 discount. License, $43; insurance, $327.

(1) Depreciation at 2¼% per month from sale price. On 2-year lease, use 2½%; on 1-year, 2.75%.

(2) 12% interest on unpaid balance of $2,498, plus 5% lost interest on $1,249 down payment.

(3) For cash purchase, assume $95 (.0057 @ 16,666 miles), plus 5% on unpaid balance of $3,747.

(4) For 2 years, .0168; for 1 year, .0138.

† Total annual fixed costs for ownership—$1,611; for open-end lease, $1,560; for closed-end, $1,680; and for maintenance, $2,082. With maintenance, total costs for ownership, at 10,000 miles per year, would be $2,314—.2314 per mile.

†† Add $250 for 2-year lease; $716 for 1-year lease.

Note: Mr. Israel, naturally, tries to make a good case for leasing, but the mileage is high—16,666 miles per year, some 66% above the average car travel; the purchase price is well below list—this is a hard-to-pin-down figure when you are trading in your old car and not inclined to do a lot of shopping; the repairs are low (especially if your wife parks in shopping centers where there are frequent opportunities for damaged fenders from careless parkers (realistically, you'll pay for such annoyances anyway); these days, more people keep their cars for 5 or 6 years, so their costs are substantially less than shown. In many cases, the trade-in value of the old car is almost as much as it used to be when you traded every 3 years.

XXIV

How to Meet College Costs—by Savings, Scholarships, and Loans

In a world growing more dynamic, more competitive, and more technically oriented, a college education can be the most important investment a family can make for its children's future. There's little question that the more education a person has, the greater his or her income will be. A college graduate earns approximately $250,000 more in his lifetime than does an individual with only a high school diploma. In 40 years, that works out to an average of over $6,000 more income a year! And in most cases, that difference starts with the first job.

But money is not everything, nor is a college education worthwhile for everyone. Do not force any child to go to college. By age 18, most youngsters are mature enough to make up their own minds. If they balk, they will probably be the losers. But as many colleges are finding out, education is no longer a straight 16-year process. More students are dropping out for a year or two of military service, work, or pleasure, and think nothing of taking 6 or 8 years to complete what was traditionally a 4-year program. This makes financial planning more difficult.

A college education is important; the way it is achieved and the college attended are no longer paramount. Anyway, with ever-increasing competition, chances are that Junior won't be accepted at Dad's Alma Mater!

372

For most students, any one of half a hundred colleges can provide a worthwhile, meaningful education.

There is one excuse for not attending college which you should *never* accept—financial inability. Except under unusual circumstances, every qualified student can get a college education through grants, scholarships, awards, and—directly or through parents—loans. Your children may have to settle for a local school or a 2-year college, and your own living may be tight for a while, but the funds are available. Every major college and most smaller ones provide financial aid and help students to get part-time and summer jobs. You may be surprised to find that the net cost of sending Junior to Yale is little more than that of Siwash U.—not counting board-and-room and transportation expenses.

The best solution to financing a college education is to start planning and saving early—preferably right after the maternity bills are paid, but certainly no later than age 5. And that goes for *every* child.

That does not mean that you have to stretch your resources too thin. If you have to support an elderly parent or pay heavy medical bills, be realistic. Start a college savings plan with flexible contributions. If you will have 3 children in college at the same time, maybe one of them will be happier at a small, less expensive local institution. Later, perhaps, he or she can transfer.

Overall Costs

The one sure thing about a college education is that it's expensive and growing more so. By 1982, the experts predict, the costs of 4 years at a private college will be about $46,000, versus some $25,000 today; at a state university, $26,000, versus $16,000 now.

Costs vary widely. The most expensive education is at a private institution; the least costly, at evening courses at state or city colleges. Yet they award similar degrees!

Following are typical budgets from 2 private schools (1974) —Yale University and small Upsala College in East Orange, New Jersey. Most public colleges are less expensive.

	Yale	Upsala
Tuition, health service, fees	$3,650	$2,301
Room and board	1,700	1,527
Miscellaneous living costs	650	141
Travel allowance	175	. . .
	$6,175	$3,969

In making your plans, aim high but don't damage your family life. The youngster may not want to go to college, or hopefully, will be smart enough to win a scholarship.

A handy general guideline to estimate future college costs: Multiply the total number of years of college, for all of your children, by $4,000. Then add 8% a year for each year until graduation. Thus, if you have 2 children, aged 8 and 10, you will have to come up with $64,000—$4,000 × 2 × 8. Since very few people make enough money to sustain such a large line of credit, a good chunk of that small fortune has to come from savings and/or from earnings by the children.

> Note: Costs can be cut substantially by living at home. According to recent studies of 2,200 colleges, commuting students got by with $980 less a year than those who lived and boarded on campus. Besides, Mom's cooking is better!

Financial Aid—How Much and Where to Get It

Even with an early start, careful planning, and steady savings, most families will need some sort of financial assistance to pay for their children's college. Except for buying a home, these bills will be the single biggest family outlay. Almost without exception, parents should expect to be strapped for cash or deeply in debt.

The easiest, best, and surest form of aid can be provided by the youngster—earnings from summer jobs and part-time work during high school and college. Yale estimates that a typical student contributes $800 a year. That's probably higher than can be attained in most areas where job opportunities are fewer and pay scales lower. In making your own plans, count on a total 4-year $2,000 to $3,000 per child.

The next major source of financial aid is from the college, governments, and in some communities, from industry, foundations, and service organizations. While some of the scholarships-awards will be for achievement, the majority will be based on need. On the average, 60% of students in private colleges receive some sort of financial assistance. For details on how your child can benefit, consult the student aid department of the college of his choice.

Many states (28 at last count) provide financial aid to undergraduates. The funds, usually awarded according to financial need, come in many forms—flat monetary payments; grants for tuition, special training, incentives, and college continuation; scholarships; and tuition-equalization plans.

Even the programs which start with need may be decided on a competitive basis because of the tremendous demand. Generally, but not always, the student must attend a college within the state.

Here are typical programs:

State	Program	Average Grant	Usable Out of State	Usable at 2-Year Colleges	Public or Private
California	State scholarship	$1,010	No	Yes	Both
	College opportunity	1,267	No	No	Both
	Occupational training	1,000	No	No	Both
Illinois	Monetary awards	733	No	Yes	Both
Massachusetts	General scholarships	594	Yes	Yes	Both
Missouri	Grant program	495	No	Yes	Both

For information, write to the Department of Education at your state capital.

Each college and state board sets its own financial criteria, but the following table gives a rough idea of how much money financial-aid officers expect parents to contribute each year toward the support of one child in college. These are estimates for a "typical" family in 1974:

Net Income
Before Federal
Income Taxes

Net Income Before Federal Income Taxes	Number of Dependent Children				
	1	2	3	4	5
$10,000	$1,260	$ 890	$ 640	$ 440	$ 340
15,000	3,030	2,400	1,900	1,580	1,380
18,000	4,320	3,640	3,030	2,600	2,340
20,000	5,160	4,480	3,870	3,430	3,150
22,000	5,970	5,310	4,710	4,270	3,990
25,000	7,160	6,520	5,920	5,480	5,220

Students are expected to earn more as they complete each year of college—from work during vacations, summers, and after classes.

Student Earnings—Annual

Prefreshman	$400	
Presophomore	500	With inflation, plan
Prejunior	600	to boost these figures
Presenior	600	10% *every* year.

Source: Helping Students Meet College Costs. College Scholarship Service of College Entrance Examination Board, Palo Alto, Calif.

Do not despair just because these figures seem overwhelming. Society has determined that more children will get a college education and is providing means to help you afford it. There are a surprising number of ways to save and make repayments over a long period of time.

For information on unusual scholarships and standard sources of college aid, write Scholarship Search, 7 West 51st Street, New York, New York 10019.

How to Finance College Educations

There are 4 general ways to come up with all or part of the money needed to supplement student earnings—savings-investments, directly or through a trust; insurance; loans to parents; and loans to students. A combination is the best solution for most families.

Another Way to Measure Costs

This table presents college costs from another angle:— the present age of your child and the annual savings required, based on after-tax return of 5%, and 7% inflation.

Age of Child (1975)	State University		Private College	
	4-Year Cost	Annual Savings	4-Year Cost	Annual Savings
1	$56,160	$1,860	$98,280	$ 3,250
2	52,480	1,890	91,840	3,310
3	49,120	1,930	85,960	3,380
5	43,200	2,050	75,600	3,590
6	40,000	2,100	70,000	3,680
7	37,440	2,190	65,520	3,830
9	32,640	2,410	57,120	4,220
10	30,560	2,580	53,480	4,510
11	28,480	2,770	49,840	4,850
12	26,720	3,050	46,760	5,340
13	24,960	3,410	43,680	5,970
14	23,360	3,930	40,880	6,880
15	21,760	4,700	38,080	8,220
16	20,320	5,990	35,560	10,490

Source: Oakland Financial Group, Inc.

Savings

This is the cheapest and most difficult method. It's also the most convenient. The trouble is inflation—if you put your money in a savings account, rising costs will wipe out the interest and cut into capital. But savings accounts are safe and sure. At $150 a month, at 5% annual interest, you will have $23,778 at the end of 10 years. With quarterly compounding, the total will be greater, but the experience of savings banks shows that people tend to skip some months and make it up later.

Following is a table, and formula, to show the benefits of compound interest over the years:

A Regular Investment
of $100 Per Year   Number of Years—Will Be Worth
Invested at   5   10   15   20

Invested at	5	10	15	20
5%	$580	$1,321	$2,266	$3,472
6	598	1,397	2,467	3,899
7	615	1,478	2,689	4,387
8	634	1,565	2,932	4,942
9	652	1,656	3,200	5,576
10	671	1,753	3,495	6,300

To get the corresponding total for any other annually invested amount (A), multiply the dollar total given above for the interest rate and the number of years assumed by $\frac{A}{100}$.

Example: You plan to invest $150 a month for $1,800 a year. What capital sum will that provide after 10 years at 5% compounded annually? Check where the lines cross for 5% and 10 years—$1,321. Then multiply by $\frac{\$1,800}{100} = \$23,778$.

Investments

The same monthly savings approach can be used to buy stocks listed on the New York Stock Exchange or shares in investment companies. (See Chapter XXV, on Investments.)

There's greater safety in the diversification of mutual funds and, hopefully, in their professional management. Despite poor performance in 1973 and 1974, many funds have had total returns, over a 10-year period, well above those available from savings accounts. There is no reason why you cannot count on an average annual return of at least 8% from a well-managed, flexible investment company. This return could be even higher if the fund is designed for income, or when there's a strong stock market, for income and growth.

Thus, with that same $150 per month invested in a no-load mutual fund, you should end up with from $28,178 to $31,554 in 10 years.

Other alternatives: (1) Buy shares in the company where

you work through a payroll-deduction plan. (2) Invest in stock of a profitable, dividend-paying corporation which reinvests dividends and permits you to add funds quarterly. (3) Sign up for a stock-purchase, dividend-reinvestment plan sponsored by a bank. In all of these, the extra benefit is the magic of compounded earnings—"interest on interest."

Perhaps the best plan (though it's more difficult) is to split your investments between quality stocks and fixed-income securities. When the stock market declines, put more into bonds. Move back into growth situations when there's a substantial recovery.

Trusts

Trusts add to college-needed capital by avoiding taxes. *You must have assets to begin with*—inheritance, gift, or investment profits.

The money–stocks–real estate are set up in a "living trust," with the college-bound child as beneficiary. This shifts income which would have gone for taxes into money to pay for education.

A "living trust" is temporary—by law, a minimum of 10 years, and usually longer. It is most valuable when the parents, or donor, are in a fairly high tax bracket—40% or more. By putting assets in the trust, you move income from your well-taxed return to the child's 1040 Form, where there will be little or no taxes.

Example: Mr. Horner has a taxable income of $35,000 and inherits property worth $26,000 that provides $1,800 annual income, on which he pays $615 in taxes.

Son Jeffrey is 9 years old, so Mr. Horner plans to earmark this extra money for his college education. He establishes a living trust with the property and names Jeffrey as the income beneficiary.

The boy will pay $140 on the $1,800 income, so $1,660 can be invested. At 8% compounded, the college kitty will be a welcome $27,740. And Mr. Horner gets back the original trust property.

Warning: Continue to check with your lawyer. Congress is changing tax laws, and it is possible that the IRS could hold the trust taxable to the father. *Basis:* It's his duty to support the child through a college education. So far, there's been no such ruling.

A custodian account offers similar tax benefits plus the advantage that either parent may manage the assets. But all of the property goes to the child when he or she reaches age 18. There's no guarantee that the money will be used for education!

Insurance

Insurance is primarily valuable for family protection in case of death or disability, but the premiums are a form of forced savings. When the child is an infant, buy straight life; when he's ready for college, buy term insurance.

Example: A 30-year-old man, elated at the birth of a son, buys an additional $20,000 of straight life insurance with annual premiums of $390.

In 18 years, the premiums will total $7,020 and the policy will have a cash value of about $8,300. If the father dies, the proceeds of the policy will help ease educational costs. If Dad survives, he can cash in the insurance or borrow against its cash value.

For extra protection: He could pay about $12 a year for a waiver of premium if disabled, or for another $18, he could get the right to add $20,000 extra coverage without a medical exam.

If Father just cannot come up with that $390 a year and gets worried about being able to meet all expenses when Junior enters college, he should buy term life insurance. At age 48, it will cost about $100 a year for 4 decreasing-term policies— $20,000 the first year, $15,000 the second, etc. These cover both death and disability.

Loans

The government-backed student-loan program is being revised by Congress, but at the time this was written, the student could

borrow up to $2,000 at 7% interest. Repayment starts 9 months after graduation.

These loans are limited to children of families with gross annual income of $20,000 or less, and generally are judged on the basis of the table shown earlier. The total of such low-cost loans is limited by the amount of federal subsidy which pays the bank the difference between the 7% and the interest rate prevailing at the time the loan was approved.

As parents, you have several options in borrowing:

REFINANCING YOUR HOME MORTGAGE. This will probably provide all the extra money needed, but it can be expensive—at least 3% to 5% more than you are now paying in annual interest charges.

BORROWING ON OLD INSURANCE POLICIES WITH HIGH CASH VALUES. Under the original contracts, many older policies permit loans, against cash value, at 5% or 6%. That's far less than the cost of a bank loan today and probably for many years to come.

BORROWING AGAINST A SAVINGS-ACCOUNT PASSBOOK. You can get a loan up to 95% of your deposits in most savings institutions. *Advantage:* Your savings will continue to earn interest, so your net cost will be about 5½% below that of the actual loan rate.

BORROWING AGAINST SECURITIES. Here again you will benefit from the returns on the assets used as collateral—interest/dividends and, hopefully, capital appreciation. Because the total income is likely to be greater than that available from savings accounts, your net costs will be lower. But if your securities drop in value, you may have to come up with additional collateral!

GETTING A LOW-COST TUITION LOAN FROM BANKS WHICH OFFER SPECIAL COLLEGE EDUCATION FINANCING. Shop your local banks to see if they have a plan similar to that offered by The National Shawmut Bank of Boston.

Under this tuition-aid plan, you establish a line of credit to pay for specific college expenses. As bills come in, you write checks against your loan commitment. The maximum loan is determined by your credit standing, but while you borrow for the 4 years—or more—you pay only on the money spent. And then only at a 10.5% interest rate.

Repayment starts 1 month after you sign the first check on the special account. The monthly amounts are fixed over a period of 4 to 8 years, as you select. Prepayment is permitted with reasonable adjustments.

The bank provides life insurance so there will be money for the full 4 years if you should die or become disabled, and it also sends statements of payments, interest charges, etc., for income tax returns.

Example: You borrow $16,000 for 4 years with 48 monthly payments at $345.08. Total cost: $16,563—only $563.84 more than your part of the college bill. (*Note:* This is a pro-forma example. Actual terms will depend on how the money is disbursed, etc.)

Setting Up Your Own Scholarships

Any private corporation—small business, large enterprise, or professional organization—can set up a benefits trust to pay for the education of the children of its employees. This is a valid fringe benefit even if there are only 1 or 2 people involved!

The corporation puts aside pretax dollars and deducts the contribution as a business expense. With more cash working, the money compounds rapidly and in a few years should provide ample funds for college costs.

The corporation must pay taxes on earnings of this

"trust" money, and when the funds are disbursed, the employee may have to pay income taxes on the amount distributed each year. (The IRS has made no formal ruling as yet.)

Advice: If you have a small corporation, consult a tax-skilled attorney. This is a new concept which requires careful drafting of the agreement. But it is legal and approved by the IRS.

XXV

How to Make Your Savings Grow

Much of the material in this chapter is digested from *Your Investments*, published annually. As editor of this fact-packed investment guide, I made several points which are pertinent to successful personal money management:

Every Investor Should Look for at Least a 10% Annual Total Return on Dividends-Interest Plus Capital Appreciation

Experienced investors should do better.

The Best Profits in the Stock Market Are Made with the Best Companies

Over the long term, the highest safe returns can be achieved with stocks of high-quality, financially strong, profitable corporations—by buying their shares when they are undervalued and selling them when they become fully priced. Both determinations can be made on the basis of historical standards and future prospects.

Over the Short Term, the Best Profits Can Be Made by Being Flexible

Being willing to shift part of your holdings according to temporary conditions—in periods of high interest rates, to fixed-income securities; in bear markets, to use leverage, trade in warrants, hedge, sell short, and take advantage of investor pessimism.

Be Patient

Rewarding investment returns seldom accrue in less than 24 months, and on the average, take even longer. Sizable estates are built slowly by *wise* rather than *smart* investments.

Concentrate on Investments That Make You, and Your Wife, Comfortable

These may not make the most profitable use of your savings, but it's better to sleep well than to gain an extra 10% to 20% return.

To invest, you must have extra funds—money saved, inherited, or earned by other investments. Whether it's $100 or $10,000, these savings should be kept hard at work to grow rapidly and provide the funds needed for better living, future wants, and building your estate for retirement and/or your heirs. Money should ALWAYS work for you as hard as you worked to make it. The most stupid mistake anyone can make is to carry a large bank balance on which there are small or no returns!

I happen to believe in the moneymaking, money-growing power of investments in common stocks of major American corporations. Other people prefer the security of bonds and savings accounts; still others enjoy the rewards (and tax advantages) of real estate, or if they are wealthy enough, participations in drilling oil wells, breeding or raising cattle, owning a motel, etc. And a few swingers like to speculate in commodities, international currency, and precious metals. *Each to his own taste—as long as you know the risks and can afford the losses.* In successful investing, it is just as important not to lose, as to make, money.

This chapter is about INVESTING—how to secure unearned income from your savings. You don't have to be an expert to make money in the stock market, but you do have to investigate first, set targets, act on facts, and use your common sense. Despite the gobbledygook of Wall Street, there's nothing difficult about making money with securities over the long term.

In the past several years, the stock market has been dismal, but that's temporary and one of the hard facts of the free-enterprise system. I believe that American business has enormous powers of recuperation and over the years will continue to move ahead in sales and earnings. This growth will assure ever greater returns to its shareholders.

Major corporations have the financial strength and managerial skills to produce high yields on stockholders' investments. Eventually those gains will be reflected in the prices of their stocks. This has always been so and, I believe, will be true in the years ahead. *You gotta believe.*

About 40 years ago, the Dow Jones Industrial Average, a standard measure for the stock market, was at 41! In 1973, it rose to 1051, then fell below 600 in 1974 but is moving up again and is expected to be close to 1500 by 1980. This prediction is based on past performance, historical ratios of prices and earnings, and the built-in gains of profitable companies that reinvest a large portion of their earnings in new products, new plants, new equipment and new markets. Business in America and the Free World is still growing. And that growth has been, and will be, fueled by profits.

In rising markets, almost any intelligent investment will make money. The trick is to find the most rewarding, and secure, opportunities.

In erratic markets, it is essential to use different tactics. The only people who made money in the stock market in the early 1970s were those who bought fixed-income securities, utilized special techniques, or put some of their money in precious metals, commodities, and other offbeat operations. When conditions change, you must change, too!

At all times, be realistic, be logical, and rely on facts—the same general approach that assures success in any business or profession. As Charles H. Dow, a pioneer in stock-market analysis, wrote at the turn of the century: "The man who is prudent and careful in carrying on a store, factory or real estate business seems to think that totally different methods should be employed in dealing with stocks. Nothing could be further from the truth."

The explanations and recommendations here have two goals —to help you build capital and to boost your income. They are NOT gospel. They should be followed only when common sense tells you they will enhance your profits or reduce your losses. Discuss your plans with your broker and/or investment adviser. He can keep you up-to-date on changing tax laws, corporate accounting, stock-market rules, and new investment opportunities.

Be flexible in your approach and in your allocation of savings. If you are young, you can invest most of your savings for the long term. If you are older, you will probably look more for tax benefits, and at retirement, high income. *Have a plan, do your homework, and never take any action you do not understand or which does not meet the tests of your own business experience.*

The Magic of Compound Interest

Few people appreciate the magic of compound interest. With consistent investment and reinvestment, you can make your savings grow at an astonishing rate over a lifetime.

Any investor should be able to earn a total return of 10% a year. Currently, this is attainable as interest from well-rated bonds, from dividends of many stocks, and from total returns of other equities. Even with a conservative holding such as American Cyanamid, the current dividend is 5.7%, so the stock has to move only 4.3% (less than 1½ up from its price of 24) to provide a 10% annual return. *Stocks appreciate; many fixed-income investments do not.*

If you start at age 25 to invest $1,000 a year ($66.67 per month) and reinvest all income and gains promptly, you will have $442,593 at age 65—on an annual return of 10%. You will, of course, have to pay taxes from other income.

If you are able to boost that average annual return to 15%, you will be a millionaire—all on a total investment of $40,000!

Years	Original Investment	Market Value
10% Average Annual Rate—Compounded Annually		
10	$10,000	$ 15,397
20	20,000	57,275
30	30,000	164,494
40	40,000	442,592
15% Average Annual Rate—Compounded Annually		
10	$10,000	$ 20,304
20	20,000	102,444
30	30,000	434,745
40	40,000	1,779,090

Plan Your Investment Program

As with all money management, the first step is to count your savings and in a family conference determine how much you want to add and how often. This is an essential part of your overall financial plan, but for most people it's a rare action. *Only one of every 20 families has a systematic, sensible, long-range plan for investing.*

You already know your goals, so the next steps to decide are:

What Type of Investor You Are—or Should Be

CONSERVATIVE. This means stressing safety: (1) preservation of capital, (2) moderate, sure, and stable returns. Usually, such an individual will buy and hold securities for a long time, through recession and boom. It's not the most profitable way to invest.

ENTERPRISING. This requires the willingness to take more risks, to strive for substantial capital gains, to accept small-to-modest income, and to be willing to face the possibility of losses. This type of investor should remain flexible and try to buy low and sell high.

SPECULATIVE. This approach should be used only with money you can afford to lose. To a limited degree, speculation can be an integral part of estate building, but it should be utilized only by those with extra funds and a thorough knowledge of the markets in which he is dealing—or with the aid of a competent broker/adviser.

Who Will Assist You and to What Extent You Will Handle Your Own Investments

Despite some advertisements, stockbrokers are seldom successful investment advisers. They make their money on commissions from buying and selling. They can be helpful in providing information and in timing transactions, but the good ones will insist that you make the decisions.

With less than $25,000, the amateur will probably do better by buying shares of investment companies. But if you want on-the-job training, invest some of your money yourself.

With $50,000, you may want to split your holdings—half in mutual-fund shares, the balance under your own judgment.

With $100,000, it's time to consider outside counsel—an investment advisory firm or subscription to investment services such as Babson's Reports, Moody's Investors' Service, Value Line, Standard & Poor's Outlook, etc. Costs will run from $100 up. Stay away from promoters who run splashy ads in the financial press. You're investing, not speculating.

Do It Yourself

The best investment counsel is your own common sense. If you are successful enough in business or professional life to benefit from this book, you have the brains and experience needed to be a successful investor.

You will need he!p from your broker and financial information that is available from books, lectures, forums, and advisory services. *Always buy ONLY stocks of profitable corporations* whose managements have shown a generally consistent ability to report better-than-average profits. Buy those stocks when they are undervalued and sell them when they become fully priced.

Stockbrokers should supplement, not lead, your choice. A registered representative is a salesman, not an investment counselor.

Lawyers are a poor choice. They are concerned primarily with preservation of capital and thus tend to buy bonds. You will be wasting your money by paying a fee when you can find well-rated bonds yourself.

Bankers are just as bad. You may get security, but in recent years the performance of bank-administered trust-pension funds has been far worse than that of the stock-market averages.

Most important, do your homework. Invest only in quality securities—bonds rated Bbb or higher by Moody's; stocks tagged B or better by Standard & Poor's. And don't buy anything (except short-term bonds) and lock it in your safe-deposit box.

Let me repeat: Investigate before you buy, review all holdings every six months; set target prices. If you are worried about the economic future of the country, the stock market, or the corporation, stay flexible and move into fixed-income securities until you are optimistic again.

Successful investing requires surveillance. If you have neither the time nor the interest, turn your money management over to a professional. But we still insist that you are your own best investment counselor!

DOs and DON'Ts for All Investors

DO Investigate before You Invest

Never buy or sell on impulse, hunch, or rumor. Make all investments by specific plan and stick to your program until there are strong, logical reasons to change.

Write down the facts you know. Fill in the gaps with information from the library, your broker, and the press. Take nothing for granted. Get the facts before the "facts" get you.

DO Investigate after You Invest

There is no such thing as a permanent investment. All securities should be checked to take into consideration the ever-changing conditions in the market, in corporate prospects, and in your own personal situation.

DO Be Patient

Avoid flitting from one stock to another. This will make your broker rich, but it will cut your potential profits and will seldom increase your capital. Few investments achieve substantial appreciation in less than 24 months.

DO Concentrate Your Holdings

Do not acquire more than 5 stocks for small portfolios; 10 for larger ones. Keep another list for future changes.

DO Act Promptly

Once you have made a decision to buy or sell, give the order to your broker. If you are shooting for a 30% gain, a quarter of a point won't make much difference.

DO Stand by Your Investment Rules

There are few occasions when the opportunity is so great and the profits so certain that it is worthwhile to break your rules. There are some 10,000 widely traded securities, so there will always be equal or better opportunities.

DO Be Ready for the Unexpected

Even when you are bullish about an industry or a company, do not let your enthusiasm overcome your judgment. Always be prepared to adjust your plans quickly—to sell when your "facts" prove to be wrong or there are unexpectedly negative developments.

DON'T Be a Nervous Nellie

Don't get panicky just because there are temporary, irrational, illogical actions in the stock market or your stocks. Wall Street is not noted for its short-term wisdom.

DO Set Targets When You Buy

Decide how much you hope to make and how long you expect this to take. Aim for total annual returns of at least 15%—3% to 5% from dividends-interest, the rest from appreciation. Because you will have to pay commissions and, possibly, interest on loans, buy only stocks which you can logically anticipate will rise 35% in the next 24 months. You will not always hit your target, so you must shoot high to maintain your average.

DO Be Sure the Economic and Stock-market Prospects Are Favorable for the Industry and the Company for at Least the Next Year

DO Take Your Losses Fast

The cheapest loss is the first one. Never let pride or stubbornness stop you from correcting an error. Sell if conditions change, you discover your facts were incorrect, or if you find your decision was faulty.

Ask your broker about setting stop orders 15% to 20% below purchase price. This makes sense in a bear market with a quality stock but can be expensive if you are dealing with a volatile equity.

DON'T Average Down unless It's an Unusual Situation

Take your beating and put the proceeds into a situation where there's a profit potential.

DO Let Your Profits Ride

But don't let them ride too far. If the rise in the price of the stock is rapid, review the situation when it reaches your target price. If the prospects are still promising, you may want to set a new target range. Otherwise, *sell*. It is always better to sell "too soon" than "too late." When an overvalued stock starts to decline (Avon, Disney, Polaroid, etc., in 1973–74), the descent can be rapid and steep.

DO Upgrade Your Portfolio Periodically

Every 6 months, review your holdings and consider selling at least one of the securities. Replace your weakest stock with one of greater potential. Do this slowly and carefully and only when the facts clearly indicate that the anticipated potential has dimmed or vanished. Commissions are expensive.

DON'T Be in a Hurry

Before you pay out any of your hard-earned savings, review all investment possibilities—savings accounts, stocks, bonds, etc., to determine the best prospects for profits.

DON'T Worry if You Miss a Quick Rise in the Price of the Security You Are Considering

If it's only a few points and you hope to double your money, start buying; you'll make 90% instead of the hoped-for 100%. If the rise was substantial, forget it. There will be other opportunities in the 10,000 frequently traded public securities.

DON'T Buy Any Stock Solely because It Appears to Be a Bargain

Wall Street is slow to change its negative attitudes. *It's not the winners you don't buy, it's the losers you do NOT buy that make the difference.*

DON'T Invest on Emotion

Never let enthusiasm or pessimism override your common sense. And that caveat applies to your broker's recommendations, too.

DON'T Change Your Goals or Plans until You Are SURE This Is Necessary and Not a Short-term Accommodation

DON'T Forget That the Name of the Game Is PROFITS

It's not cocktail-party conversation to impress your friends. It's almost always easier to lose money than to make it.

What Securities to Choose

For convenience, investment opportunities in securities can be divided into 4 broad categories—common stocks, preferred stocks, convertibles, and bonds. All have merit, yet each has unique characteristics that can be used to achieve specific investment goals, or as is more important to some people, to provide security and income.

Bonds, especially tax-exempt bonds, seldom provide adequate total returns over the years and always decline in purchasing power. But if their possession makes your wife more comfortable, add them to your portfolio. The few thousands of dollars of lost profits will be more than offset by peace in the family. Profits—from dividends, interest, and appreciation—should be the primary reason for buying any security, but don't overlook the comfort quotient.

Investing in Stocks

The key to profits in common stocks is *quality*. There are many ways to measure this essential ingredient, but basically, the criteria are:

Financial Strength

- Plenty of cash, no more than 40% of total capital in debt issues.

Investment Acceptance

- Wide institutional and public ownership with, preferably, listing on the New York Stock Exchange.

Profitability

- A minimum return on stockholders' equity capital of 11% annually.

Strong Growth

- At least 4% a year in equity, dividends, and revenues.

Your broker can help you find such companies, but an easy way to start is to check Standard & Poor's *Stock Guide*, which rates thousands of common stocks according to their records of earnings and dividends—A+—Highest; A—High; A— — Above Average; B+—Average. For investments, concentrate on companies rated B+ or better.

Only rarely will quality stocks move up rapidly in price, but steady, consistent growth is better, anyway. *Remember: The tortoise did defeat the hare.*

Checkpoints for Real Growth

Younger investors should always choose growth over income. It's nice to receive a hefty check for interest-dividends, but that income will be taxed at a comparatively high rate and most likely will be spent quickly. If the corporation plows back most of its profits, it's a tax-free savings for you.

Older investors will probably want to invest with an eye to retirement when they will need more unearned income. But realistically, quality growth stocks will provide greater total returns—again largely because so much of your profit will be withheld for corporate growth.

Two fundamental measurements of corporate growth and profitability are: Earned Growth Rate (EGR) and Profit Rate (PR). They are easy to compile from annual reports or printed statistical data.

The EGR is the annual rate at which the company's equity capital per common share is increased by the net earnings after payment of dividends—if any. This shows the growth of *your* money.

Quality Stocks Listed on the New York Stock Exchange

Aerospace

Cessna Aircraft Company
McDonnell Douglas Corporation

Apparel

Blue Bell, Inc.
Brown Group
Interco, Inc.
Jonathan Logan, Inc.
United States Shoe Corporation
V. F. Corporation

Automotive

Champion Spark Plug Company
Dana Corporation
Eaton Corporation
Ford Motor Company
General Motors Corporation
Monroe Auto Equipment Company

Beverages

Coca-Cola Bottling Company of New York
Coca-Cola Company
Heublein, Inc.
Pepsico, Inc.
Royal Crown Cola Company
Walker (Hiram)-Gooderham & Worts, Ltd.

Chemicals

American Cyanamid Company
Big Three Industries, Inc.
Colgate-Palmolive Company
DuPont (E. I.) De Nemours & Company
Firestone Tire & Rubber Company
Goodyear Tire & Rubber Company
Hercules, Inc.
International Flavors & Fragrances, Inc.
Lubrizol Corporation
Nalco Chemical Company
Procter & Gamble Company

Purex Corporation, Ltd.
Rubbermaid, Inc.
Stauffer Chemical Company

Construction

Caterpillar Tractor Company
Ferro Corporation
Halliburton Company
Johns-Manville Corporation
Marley Corporation
Masco Corporation
Masonite Corporation
Skyline Corporation
Stone & Webster, Inc.
Trane Company
Weyerhaeuser Company

Diversified

Diamond International Corporation
FMC Corporation
Minnesota Mining & Manufacturing Company
National Service Industries, Inc.
Scott & Fetzer Company
Sybron Corporation
Textron, Inc.

Drugs

Abbott Laboratories
American Home Products Corporation
American Hospital Supply Corporation
Avon Products, Inc.
Bard (C. R.), Inc.
Baxter Laboratories, Inc.
Bristol-Myers Company
Chesebrough-Pond's, Inc.
Gillette Company

Johnson & Johnson
Lilly (Eli) & Company
Merck & Company, Inc.
Pfizer, Inc.
Revlon, Incorporated
Richardson-Merrell, Inc.
Robins (A. H.) Company, Inc.
Schering-Plough Corporation
Searle (G. D.) Company
Smithkline Corporation
Squibb Corporation
Sterling Drug, Incorporated
Upjohn Company

Electrical

Emerson Electric Company
General Electric Company
Hobart Corporation
Maytag Company
Square D Company
Thomas & Betts Corporation

Electronics

AMP, Inc.
Burroughs Corporation
Digital Equipment Corporation
Harris Corporation
Hewlett-Packard Company
Honeywell, Inc.
International Business Machines Corporation
Motorola, Inc.
Perkin-Elmer Corporation
RCA Corporation
Schlumberger, Ltd.
Texas Instruments, Inc.
Zenith Radio Corporation

Financial

C.I.T. Financial Corporation
Chase Manhattan Corporation
Citicorp
Heller (Walter E.) International Corporation
Household Finance Corporation
Marine Midland Banks, Inc.
Ryder System, Inc.
Trans Union Corporation

Foods

Beatrice Foods Company
CPC International, Inc.
Campbell Soup Company
Central Soya Company, Inc.
Consolidated Foods Corporation
General Foods Corporation
General Mills, Inc.
Heinz (H. J.) Company
Kellogg Company
Kraftco Corporation
Nabisco, Inc.
Quaker Oats Company
Ralston Purina Company
Standard Brands, Inc.

Machinery and Equipment

Baker Oil Tools, Inc.
Black & Decker Manufacturing Company
Briggs & Stratton Corporation
Bucyrus-Erie Company
Chicago Pneumatic Tool Company
Clark Equipment Company
Combustion Engineering, Inc.

Diebold, Inc.
Dover Corporation
Ex-Cell-O Corporation
Gardner-Denver Company
Ingersoll-Rand Company
Joy Manufacturing Company
Otis Elevator Company
Smith International, Inc.
Warner & Swasey Company
Xerox Corporation

Metal Producers

Amax, Inc.
Cleveland-Cliffs Iron Company
Continental Can Company, Inc.
Crown Cork & Seal Company, Inc.
Emhart Corporation
Harsco Corporation
Illinois Tool Works
International Nickel Company of Canada, Ltd.
Phelps Dodge Corporation
St. Joe Minerals Corporation
Signode Corporation

Oil and Gas

Ashland Oil, Inc.
Continental Oil Company
Exxon Corporation
Gulf Oil Corporation
Kerr-McGee Corporation
Louisiana Land & Exploration Company
Mobil Oil Corporation
Quaker State Oil & Refining Corporation
Standard Oil Company of California
Texaco, Incorporated

Paper

Hoerner-Waldorf Corporation
Union Camp Corporation

Printing and Publishing

Donnelley (R. R. & Sons) Company
Dun & Bradstreet Companies, Inc.
Gannett Company, Inc.
Times-Mirror Company

Recreation

AMF, Inc.
CBS, Inc.
Disney (Walt) Productions
Eastman Kodak Company
Howard Johnson Company
Milton Bradley Company
Outboard Marine Corporation

Retailers

ARA Services, Inc.
Associated Dry Goods Corporation
Carter Hawley Hale Stores, Inc.
Eckerd (Jack) Corporation
Federated Department Stores, Inc.
Jewel Companies, Inc.
Kresge (S. S.) Company
Kroger Company
Lucky Stores, Inc.
Macy (R. H.) & Company, Inc.
Melville Shoe Corporation
Mercantile Stores Company
Penney (J. C.) Company
Petrolane, Inc.

Safeway Stores, Inc.
Sears, Roebuck & Company
Servomation Corporation
Southland Corporation
Winn-Dixie Stores, Inc.

Textiles

Collins & Aikman Corporation

Tobacco

American Brands, Inc.
Reynolds (R. J.) Industries, Inc.
United States Tobacco Company

Transportation

Delta Air Lines, Inc.
Transway International Corporation

Utilities

Allegheny Power System, Inc.
American Electric Power Company, Inc.
American Natural Gas Company
American Telephone and Telegraph Company
Atlantic City Electric Company
Baltimore Gas & Electric Company
Central Illionis Public Service Company
Central Louisiana Electric Company
Central & South West Corporation
Cincinnati Gas & Electric Company
Cleveland Electric Illuminating Company
Columbia Gas System, Inc.
Delmarva Power & Light Company
Florida Power Corporation
Florida Power & Light Company

Gulf States Utilities Company
Houston Lighting & Power Company
Houston Natural Gas
Indianapolis Power & Light Company
Lone Star Gas Company
Long Island Lighting Company
Louisville Gas & Electric Company
Middle South Utilities, Inc.
Northern Illinois Gas Company
Northern Indiana Public Service Company
Northern Natural Gas Company
Ohio Edison Company
Oklahoma Gas & Electric Company
Pacific Gas & Electric Company
Panhandle Eastern Pipe Line Company
Peoples Gas Company
Public Service Company of Colorado
Rochester Telephone Corporation
Southern Company
Southern Natural Resources, Inc.
Tampa Electric Company
Texas Eastern Transmission Corporation
Texas Gas Transmission Corporation

Miscellaneous

Anchor Hocking Corporation
Automatic Data Processing, Inc.
Avery Products Corporation
Engelhard Minerals & Chemicals Corporation
Genuine Parts Company
Nashua Corporation
Owens-Illinois, Inc.
Pittston Company
Purolator, Inc.
Simplicity Pattern Company, Inc.

Source: Wright Investors' Service.

A top growth company will increase its equity capital at a rate of at least 6% per year.

The PR assesses true profitability by measuring the ability of corporate management to make money with your money. It shows the rate of return produced on shareholders' equity capital at corporate book value. Be very cautious about *investing* in any corporation that has not been able to show a PR averaging over 11% a year.

The advantage of both of these yardsticks is that they can be applied to any type of company—fast-food franchiser, steel manufacturer, retailer, or financial institution.

To get these checkpoints, take the latest annual report and look for the summary of financial results, usually at the end of the booklet. Find the book value per share of common stock. (It's also called stockholders' equity or shareholders' equity.)

This is the net value of total corporate assets—what's left over when all liabilities, including bonds and preferred stock, are subtracted from total assets. That's what each share of stock really owns.

The following table shows why Eastman Kodak qualifies as a top growth company—it has shown consistently strong growth and high profitability.

Eastman Kodak Company

Year	Book-Value Beginning Year	Per Share Earnings (Adjusted for stock split)	Per Share Dividends	EGR	PR
1969	$11.39	$2.49	$1.25	10.9%	21.9%
1970	12.63	2.50	1.32	9.3	19.8
1971	13.81	2.60	1.34	9.1	18.8
1972	15.07	3.39	1.39	13.3	22.5
1973	17.05	4.05	1.81	13.1	23.8
1974	19.30	3.90	1.99	9.9	20.2

Here are the formulas for EGR and PR:

EGR = Earned Growth Rate
E = Earnings
D = Dividend
BV = Book Value

$$EGR = \frac{E - D}{BV}$$

For 1973, take the per-share earnings of $4.05, subtract the $1.81 dividend to get $2.24. Then divide by the book value at the beginning of the year—$17.05—to get an EGR of 13.1%.

$$EGR = \frac{4.05 - 1.81}{17.05} = \frac{2.24}{17.05} = 13.1$$

For the PR:

PR = Profit Rate

P = Profit per common share for the last year reported $\qquad PR = \frac{P}{BV}$

BV = Book Value

$$PR = \frac{4.05}{17.05} = 23.8$$

Both of these rates were about double those of the 30 giant corporations which make up the Dow Jones Industrial Average (of which EK is a component).

Year	Book Value Per Share	Per-Share Earnings	Per-Share Dividends	EGR	PR
1969	$521.08	$57.02	$33.90	4.4%	10.9%
1970	542.25	51.02	31.53	3.6	9.4
1971	573.15	55.09	30.86	4.2	9.6
1972	607.61	67.11	32.27	5.7	11.0
1973	642.87	86.17	35.33	7.9	13.4
1974	690.22	99.04	37.72	8.9	14.3

Source: Wright Investors' Service.

Use these tables as a frame of reference when you are rating potential purchases. The majority of quality stocks on the table will have records as good or better than the Dow. Just as with Kodak, most of these companies will falter once in a while, but they will come back—probably with a new president. In the big leagues, executives either produce or are replaced.

Note: Just because a corporation continues to show strong, profitable growth is no guarantee that the price of its stock will stay high. One of the dangers of buying—or holding—any stock after it has become fully valued is that a slight drop in the rate of growth (or even flat earnings) can trigger a sharp decline in its market value. Too often, Wall Street expects miracles and turns sour if these super results are not produced according to what the analysts (not corporate management) anticipate. Once the pros turn thumbs down on any industry or company, it's best to take your profits and move to another area where there is greater investor enthusiasm. Don't try to buck the stock market, no matter how favorable your interpretation of the facts.

Common Stocks for the Best Profits

Over the years, few investments provide such consistent, increasing returns as common stocks of growing, profitable, quality corporations. You gain in 4 ways:

Ever-Higher Dividends

For Eastman Kodak, in 5 years, from $2.50 to $3.90 per share.

Constantly Greater Underlying Values

In the same period, total assets rose from $1,590 million to $2,491 million. Since the company paid out only about 50% of its profits, an equal amount was plowed back into making the company more efficient, more productive, and more profitable.

Rising Prices for the Common Stock

The price rose from about 58 in 1970 to 152 in 1973. Or to put it another way, $5,800 invested in Kodak stock would have grown to $15,000 plus $586 in dividends.

An Effective Tax Shelter

The earnings not paid out represent tax-deferred income. You pay no taxes on these "gains" until you sell, and then, probably at the low capital gains rate.

Those are the good features of a quality stock. The bad side came in late 1973 and 1974 when the price of Eastman Kodak dropped below 60, the extra dividend was eliminated, and the company moved into Wall Street's doghouse. But quality will win. By mid 1975, the stock was selling over 100!

This points up the major financial—and psychological—disadvantage of common stocks. Their prices will fluctuate because they reflect investor enthusiasm or pessimism—factors over which the individual has no direct control. Even the highest-quality stocks will move up or down about 25% a year! That's a pleasant gain if you bought low, but a harsh loss if you bought high.

And of course, if you were foolish enough to buy poor-quality equities, you can lose a good chunk of your capital. Usually, the mistake is yours, not the company's. When you forget quality and buy for a "quick gain," you are speculating, not investing. This does not mean that you won't lose capital if you buy a quality stock at the wrong time (as many people learned in 1974), but if there's real quality, hang in there and enjoy the dividends while the price of the stock slowly works up again.

Obviously, the smart investor bought Kodak when the stock was undervalued (in 1970–71) and sold it when it became fully priced (in 1972). But how do you know these key price areas?

The Usefulness of Price/Earnings Ratios

Professionals have many complicated criteria, but for amateurs, a good place to START is with the P/E ratio. *There are always other factors to consider before you make the final decision.*

The P/E ratio is the market price of the stock divided by last year's per-share earnings—e.g., when Eastman Kodak was at 75 and its per-share profits, in 1970, were $2.50, the P/E was 30. In most stock tables, you will find the figure listed in the daily quotations.

Over the years, stocks tend to sell within fairly well-defined P/E ranges. There are exceptions in depressive and ebullient stock markets. With EK, the P/E ratios for the 1964–73 decade ranged from an average high of 37 to an average low of 26. When the price of any stock rises too high or falls too far, the P/E ratio gets out of line and the stock should be sold or bought.

In 1972, for example, Kodak's earnings were $3.39 per share. Using the high P/E of 37, this would mean that the stock should be sold at 125 (37 × 3.39). At any higher price, the stock was, by historical standards, overvalued. This was an important signal.

It's true that investor enthusiasm for Famous-Name, Glamour-Growth stocks did send EK to 152, but the wise investor would have sold at the target price. As Baron de Rothschild said, when asked the secret of his financial success, "Always selling a little bit too soon."

Note: The P/E ratios of EK, as befits a high-quality, strong-growth stock, are high; almost double those of most equities. Over the years, only a few stocks sell at multiples over 17, and at the end of 1974, the stocks of the Dow Jones Industrial Average had a dismal P/E of 6.2! But in investing, *the only criterion is past performance.*

Conversely, when EK dropped to 65 in anticipation of lower earnings in 1974, its P/E was a bargain 18. This was the time to buy.

The P/E can also be used to set target prices when you buy a stock. Such projections can be made *only* with stocks of quality corporations with long, consistent records of growth. They are useless with corporations that have erratic records of growth and profitability.

P/E ratios are only one factor in analysis. You must always consider the outlook for the stock market, the prospects for the particular company, and the possible problems which may be beyond corporate management's control—a recession, governmental rulings, antitrust suits, international complications, etc.

Here's how to make projections with P/E ratios. EK is at 65. Its anticipated earnings are $3.80 per share, so the P/E is just

Price/Earnings Ratios

Industry Group	1964-68 Hi-Lo	1969-73 Hi-Lo	Industry Group	1964-68 Hi-Lo	1969-73 Hi-Lo
Aerospace	21-10	33-17	Oil: Explor. & Drill.	17- 8	24-13
Agric. Machinery	14- 9	16- 9	Oil: Crude Producers	26-16	33-18
Airlines	30-15	29-14	Oil: Domestic	16-11	19-12
Adv. Agencies	18-11	16-8.1	Oil: International	17-12	16-10
Aluminum Prod.	20-13	17-10	Oil: LPG Distrib.	18-11	17- 9
Apparel Chains	12- 8	23-13			
Bakers	21-13	39-21	Paper	18-12	17-10
Bus. Machines	45-23	46-24	Printing-Publish.	23-14	20-11
Canners & Proc.	19-12	21-13	Radio-TV	27-14	27-13
Const. Machinery	13- 8	19-12	Railroads	15-11	20-12
Copper Producers	15- 9	14- 8	Restaurants	35-14	32-14
Cosmetics-Toilet.	28-16	37-22			
Department Stores	17-11	22-13	Service Orgs.	37-16	52-25
Discount Stores	14- 7	24-12	Shoe Stores	12- 8	17-10.5
Diversified Food	21-14	20-14	Steel: Integrated	16-12	12- 8
Drug Chains	15- 9	26-14	Steel: Specialty	14-10	15-9.2
Drug Mfs.-Divers.	30-20	33-22	Surg. & Dental Supply	31-18	46-27
Drug Mfs.-Ethical	29-19	31-20			

Elec. Appliances	20–11	24–13
Elec. Companies	21–12	22–13
Elec.-Industrial	21–11	22–13
Food Chains-Local	24–15	22–12
Food Chains-Nat.	16–11	19–13
Gold Producers	38–23	32–15
Hospital Mgt.	. . . . .	42–18
Hotels-Motels	32–13	74–37
Machinery & Equip.	17–10	24–14
Machine Tool Mfs.	13– 7	29–17
Metal Producers	20–12	16–9.3
Mining Cos.	20–12	17–10

Textiles	17–9.4	17–9.3
Tobacco	14–8.6	13– 9
Trucking	14–8.1	24–12
Utilities: Elec.*	22–18	15–12
Utilities: Elec.**	19–16	14–11
Utilities: Elec. & Gas	19–16	14–11
Utilities: Gas	17–13	13– 9
Dow Jones Indust.	18–15	17–14
Dow Jones Util.	18–16	13–11
S & P 425 Ind.	18–15	19–16

* Quality Companies; ** Others.
Source: Wright Investors' Service.

over 18. Research shows that, over the years, profits have risen
at an average annual rate of about 13%. But since these are difficult times, you lower the expected gain to 8% a year and hope
the P/E will rise modestly.

Year	Per-Share Earnings	If the P/E Ratio Is: 20	22	24	26
1	$3.80	76	84	91	99
2	4.10	82	90	98	107
3	4.42	88	97	106	115

In 24 to 36 months, you can hope for gains of from 40% to
77%, plus modest dividends (originally $1.56, and if past is
prologue, higher each year). On an annual basis, total returns
will be about 25%.

There's no assurance that these targets will be reached, but
this is the approach to take whenever you make any investment:
Project the potential on the basis of facts, not hopes.

Remember: Investing is for the long term. The stock market
repeats historical patterns. Use the following table only for
stocks of companies that have proven records of past performance for at least 3 and preferably 5 years.

Preferred Stocks for Income-Security

A preferred stock is just what the name states—it has preference on all income available after the payment of bond interest
and amortization. Dividends, usually at a fixed rate, are paid
before any money is distributed to common shareholders. Compared to common stocks, preferreds are safer, will bring higher
income for some years after issue, and provide tax benefits for
investing corporations—85% of the income is tax-deductible.

Straight preferreds have limited appeal to individual investors.
They should be bought only when they have a yield advantage of
at least 1% over bonds, are selling at a discount, and when the
investment goal is income and security. As fixed-income invest-

ments, their long-term value, in purchasing power, will decline under the pressure of inflation.

Seldom buy straight preferreds at issue. There's little chance of appreciation. If your wife insists on safety, look for preferreds that pay modest dividends and because of high interest costs are selling well below their face value—e.g., a $4 preferred at 50 when interest rates were about 8%. This will provide a good return, and if the cost of money drops, will rise in price.

Convertible Securities (CVs)

These combine the fixed income of senior securities with the growth potential of common stocks. They are bonds or preferred stocks that can be converted into shares of the related common stock at a specified ratio, usually until a specified date. CV bonds, called debentures, represent a debt of the issuing company. They are redeemable at par—generally $1,000—and after the first few years, may be callable by the corporation. When backed by a strong company, CVs can be excellent investments.

For conservative investors, they provide adequate income— from 6% to 9%—and if the value of the related stock rises, can bring substantial appreciation. Retired people often use them for current income and, for their children, future growth. To a certain degree, CVs permit you to have your cake and eat it, too.

Typically, CVs are issued at a premium of about 15% over conversion value. The hope is that the proceeds from the sale of the CV will enable the corporation to prosper so that the price of its stock will rise and make conversion profitable. For that privilege, investors are willing to accept CVs with interest rates as much as 2% below those of regular bonds.

Thus, a debenture convertible to 20 shares of stock (at $50 a share) might carry a coupon of 6½% when a comparable bond would pay 8%. At that time, the stock would be selling at about 42, so the premium on the CV would be just over 15%.

The price of a CV is determined on 2 bases:

Investment Value

This is the theoretical worth as a conventional bond or preferred stock without consideration of the benefits of conversion. This is supposed to be a floor price under which the CV will not decline, regardless of the action of the related stock. Thus, a 6% CV will sell at around 60 when interest rates are about 9%, even though the price of the related stock might be down 50% or more.

This floor is more theory than fact. When there's a real bear market, the investment value gets clobbered along with the stock. But as long as the corporation remains solvent, the interest-dividends will be paid.

Conversion Value

This is the amount the CV would be worth if it were exchanged for shares of the common stock. The CV moves with the price of the stock. When the corporation does well, the price of the stock will rise, and with it, the CV.

New issues of CVs are floated most frequently when stock prices are high. There are no commissions, but except in strong bull markets, new offerings are not the best investments. The time to buy CVs is when the premium is low and the prospects for the common stock high.

Your broker can give you the premium on any CV, but if you want to do your own figuring, use this formula:

PC = the price of the common stock
SC = the number of shares by conversion
PB = the current price of the convertible
$\$P$ = the dollar premium you pay
CV = the present value of the convertible
P = the percentage of premium

First, $CV = PC \times SC$; then $PV - CV = \$P$; finally, $\dfrac{\$P}{CV}$ P

Example: Becton Dickinson convertible debentures 4⅛s, due in 1988, were selling at 91.25 ($912.50). Each bond was convertible into 20 shares of common stock, then at 39.

$$CV = 39 \times 20 = 780$$
$$912.50 - 780 = 132.50$$
$$\frac{132.50}{780} = 17\%$$

This premium is just about what most analysts feel is a fair price to pay.

Here are Moody's recommendations for "Selected Convertibles for Appreciation" as of early 1975:

Company	Conversion Rate	Dividend Minus Interest	Recent Price Common	Recent Price CV	Yield Per Cent	Conversion Value	Premium
Amer. Hosp. 5¾, '99	3.39	$5.75	28½	111	4.97	96⅝	14.9%
Beatrice Fds. pfd.	5.00	4.00	14¾	75	5.33	73¾	1.7
Int. Min. & Chems. 4s, '91	2.62	4.00	33¾	89½	4.96	87½	2.3
Monsanto, pfd.	1.12	2.75	44¼	50¾	5.42	49½	2.5
Sun Oil, pfd.	0.984	2.25	36	37¼	6.04	35½	1.4

Bonds for Income

Bonds are loans to corporations. They are promises to pay interest at a specified rate until the debt is repaid at face value at a specified future time, from 1 to 40 years hence.

Broadly speaking, there are 2 types of bonds:

• Taxable bonds—issued by corporations and by the federal government and its agencies.

• Tax-exempt bonds—issued by states, local governments, and certain public authorities.

The prices of bonds are determined by the prevailing interest rate, not by supply and demand as with common stocks. Bond values rise when interest rates decline, fall when interest rates go up. The lower the quality of the issuer, the higher the coupon rate (the rate of interest paid at issue). Thus, long-term AT&T bonds, with the highest rating of Aaa, carried an 8.7% coupon at the same time short-term, lower-rated Baa bonds of Detroit Edison Co. were floated with a 12¾% yield.

The trouble with bonds is *inflation*. Bonds can provide good-to-high income, but they cannot maintain the purchasing power of either principal or income. With inflation a permanent factor in our economy, the *real* value of a bond will be cut almost in half in just 7 years! At the end of 20 years, you will get back your original $1,000, but it will buy only 20% (or less) of what it did when the original purchase was made. Common stocks of growing, profitable corporations will rise in value and dividends and thus offset a good portion of the ravages of inflation.

Yet, to many people, bonds are preferred investments. They provide peace of mind, security of principal, and the assurance of regular income. Unlike stocks, which can plunge 25% (more in a recession), high-coupon bonds are not likely to drop far in market value and will go up when interest rates decline. Capital gains can be made with bonds, but in most cases, these securities are bought for long-term income. To varying degrees, there's a time and place for bonds in almost all investment portfolios.

How to Make Profits in Bonds

The key to making money with bonds is the cost of money. Buy short-term, high-coupon bonds when there is a probability of higher interest rates—as in 1957, 1964, 1971, and 1974. Their prices will hold because of the approaching redemption.

Buy long-term, low-coupon bonds where you anticipate a drop in interest rates in the next 6 to 12 months—as in 1967, 1970, and 1975.

Example: In late 1969, a 4% U.S. corporate bond, issued at $1,000 and maturing in 21 years, was selling at 64 when the prime bank rate was 8.5%. By the end of 1970, when the bank rate was down to 7%, the price of the bond moved up to over 73. This was the time to sell—before the interest rate moved up and the price of the bond went down again: to below 50 when interest rates were at a peak.

The greatest profits in bonds can be made by buying on margin. Except in periods of tight money, you can borrow 80% or more of the market value of quality bonds at interest rates close to the yield on the bonds. By buying long-term bonds at a discount, you can hold them at practically no cost and hope for capital appreciation.

Example: In the spring, you buy 50 Sore Tooth 4¾ s, 1988, at 60 ($600), for a total cost of $30,000. You put up $6,000 cash and borrow $24,000 (80% of market value) at 8% interest ($1,920). The income from the bonds is $2,375, so you have a net income of $455, not counting the small commissions.

By winter, the interest rate drops and the price of the bond moves up 3 points, so you have a $1,500 profit if you sell.

With bonds approaching maturity, there's not as much leverage by borrowing, but profits can come quickly.

Example: In early 1973, Pacific Gas & Electric 3s, 1974, were selling at 95. You bought 10 bonds for $9,500 (omitting commission). You had a certain income of $500 when the bond rose to its $1,000 redemption price plus $300 interest. At that time, you would have had to be mighty smart to make as much by buying common stocks. And the risks would have been greater.

DOs and DON'Ts on Bond Investing

DO Check the Rating of the Bond

Buy only those rated Baa or higher. Moody's and Standard & Poor's rate bonds on the basis of the issuer's ability to pay principal and interest.

Moody's Bond Ratings

Aaa—gilt-edge.
Aa —high-quality.
A —upper-medium.
Baa—medium.
Ba —uncertain.
A/1 (municipal bonds)—strongest investment attributes.
From B to C—skip 'em unless you want to speculate.

DON'T Sacrifice Safety for Yield

Buy the highest-yielding obligation of a sound issuer. For best sleeping, buy no bonds under A. For highest income, take the 12¾% that went with the Baa rating of Detroit Edison bonds.

DON'T Buy Bonds Close to or above Their Call Price

The call price is the price at which the issuer can redeem them, usually 3 to 5 points above par. A downward shift in interest rates can lead to a call; an upward move in interest rates will mean a price decline.

DON'T Buy Foreign Bonds

No matter how attractive the yield may be, there are dangers of devaluation, default, or taxation.

DO Buy Quality Bonds at Discounts

You can be sure of good income and price appreciation— soon, if interest rates drop; later, when the maturity date approaches.

Tax-Exempts for the Wealthy

In recent years, tax-exempt bonds have become popular investments for individuals who want to avoid paying taxes on the interest. Generally, tax-exempt securities are not worthwhile if

Tax-Exempt versus Taxable Income

How to Use Table

Find your own income bracket in column A and read columns across. Take, as an example, a husband and wife who file a joint return on $25,000 after deductions and adjustments. They are in the 36% federal income tax bracket (column B) and must turn over to the tax collector 36 cents out of the next $1 of taxable income they earn. Whereas the income from a municipal bond paying them 6% would be all their to keep (C), in the 36% tax bracket they keep only 3.20% from a savings account paying 5% taxable (D). They keep 3.84% from a U.S. government obligation paying 6% (E). They keep 4.80% from a 7½% corporate bond (F).

A If Your Net Joint Taxable Income Is	B Your Federal Tax Bracket Is	C Your Takehome From a Tax-Free 6% Bond Is	D Your Takehome from a Bank Paying 5% Taxable Is	E Your Takehome from a US Govt. Bond Pay- ing 6% Taxable Is	F Your Takehome from a Corporate Bond Pay- ing 7½% Taxable Is	G To Keep 6% from a Taxable Bond It Would Have To Pay You
$ 16,000	28%	6%	3.60%	4.32%	5.40%	8.33%
25,000	36	6	3.20	3.84	4.80	9.37
35,000	42	6	2.90	3.48	4.35	10.34
50,000	50	6	2.50	3.00	3.75	12.00
75,000*	55	6	2.25	2.70	3.38	13.33
$100,000*	62	6	1.90	2.28	2.85	15.79

*Taxable income from all sources, "earned" and otherwise.
Source: Lebenthal & Co., Inc.

you are in a 25% tax bracket, are of minimal benefit for those in the 36% tax bracket, and are really valuable when you have to pay federal taxes at a rate of 42% or more—with limited exceptions for those who have to pay state and city income taxes.

Before you answer any ad offering to double your after-tax income, do your homework, check the tax tables (using your adjusted tax rate), and consult your tax adviser. For most people, tax-exempt bonds are a better security blanket than investment.

Tax-exempts have the same disadvantage as all fixed-income securities—certain loss of purchasing power. In addition, they may be illiquid. If you have to sell in a hurry, you can lose 2 or 3 points—$20 to $30 per bond (even more after the New York City financial crisis).

If you do add tax-exempts to your portfolio, check the quality of the issuer, find a maturity date which fits your estate plan, select an issue which has an active market (big cities rather than small villages), and look for bonds selling at discounts so you can enjoy capital gains.

Most important, deal only with a reputable brokerage firm. The growing popularity of tax-exempts has spawned a modern version of the old bucket shop—glib salesmen telephone prospects to offer bargains, lie about the bond's quality, issuer, rate of return, maturity date, and true market price. *Never buy bonds from a stranger.*

Finally, be wary of switching bonds at year-end. Competition keeps the price and yields of tax-exempts in line. Switching is more profitable for the dealer than the investor.

How to Read Bond Quotations

Corporate bonds are quoted in ⅛ points. A typical daily report of bonds traded on the New York Stock Exchange would read:

Bonds	Current Yield	Volume	High	Low	Last	Net Change
AT&T 4⅜s, '85	5.8%	76	76	75¼	75¼	+¼
Ford Credit 4½s, '96	CV	150	61	61	61	....
GAC 11s, '77	17%	30	62¾	62½	62¾	....

The first line shows that 76 AT&T bonds due in 1985, with a coupon of 4⅜s, were sold at prices between 76 and 75¼, with the last sale ¼ above the closing price of the previous trading day. Each bond pays $43.37 annual interest, so the current yield on the $760 price is 5.7%.

Note: (1) the low price of the Ford Credit CV (which is convertible to stock of the Ford Motor Company) and so reflects the depressed state of the auto industry; (2) the very high 17% yield of the low-quality GAC bond, which investors are not so sure will be paid off in 1977.

Government bonds, which are traded over-the-counter, are quoted in 32/100s on a bid-and-asked basis.

Rate	Maturity Date	Bid	Asked	Bid Change	Yield to Maturity
4s	February, 1980	86.10	86.20	....	7.19%
7½s	August, 1988–93	97.28	98.28	+.2	7.61

The first line shows that at the close of the market, some bond dealer was willing to pay 86 1/32nd ($863.12), plus interest accrued since the most recent semiannual payment, for each $1,000 face value of 4% bonds due in February, 1980; that some seller was willing to sell such bonds for 86 2/32nds ($866.24). There was no change from the closing prices of the previous day. The 7.19% yield to maturity includes a capital gain of $136.88, plus the proportionate share of the annual $40 interest.

The 7½s provide greater income (but less appreciation), so are priced closer to par.

How to Mix a Bond Portfolio

Here are guidelines for conservative bondholdings:

Age Bracket	Corporate Bonds	CVs	Tax-Exempts	Governments
30–39	50%	50%		
40–49	33	33	33	
50–59	25	25	25	25
60+	20	20	20	40

Extra Profits from Tax-Exempts

Bonds with mandatory sinking funds can be unusually attractive when there are provisions for early call by lot. With toll-road bonds, the trustee must go into the open market and buy a certain number of bonds each year. The bonds to be called are selected by lot, so every bondholder has a chance for substantial capital gains before normal redemption date.

These securities have a *yield to average life* that is higher than *yield to maturity* and *current yield*.

Example: When New York State Thruway Series D 3.10s, 1994, rated Aa, were selling at $590, they provided a current yield of 5.25%, a yield to maturity of 6.90%, and a yield to average life of 8.27%—all tax-free.

If you own such a bond, your $590 might become $1,000 quickly.

Saving Estate Taxes

One of the most rewarding investments for older people is "flower bonds." These are direct obligations of the U.S. government that, at death, are worth par when used to pay estate taxes. They carry low coupons, so can be bought at substantial discounts.

Example: U.S. Governments 4¼s, 1987–92, are selling at about 77. Your mother, who is old and ailing, has a modest estate on which you anticipate federal taxes will be about $5,000.

You buy 5 bonds at 76 for her account. When she dies, that $3,800 investment will have a tax-payable value of $5,000. Meantime, she receives $212.50 in interest, paid semiannually.

Flower Bonds

Rate	Maturity Date	Approximate Price	Yield to Maturity
4½%	May, 1975–85	80	6.93%
3¼	June, 1978–83	77	6.88
4	February, 1980	86	7.19
3½	November, 1980	84	6.70
3¼	May, 1985	76	6.32
4¼	August, 1987–92	77	6.39
4	February, 1988–93	76	6.16
4⅛	May, 1989–94	77	6.16
3½	February, 1990	76	5.85
3	February, 1995	76	4.84
3½	November, 1998	76	5.24

Savings Bonds

Savings bonds are issued in two series—E (in denominations of $25, $50, $75, $100, $200, $500, and $1,000) and H (in denominations of $500, $1,000, and $5,000). Both bonds are bought at discounts—E bonds, for example, at $18.75, $37.50, $75, etc. With E bonds, interest accrues through the increase in the redemption value at the beginning of each successive half-year period after issue date, with an additional increase in the last 4-month period.

H bonds pay semiannual interest with checks mailed to the

holder. When held beyond maturity, both types of bonds continue to pay interest.

The best thing that can be said about savings bonds as investments is that they are safe, convenient, and permit postponement of taxes on interest until redeemed. Their yields, currently 6%, are well below those available from other fixed-income investments, and there is no chance of appreciation above face value. You can, however, avoid taxes on interest by switching from E to H bonds.

If you give savings bonds to a minor, be sure to type GIFT above your name and list your Social Security number. On the bond itself, write the name of the child and his (her) Social Security number. Otherwise, you will be liable for taxes on the interest.

How to Get the Most from Investment Companies

Investment companies can be divided into two categories—open-end (commonly called mutual funds) and closed-end. Both invest shareholders' money in diversified portfolios according to stated investment objectives—for income: bond and high-yielding stocks: for growth: common stocks; for balanced income-growth: mixed holdings. There are also specialty funds which invest only in certain securities or industries—convertibles, liquid assets, foreign securities, etc. *You name it, and one of the 800 investment companies has it.*

Shares of investment companies have been available for more than 50 years but are still not nearly as popular as publicity would indicate—only 8% of Americans own shares in any investment company, and 70% of these admit knowing little about them. But they can be important, profitable, and convenient depositaries for savings.

Open-end funds are always ready to sell more shares or redeem outstanding ones at net asset value at the close of stock-market trading. Closed-end funds are similar to corporations.

They have a fixed number of shares which are bought and sold just like regular stocks—with standard commissions.

There are 2 types of mutuals:

Load Funds

These are *sold*—primarily by registered representatives of brokerage firms—with a sales charge of about 8.5%, which is deducted from your investment. Thus, you have only $91.50 of every $100 working for you. (On large purchases, the rate of commission drops to about 3% on a single $100,000 purchase.) There's no charge for redemption.

No-loads

Shares are bought directly from their sponsoring company without sales charge. All of your savings go to work.

All types of investment companies operate much the same and charge similar management fees—usually a maximum of one-half of 1% of portfolio value.

Investment-company shares are best for small investors and for those who have neither the time, the patience, nor the interest to handle their own investing.

They provide:

DIVERSIFICATION. Unless you have $50,000, it is difficult and costly to build a properly diversified portfolio. It's expensive to buy odd lots, and acquiring 100 shares in a quality company will cost about $65 (at an average price of 40). With limited capital, it is difficult to spread the risks by holdings in different industries. Investment companies seldom own stocks in less than 50 corporations.

PROFESSIONAL MANAGEMENT. While the records of a few funds look as if their money had been allocated according to the phase of the moon or to interpretations of tea leaves, the majority reflect the time, experience, and knowledge of skilled money managers.

By and large, amateur investors do not understand the art of making money. They are slow to act, rely on tips rather than facts, buy when stocks are popular (and thus high-priced), and sell when they are depressed (and, often, bargains). The true professional money manager establishes strict standards for the stocks he wants to buy and hold, acts primarily on facts, and makes decisions unemotionally.

AWARENESS. The professionals have access to more, and more recent, information than is available to most amateurs. By the time the individual gets the news or understands its significance, a stock may have moved a couple of points.

BETTER PERFORMANCE. Don't let adverse publicity about the performance of investment companies dismay you. Look at their records. Only a small percentage of investors have done as well as the average professional. Check the 10-year records yourself!

EXTRA SERVICES. Not all funds offer all services, but here are some of the most frequently available extras:

• AUTOMATIC REINVESTMENT. All dividends-interest and capital gains can be automatically reinvested to compound your earnings. In effect, this is a form of dollar-cost-averaging. More important, your money is kept almost constantly at work.
Note: This feature may not always be in your best interest. Funds make the largest disbursements when the stock market is high, so your money is reinvested when stocks are expensive. The experienced investor may do better to take a check and buy more shares when the market declines.

• BENEFICIARY DESIGNATION. You can bypass probate by naming your beneficiary under a trust agreement. Consult your attorney, as some states prohibit such a transfer.

• TERM LIFE INSURANCE. This is available with long-term contractual plans. The insurance guarantees that your survivors will receive the insurance at reasonable cost and without examination if you are under age 55 and have a total investment under $18,000.

• CONVERSION PRIVILEGE. This permits you to switch when your investment objectives change—from a growth fund to an income fund when you retire. Most investment-management companies handle several types of funds with different investment goals.

• REGULAR INCOME CHECKS. These are available (by month, quarterly, semiannually) by: (1) buying shares in several funds, each with different dividend months; (2) arranging for regular quarterly dividends to be paid in monthly installments; (3) opting for a fixed income each month by permitting the sale of some shares to supplement the dividends–capital gains.

• MASTER RETIREMENT PLAN. Almost all investment companies are set up to handle personal retirement plans. They have special forms to save you paperwork and to provide the information needed for tax returns.

How to Judge Investment Companies

In selecting investment companies, consider buying funds which have:

A 10-year Record

Look for a 10-year record of total returns (realized capital gains, reinvested dividends, and unrealized appreciation) that has reported an annual average rate of return of 10% in up market years.

In Good Market Years, a Record of Gains

Look for a record of gains that is consistently (rather than erratically) better than those of the market as a whole.

In Bear-Market Years, a Record of Annual Losses Less or Only Slightly Greater than Those of Stock-Market Averages

Ability to Perform Comparatively Well in Both Bull and Bear Markets

Avoid buying funds which:

Are Highly Publicized and Aggressively Promoted

Risks do not vanish just because there's professional management.

Have Had Less than $50 Million in Assets for the Past 10 Years

The fund is either so new that it has not had time to grow, or its performance has been so poor that new shares could not be sold widely.

Note: If you want to speculate, look at small funds and take the risk you can pick a winner. One or 2 good selections and a $10-million fund can double its portfolio value in a couple of years.

Have Been Highly Successful for 1 or 2 Years

A small fund can be lucky with a couple of "hot" stocks. The real test comes when fund management is entrusted with large sums and must concentrate on stocks of major corporations.

Almost without exception, the man who is a "genius" with a $20-million fund is a "bum" when he has to handle a $100-million portfolio. (This advice may sound out of place after the 1973–74 debacle, but it's sound counsel for the long term. In 1967 and 1968, Enterprise Fund was THE fund; in 1969, it ranked 343rd in performance.)

Fund	1964 Up	1965 Up	1966 Down	1967 Up	1968 Up	1969 Down	1970 Mixed	1971 Up	1972 Up	1973 Down	1974 Down
Balanced											
Stein Balance*	+10.9	+11.2	− 3.0	+20.1	+12.6	− 7.4	− 3.2	+21.8	+18.2	−14.0	−25.2
Super. Invest.		+10.3	− 3.3	+20.6	+22.7	−11.7	+ 9.8	+15.2	+10.2	− 9.1	−16.2
Putnam, Geo.	+11.1	+12.7	− 3.5	+18.1	+ 9.2	− 6.3	+ 2.5	+17.7	+19.6	−10.4	−22.4
Axe-Houg. A	+17.5	+18.6	− 0.4	+56.2	+18.5	−26.7	− 6.2	+16.0	+ 6.9	−15.5	− 3.9
Whitehall	+10.6	+ 8.4	− 5.3	+27.9	+16.2	− 1.7	− 7.8	+21.6	+19.8	−15.7	......
Income											
Decatur	+21.5	+19.0	− 6.6	+32.9	+25.0	−12.8	+ 7.7	+16.4	+ 6.1	−13.8	−11.2
Provident	+14.0	+25.7	− 6.8	+40.5	+32.6	−19.4	+ 3.8	+27.1	+ 1.4	−15.3	− 9.8
Puritan	+16.4	+23.3	− 6.2	+26.4	+17.1	−14.8	+ 6.2	+13.0	+10.6	− 7.2	−11.8
Northeast*	+11.4	+ 7.9	− 5.8	+10.3	+14.3	− 9.3	+ 6.7	+14.4	+ 9.2	......	− 7.5
Eaton Income	+ 9.8	+ 9.5	− 5.3	+15.7	+20.6	−14.0	+ 4.9	+19.5	+ 9.8	− 2.0	−10.1
Bond & Pref.											
Harbor Fund	+10.1	+17.8	+ 4.1	+49.7	+24.2	−17.6	− 5.6	+19.9	+ 4.8	− 7.2	−11.3
Investors Sel.	+ 4.8	+ 3.6	− 1.3	+ 3.1	+ 5.7	− 0.1	+ 7.3	+13.4	+ 8.3	+ 2.1	− 3.1
Keystone B-4	+14.8	+ 7.7	− 3.8	+ 6.1	+15.1	− 6.5	− 2.3	+20.8	+11.6	− 7.1	− 7.7
Keystone B-2	+ 7.5	+ 6.1	− 3.5	+ 5.1	+ 4.6	− 8.0	+ 7.3	+17.1	+ 9.5	− 0.8	− 7.3
Keystone B-1	+ 3.9	+ 1.5	− 0.2	− 3.4	+ 2.8	− 6.0	+10.7	+10.8	+ 7.5	+ 3.4	− 1.3
DJIA	+14.6	+10.9	−18.9	+15.2	+ 4.3	−15.2	+ 4.8	+ 6.1	+14.6	−16.6	−28.0
DJ Bond Yield	4.6%	4.7%	5.4%	5.9%	6.6%	7.4%	8.6%	8.0%	7.7%	7.9%	8.0%

* No load

Source: *Fundscope* magazine.

How Funds Fared—10-Year Results, 1965–74
(Based on original investment of $10,000, with all distributions reinvested in additional shares)

Fund	Cash Dividends	Final Value
Inter. Investors	$4,032	$42,871
Templeton	2,248	30,186
Price New Horizons*	1,518	21,460
Istel Fund	3,507	20,898
Investors Research	2,325	20,257
Security Equity	2,373	19,289
O-T-C Fund	2,844	18,969
Axe-Houghton Stock	3,322	18,348
Financial Income*	6,273	18,139
Harbor Fund	6,636	17,422

* No-Load.
Source: *Fundscope* magazine.

Concentrate on Any Particular Type of Stock— Chemicals, Electronics, Convertibles, etc.

This is probably a better merchandising gimmick than investment approach. These funds do not provide diversification. If the industry—or the type of securities—in which they are investing become unpopular, the profits will be small, if any.

Hold Letter Stocks

These are securities of new, small corporations which are bought at bargain prices with the provision that they will not be traded publicly for a set period of time, sometimes as long as 4 years. They reduce the fund's liquidity, have no real market value, and may become practically worthless if the company is not successful.

Buying Bargains with Closed-End Funds

Like to buy IBM, Xerox, P&G, and other quality stocks at discounts of 20% or more? Ask your broker about shares of closed-end funds. Usually, these sell at a discount. Apparently, investors feel their fixed capitalization limits opportunities to move quickly with changing markets. With the same amount of money you have in 2 stocks, you can buy part ownership in 50 or more corporations and probably receive higher income. These shares are good buys for anyone, but are especially satisfactory for retirees.

Example: You are starting to plan for retirement and want to shift from your $100,000 low-income portfolio ($2,200 in annual dividends) to a more diversified, better-yielding portfolio.

After selling your shares and paying the capital gains tax, you have $80,000. You locate a closed-end fund which is selling at a 20% discount. You buy 4,000 shares at 19, pay the commission costs of about $2,530, and have enough left over for a vacation.

Your share of the underlying stocks of the fund has a market value of $100,000. Annual income is about 5%, so you have doubled your dividends and still have hopes of capital gains. In a strong market the discount will narrow but the prices of closed-ends tend to lag behind the market.

Diversified Closed-End Funds

Fund	Net Asset Value	Stock Price	% Difference (Discount)
Adams Express	$11.18	10	−10.6%
Advance	9.36	8½	− 9.2
Carriers General	13.01	10¾	−17.4
Central Securities	5.79	3½	−39.6
General American	10.14	9	−11.2
Inter. Holdings	11.23	7	−37.7
Lehman Corp.	10.98	9½	−13.5
Madison	10.85	8⅛	−25.1
Niagara	11.65	11⅝	− 0.2
Tri-Continental	19.38	18½	− 4.5
United Corp.	8.66	6¾	−22.1
U.S. & Foreign	16.96	13⅝	−19.7

Funds for Income
10-Year Results, 1965–74
(Based on original investment of $10,000, with all distributions invested in additional shares)

Fund	Cash Dividends	Final Value
Harbor Fund	$6,636	$17,422
Provident	6,531	16,084
Decatur	5,881	15,236
Puritan	5,316	14,850
Security Investors	5,898	14,618
Northeast*	6,034	14,488
Eaton Income	5,213	13,857
Investors Select.	5,115	13,683
Founders Inc.	5,049	13,241
United Bond	5,485	13,124

* No-Load.
Source: *Fundscope* magazine.

How to Get $2 for Every $1 Invested

An interesting variation of closed-end funds is the dual fund. This offers 2 separate investment vehicles—capital shares for growth and income shares for high returns and assured redemption.

All money paid in, for both types of shares, is placed in a single pool. All capital growth is retained by holders of capital shares. All income received by the entire fund is paid to holders of income shares. Thus, every shareholder has at least $2 serving his investment goal for every $1 he invests. Actually, it's more because of that discount that characterizes all closed-end funds.

The income shares resemble preferred stocks in that they have stated minimum dividends which are cumulative. The rate of payout ranges from about 5% to 8% on the original offering price. Since the shares are below that figure, the real returns are higher.

The life span of dual funds is limited to 12 to 18 years from the date of the fund offering. At termination, from 1979 to 1985, all income shares will be paid off, at a price guaranteed in the prospectus, or swapped, on a dollar-for-dollar basis, for capital shares. As with preferred stocks, 85% of the dividends are tax-deductible by corporations.

Capital shares provide a long-term tax shelter. Since no dividends are paid, the increase in value is taxable at the low capital gains rate. If fund management is able to achieve average annual gains of 10% (the total on both types of stocks), the investor can hope to double his money about every 7½ years.

Example: At the end of 1974, Scudder Duo-Vest Income shares were selling at 7¼, a discount of 23% from the net asset value of the underlying securities. The dividend was .825¢ per share for a hefty 11% return. By 1982, the shares will be redeemed at $9.15, to assure a capital gain of $1.90 per share.

At the same time, Scudder Duo-Vest Capital shares were available at 3⅞, a whopping 34% discount from the $5.85 net asset value. With an average annual boost of 10%, each share may be worth about $8.32 in 1982, plus the possibility of a rise to the net asset value of approximately $12.50 per share.

Dual-Purpose Funds

American Dual Vest	Leverage
Gemini	Puritan Duo-Fund
Hemisphere	Putnam Duo-Fund
Income and Capital	Scudder Duo-Vest

Money-Market Funds

These funds started to become popular in 1973. They invest only in liquid assets—Treasury bills, certificates of deposit, and similar short-term money-market instruments. Once you've put in a minimum deposit ($1,000 to $5,000), you can withdraw or deposit any amount you like on a day's notice.

In 1974, the yields were 11% to 12%, but with the lower cost of money, they dropped to below 10% and very likely will go much lower. They are fine for temporary holdings, poor for long-term investments. You will do better in high-coupon bonds (which will pay well for 20 years or more) or high-dividend-paying stocks (which, hopefully, will appreciate in value).

For a clue of what you will receive in the next few months, watch the yield on Treasury bills. If the interest rates drop, your returns will dwindle. If the yields stay high, watch out—the fund manager may be speculating with high-interest notes of comercial paper of low-rated corporations.

Some Money-Market Funds

Fund	Smallest Investment	Sales-Service Charge
Am. General Reserve	$5,000	1%
Capital Preservation	2,500	none
Dreyfus Liquid Assets	2,500	none
Fidelity Daily Income	5,000	2.50%
Money Market Management	1,000	none
Reserve Fund	5,000	none

The Benefits of Dollar-Cost-Averaging (DCA)

For those who want to schedule their savings-investments, a good approach is Dollar-Cost-Averaging. This eliminates one of the most difficult problems of investing —timing.

Time, not timing, is the secret of success of DCA. For best results, select a quality growth stock. DCA is a formula plan that will prove profitable—almost always when you choose the right securities, usually when you settle for mediocre equities—IF you are consistent and patient.

DCA is based on the obvious fact that the same number of dollars will buy more shares of a stock when its price is low than when it is high. Therefore, over the years, you will accumulate more shares than you would with an outright purchase.

When the price of the stock goes up, you will make a greater profit on the larger number of shares than if you had bought all of your stock at the same average price.

Example: You buy 100 shares of stock A at 10, and after a temporary decline, it moves to 18—an 80% gain. Your son, who has limited funds, invests $200 a month in the same stock—at 10, at 8, at 5, at 10, and at 18. He buys 116 shares, which rise to a value of $2,088 compared to $1,800 for your holdings.

Note: This is an *example,* not a case history. The costs of commissions would just about wipe out the extra gain. One way to minimize these charges is to buy shares of a company with a Dividend Reinvestment Plan. All of your dividends will be reinvested, and you add cash regularly.

Total commissions are small, as they are prorated among participating shareholders—on the DCA example, less than $5 per transaction, about half the costs of straight purchases. Similar automatic stock-investment plans—for shares of a limited number of major corporations—are also available through some banks.

Stocks for the Times of Your Life

These recommendations have been updated and digested from an article I wrote for *Money* Magazine in April, 1974. At that time, some of these stocks were selling at higher prices than almost a year later. Without exception, these declines were due to circumstances beyond corporate management's control—inflation, governmental policies, economic pessimism, etc.

To the investor, this was a benefit because he could acquire these worth-holding securities at more favorable prices. Based on fundamental analysis, all of these are quality stocks that were undervalued in 1974 and were even greater bargains in 1975.

Each of the portfolios is designed to give the investor a compound average return, with income and capital gains reinvested, of at least 10% a year.

Young or old, carefree or committed, investors should seek out shares of companies maintaining a respectable rate of growth—an EGR of at least 6% annually and a PR of 15%.

In selecting his own stocks, each investor must decide whether he has a speculator's aplomb. The sample portfolios vary in risk—all stocks are suitable for all ages. Once a strategy is set, stay with it until objectives change.

Note: For portfolios for retired couples, see Chapter XIX, on Retirement.

Young Novices

If they have no children to support and $5,000 or more to invest, people in their 20s can speculate a bit.

Company	Shares	Recent Price	Cost	Current Dividends	Yield
Warner-Lambert	100	26	$2,600	$ 84.00	3.2%
Eastman Kodak	10	66	660	15.60	2.4
Tektronix	100	19	1,900	20.00	1.1
			$5,160	$119.60	2.3%

All of these stocks were selected as prospects for annual increases in price averaging over 8%.

WARNER-LAMBERT AND EK. These companies have established enviable records of growth. One analyst predicts that W-L earnings will rise in the next few years at an 11% compound annual rate. Kodak, which has also managed to come up with successful new products, has earned over an average of 20% on shareholders' equity during the past 10 years.

TEKTRONIX. This, the most speculative entry, has become a leader in the electronic instrument industry, where stocks are selling at close to 20 times their annual earnings. Tektronix seemed undervalued at about 7 times earnings.

Parents in Their 30s

Families earmarking $15,000 or so for college costs a few years hence need stock combining growth and income with low risk.

Company	Shares	Recent Price	Cost	Current Dividends	Yield
Blue Bell	100	16	$ 1,600	$ 80	5.0%
Beatrice Foods	200	17	3,400	144	4.2
Coca-Cola	100	57	5,700	213	3.7
Pfizer	100	28	2,800	76	2.7
Textron	100	14	1,400	110	7.9
			$14,900	$623	4.2%

BLUE BELL. A leading manufacturer of Western, sports, and work clothing, Blue Bell has had an average EGR of over 10% and a PR above 14%. Its stock price is just over half corporate book value and far below its normal price range.

BEATRICE FOODS. After achieving remarkable success as a manufacturer of dairy products, groceries, and candy, Beatrice Foods has diversified into nonfood products and financial services. Sales and earnings have climbed for 23 straight years.

COCA-COLA. Company has a very strong cash position (valuable in these days of high interest rates). Through diversification, its growth continues in the United States and abroad. Return on equity—over 20%—is one of the highest in the industry. Dividends have almost tripled in the past decade.

PFIZER. A leading drug manufacturer, Pfizer has a strong position in world markets and an active research program which has recently produced several new drugs for clinical testing. The annual growth rate can be expected to be around 11%, which has not been reflected in share prices.

TEXTRON. A conglomerate in industries ranging from aerospace to zippers, Textron has performed well in an erratic market. Earnings per share over the past 10 years have risen an average of 13% annually.

Working Couples

Predictable corporate growth is sought in this portfolio for business or professional couples with $20,000 to invest and a high tax bracket which will eat up dividends.

Company	Shares	Recent Price	Cost	Current Dividends	Yield
So. Nat. Resources	100	45	$ 4,500	$165	3.7%
Joy Manufacturing	100	44	4,400	150	3.4
Reading & Bates	100	16	1,600	35	4.4
Honeywell	100	24	2,400	140	5.8
Melville Shoe	200	7	1,400	92	6.6
Emerson Electric	100	24	2,400	70	2.9
Norton Simon, pf. convertible	100	31	3,100	160	5.2
			$19,800	$812	4.1

SOUTHERN NATURAL RESOURCES. This major utility, which distributes natural gas, develops gas and oil wells, and has interests in forest products, is selling at 8 times earnings, versus a decade average of 14. It may average 20% to 25% compound annual rate of return to investors over the next 5 years.

JOY MANUFACTURING. This company is in the happy position of making both coal-mining machinery and equipment to control air pollution.

READING & BATES OFFSHORE DRILLING CO. Reading & Bates has oil-drilling contracts in several key spots around the world.

HONEYWELL. The stock of this computer-instrument, electronics manufacturer has sagged to little more than 10% of its 1972 high. Its present price appears to overstate its problems.

MELVILLE SHOE. Through aggressive marketing, earnings of Melville Shoe over the past 10 years have risen faster than those of many well-known glamour-growth stocks. It has always maintained high EGR and PR rates.

EMERSON ELECTRIC. Emerson Electric has had a PR of more than 23% over the past 10 years, yet is selling 25% below the low end of its historic average P/E multiple.

NORTON SIMON. Convertible preferred shares of Norton Simon, which has interests in foods, soft drinks, distilleries, and packaging, have been selling at just over conversion value in common shares while yielding more than the common.

Note: These stocks are all the TYPES of securities that should be included in the portfolios chosen for long-term growth and income at any age. These are corporations whose managements know how to make money. Their stocks will reflect this important ability—certainly, later; hopefully, sooner.

But do not spend any money until you have investigated thoroughly and are sure that their growth and profitability are continuing, that the stocks are still undervalued, and that the prospects for the stock market and these equities are promising. Unless there are drastic changes, all of these recommendations will be worth much more in the years ahead.

At all times, stay flexible. Invest most of your savings for the long term, but keep some funds for short-term opportunities. In bull markets, use margin to leverage your profits. In bear markets, don't be afraid to sell short or hedge. These techniques are neither as difficult nor as risky as you may think.

For details of how to use warrants, rights, options, and convertibles, see the latest edition of *$Your Investments$*. This is issued annually, so it will keep you up-to-date on what's happening in the investment world. The fundamentals of quality and value are constant (even though there may be temporary aberrations due to stock-market depression), but the timing and techniques of making money with investments change frequently.

What You Can Get for Your Income Dollar

If You Put Your Money in	1975 (Jan.)	Your Yields Would Have Been 1974	1973	Average 1970–74
U.S. Treasury Bills (90 days)	6.95%	7.60%–7.86%	4.49%–8.75%	5.72%
U.S. Treasury Bills (180 days)	6.95	8.15–8.62	4.50–7.52	6.65
Canadian Bills (90 days)	7.05	9.10	5.74	....
Euro-dollars (90 days)	10.10	13.75–13.94	5.53–11.50	....
Bankers Acceptances (90-day)	8.50	11.75–12.03	4.85–9.65	6.70
CDs (under 90 days)	8.56–8.62	11.50–11.75	4.62–9.88	....
CDs (over 180 days)	8.0–8.12	12.25–12.42	4.85–8.25	6.81
Government funds (under 1 year)	7.03	9.10–9.33	5.02–8.78	6.65
Government (long-term)	6.69	6.62–7.82	5.87–7.85	6.07
Municipals (long-term)	7.08	5.75–7.50	5.19–5.48	5.60
Corporate Bonds	9.60	8.90–9.59	7.65–7.83	7.98
Stocks (Dow Jones)	6.4	4.6–4.9	3.1–3.8	4.3–4.4
Utilities		6.9–11.0	5.84–7.48	6.02
Savings Banks and S&Ls	5.47–8.17*			
Savings- Commercial Banks	5.20–7.90*			

* Ceiling—based on daily compounding from under 90 days to over 6 years.
Source: Continental Bank.

The purpose of this table is to show how temporary are the high interest-dividend rates of 1974–75—about 25% greater than the average yields over the past 5 years (and as your parents will tell you, double or more those of post–World War II years).

The cost of money may not go as low as in the "old days," but it's not likely to stay as high as it has been in the early 1970s. "Fixed" income is a lot more transient than most people remember. Those high-rate CDs and Treasury bills look good for a short time, but when they mature, you will probably have to settle for a much lower return.

How to Transfer, Endorse, and Replace Stock Certificates

Stock certificates may be your only proof of ownership, so it is important to keep them in a safe place and to know how to transfer them legally. These pieces of paper are the corporation's acknowledgment of your partial ownership. Usually, certificates are engraved to prevent counterfeiting and are numbered for identification. This situation may change because of the high cost and the development of new electronic techniques.

For quick reference, keep a complete record in your home file of the name of the company, number of shares, date of purchase, price paid, name of broker, identification number, and transfer agent (printed on every certificate).

A safe-deposit box is secure, but it's inconvenient. If you trade frequently, you have to take out the certificates when you sell and put back new ones when you buy. An easy solution is to deposit the certificates with your broker. *Added advantage:* The shares can be used as collateral for margin-account loans.

You will get a receipt, and if the securities are registered in your name, you will have written proof of ownership. This will enable you to get your shares or money quickly if the broker should run into financial problems such as occurred in the late 1960s.

Many people, and most brokers, prefer to have shares in the "street" name—that of the brokerage firm. This facilitates trading and makes the stock available, with your permission, for lending for short selling. Such a practice was risky when Wall Street firms were failing, but today most brokers provide their own insurance, and under the Securities Investor Protection Corporation (SIPC), $50,000 coverage for each account.

The SIPC is to brokers what the Federal Deposit Insurance Corporation is to banks. If a brokerage firm runs into financial trouble, a trustee is appointed to supervise liquidation, return cash and identifiable securities to owners, and pay debts from the broker's assets and the SIPC.

> *Note:* If you are queasy about the financial solvency of your broker, spread your investments with no more than $50,000 in any one firm.

When new certificates arrive, check the spelling of the owner's name, and if corrections are needed, return the shares to the transfer agent.

Transferring Stock

When you sell securities, there's usually no fuss, as your bank or broker will handle the transaction routinely. If you want to do it yourself, contact the transfer agent of the corporation to find out what documents will be required.

Making a gift is more complex. It requires a letter of authorization instructing the transfer agent to issue the stock in the name of the new owner and proper signatures on the back of each certificate—your name and that of the "attorney to transfer" (the bank or broker who will guarantee the signature as that of the owner).

This procedure applies to all gifts—within the family or to your college, charity, or cause. Be sure to file a federal gift tax return and make a notation on your tax return. Even if there's no tax to pay, you will need the record.

A custodian who turns stock over to a minor-turned-adult follows the same procedure, with the addition of Social Security number, mailing address, and proof of age (preferably a birth certificate) of the new owner.

When you inherit property, the executor-administrator of the estate must initiate the transfer and supply, to each heir, court-certified copies of the death certificate, proof of his authority (a copy of the will or letter of appointment), an affidavit of domicile, and a waiver certifying that the proceeds from the property are not needed to pay taxes or other claims against the estate.

If stock is owned jointly with the deceased, the survivor can

have new certificates issued by providing the same sort of proof.
For safety, send certificates by registered mail. Brokers use special messengers for hand delivery.

Endorsing a Stock Certificate

Proper endorsements save time, trouble, and expense—for you and your stockbroker. In most cases, it is no longer legally necessary to have someone witness your signature when a stock is sold. But as noted earlier, when there's a gift or inheritance

When you deliver your Security (Certificate) for sale ... here is how to endorse it properly

(1) *For Value Received* _____ *hereby sell, assign and transfer unto*

_____
(NAME AND ADDRESS OF TRANSFEREE SHOULD BE PRINTED)

_____ *Shares*

of the Stock represented by the within Certificate and do hereby irrevocably constitute

and appoint (2) _____ *Attorney*

to transfer the said stock on the Books of the withinnamed Corporation with full power

of substitution in the premises. *Dated* (3) _____ *19*____

In Presence of

_____ (4) X _____

(1) Please leave blank

(2) Please write in "Reynolds Securities Inc." (to restrict negotiability in case of loss)

(3) Please fill in the date

(4) Please sign your name exactly as it appears on the face of the certificate. Stocks registered as joint tenants, must be signed by all parties.

Reynolds Securities Inc.

involved, check with your lawyer or broker first to get the transfer handled right the first time.

When you sell a stock, follow these steps:

1. DO NOT COMPLETE ITEM 1. It has nothing to do with you.

2. FILL IN THE FULL, OFFICIAL NAME OF YOUR BROKER. (In this case the name is Reynolds Securities, Inc.) This authorizes the firm to act as your attorney in transferring the shares. Without a specific agent, the certificate becomes fully negotiable if lost or stolen.

3. WRITE IN THE DATE YOU SIGN. If you prefer, your broker can complete this later, but it's wise to do things properly from the outset.

4. SIGN YOUR NAME EXACTLY AS IT APPEARS ON THE FACE OF THE STOCK CERTIFICATE. If your grandmother bought the stock for you when you were Chauncey William Wigglesworth and you are now known as C. William Wigglesworth, sign your *full* name at the top and your current cognomen below.

The same precision is necessary when your original name is misspelled or if the stock was issued in a maiden name before marriage. The lady must sign her family and her married names—*Ruth Elizabeth Hart;* then *Ruth Elizabeth Hart Wigglesworth.*

When shares are in joint ownership, both owners should sign. If one is deceased or unavailable, consult your lawyer. He can advise whether a power of attorney is acceptable or whether more formal procedures are needed.

5. IF YOU DECIDE NOT TO SELL THE STOCK AFTER YOU HAVE SIGNED. In this case fill in the name of your broker and turn the certificate over to his firm for safekeeping. Your signature makes the stock negotiable, and besides, you are likely to change your mind again!

United States Savings Bonds

U.S. Savings Bonds, series E and H, usually bought through a payroll savings plan, are NOT transferable. They must be reissued in new names. When there's joint ownership, however, death automatically makes the survivor the sole owner.

These small-dollar bonds can be replaced with minimal expense. If the bonds have been lost, stolen, or damaged, write for forms from the Bureau of Public Debt, Treasury Department, 536 South Clark Street, Chicago, Illinois 60605.

This office is also the one to contact if you believe you have bonds that have not been reclaimed or redeemed and you have no safekeeping receipt or other confirming records.

Send your name, the address that would have been inscribed on the bond at the time of purchase, and any other helpful information such as approximate date or year of issue.

If you do have a safekeeping receipt or other records (payroll allotment form, check stubs) write to: Treasurer of the United States, Securities Division, Washington, D.C. 20220, for a copy of Treasury Form 5114 (Request for Release of United States Savings Bonds Held for Safekeeping). If the receipt shows the depositary to be a Federal Reserve Bank, contact that bank.

How to Replace a Lost Certificate

When a stock certificate is lost, stolen, or burned, contact the transfer agent directly, through your broker or through the office of the secretary of the issuing corporation. Such action will initiate procedures to prevent the sale of your certificate.

(Think how much easier this will be if you remember to keep up-to-date records in your home office file!)

It's expensive to secure a new stock certificate. You must furnish the corporation with a perpetual indemnity bond covering any losses that might be incurred by reissuing the shares. The cost is about 4% of current market value—$200 for $5,000 worth of stock.

If the certificate is found within 12 months, you will get back 50% of the premium, minus $10.

Safeguarding Your Personal Papers

A safe-deposit box is a *must* for everyone. But DO be careful what you put into it, and DON'T overlimit access.

In today's complex world, with changing legal precedents, expanding governmental programs, and more extensive tax audits, an increasing number of documents are needed to assure benefits and to avoid penalties. Cards, records, receipts, and policies must be retained and be readily available. That's when a safe-deposit box comes in handy. Fortunately, it's one of the few services where the cost is low—at some banks, a standard lock box is part of a $3-per-month package deal, and in all banks, the costs are seldom over $15 a year.

Most people make 2 mistakes in using a safe-deposit box—they store too many of the wrong papers, and they fail to permit other responsible people to have a key, so that important documents can be obtained when they are most needed.

To determine what should be safeguarded in the lock box, keep in mind that there should be *nothing* that you or your survivors wish wasn't there, and there should be almost *everything* that you would hate to lose (assuming it's small enough to fit).

If you've read any good detective stories lately, you'll remember at least one thriller in which the telling clue is found, after the death of one of the suspects, in the safe-deposit box—hordes of cash, jewelry, dope, or secret account books.

For ordinary people, these are exaggerations of what might happen, but you get the idea! *Some things, no matter how valuable, should not be in a safe-deposit box without a clear explanation!*

At death, an individual-access lock box can be opened by the widow, executor, or known heir *only* in the presence of a bank officer and for the specific purpose of locating essential documents such as the will, deed to cemetery plot, or life insurance policy.

Under such conditions, a receipt for removed articles must be signed by the banker and be made available to tax authorities. The box is then sealed and reopened only in the presence of a governmental official, usually a representative of the state tax commission. If he sees piles of cash or jewelry and your wife or other authorized people cannot prove ownership, the official will probably call in the IRS and the inheritance tax on your estate may be far greater than planned.

Easy solution: Arrange for regular access by a deputy, preferably one trustworthy individual who is in a position to do the chores of rummaging through the box for papers when needed. The choice could be your wife, son, daughter, attorney, executor, or once in a while, private secretary.

If you have a professional corporation (often used by physicians, dentists, etc., for their practice and pension plans), rent the box in the corporate name and give keys to the officers who, presumably, have your best interests at heart.

Or if you are reluctant to have information on your affairs go outside your family, rent the box in your wife's name and arrange for power of attorney for yourself. This works well if the husband is considerably older than the wife.

With all safe-deposit boxes:

DON'T Put in:

All insurance policies. Keep a small one ($1,000 or so) at home, so it can be used for prompt payment to provide cash needed for your family when you die.

All copies of wills. Arrange for the originals to be kept with your lawyer.

Deed to cemetery plot.

DO Deposit: Length of Time

Permanent personal documents:
Certificates of birth, marriage, and
death (of relatives who have died   } Indefinitely
in recent years)
Military discharge and service records

Stock and bond certificates
Mortgage and loan agreements, in- } Until sold or
stallment notes, paid-up receipts   superseded
(owed by and to you)

Insurance policies on home, car, health,
disability, and life (except as noted above)
Warranties on expensive equipment—e.g., for } Until final
physicians' X-ray machines, lab testing units   disposition
Legal papers
Jewelry not worn frequently

Checkpoints: Does it have great value? In dollars, not just sentiment?

Note: If your wife has access to the safe-deposit box, keep her key separate from yours. If both keys are lost or misplaced, it will cost about $50 for drilling and replacement of locks—plus plenty of embarrassment!

Be sure to weed the contents annually and keep your attorney advised on what you are protecting. He may suggest changes in your will or trust agreements to avoid future trouble. *Example:* The husband died, leaving a large block of negotiable bonds in the safe-deposit box held jointly with his wife. The will bequeathed some bonds to his children by a previous marriage.

The widow claimed all of the bonds on the grounds that she could have entered the box and taken the bonds at any time. Fortunately for the children, the judge did not agree.

To avoid such a possibility, rent a separate box for special securities and spell out your wishes in your will.

Safe-Deposit Insurance

Fearful that your lock box will be looted?

Buy a customer-safekeeping policy that will insure the contents. Some banks provide such coverage automatically, but you can get an individual policy from Aetna Life & Casualty. Cost: 50¢ per $1,000.

The Aetna policy also provides protection if your stockbroker can't come up with the stock he has been holding, or if a dealer storing your collection of art, china, antiques, etc., is robbed.

Your Handy Home File

You should also have a home file that is safe and convenient. If it's locked, be sure that someone you trust has a key or knows the combination. Getting it open in an emergency can be difficult and complicated, especially if the IRS is questioning the valuation of your estate.

Here again, start by retaining only useful records and documents that are difficult to replace. This time, of course, you will be dealing with less valuable and more frequently used items.

What to Keep — Length of Time

What to Keep	Length of Time
Unpaid, current bills	Separate until paid
Paid bills, receipts	3 years
Current bank statements	3 years
Canceled checks	
Income tax duplicates	
Records of other taxes paid or assessed	3 to 6 years
Employment records	

What to Keep	Length of Time

Booklets on employee benefits
Inventory of safe deposit box
List of credit cards: name, number, expiration dates
List of insurance policies: company names and policy number
Unsigned copies of will
Family health records
Appliance warranties
School records of children
Serial numbers of portable appliances (so police can check pawnshops if your home is robbed) } Keep current
Xerox of driver's license, car registration, record of blood type and any allergies
List of items usually carried in your wallet and your wife's pocketbook (just the valuables)
Important addresses and phone numbers for emergencies
Biographies of everyone in the immediate family
Duplicate keys, with identification tags

Set an annual date on which you and your wife can go through the home file and eliminate unwanted items—not only outdated records but also news clippings, brochures, Christmas catalogues, recipes, faded photos, and memorabilia which takes up valuable space and which, if sentimentally important, should be kept in a special corner of the attic or basement.

Dead-Storage File

Generally, 6 years is long enough to keep any legal, financial, or tax records, but when property is involved, keep them until there has been a sale or other disposition. You will need dates and costs for income tax purposes. These long-term files should be kept in a safe, dry place, in a durable container, in the cellar or attic, with the subject clearly marked on the exterior.

What to Keep	Length of Time
Superseded legal papers Old canceled checks (sort and keep only tax-insurance- property payments) Old income tax duplicates	Indefinitely

XXVI

How to Save on Taxes

Tax savings are useful, enjoyable, and when they are handled properly, profitable. They are net income that does not have to be shared with any government. *But tax savings should never be the sole reason for any important money management decision!*

For most individuals, the tax benefits are limited to almost standard income tax deductions. But there are legitimate ways by which present taxes can be lessened or deferred and future taxes minimized. Broadly speaking, the tax advantages of losses are greater than those of gains. But the objective of successful money management is to *make*, not to *lose*, money.

Too many people worry too much about taxes. They forget that in all business the government is their partner. Whenever you make an investment, the potential profit should be reduced to reflect the tax bite, which in most cases increases with the margin of profit.

This chapter will outline some broad principles, explain special techniques, and suggest worth-exploring ideas on how to save taxes. For specific information, read a tax guide, consult your local IRS office, watch for explanations of new tax legislation enacted by Congress, and if you have sufficient funds, retain a tax adviser. Taxes are *an*—but not *the*—important factor in personal money management.

452

Do Your Homework

There are few areas of finance where advice is so abundant, so confusing, and so inaccurate as taxes, especially tax avoidance or deferment. Almost every conceivable situation is spelled out in official booklets, and all you have to do is ask the IRS. If you don't want to reveal your name, telephone and present the problem. You will find that, with few exceptions, the answer will require only common sense, the ability to make simple calculations, and the willingness to recognize that the IRS is seeking to follow the terms set by Congress and the courts.

Do NOT be "smart" and try to outfox the IRS. Even small offices have people who are familiar with every kind of tax-dodge gimmick. And remember that these agents are human, too. Most will make every effort to be fair, to overlook honest mistakes, and to accept the excuse of misinterpretation.

Once the IRS has had a bad experience, the taxpayer, no matter what his tax bracket, is flagged for future checking. And once you have established a pattern, especially on deductions, it will be recognized in future tax returns.

There is not much most people can do about withholding taxes, so the area to concentrate on is unearned income—from interest, dividends, and capital appreciation. With the exception of tax shelters, the examples here focus on securities because, generally, the same rules apply to other types of property (with extra benefits from ownership of real estate as explained in another chapter).

It's OK to avoid taxes legally, but not to evade them. To some people, unfortunately, tax avoidance becomes a mania. They stay up nights looking for ways to deprive Uncle Sam of his just dues. In most cases, this is foolish, and in some situations, it is stupid. Taxes, like it or not, are the price you pay for living in a modern society.

What the IRS Looks For

The higher your income, the greater the chance that your annual tax return will be checked, if not audited. By and large, the IRS's extra interest is triggered by unusual figures—high unearned income, large losses on securities or from bad debts, tax payments that fluctuate widely from year to year, and most important, deductions that are far from the norm—not only that shown in the table but your own previous tax returns.

The IRS examiners are not overly concerned with high medical deductions, but they tend to dig deeper if the amount of reported sales taxes takes a big leap or charitable gifts suddenly double.

If your deductions are well above the average, always be prepared by retaining all pertinent receipts, bills, checks, and gift acknowledgments.

The following table is based on a sampling of itemized deductions on 1972 income tax returns by taxpayers with adjusted gross incomes up to $50,000:

Average Deductions on Federal Income Tax Returns

Adjusted Gross Income	Medical Expenses	State and Local Taxes	Contributions	Interest Paid	Miscellaneous	Tax Paid
$15,000–$20,000	$294	$1,404	$ 424	$1,097	$352	$2,026
$20,000–$25,000	291	1,778	544	1,208	372	3,069
$25,000–$30,000	336	2,184	691	1,360	420	4,236
$30,000–$50,000	393	2,983	1,031	1,686	629	6,961

The No. 1 rule on tax savings is to delay taking profits for over 6 months. The taxes will then be paid at a lower rate—one-half of the regular income tax rate up to a maximum of 25%, for most people. Thus, if you are in a 36% tax bracket, your tax on long-term capital gains will be 18% of your profits.

Above $50,000 income, this rate rises to 35%. That means you still keep 65% of your profits.

There are times when a tax loss can be beneficial, but usually it does not pay to consider selling at a loss unless the tax savings are greater than 20% of the market value of the property, or $4 per $100.

Here's Why

For easy figuring, let's assume a tax rate of 25% (the maximum for most people). If the loss is 20%, the net savings are 5%. Commissions for selling the present stock and buying other shares is about 2%, so the real benefit is 3%. Even that is iffy because some states and municipalities levy further taxes on profits. This is not really a savings but a postponement of inevitable taxes on gains made with the reinvestment of your money. The savings are too small and too costly to achieve for any but the wealthy.

To consider any tax-loss sale, you should have: (1) a stock in which there is a substantial loss, (2) a stock that has dim prospects of appreciation, (3) another stock in which you hope to make a handsome profit.

As we'll see, losses can be used to offset profits, but here again the benefits are limited.

In what is usually a mistaken effort to minimize taxes, some people:

Let the Value of Their Assets Decline

They do this so they can sell at a loss for "tax purposes." *Nothing could be more foolish.* No intelligent person should ever try to lose $1,000 in order to save $100 in taxes!

Wait until Death

They do this so that their estate will get the stocks at current value and the heirs can use this higher price as a base for future taxes. Once in a while this makes sense, but only when the gains are substantial—over 100%.

Give Away a Stock and the Tax Burden with It

The wisdom of such action depends on the financial affluence and the needs of the present owner. It can be worthwhile when fairly large sums are involved. (See Chapter XI, on Charitable Gifts.)

Concentrate Tax Selling in December

This makes little sense because proper money management is a year-round effort. Every investor should keep running records, be able to approximate his tax position at the end of each quarter, and be ready to sell at that time.

Go Overboard with Tax-loss Selling

Losses—100% of short-term and 50% of long-term—can be applied against ordinary income and short-term gains to a maximum of $1,000 a year. Any excess loss can be carried forward indefinitely until exhausted, up to a maximum of $1,000 a year on the same basis as the original losses were taken—i.e., a long-term capital loss last year can offset a long-term capital loss next year. But since long-term losses are deducted at only 50%, twice the amount is needed to reach the limitation.

The only real advantage of such losses is that they occur at the top of your income tax bracket. The higher your tax rate, the more important and beneficial is the tax loss.

How to Line Up Your Fiscal Year Gains and Losses

Even if there are changes in the tax law, these general guidelines are likely to continue. Ask your broker for the proper working sheets and then record all transactions during the year —gains, losses, and whether short- or long-term.

To get ready for tax filing:

1. Add all actual long-term gains and—separately—all actual long-term losses. The difference between them is your *net long-term gain or loss*.

2. Do the same with short-term gains and losses to find your *net short-term gain or loss*.

3. Compare the total of items 1 and 2. If you have gains for both, treat each item separately.

4. If you have greater net long-term gains than net short-term losses, offset them and treat the net result as your *long-term capital gain*. This is taxable at half the ordinary rate—i.e., at a rate up to 25% (up to 35% for amounts over $50,000).

5. If you have more net short-term gains than net long-term losses, treat the net result as your *short-term capital gains*. This is added to ordinary income and taxed as regular income.

6. If you have only losses or even a net loss (either short- or long-term), your total loss can be used to offset your ordinary income up to $1,000 in the current fiscal year. Deduct the short-term loss first. Long-term losses can be applied against ordinary income only up to 50% of the total net long-term loss. If total applicable losses are more than $1,000, you can carry the excess forward into the future year with no time limit.

7. Note down all unrealized losses and gains. Arrange them and total them just as you did the actual results. You will then be able to select those securities that seem doubtful for the future. They should be your first choices for sale. But before you place the order, find out the tax benefits, *if any*.

In most cases, the sale should be made only when the stock has small prospects for future gain and your money can be invested more profitably elsewhere. You are invest-

ing to make, not to lose, money. Do not try to kid yourself
—or your wife!

Complete this itemization before the end of October each year,
so you will still have time to decide if you want to sell any holdings or to take advantage of a wash sale.

How the Wash-Sale Rules Work

A *wash sale* is a sale for a capital loss where you buy the
"same or substantially identical" securities within 30 days *before*
or *after* the loss sale. That means a span of 61 days. The rules do
not apply to securities acquired through inheritance, gift, or tax-
free exchange.

"Substantially identical" means just that—a common stock,
a call on a stock, or a voting trust certificate representing that
stock. Voting stock and nonvoting stock paying the same dividend and selling at about the same price are not covered. Nor are
2 or more series of bonds of the same corporation with different
coupon rates or maturity dates; nor a stock and a related warrant.

Here are the tax consequences:

1. Losses from wash sales are not deductible; gains are taxable.

2. The loss is *added* to the purchase price of new securities
to establish the base for determining a gain or loss on the future
sale of these securities.

3. The holding period (over 6 months for long-term tax benefits) for the repurchased securities is extended to include that
for the original securities.

Example: You buy 100 shares of All-American Shoelace at 40
on July 1. On October 15, when the stock is at 30, you sell in
anticipation of using the $1,000 loss as a tax offset against other
realized capital gains.

To take advantage of the loss, you cannot rebuy the stock until
after December 15. If you should buy on November 10, when the

stock is down to 25, you would lose the tax benefit but have a lower base price for future taxation.

But if you delayed the repurchase until November 16 (30 days after your sale on October 15), your new purchase would not become long-term until mid-May the next year. But that November 10 wash-sale repurchase would throw back the start of the holding period to July 1, so you could take a long-term profit, if any, in January.

The IRS frowns on trick deals—between relatives or between family-controlled corporations and trusts. *The only solace:* When the securities are subsequently sold for a capital gain, only that portion of the gain in excess of the disallowed loss will be taxable.

A wash sale permits you to save taxes if you follow the rules.

Selling Short Against the Box

This is a technique that freezes paper profits and postpones taxes. You sell short against stock which you already own.

Normally, an investor buys a stock long in hopes of appreciation. Short selling is just the opposite. You sell in the expectation that the price of the stock (or commodity) will decline and that you will be able to buy it back at a lower price. Usually short sales are made with borrowed stock.

When you sell short against the box, you (1) believe the price of the stock is too high, (2) look for a general market decline, (3) want to avoid, reduce, or postpone taxes. Keep in mind that tax factors alone are never a sound reason for selling of any type.

Once you have made the short sale, there are 3 possible developments:

The Price of the Stock Declines

You were right. If you cover by buying new stock at the lower price, you will have a short-term capital gain and you will still own the original stock. Your profit on a short sale is always short-term. If you use your own stock to cover the position, you will have a capital gain as you had on the stock at the date and price you sold short.

The Price of the Stock Rises

You were wrong. If you buy new stock to cover the short position, you will have a capital loss—the difference between the price of the new shares and that at which you agreed to deliver the stock under the short sale.

But if you cover with your own stock, you will avoid a loss and will have a capital gain on your own stock based on the date and price at the time of the short sale.

The Price of the Stock Remains Almost Unchanged

Your fears were unwarranted or your hopes premature. You can cover with your own stock and close out the position. Your capital gain will be the same as it was on the date and price you sold short.

If you want to retain your position, buy new shares. You will break even except for commissions, fees, and taxes. But first check your tax situation to determine the dollars and cents involved.

Selling short against the box postpones the effective date of the gain, for income tax purposes, until the day you cover the short position. By doing this at year-end, you assure the current profit you have and push the tax date ahead to the next year, have use of the money which would have been paid in taxes, and hopefully, set the stage for further tax savings.

You can sell short against the same stock as many times as you want, but you must cover sometime, and of course, commissions can be costly. And remember, you must hold the same or substantially identical stock for more than 6 months (the wash-sale situation). Taxwise, the long-term loss must be used to offset long-term gains, so the effect is to reduce taxes only one-half as much as would a short-term loss.

Be careful: The tax savings are intriguing, but do not get too enthusiastic about this technique. Stocks which make sizable gains in 6 months tend to have sufficient momentum to continue to rise. If you sell short, you incur 2 selling commissions. A rising stock, usually, is a better buy than sale.

These techniques sound difficult, but sit down and work out the arithmetic and you'll see they are logical, safe, and when you guess right, profitable—directly through gains or indirectly in tax savings.

How to Use an Installment Sale to Save Taxes and Boost Income

If your parents or older relatives have stock or real estate which has appreciated handsomely over the years, an installment sale can be worthwhile. It will shift the burden of high capital gains taxes, permit investment diversification, and usually provide larger current income.

This ploy is valuable when the stock will be inherited by one person—a son or daughter. The installment sale must be genuine, paid for by a long-term note, and bear at least 4% interest.

Here's How It Works

Father Beane has 1,666 shares of XYZ stock with a market value of $250,000. This is the result of a $25,000 investment in 200 shares of XYZ stock in 1963.

Mr. Beane is retiring, so he needs more income than the skimpy $1,399.44 dividends. If he sold the stock outright, he would have to pay over $60,000 in taxes!

So Mr. Beane sells his shares to his son for a note requiring payments of $1,666.50 per month for 19½ years. The total payments will be $389,961—$250,000 for the stock at its current market value, plus $139,961 interest at 5%. Since there is a 10 to 1 ratio between the cost and the current value, 10% of the monthly payment would be tax-free as a return of capital and the 90% would be taxed as long-term capital gains. For Beane, Jr., the interest is a tax-deductible expense.

To provide more income for his father, Beane, Jr., sells the XYZ stock and reinvests the $250,000 (less commissions) in shares of no-load mutual funds that provide a total return (dividends-interest and appreciation) of 8% annually. At this rate, the capital will be maintained despite a withdrawal of $1,666.50 per month. Now Beane, Sr., gets $19,998 per year, more than 14 times the old dividend income.

In 234 months, the loan will be paid off and Beane, Jr., will have a portfolio which, hopefully, will be worth more than $250,000. He can then decide whether to hold the shares or sell and do his own investing.

IRS requirements for such installment sales:

- The purchase price must be at least $1,000.
- Payments received in the year of sale must not exceed 30% of the purchase price.
- The purchaser must make at least 2 payments in 2 different tax years.
- Details of the sale must be reported in the tax returns of the year in which the sale is made.
- No hanky-panky.

What about Tax Shelters?

Tax-sheltered investments (1) provide either wholly or partially tax-free income, (2) produce capital gains rather than ordinary income, (3) reduce taxes because of special provisions of the Internal Revenue Code, (4) postpone taxes until you are in a lower tax bracket.

Since dividends are taxable under some circumstances and not under others, every investor should explore often-overlooked approaches that avoid overexposure to taxes.

Dividend Exclusion

Each taxpayer is entitled to a $100 exclusion on dividend income. Obviously, securites should be divided so that both husband and wife receive $100 each in dividends. When a stock is held jointly (not a good idea), each individual is considered as receiving half the dividends.

If all securities are now held in one name, a transfer to the spouse will produce an extra tax-free income up to $100.

Such an arrangement is subject to a gift tax. Since everyone can give away $3,000 to one person each year, this is a simple process. With a 5% dividend, a transfer of $2,000 in securities can assure the dividend exclusion.

Shift Assets to a Business Corporation That the Investor Controls

The corporation can accumulate up to $100,000 of dividend income without tax penalty. Furthermore, the corporation gets an 85% dividend-received credit.

If the corporation's taxable income is less than $25,000, only 15% of the dividends are taxed and then at a rate of only 22%, versus 35% to 50% for a well-to-do individual. This is the same as the entire dividend being taxed at about 4%.

When the corporate taxable income is over $25,000, the tax on dividends is only a bit over 7%.

Disadvantage: The tax shelter is temporary. Someday the accumulated dollars must be distributed.

Shift Dividend Income to Other Members of the Family

As described elsewhere, this can be done by means of a trust for children or older people or under the Uniform Gift to Minors Act.

Be careful that the income is not used to pay for parental obligations when children are involved. In a recent decision, the U.S. Court of Claims ruled that trust fund dividends used for private schooling were taxable because the father had no obligation to send his children to private schools.

Look for Investments in Companies That Pay Little or No Dividends

If the corporation is profitable, the retained profits will accumulate with little or no taxes and the money will be used to expand corporate capabilities and profitability.

Invest in Companies That Pay Stock Dividends

The idea is to sell the dividend stock and have the profit taxed at favorable capital gains rates rather than to have a cash dividend taxed at ordinary rates. Tax laws permit this.

Invest in Stocks of Companies Whose Dividends Are Fully or Partially Tax-exempt

These include corporations which benefit from depletion allowances (mining and natural resources), public utilities (which take advantage of accounting practices), and real-estate investment companies (where capital gains may account for a good portion of the dividends).

Tax Benefits of Municipal Bonds

For many years, the interest on bonds issued by states, local governments, and many public authorities has been exempt from federal, and in some cases, state and local taxes. Now it seems probable that Congress will eliminate all or part of this tax shelter. But existing bonds are likely to continue to offer substantial tax benefits. (See Chapter XXV.)

Tax Shelters with Nonstock Investments

For most people, the best tax-sheltered nonstock investment is real estate, primarily their own home. As the accompanying table shows, homeowners' deductions account for over 70% of the tax savings by the family in the $15,000-to-$20,000 income bracket and almost 50% for the $20,000-to-$50,000 adjusted gross income taxpayer.

But lured by the hope of huge, quick, nontaxable gains, too many people become involved in such offbeat ventures as oil and gas drilling, cattle feeding and breeding, timber, Scotch whiskey, citrus and pistachio groves, leasing ranch land, or through limited partnerships, in ownership of athletic teams, financing TV shows, leasing equipment, and even racing horses. *All of these are speculations and should be made only with money you can afford to lose and by people who are in the 50% or higher tax brackets!*

Tax shelters have one thing in common—they divert money that would have been paid to the government in the form of taxes to the use and possible profit of the private investor. They are seldom wise for anyone who needs income rather than tax deductions.

The term "tax shelter" refers to an "expense"—a payout of cash or a charge representing the using up of capital that can be deducted from gross income before the income is taxable.

All tax-shelter deals are complex, most are risky, and few pay out in less than 3 years. But they can be rewarding in tax savings and in long-term capital gains. D. Bruce Trainor, the head of Tax Shelter Advisory Service, Narberth, Pennsylvania, warns: "Less than 5% of all deals being offered for tax shelters are worthwhile. If anybody is thinking about tax shelters to make money, somebody is going to have to do a lot of hard work. You have to have an independent expert—a mining engineer, geologist, or cattleman—to check the procedure used in packaging the deal. Then you have to study the structure to make sure it benefits you."

Average Tax Savings from Tax Shelters

Adjusted Gross Income	Long-term Capital Gains	Tax-exempt Bond Interest	Real-Estate Depreciation	Oil Drilling—Drilling Costs	Farm Capital Gains and Expense Write-offs	$100 Dividend Exclusion	Homeowners' Deductions	Average Total Tax Savings	Average Total Tax Paid
$15,000–$20,000	$ 32.21	$ 3.08	$ 4.15	$ 2.46	$ 13.85	$ 7.08	$ 161.23	$ 224.15	$2,217.85
$20,000–$50,000	218.18	22.73	24.09	15.00	38.64	22.50	320.23	661.36	4,547.27
$50,000–$100,000	2,300.00	750.00	157.50	142.50	137.50	67.50	852.50	4,407.50	18,337.50
$100,000 and over	29,700.00	3,600.00	810.00	870.00	450.00	90.00	1,690.00	37,210.00	67,560.00

Source: *Money Magazine.*

In tax shelters, most of the "expense" items are noncash charges—depreciation, interest, the cost of feed in fattening livestock, the intangible drilling costs connected with oil and gas exploration, etc.

Example: You are in the 50% tax bracket and make a $10,000 investment in a tax shelter that will, hopefully, generate $10,000 in tax deductions. As income, that $10,000 would be cut to $5,000 after taxes. If the investment can generate a $10,000 deduction, you have "saved" $5,000 in taxes.

Deductions are normally heaviest in the first year before operations are profitable. Most tax shelters pyramid these initial deductions by structuring the deal so that the money invested by outsiders pays only for deductible items. There's extra leverage by borrowing. This boosts the investment and makes available, for tax benefits, the interest costs. But that money has to be repaid, usually, before there's any payout to investors.

The most common tax shelter is built around a limited partnership. This involves a general partner who has experience in the operations of oil, cattle, crops, etc., and limited partners who put up the money and receive the majority of tax deductions.

The general partner makes the decisions. Under recent IRS rules, he must have a minimum 1% interest in partnership losses as well as in gains. He puts up a little money but gets a sizable income and share of the profits. He must accept losses in excess of partnerhip capital. With public offerings (more than 100 investors) the SEC sets some standards. In an oil-gas deal, for example, the manager must have a net worth of $250,000.

In case of failure, the limited partners can claim total tax losses not greater than their equity investment in the last 2 years. A minimum investment, usually, is $10,000. This can be supplemented by an $8,000 loan, so the real exposure is $2,000 IF the project is successful or breaks even.

Checkpoints for Sound Tax Shelters

Before you invest (?) any money in any tax shelter, look for these qualities:

ECONOMIC FEASIBILITY. Tax advantages are not enough. You should always have a better-than-even chance to get your money back with a respectable return.

MAXIMUM CURRENT DEDUCTIBILITY. You want the benefits now—when you know that your income is likely to be high.

ALL INCOME SHOULD BE FULLY, OR MOSTLY, DEDUCTIBLE. You did not invest for returns on which you would have to pay high taxes.

ABILITY TO GET OUT QUICKLY AND WITH A PROFIT—AFTER A REASONABLE PERIOD OF TIME. What would your widow do with shares in a South Seas oil well? Or a Mexican vegetable farm?

> *Note:* Under a recent court decision, if a tax shelter goes bankrupt, "investors" can look for relief from third-party promoters—lawyer, accountant, salesman. Previously, they could hide behind bankruptcy. Contact an experienced tax lawyer for assistance.

Here's how a typical tax shelter (oil-well drilling) works out for an individual in the 50% tax bracket:

First Year

Investment	Assumed tangible drilling cost deduction	Tax saving		After-Tax investment
$10,000	$9,000	$4,500		$5,500

Second Year

Assumed net income	Assumed depletion	Taxable income	Tax	Net cash received
$1,000	$330	$670	$335	$665

Third Year

Assumed net income	Assumed cost basis	Capital gain	25% capital gains tax	Net receipts
$9,000	$1,000	$8,000	$2,000	$7,000

Final Result

After-tax cash from income and sale	After-tax investment	After-tax profit	After-tax profit on investment
$7,665	$5,500	$2,165	28%

Source: *Business Week.*

Foreign Tax Havens

If you have substantial funds ($50,000 or more) which you can do without, consider a foreign tax haven. This will permit you to squirrel away savings in an irrevocable foreign trust under circumstances that will permit your wealth to accumulate for years without having to pay taxes. *But you must relinquish all rights to income and principal as well as management or the trust will lose its U.S. tax immunity.*

These havens are no good for fixed income because the IRS withholds 30% of all dividends, interest, and rental income. And you may have to pay taxes in the foreign country, too.

When the foreign trust capital is eventually repatriated to your American beneficiaries, they will be taxed on the accumulated income as if it had been distributed to them each year during the trust's existence. *One benefit:* The 30% which the IRS withheld is credited against your tax bill.

Tax havens that make special legal provision for trusts include Bermuda, the Bahamas, New Hebrides, Cayman Islands, and Hong Kong. The Caymans specialize in "exempt trusts" which provide an official guarantee against all future taxes for 50 years. For this peace of mind, you have to pay a base fee of $250 plus an annual service charge of $125.

To ensure tax immunity, you must:

Appoint a Foreign Trustee

Foreign branches of U.S. banks are no good.

Appoint an American Adviser

He is appointed to assist the foreign trustee (but his recommendations won't be binding).

Set Broad Trustee Powers

Do this to avoid any implication that you retain control.

Set Up the Trust Formally and Deliver the Assets to the Foreign Site

Not Do Any Business in the U.S.

You may not own real estate, run a ranch, etc.

Be Careful Not to Involve a U.S. Gift Tax on the Total Value

For detailed information, consult an experienced attorney, or send $5 to Manacon Services, Ltd., 400 City National Bank Building, Miami, Florida.

Interested in a Swiss Bank Account?

In recent years the traditional secrecy of Swiss banks has been pierced. But anyone can open an account—with restrictions.

Most Swiss banks ask potential American depositors to sign statements swearing they will fulfill all U.S. tax obligations (though it's doubtful that this is legally enforceable). They also want proof that deposits of more than $50,000 were legitimately accumulated and will require personal references, proof of signature, etc.

All currency transactions over $5,000 are supposed to be reported to the U.S. government. This is done automatically if you open your account through the U.S. office of the Swiss bank. With all accounts of $10,000 or more, details must be reported to the IRS.

There are also restrictions on the other side. Swiss banks are prohibited from paying interest on new deposits of more than 50,000 francs per person (about $15,000). Even then, the interest is not attractive—3¼ % to 5%, minus the 30% Swiss withholding tax (which can be used as a credit against U.S. taxes).

Unless you are very wealthy or want to go to the expense of skilled legal tactics, skip this method of tax avoidance. It may sound great in the locker room, but it's seldom a profitable investment by any standard.

Tax Tips

Keep ALL records for 3 years after the April 15 filing date. Normally, the IRS completes audits in 26 months, but keep your notes in case there's a need to reconstruct.

Keep purchase data on all property—home, real estate, securities, etc. You'll need the information to figure your gain or loss when you do sell.

Keep your copy of each tax return in your safe-deposit box—to verify earned income for Social Security, for possible income averaging, and in the case of trusts, for review.

If you've lost a return, the local IRS office will obtain a copy for a small fee.

DOs and DON'Ts for IRS Audits

Almost every family with an income of over $20,000 can expect at least one tax audit over a working lifetime. There is no way to anticipate such a situation, but if it does occur, here are some DOs and DON'Ts:

DO Relax

The majority of audits are routine. You have nothing to worry about if you have tried to be honest, can prove your income, and can verify your deductions.

The IRS agent is an accountant with a job to do. He or she works within strict limits defined by law and regulation. His job is to see that Uncle Sam collects his proper share of your income. He is a professional who expects to be treated as such—in a businesslike manner with businesslike procedures. Relax—you may find it an enlightening experience!

DO be Courteous, Cooperative, and Careful

Be prepared with canceled checks, ledgers, etc. Be friendly but firm. If you have any problems, call your tax adviser.

Keep cool if the agent appears to be abrupt or arbitrary. By making his job easier, you can avoid the grave possibility that he will want to dig deeper into your return or go back to those of previous years.

The best you can hope is that your arguments will be included in the "Revenue Agent's Report." That can be important if the case goes to higher authorities.

Do Find Out if This Is an OFFICE or FIELD Audit

An *office* audit is the easiest, as it usually requires only that you bring to the IRS office canceled checks, signed receipts, etc.

A *field* audit will be held in your place of business and will need more detailed information—your books, files, bills, etc.

If 2 agents show up, you may be in trouble, probably under suspicion of fraud. Call your attorney and tax adviser immediately and say nothing until one or both are on the scene. This special agent is an expert in getting information which may be used against you in criminal prosecution. He is not concerned with back taxes as such. There's little chance he will go away if you agree to pay for minor miscalculations.

DON'T Turn Over any Records or Information Voluntarily Without the Approval of Your Tax Adviser-Attorney

Be careful that you, and your staff, do not supply any information that is not specifically requested.

DO Ask the Agent for Identification and a Description of What his Job Entails

If there's a search warrant, read it carefully after you have called your lawyer. As soon as any case against you takes on a criminal aspect, you must be advised of your rights—that you have the right to remain silent, that anything you say may be used against you, that you can refuse to turn over any records, and that you have the right to counsel.

DO Limit the Area in Which the IRS Agent Can Work on Your Premises and the Material and Records He May See

DON'T Agree to Let the IRS Agent Take any Records unless He Has an Authoritative Search Warrant

If he takes them away, the records may not be allowed in evidence against you.

DO Keep Your Records for 3 Years—After the April 15 Filing Date

Usually, audits are restricted to a review of tax returns for the past 3 years. If you want to be supersafe, hold records for 6 years. Even the IRS shreds old returns after that period.

DON'T Sign Anything Without Legal Advice

If the 3-year statute of limitations is running out, the agent will not be able to assess any deficiency unless there's an extension. By signing Form 872, "Consent Fixing Period of Limitation upon Assessment of Income and Profits Tax," you OK a time extension.

If you refuse to sign this form, the agent might slap you with a large, out-of-his-hat deficiency assessment. This will protect his position if he finds errors-omissions. But it will scare you silly!

Exception: If the agent suspects you understated your income by 25% or more, he can go back as long as 6 years. With fraud, there's no statute of limitations.

DO Tell the Truth

If you don't know or remember the answer, say so. If the agent suspects you have tried to trick or mislead him, he can broaden his investigation. That includes reopening past returns and bringing in a special agent.

DO Take Advantage of Errors in Your Favor

If the audit shows you did not take all legal deductions, press your case. These benefits may cancel out the assessments. By insisting on your rights, you will limit the probe and probably cool the agent's desire to expand the review.

DO Be Slow to Compromise

If it's a small sum, make a deal. If you are arguing about $1,000 or more, keep in mind that: (1) The longer your case is unsettled, the greater the chance that new and more difficult issues may be raised. (2) The earlier the tax is paid, the smaller the penalty assessment. With interest now at 9%, the extra payments can mount rapidly. (3) The longer the decision is delayed, the more fixed the "facts," as reported by the agent, become.

The general procedure is for the agent's report to be forwarded to a reviewer, then to the review staff, and finally to the appellate staff.

You always have the right to protest by:

Asking for a District Conference

The job of this district official is to ensure that the agent is right. You are entitled to present your arguments. The reviewer (not the agent) can compromise the case if the dispute is over $2,500 or less.

Requesting a Conference With the IRS Appellate Division

This group can overrule the agent and effect a compromise if there are "hazards of litigation." This is a wise course only if more than $2,500 is involved.

Filing a Petition With the U.S. Tax Court

Here you can try your own case without paying the contested tax. Claims must be under $1,500. For a hearing date, write to the Clerk of the U.S. Tax Court, Box 70, Washington, D.C. 20041, within 90 days of your receipt of the formal note of deficiency. *But there's no appeal.*

Paying the Tax and Seeking a Refund Through Suit in Either the Federal District Court or the U.S. Court of Claims

This will require legal counsel and considerable expense.

XXVII

Added Advice

It's Your Funeral—Why Not Arrange for It Now?

One of the biggest favors you can do your family is to arrange for your own funeral—in general terms, with your heirs; and specifically, with a funeral director. Such preplanning will make certain that the ceremony follows your wishes in format and in cost.

Much has been written about the expense of funerals and the high-pressure tactics of some morticians who take advantage of the emotional state of the widow and children. There are, of course, abuses but the majority of all funerals are conducted in accordance with family traditions and social amenities.

To many people, the cost of a funeral, as such, is not important. The tribute to the deceased should be the finest regardless of expense. It all depends on the viewpoint. It's very difficult for an affluent Boston Unitarian, who prefers a simple $1,000 memorial service and cremation, to understand how or why her Spanish-speaking maid will insist on an expensive wake and an elaborate church ceremony for her unemployed husband.

The *average* funeral costs between $1,400 and $2,000, depending on the location. In most cases, the differences are in the extras, not the coffin as some writers would have you believe. Caskets, priced between $200 and $2,500, account for only about 20% of total expenses. The other $800 to $2,400 represents services—preparation of the body, restoration of lifelike appearance, use of the parlor at the funeral home, music, grave-opening expenses, limousines to the cemetery, press notices, clergymen's fees, etc. As every funeral director will be glad to explain, a funeral does not have to be expensive to be dignified and to provide a fitting memorial to the deceased.

Ranges of Funeral Costs

Coffins	$150–$2,500
Basic charges*	400– 900
Clergyman	25– 100
Grave	255– 1,200
Interring body	100– 450
Crematory charges	75– 100
Direct cremation†	250– 800
Legal documents‡	25– 75

* Use of facilities and staff, hearse, embalming, sanitary care, removal, filling out forms, etc.
† Without a funeral service.
‡ Burial permit, copies of death certificate, etc.
Source: Federated Funeral Directors of America.

Planning Ahead

If you are worried about future problems with your own or a relative's funeral, make arrangements at the same time you prepare or update your will. This can be done either by signing an agreement with a funeral home or by detailing your wishes with your spouse, your children, and your executor.

In smaller communities, the preplanning can be on an informal basis. You probably know personally or by reputation several funeral directors. Select those whose homes will be convenient to your family and friends and whose range of services fits your financial resources and will be socially acceptable to your family.

Then make an appointment to discuss your desires and their financial terms. The final decision, however, should consider which home will be most comfortable for your heirs.

Once you have made your selection, get down to details—the coffin, help in checking a family plot or buying a new gravesite, arranging for cremation, the advisability of an outside container or vault for additional protection, type of grave marker, names of monument makers, and most important, the estimated costs.

In most cases, the funeral director will confirm your instructions and quote price ranges in a written agreement (often with a prepared list which can be checked quickly). A copy should go to your attorney and executor.

Finally, you may want to make arrangements for payment—from proceeds of an insurance policy (supplemented by Social Security benefits) or from a savings account or small trust fund. On death, this will be payable to your heirs or to the funeral home. The interest should compensate for some of the inevitably rising costs. And if you start early and live long, there could be a surplus for your heirs!

If you're a city dweller, follow the same procedure after narrowing your targets by recommendations from your banker, lawyer, business friends, and neighbors.

Be sure to keep records and inform some younger, responsible person of all of your arrangements. In the confusion of accidental death, your carefully laid plans could be ignored.

Cemetery Plots

Many families have several burial plots. Check their condition, find out how much space is open, whether perpetual care is provided, and then decide which to choose. If you are very sentimental, you may even want to go to the substantial expense of having graves moved so that close members of the family will be together.

If you buy a plot, make sure that the cemetery is a member of the National Association of Cemeteries' Lot Exchange Plan, the address of which is Suite 409, 1911 North Fort Myer Drive, Arlington, Virginia 22209. This provides a central service so that you have a chance to get rid of a lot you don't want. Such a file is especially valuable if you move to a retirement community and live long enough to want to be buried in that area rather than in your old hometown.

Warning: When buying a cemetery plot, watch out for bargain plans and telephone solicitations. State laws have eliminated most of the unethical promoters, but check with your attorney before you sign any installment-payment plan. Carrying costs and redemption charges can be very expensive.

> *Note:* Any person honorably discharged from military service who served during a designated war period is entitled to a government burial allowance and an interment lot in a national cemetery. The government will also supply a flag and grave marker or headstone without charge. To make arrangements, contact your local postmaster.

Donation of Vital Organs

People who would like to give their eyes, heart, kidney, or other vital organs for transplants should be sure that state laws permit such donations. Before you issue firm instructions, discuss your plans with your physician and, with his approval, with a responsible member of the staff of the cooperating hospital.

You must trust your survivors to carry out your wishes. At death, prompt action is essential, so make certain that your plans are clear to your heirs, your attorney, your executor, and the director of the funeral home which you have selected.

It's also wise to make alternate plans in case the receiving institution feels your body or organ is not acceptable because of age, damage from accident, lack of immediate need, etc.

Checkpoints for Funeral Arrangements

PROMPTLY AT DEATH:

CALL THE FUNERAL DIRECTOR TO CHECK WHETHER THERE IS A NEED FOR A CORONER OR MEDICAL EXAMINER. Generally, this is required only in the case of accidental death or the demise of someone not recently under the care of a physician. (If you have not decided on a funeral home, call the police department, or in rural areas, the sheriff's office.)

ASK THE FUNERAL DIRECTOR TO START MAKING ARRANGE-MENTS. He should provide a list of days and hours convenient for viewing and burial.

CALL YOUR CLERGYMAN. If you are not a church member or are new in the community, ask the funeral director for help.

PREPARE INFORMATION FOR THE NEWSPAPER OBITUARY. With older people, especially those who have been ill, this should be readily available. For you and your spouse, such data should be updated whenever you check your will, move up to a new position, or have a new child or grandchild.

Note: Be sure to include the names of *all* blood relatives. It's easy to forget Aunt Martha, who now lives far away but once was your mother's favorite sister.

AS SOON AS POSSIBLE:

SET THE DATE AND HOUR OF THE FUNERAL. The funeral should be held at the convenience of the major heirs and the clergyman. Don't be hasty. It takes time for older people to travel long distances.

COMPLETE THE ARRANGEMENTS WITH THE FUNERAL HOME. The arrangements comprise the type of funeral, fraternal participation, order of events, music to be played, hymns to be sung, etc. Provide the director with a list of the pallbearers (if any) and of relatives and friends who will drive or will need limousines in the procession to the cemetery.

If the deceased is well known, make arrangements for extra parking facilities and attendants at both the home and the cemetery.

GET A CERTIFICATE OF DEATH. This is usually filled out by the attending physician. If death should occur out of town, rely on the local funeral director to handle the legal details, prepare the body, and make arrangements for transportation.

NOTIFY THE INSURANCE COMPANIES. This requires certified copies of the death certificate and can be handled most easily through one agent. The funeral home will advise you on Social Security.

WHEN AGREEMENT HAS BEEN REACHED, HAVE THE NEXT OF KIN SIGN THE CONTRACT WITH THE FUNERAL HOME. If you are asked to sign, too, read the contract carefully. In some states, your signature is a formality, as payments must be made from the estate or by the original signer—if the estate is insolvent.

But the funeral home may look to you if there should be a default. Legally, he may have a weak case, as indicated by a recent decision in New York City. A brother-in-law of the deceased made arrangements for the funeral, picked out a $1,500 coffin, and cosigned the printed agreement. The widow had already signed and approved an itemized statement of anticipated costs. After the ceremony, the widow paid $500 and left for Florida.

Unable to collect, the funeral home sued the brother-in-law. The judge ruled that he was not liable as "his signature was not sufficient to depart from the general principles of primary estate liability." (*Riverside Memorial Chapel, Inc.* v *Edward Albert*).

Memorial Societies

In recent years, there has been growing interest in memorial societies. These are local volunteer organizations which help to arrange "simple, dignified, and economical services." Usually, they involve cremation. Savings can run from $500 to $1,000 per funeral.

For modest dues ($10 to $25 on a one-time basis), memorial societies send forms, a list of services and costs, and names of undertakers who will contract for services at set prices or price ranges. (In some states, fixed fees are illegal.) For information on memorial societies in your area, contact the Continental Association of Funeral and Memorial Societies, 59 East Van Buren Street, Chicago, Illinois 60605.

The cost of the simplest ceremony—cremation prior to a memorial service—can be as low as $300. After-memorial costs, which include embalming and a coffin, are more expensive— $800 and up. These figures do not include expenses for the funeral parlor, death notice in the papers, minister, legal papers, limousine, etc. Overall, however, the simplicity of the ceremony saves money and in many cases provides funds for donations to church or charity.

Remember that, unless you have made firm contracts, your heirs are under no obligation to carry out your wishes (nor are you required to fulfill the request of your relatives). In almost all cases, the funeral will be conducted in a manner and at a place and cost which the major survivors feel is most meaningful.

If you have strong doubts as to what may happen, go over your wishes with your spouse, children, and executor and explain exactly what you have in mind. If you are worried that your widow will use the occasion to impress her friends, provide safeguards while you are still living—by a contract with a funeral home or written instructions to your lawyer and/or executor.

Suggestions: If you anticipate a special tribute because of fraternal, community, or military involvement, make arrangements with the one or two "permanent" members (often the secretary or treasurer). They will be honored by the opportunity and will probably ask you to do as much for them.

Costs are important in a funeral, but they are never the most important consideration. That's a fitting tribute to a worthwhile life.

Note: If death occurs in a Veterans Administration hospital or is paid for by the VA, the government may pay the costs of transporting the body to the place of burial and up to $250 in expenses. For information, check the nearest VA office or the local chapter of the American Legion, Veterans of Foreign Wars, or other military-service groups.

For the Minister's Files

Don't forget to keep your clergyman informed as to your final wishes. He can provide practical as well as spiritual help. Many parishes provide a mimeographed form to be kept in the confidential file of the house of worship.

This provides space for your name, address, date and place of birth, names of physicians and attorney, location of will, and then for such specific requests as:

In the event of my death, it is my wish that I be given:
A coffin burial_____. Cemetery preference and lot number:_____. Cremation_____.
I am a member of a vital organ bank: Eye_____. Kidney_____. Other_____.
I prefer a funeral service: In Church_____. At home_____. At a funeral parlor_____.
I prefer a memorial service: At church_____. At home_____.
I want to discourage the sending of flowers. Alternative contributions to_____.
Special wishes_____.

Cut the Cost of Moving

It's always possible to make a do-it-yourself move, but if you have a sizable house and valuable furniture and furnishings, a professional moving firm will be surer, safer, and more dependable. Besides, unless it's a short move where you can hire a couple of husky teenage neighbors, you will avoid personal risks of hernia, strained back, and exhaustion. And there'll be far better professional supervision!

The first and most important step in cutting moving costs is to select a reputable mover. Start with the Yellow Pages and look for the local representative of an established national organization. This affiliation is no guarantee of competence, but chances are you'll be dealing with reliable people.

Then, ask for recommendations from friends and neighbors, especially those who have moved more than once. When there is criticism, try to find out whether the fault lay with the mover or the neighbor. Moving can be a very traumatic experience for some people.

When you have narrowed the list, make sure that the final firm has an office in or near the community to which you are moving. If there's future trouble, you can complain locally.

Next, ask the mover to come to your home to make an estimate. This will cover the costs of loading, transporting, and unloading, but *not* charges for packing or moving special items such as boats, skimobiles, automobiles, etc.

The estimate will be based on weight, and as professionals, the movers will estimate close to the final bill. Typically, a room contains about 1,000 pounds of furnishings.

Do not haggle over the costs. It won't do much good, as all rates for interstate moving are similar. They have to be filed with the Interstate Commerce Commission (ICC) and are based on business costs: Total charges = weight + mileage.

You can try to bargain on moves within your state. There are no set standards. Some movers charge by weight and distance, others by man-hours. And of course most estimates will reflect how anxious the mover is to get the business. Be wary when one quotation is way below those of competitors.

Charging by man-hours sounds sensible, but this can get out of hand if your beds and sofas are oversize and have to be inched up narrow staircases. Or if the weather is bad—on a hot day there will be plenty of time-outs for a cold beer, and in icy weather, things will move with incredible slowness.

If you can legally make such a deal (not possible in New York State, for example), get a price based on man-hours with a bonus if savings in time are over 5% below the estimate.

Costs can be cut somewhat if you carry personal and valuable items in your car and do your own packing. The mover will sell you boxes and barrels. But remember, no matter how agile your wife and daughters, they are not professionals! Chances are the boxes won't be ready, so whatever you save on packing will probably be more than spent for overtime.

One important deed: Before the big day, make a *complete* inventory of all possessions. You will need it at the destination.

When Your Company Pays

If your company is planning to move you, find out exactly what will be paid for.

BEFORE THE MOVE. How many house-hunting trips? For yourself? For your wife?

DURING THE MOVE. Motel accommodations? Meals? Family transportation? Housing compensation?

AFTER THE MOVE. Temporary help? Appliance-servicing fees?

Don't make your plans on the basis of what happened last time. Corporations are tightening up. The total cost of moving a family to a new city, reports Atlas Van Lines, was $2,994 in 1973. This was 9.2% less than a year before. The savings were in the extras allowed employees—down an average of 22.4%, or $432!

Payments and Claims

Unless credit arrangements have been made in advance (usually when you, not your employer, are paying the costs), payment must be made in cash or certified check at the completion of the move. If the bill exceeds the estimate by more than 10%, you must pay the estimated cost and will have 15 days to pay the balance.

The bill will be based on weight registered on a certified scale when the truck is loaded. If you are suspicious, ask for a reweighing at the destination. It may cost you a few dollars more, but the added expense will ease your mind.

If the goods have already been unloaded at the destination, you may be lucky. You can refuse to pay the *extra* charges, as the mover cannot reload without going to court.

If the truck is full but you still feel you are being overcharged, pay up, then complain, in writing, to the ICC in Washington or to the supervisory agency in your state (probably the Public Utilities Commission).

Advice on handling claims from James F. Harley, ombudsman for New York's Office of Impartial Chairman of Moving and Storage Industry: "Make sure that everything has been delivered and note any visible damages on the receipt. When you sign, add 'Accepted subject to further inspection for concealed damage or loss.' This keeps your legal options open."

It is your responsibility to complete your check for broken glass, dishes, etc., and to file claims promptly—in writing. Reputable movers settle minor damages in a couple of weeks, but you can't blame them for protests or refusals if, 2 years after the move, your mother-in-law discovers one of her favorite perfume bottles is broken.

If you do not get satisfactory service-payment, contact the local Better Business Bureau or city or state Consumer Protection Agency. *Do not delay, and do be specific.*

Before the move, it's wise to pay the mover to increase his liability coverage. Normally, movers are liable only for 60¢ a pound per article. That's not much. If your 50-pound TV set should be smashed, you'll get back only $30!

Best coverage: Add a temporary rider to your homeowner's insurance policy or get a full-value policy from the mover. This broad policy will raise the liability to $1.25 per pound and also provide for full replacement value of anything destroyed. Be sure to get a copy of the full-value insurance, so if the mover refuses to pay later, you can sue him and know he's covered.

Harley summarizes: "You'll have a smooth move if you choose your mover with care, plan your relocation, and accept your responsibility. If you make the mistake of hiring a poor firm, you can still get satisfaction if you are willing to take your complaints to local or state agencies. And if you are really angry, contact the ICC in Washington or at the nearest regional office."

Bibliography

General

How to Have More Money by John Barnes. Morrow.
Personal Finance by Jerome B. Cohen and Arthur W. Hanson. Dow Jones-Irwin.
Save Time, Save Money, Save Yourself by Dorsey Connors. Hawthorn Books.
How to Manage Your Money: A Woman's Guide to Investing by Elizabeth M. Fowler. Little, Brown.
Personal Finance by E. Bryant Phillips and Sylvia Lane. John Wiley.
The Money Book by Sylvia Porter. Doubleday.
Managing Personal Finances by W. H. Rodda and E. L. Nelson. Prentice-Hall.
Guide to Personal Finance by Richard J. Stillman. Prentice-Hall.
Time-Life Book of Family Finance. Time, Inc.
Consumer Problems and Personal Finance by A. C. Troelstrup. McGraw-Hill.
Dollars and Sense by Art Watkins. Quadrangle.

Estate Planning

Personal Financial Control by Richard B. Bibbero. MMC Publishing.
The Complete Estate Planning Guide by Robert Brosterman. McGraw-Hill.

488

Home

Home Owners' Legal Guide by Robert Schwartz. Macmillan.

Personal Pension Plans

Retirement Dollars for the Self-Employed by Steven R. Anreder. Thomas Y. Crowell.
A Financial Guide for the Self-Employed by John Ellis. Henry Regnery.

How to Meet College Costs

Barron's Profiles of American Colleges. Barron's Educational Series.
Comparative Guide to American Colleges by James Cass and Max Birnbaum. Harper & Row.
The College Handbook by Douglas Dillenback and Sue Wetzel. College Entrance Examination Board.
Einstein's College Entrance Guide by Bernice Einstein. Grosset & Dunlap.
Lovejoy's College Guide by Clarence Lovejoy. Simon and Schuster.
The New York Times Guide to College Selection by Ella Mazel. Quadrangle.

Lawyers

Law for Executives by Russell F. Moore. American Management Association.
Time-Life Family Legal Guide. Little.

Real Estate

Profits in Real Estate by Bill Adler and Catherine J. Greene. Cornerstone Library, New York.
Real Estate Investment by William R. Beaton. Prentice-Hall.
Real Estate Manual by Maurice A. Unger. SW Publishing Co.
Real Estate Finance by Henry E. Hoogland and Leo D. Stone. Dow Jones-Irwin.
Real Estate Investment Strategy by Maury Seiden and Richard Swesnik. John Wiley.

The Family Car

Time-Life Book of the Family Car. Time, Inc.
The Car Owner's Handbook by Ray Stapley. Doubleday.

Retirement

Retirement Handbook by Joseph C. Buckley. Harper & Row.
Where to Retire on Small Incomes by Norman D. Ford. Harian Press.
Your Personal Guide to Successful Retirement by Sidney K. Margolius. Random House.

Insurance

Life Insurance by Joseph M. Belth. Indiana University Press.
Introduction to Insurance by Allen L. Mayerson. Macmillan.
Insurance Principles & Practice by Robert Riegel and Jerome Miller. Prentice-Hall.

Investments

Investments by Frederick Amling. Prentice-Hall.
Investments: Principles and Practices of Analysis by Douglas H. Bellemore and John C. Ritchie. SW Publishing.
Investment Analysis and Management by John W. Bowyer, Jr. Dow Jones-Irwin.
The Sophisticated Investor by Burton Crane. Simon and Schuster.
Dow Jones Investor's Handbook by M. L. Farrell. Dow Jones-Irwin.
The Intelligent Investor by Benjamin Graham. McGraw-Hill.
Security Analysis by Benjamin Graham. McGraw-Hill.
$Your Investments$ by C. Colburn Hardy. Dun & Bradstreet.
Success with Your Investments by John W. Hazard. Doubleday.
The Battle for Investment Survival by Gerald M. Loeb. Simon and Schuster.
The Battle for Stock Market Profits by Gerald M. Loeb. Simon and Schuster.
How to Make Your Money Do More by David L. Markstein. Trident Press.
Financial Independence Through Common Stocks by Robert D. Merritt. Simon and Schuster.
How to Make Money in Wall Street by Louis Rukeyser. Doubleday.
Investing for Your Future by Sam Shulsky and J. K. Lasser. Simon and Schuster.

Investment Advisory Services

Babson's Reports, Wellesley Hills, Massachusetts 02181.
*James Dines & Co., Inc., 18 East 41st Street, New York, New York 10016.
*Indicator Digest, 451 Grand Avenue, Palisades Park, New Jersey 07650.
The Granville Market Letter, P.O. Box 2614, Ormond Beach, Florida 32074.

* Emphasis on technical analysis.

Stock Research Corporation, 55 Liberty Street, New York, New York 10005.

United Business Service, 210 Newbury Street, Boston, Massachusetts 02116.

Value Line Investment Service, 5 East 45th Street, New York, New York 10017.

Mutual-Fund Information

Fundscope, Inc., 1900 Avenue of the Stars, Los Angeles, California 90067.

Arthur Lipper, 140 Broadway, New York, New York 10005.

Mutual Funds Almanac, The Hirsch Organization, 6 Deer Trail, Old Tappan, New Jersey 07675.

Vickers Associates, 48 Elm Street, Huntington, New York 11746.

Arthur Weisenberger Services, 61 Broadway, New York, New York 10006.

How to Make Money with Mutual Funds by David L. Markstein. McGraw-Hill.

Index

493

494 / Index

About the Author

C. Colburn Hardy started a second career as a professional writer after early retirement as a public relations executive with one of America's largest corporations. He has written over 700 articles on investments, finance, and money management and is the author of five books in these fields—three over his own name and two as collaborator for two well-known investment advisers.

A Phi Beta Kappa graduate of Yale, he is registered as an Investment Adviser with the Securities and Exchange Commission and the State of New Jersey. He has lectured on investments and money management before a number of organizations, taught at local colleges and appeared as a guest on local and national radio and TV programs.

Mr. Hardy lives in East Orange, N.J., where he is active in community affairs. Currently, he is researching material on investment techniques and personal pension plans.